The Story of Huey P. Long

BY

CARLETON BEALS

GREENWOOD PRESS, PUBLISHERS
WESTPORT, CONNECTICUT

CONTENTS

6 *Contents*

The Story of
Huey P. Long

I—CHALLENGE

"WHO'S this scaffold for?" asked Huey Long.

"Governor, they're fixing it for you," was the reply.

The Kingfish was threatened—that momentous year of 1929—with impeachment by the Senate of Louisiana. Reform governor, with a hostile, Old Ring legislature, his attempt to force through a new tax on the refining of petroleum had brought the gang politicians out baying in full force against him.

Eight years previous, Huey had beaten the old crowd when they tried to boot him off the Railroad Commission, but now his enemies were determined to cut off his political head once and for all. They raked up every charge from bad manners to a murder plot. Halitosis was not included; Mr. Ickes is not from Louisiana. But there were many serious items—bribery, petty embezzlement, the awarding of contracts without legal bids. The outlook was dark.

Huey's campaign supporters, the New Regulars, had broken with him. Colonel Robert Ewing, Democratic national committeeman and editor of the *New Orleans Daily States,* had broken with him. The Independent Regulars had thrown him over long ago. The Old Regulars, the Tammany Ring of New Orleans, had always bucked him. All the powerful interests of the state hated him. The old plantation-owning class detested him. Every newspaper was shouting for his head. He had only a slender minority in either house. As he had not yet built up much of a state-wide machine, and only a few friends stuck by his side, all cards seemed stacked against him. He looked like a dead cock in the pit.

His only hope was to appeal to the voters. He made a whirlwind campaign, put out tens of thousands of circulars, and in dozens of speeches, from the bayous to the Red River hills,

he whacked "the interests," even accused them of bribing legislators.

Returning to the capitol from one of his speeches—it was
near daybreak—he dropped off to sleep in the governor's
office. Hours later he was awakened by the noise of saws and
hammers.

He raced upstairs to investigate the unusual racket. The
whole inside of the Senate Chamber was being made over with
a big platform and high benches. "It seemed like preparations
for a pre-revolution French hanging," Long later remarked.
But they were unable to hang him. His neck slipped out of
the noose. He was too "slick" for them. His backwoods barnstorming rallied the state behind him. With jobs and other in-
ducements, he secured the support of the requisite number of
Senators to block proceedings. The impeachment bubble was
suddenly pricked. His frustrated enemies retired furious.

The charges were never aired. The October stock-market
crash changed the whole picture of Louisiana and the nation.
Soon the guardians of prosperity were too dazed to fight. And
in the growing confusion of the depression, Huey sidetracked
all effective opposition and cemented his power. The impeachment publicity, his clever victory, enhanced his popularity,
helped make him lord and master of his state. His enemies
made him a national figure.

He was thirty-five then. Before 1929 his name was rarely
found in any New York daily. From that date on the news
weeklies found him good copy. Article after article has appeared in magazines of wide circulation. In a few years he became the most arresting personality in public life.

In 1893 Huey Pierce Long peered over the cradle and
squalled—it may be for a crown.

In 1910 or thereabouts, Huey was peddling Cottolene from
door to door. Housewives would look out to see a slim athletic
boy with eager dancing brown eyes, red curly hair, large snub
nose, an engaging cleft chin and a wide smile, who instantly
deluged them with rapid-fire sales talk.

In February, 1930, Huey was saying to Calvin Coolidge,
"When I was elected, I found the Governor's mansion in such

rotten shape, I had to tear it down and rebuild. I don't want to have to rebuild the White House."

"What part of Louisiana are you from?" Coolidge asked drily.

"I'm a hillbilly like yourself."

Almost as soon as he could work, Huey as a boy was out hoeing long rows of potatoes, picking cotton, cutting wood. Years later, he was to speak bitterly of the harshness of that toil, the hot sun, the lack of companionship. He rebelled against it early.

By twenty-one he had been sworn in as a full-fledged member of the bar.

By twenty-five he was a member of the Railroad Commission.

By thirty-five he was Governor. "Stick by me, you fellers; I'm gonna be President some day."

At thirty-seven he was elected to the United States Senate.

At thirty-eight he was leading the Democratic delegation from Louisiana to the Chicago convention to break the power of John K. Raskob and nominate Franklin D. Roosevelt.

There the son of William Jennings Bryan gave him the gold fountain pen presented to his father by the school-children of Mexico; and there at the Chicago convention, or earlier, Huey discovered in Bryan's "Cross of Gold" speech the phrase, "Every Man a King," the subsequent title of his own published autobiography. Pending universal kingship, Huey was bent on making at least himself king.

There at the Chicago convention, he shouted, "The Democratic Party in Louisiana! *I* am the Democratic Party in Louisiana."

Equally he could have said, "I am Louisiana." The Democratic Party there *is* Louisiana. Earlier in his career, during a wild fracas on the floor of the House in Baton Rouge, an irate member flung a copy of the Constitution at him. He shouted back, with unconscious Louis XIV ventriloquism, "I am the Constitution in Louisiana."

He imposed his absolute power in every corner of the state. Even New Orleans, which resisted longest, had to bow to his will, all except Mayor Walmsley—"Old Turkeyhead," Huey disrespectfully shouted at him over the radio—who was merely holding the bag until the final financial collapse of the city, whereupon Huey, had he not been killed, would have moved in and saved the day. The entire electoral machinery of the state, the militia, the highway police, Governor "Okay" Allen, the Legislature, the local judges, the police and firemen, tax-collectors, university professors, teachers, the members of all state boards, the highest and the lowliest official—all were in Huey's hands. He created the State Bureau of Criminal Identification, a mysterious body, to nose into private affairs and pass on the qualifications of state employees. Huey could ram through forty-four state laws in twice forty-four minutes. His henchmen could disqualify any voter. He could block local financing and kick out any municipal government. He did so in Alexandria. By a martial law decree for Baton Rouge, he removed elected officials he did not like. He persecuted even the relatives of those who opposed him. He had the power to increase assessments on their property. He tried to gag the independent press, and heavy gouges were made into the salaries of state employees to found and support his paper, *Louisiana Progress*. Those who refused to contribute lost their jobs. All state employees forked over 10 percent of their wages as "voluntary" donations to the Long machine. He swaggered about at the head of the state militia. He was already emperor of Louisiana in all but name, when a bullet cut short his ambitions. He had devoured the state. No ballots could pry him out, only bullets or federal intervention—and a bullet did.

Despite all his arbitrary measures, however much he was hated by the "better elements"—a phrase repeated *ad nauseum* in Louisiana—he had the loyal backing of the mass of the population of his state and carried with him to the grave the sorrow of hundreds of thousands. His good roads, his showy public edifices, his skyscraper capitol building, his free textbooks (they were given away in many parishes before his advent), his toll-free bridges, his whanging away at the corporations (however many backstage deals may have been celebrated with them), his rate reductions (his gasoline, tobacco and soft-drink taxes more than ate up the saving), his swaggering dramatics and racy language—all idolized him for the common man.

He went on to the national scene. His purpose was clear—to dominate the Democratic Party nationally or else break it and form his own party. Though a rule or ruin type, Huey's tactics were canny. He flung himself with double-barreled shotgun onslaught upon the man who is both the weakest and the strongest link in the Roosevelt machine, his old friend Jim Farley—the Mark Hanna of gilt-edge illusion, the man of lost moral prestige, who sets out the cream to keep the political alley-cats from straying. Huey told Ickes to go to hell, he would "nail his ears back." He accused floor-leader Senator Robinson of being a corporation hireling. He heaped anathema upon Christian mystic Henry Agard Wallace, the monk of scientific scarcity, and accused him of utilizing his power and program to promote his personal financial interests. He hit many a solar-plexus blow at "Barney Baruch's office-boy," Hugh Johnson. President Roosevelt reaped his share of Longish ridicule by leaving Washington to feel the pulse of the country on Vincent Astor's "five-million dollar yacht" in the company of English dukes and earls. Now that Huey is dead Roosevelt can resume those happy junkets. Huey struck effective blows in other quarters.

Besides being a persuasive orator, a billingsgate phrase-maker and a Barnum and Bailey of horse-laughter, Huey was a real organizer. He was the most efficient campaigner in the history of America. Rarely has he ever been excelled in his power to command publicity. No other politician—Coughlin was his only competitor—continuously used a national radio hook-up.

Thus he swept like a hurricane into the troubled national arena. He tore aside the sacrosanct veils of sickening eulogy for the administration and broke the solid ranks of triumphant Democracy. In the South he was gaining control in state after state—note his March whirlwind campaign through South Carolina. He was big-shot in North Dakota. He had made in-

cursions into the rest of the more insurgent Middle West. He
had laid plans for a nation-wide distribution of his propaganda
among farmers, workers, students, the middle classes, anyone
else willing to listen. At one time he received and sent out a
truck-load of mail daily—as much as all other Senators combined. He claimed over five million Share-the-Wealth members.
He had seriously menaced Roosevelt's re-election. He was a
potential President himself.

Huey P. Long became the pole-cat, wild ass, Messiah and
enigma of American politics. Last September people were
asking what will be this man's destiny. Today he provides
a lesson in American politics that should be studied, memo-
rized, and utilized. He was well on his way to becoming
America's first dictator. Perhaps he was only a bubble flashing on a stormy sea. But his popularity, his power, his rapid
rise, were the result of a deep malady in American life that
has not disappeared because Huey Long disappeared.

2

Huey was a buccaneer frontier individualist. But his growth
was conditioned directly by his Louisiana environment, where
individualism, not merely a *laissez-faire* product, has curious
quirks. For there individualism is also complementary to political absolutism in the Latin sense.

Climatically, racially, to some extent institutionally, Louisiana is closer to Cuba or Mexico than it is to Connecticut. It
is semi-colonial, sharply divided racially, still partly feudal,
partly Latin—it jostles constantly with the Latin-American
world. There the bland air, at times brutally hot, slows up
effort, produces languor, an unaffected love of joy and sensual-
ism punctuated with cruelty. Cruelty is a short-cut of slothfulness. Individualism is a short-cut. It takes periodic exaggerated
forms—reaction to slothful but arbitrary rule, not a functioning component of rule. Hence the undisciplined picturesqueness
of Huey.

There in Louisiana, some of the courtly extravagance,
cruelty and absolutism of French and Spanish domination have

survived alongside the frontier tradition of fighting Indians and hewing out farms from the shallow soil of the pine-clad Red River region. From the beginning there, American democracy has jostled, mostly unsuccessfully, with class and race rule. From the start almost, the Northern farmers there have been politically and economically under the heel of the plantation Creoles in the South, later under the banks and corporations. American political traditions have never had any rooted vitality in Louisiana. Negro disenfranchisement plus large-scale white illiteracy and poverty have prevented true democratic practices. Government by "decent" men has always been the polite fiction. But in these later years in Louisiana a "decent" office-holder has been merely one clever enough successfully to cover up grafting and underworld connections. Thus dictatorship, more or less disguised, has always ruled the state.

Colonialism, slavery, then feudalism—all were overwhelmed by Northern industrialism and now increasingly by monopoly and financial capitalism. In only the past five years the trapping industry—Louisiana produces more furs than all of Canada—has passed from a free individualist régime to one of ironclad monopoly with serf-like conditions comparable to those of the West Virginia coal industry. And just as a hierarchical state and religion are the proper expressions of a feudal economy, so the logical expression of monopoly capitalism is one-man dictatorship.

Louisiana is a conquered colonial state. The region was conquered and settled by Frenchmen and Spaniards. After the Louisiana Purchase in 1803, it was reconquered by Northern "Anglo-Saxon" immigration. The Civil War conquered it again for Northern industrialism, which changed the slave market into a wage market, substituting the previous "kennel economy" of chattel slavery into the jungle economy of exploited "free" labor. Conquest by the sword was followed by pacific financial and economic subjugation. In the train came a legal, and to some extent cultural, invasion from the North. The basic Roman law of Louisiana more and more gave way to Anglo-Saxon law—time-payment purchasing is an example. When Huey, in one of his campaigns, damned the federal courts and their injunction powers he was in part reflecting the regional hostility to this change. Louisiana is a Cuba within the borders of the Union.

Huey is not entirely a new phenomenon in Louisiana. Lawlessness and dictatorship have passed over the state in recurrent waves. Dictatorial colonialism passed into the undisputed rule of the dictatorial plantation class—from 1815 to the end of the Civil War—a pyramid resting upon the dark base of human slavery. In reconstruction days the carpetbag rule of Republican Governor Warmoth—sustained in power by federal bayonets, the long arm of Northern industrialism—bears a close resemblance to that of Huey Long. During Warmoth's arbitrary rule—with the aid of negroes and of the same poor whites and lower middle class Huey utilized—was implanted the counterpart of the recent militia, electoral and anti-home-rule laws which riveted the Kingfish's control over the state. That also was a transition period, and during transition, democracy suffers its worst defeats—especially in Louisiana.

By the time the federal army loosened its grip—after a well-countenanced counter-revolutionary terrorism—by the White Leaguers and the Klu Klux Klan—a new alliance of the old plantation class with the new Northern industrialist had been effected; they came to terms about the negro and poor white and their own mutual spheres of exploitation—almost the same pattern as in Cuba, Mexico or Peru.

New capital had hurried in. The industrial age was knocking at the door. Railroads were pushing through, oil wells were being drilled, sawmills were springing up, plantations were being industrialized, new banks were being founded, the new factory products of the Midwest were sliding down the Mississippi, and as usually happens in a feudal semi-colonial area, the negro and poor-white alliance broke down before the new feudal-industrialist alliance. It was in the midst of this break-up of rural simplicity by the thrust of modern commercialism that Huey Long's formative years were spent.

The new Southern gentleman-business class, mouthing old slogans of race-superiority and medieval privileges, held unbroken sway ever since the 'eighties and had grown ever more corporation-ridden. For a while the haughty candidates of the "best families" continued to settle their differences at dawn under the Dueling Oaks or on the Vidalia sandbar outside of New Orleans, but by the turn of the century, behind their mint-julep respectability stalked the gangster politics of the city— one of the most hybrid, riffraff and corrupt metropolises on the continent. The politics of the state had become a cesspool, the stench of which the fine gentlemen could no longer perfume away.

Soon the New Orleans "gang" was in the saddle, not only in New Orleans but in Baton Rouge. Its victory marked the first breakdown of corrupt political gentility. As is true of all capitalist conquests of backward regions, the second phase is exactly this switch from ineffective well-wishing aristocracy as political agents to more ruthless gangster elements to main-tain control in the face of cumulative economic inconsistencies. Thus in Cuba the Creole aristocracy gave way to the machine-gun gangsterism of Gerardo Machado, then to the militant one-man mulatto gangsterism of Fulgencio Batista. So in Louisiana, Huey Long was the next lógical and inevitable step. As in Cuba, as in carpetbag days, Northern financial capital, if crisis makes it necessary, may again rule with a negro coalition.

Huey peeled off the aristocratic veneer of politics. Over the radio, he dared call a respectable plantation-owning Colonel "Whistle-Breeches"; and the hillbillies guffawed; and the negro servants, largely on a pre-Civil War status, foregath-ered backstairs, rolled their eyes, and asked each other in awed delighted whispers, "Did yo heah what the Kingfish call Massah?" It upset the sacred scheme of things. It shook off decorative externalities. Such tactics exposed the core of gangster control.

3

Types like Huey Long, be it in Cuba, Mexico, or Louisiana, rise through insurgency. He rose against the hostility of the newspapers of the state, against the control of his party by the corrupt Old Regulars of the Choctaw Club, against the vile

New Orleans ring, against the old plantation control, against the enmity of powerful corporations. He endured calumny and ridicule, and both but enhanced his popularity—thus overthrowing a holy American axiom.

The insurgency involved in semi-colonial areas is in part provoked by the economic and cultural inconsistencies created by absentee monopoly capital. In Cuba and Mexico this revolt was somewhat conscious, to some extent rational; in Louisiana it has had no sensible ideological pattern. Louisiana is not a nation, nor is economic thinking a characteristic of American democracy or its leaders. Huey Long perhaps sensed the parallel when he half-jokingly proposed that Louisiana secede and ally itself with Mexico; or when he threatened a Louisiana "tea-party." For in many ways Louisiana is more unable to achieve economic liberty than is Mexico; it cannot lay hold of similar nationalistic weapons.

As in Latin countries to the south, the revolt in Louisiana is largely that of the formative lower middle classes; the farmers of the scrawny soil of the hills and hollows, where the land is too poor to be cultivated by plantation owners; the commercial class that is dependent on the independent farmer, trapper and lumber man for a profit. Here again Huey was partly the product of the Civil War and "scalawag" carpetbag rule plus present-day depression. In the beginning he forged his political strength with the ignorant and miserable whites of the backwoods, the dwellers in mud shacks and log cabins, the sufferers from pellagra, hookworm and malaria. His chosen were also the petty commercial class of the small interior towns whose little establishments long ago supplanted the commissaries of the large plantations.

The Civil War partially freed the poor whites and gave rise to this new petty commercial class. It brought about a decrease in the acreage of the old plantation aristocrats, driven to the wall by the change in the economic system and unsettled labor conditions. For a time, part of the small farming and commercial groups gained in power and importance, even found bold leaders—at least elsewhere in the South. "Pitchfork Ben" Tillman of South Carolina, who sought to run his prongs into "that old bag of fat, President Cleveland," was the first truly picturesque example.

Once more this class is being pushed back into economic misery. Roosevelt relief has buttressed up the old plantation at the expense of this group and of the tenant farmer. And as new feudal capitalism replaces the old plantation methods, installs machinery on rice, sugar and cotton estates, and establishes monopoly in oil mining, banking and fur industries, the old-style commissary reappears; chain stores also crush the free merchant (Huey tiraded against them). And so the Kingfish, with the endangered class at his heels, came storming, like Tillman, with the not too realistic slogan, "Turn out the aristocrats."

For the first time, a political leader actually promised the people of the state something. Read Louisiana political speeches since before the 'nineties. Mostly they are vapid elegant bombast of gentlemanly know-nothingness, bright banal gems about the Constitution, the sacred flag, the Fourth of July, the glorious traditions of the South, the chivalry and bravery of its men, the purity and beauty of its women—all the smug slothfulness of one-party rule unchallenged. The answer was not the birth of real democracy—but vigorous one-man rule.

As a matter of fact, this old-school virtuousness and pomposity covered up the looting of the natural resources of the state, the dishing out of fabulous concessions to favorites, the steady invasion of large outside corporations with no proper protection for local economic sovereignty—all the pseudolegal manipulations of high finance. The fine old velvet manners also covered up the growth of gangster and vice operations which provided the sinews for political control. Both were manifestations of the development of absentee financial capitalism.

Huey smashed the polite façade He changed the name and the game of Louisiana politics. In a state so utterly backward, it is not surprising that to many Huey seemed the Messiah himself, a virtual miracle worker. He came as a challenge to the senile, feather-duster politicians, to the hypocrisy, ineffectiveness and self-satisfaction of the ignorant, if occasionally well-mannered, powers that were in Louisiana. It was not so difficult, really, to make himself absolute master of the state and provide something of a showing. Certainly he promised any and everything, and—for a high price indeed—gave considerable; although actually, in real social achievements, except for showy public works, the state still remains almost at the bottom of the list.

For starving people cannot eat concrete highways or marble-coated public buildings. Even relief workers, some of them employed at as little as ten cents an hour, cannot buy back their share of Louisiana's rice. A Chinese coolie is better off than such folk in Louisiana. Transportation efficiency and administrative efficiency (a question mark here) are not answers to social problems.

Of course Huey, by smashing the past fake simulation of democracy and forging his own power unshakable, followed the only course by which he could break the old gang and create a true democracy embracing the share-croppers, the farmers, the petty business men and similar groups (he was a consistent, though not aggressive, enemy of negro rights) which helped him into control. If one surveys the old gang, the shoddy aristocracy, the intellectual barrenness of so-called "better elements" and "decent" people of Louisiana, one is tempted, indeed, to applaud him. His methods were inevitable, and in themselves not reprehensible. No intelligent critic should attack Huey Long too much for the manner in which he smashed the die-hard clique of pompous political plugs, whose present lachrymose loyalty to a constitutionalism and democracy they never respected or vitalized is merely the impotent hypocrisy of political "outs." Some of those who have fought Huey most bitterly in Louisiana are precisely those who once abused with their own excessive power, who lied, stole and banqueted smugly. Huey pursued the only intelligent and effective course to destroy their greedy and ignorant job-holding monopoly The world is better for their demise, and Farley's efforts to resuscitate them through federal patronage is one of the darkest smirches on the Rooseveltian New Deal.

Huey's methods become reprehensible only in the light of his deeper failure—the use of such drastic acts with such flimsiness of purpose, such inadequate results. *Revolution for reform*—so common in colonial entities oppressed by the nightmare of outside industrial power—is a costly tragi-comedy. [For Huey, once he had become undisputed master of the ship, did *absolutely nothing* effective to promote the economic liberation of the classes whose votes he won. Hence he created no reliable support for himself in those groups. Whatever his general popularity, inevitably he had to become the instrument of big business in his state; he had to celebrate secret deals and alliances with the corporation heads with whom publicly he shadow-boxed. Despite all his prolonged sound-and-fury battles with the Standard Oil Company, it is still able to refine oil, in large part *because of very low wage costs,* more cheaply in Louisiana than almost anywhere else in the Union.

Long's career, so far as Louisiana is concerned, repeats the tragedy of betrayal that Calles perpetrated in Mexico, that Batista has perpetrated in Cuba. Thus whatever Huey may have become in the nation, in Louisiana, in terms of real social betterment, popular economic rights, and more equitable distribution of the products of labor, he was already a complete failure.

4

In terms of personal power, of course, Huey was an increasing success. In fact he well represented the good old American doctrine that any man of ability can succeed, and success at any price was his one golden god. Huey's enemies often twitted him about his humble origin; in Louisiana one can have flat feet, degenerate ear-lobes, and a fourteen-year-old I.Q. provided one has a pedigree. Hence Huey's opponents ridiculed his superhuman personal achievements by stressing his shoddy "drummer" manners, his Cottolene salesmanship, his clownishness, his lack of Southern "cultyah." That which is usually considered the glory of America—the bold success of a self-made man—in his case was held up to derision.

But undoubtedly large masses of Americans did sense that he justly corresponded to the hoary American ideal. Certainly the great American fortunes were founded by unscrupulous "robber barons" who at no time hesitated to use almost any means to compass their ends. Huey Long carried at least the boldness of their tactics over into politics, to the conquest of the state. Thus he wore the halo of rampant individualism rather than that of the leader of a newly organized social order. He was the shining example in politics of the much touted individualism that the large financial leaders have been so desirous of preserving—for themselves.

Huey belongs, as we have seen, also to the great Southern demagogic tradition of Tillman and Thomas J. Hefflin; he has his counterpart in similar figures of today: Olin D. Johnson of South Carolina; the "prosperity rain-maker" Klansman, Bibb Graves of Alabama; Ruby Lafoon, the silk-stocking baiter of Kentucky; Eugene Talmadge of Georgia; rabble-raiser Theodore G. Bilbo of Mississippi; and others. He belongs, therefore, also to the Andrew Jackson tradition. He was a modern version of the mugwumps, the know-nothingers, the free silverites, the Populists. He was another great Commoner quoting Scripture—with a difference.

He was more efficient, more intelligent, more adaptable, more universal, and more ruthless. His drive was tremendous. In fifteen short years he rose from the obscurity of poverty in a small Louisiana town to the United States Senate, and unlike previous Commoners, Huey apparently was insatiably greedy for personal power. The world today has little opportunity to choose noble Lincoln leadership, but must choose hurriedly between gangsters. Certainly in Huey the reformer was quite subordinate to his lust for Napoleonic command. Bad manners are symptomatic. Figuratively he kicked more than one Volney in the stomach.

Thus Huey Long was the buccaneer of American politics. He was part of the gun-toting, lawless frontier turning back upon itself. His success was part of the price of Louisiana's colonialism. He was a William Walker, a Lee Christmas, come home to roost, an American Pancho Villa. Whatever jibes may have been leveled at Huey's lack of physical courage, he was of the breed of *condottieri*. In this spirit he vaulted over into the national bull-ring.

Look at him in action. The Kingfish is leaving Baton Rouge at four o'clock. By noon autos filled with state policemen begin scouring all roads leading out of town. They stop all cars, force all drivers to identify themselves. Parked cars are ordered to move on. Every quarter of an hour or so Long is advised by phone just who has been found loitering.

At four o'clock—no one but his intimate henchmen know the exact hour of departure—his car is sent for. A squad of armed men looks over the hotel lobby. Long shoots down—heavily guarded—in a reserved elevator and, surrounded by armed men, is hustled out through a double file of guards.

The procession starts. Ahead is a car of armed guards. His own car is flanked by motorcycle cops. Behind are other cars.

He had all the appurtenances of frightened tyranny. "The state is force," is an old saying. Elsewhere the fact may be veiled. In the vicinity of the Kingfish, its naked truthfulness was revealed.

Motors pop, horns toot, sirens scream. "The Lord of Louisiana is off in a cloud of dust."

Such displays invite violence. On the national scene they might have cracked the nation open in civil war. They bespoke the bitterness he had aroused in local politics, and all his guns and guards did not save him.

Before his death the questions *constantly* asked, were: Is he a potential Fascist? Is he a fearsome radical? Is he a revolutionist? Or a premature counter-revolutionist?

He defied classification. He could be defined only in American terms.

Of course at present the United States very much resembles Italy during the immediate pre-Fascist years: a rising tide of labor and farmer unrest, ever more militant war-veterans, violence, crime, crack-brained remedies, maverick agitators, insurgent groups more or less affiliated with the major parties, a noble well-wishing ineffectual group with Social Democratic tendencies anemically propping itself on slightly irritated Big

Business, shifting allegiances, cowardly political betrayals, budgetary recklessness, a crassly inefficient and bickering parliament. In Italy, also, a radical clerical party rapidly developed. Father Coughlin has his earlier parallel in Don Sturzo, the *bête noire* of Italian politics of that day. Nitti, Giolitti, Facta, Turati, Serratti, Gentile, have their present-moment American counterparts. And just as did the Fascist movement, so Huey appealed primarily to the hard-hit lower middle class.

But if these resemblances are striking, present events here must be interpreted in the light of American forces and traditions. Huey must be interpreted in terms of the great Commoner tradition, the Southern demagogic tradition, of American political corruption, revivalism, salesmanship, burlesque tap-dancing, gangsterism and holy uplift—all projected upon a scene of sharpening modern industrial class struggle in a ruthless nationalistic competitive world menaced with war and revolution. His rule in Louisiana was an odd conglomeration of "Hitlerism, hokum and Tammany Ring methods."

It is now purely academic to speculate on how far he might have gone. In 1924 Robert La Follette, with a fourth of Huey's national prominence, with a fraction of his organized national support, still carrying the stigma for many of his war stand, and hampered by his sentimental fidelity to sacred American democratic traditions, polled four million votes at a time when a third party had far less psychological and economic reason for existence.

The stock saying has been that a Southerner can never become president. Huey smashed every stock saying that stood in his way. Nor do we need Rome to teach us that in times of uncertainty new conquerors come from the frontier periphery. When political instability becomes marked, usually militant leadership comes from the most backward corners of the empire, where the contrasts between barbarism and civilization are most marked, where economic injustice is most flagrant. To rephrase it in more conventional terms, when party lines become blurred and maladjustment increases, a strong personality—such can arise most easily in the ragged fringe of a system—moves through confusion like a magnet through iron filings.

For the time being, Huey merely came among us selling Utopia cheap. In this country we have always idolized the able salesman more than the man who can invent, produce or organize. Huey was adeptly putting across a Cottolene coupon purchase of millennial security—a slip of paper and, presto! But a people which would buy Peruvian bonds or a share in orange groves in Mexico, certainly would not hesitate to spend its ballot on whatever chance, however remote, that carried a flossy sales talk. "I can sell anybody anything," was one of Huey's favorite adages.

Huey's program would have disturbed a few multi-millionaires, but would have done nothing to correct the system that created them. Basically his plan was not one of wealth-sharing for the nation, but for the pooling of the interests of the millionaire class. His proposals would create a definite class system, or rather would reform for perpetuation an existing class system. In Louisiana he built roads for a people whose standard of living was on a low Balkan level, who mostly could not afford automobiles, where the number of registered automobiles decreased steadily from the day his road program was begun; yet he won that people's undying affection. Nationally he might have presented us with a financial sewerage system without providing us any toilets.

Thus Huey Long is the mirror of both the weakness and the strength of American democracy. He represented the chaos and childishness of its thought, but also the power of its aroused might. He was trading on both.

Naturally his success would have depended upon economic conditions in the country in 1936 and up until 1940, plus a continuation of the mistakes of the Robinsons, Ickes, Johnsons and Farleys in their methods of attacking him. For Huey was the prophet of discontent. But he could not have led the masses unless they were sadly in need of being led. Deep social unrest still pervades the land. Roosevelt himself has done nothing of importance permanently to rescue the working and lower middle classes. When they finally decided to do something for themselves, they might well have turned to Long. Many a local Messiah has already gained following because of this.

But more likely the administration's gigantic slush fund of nearly six billions, generally labeled "for relief or recovery," would have whipped the cohorts into line for 1936. But every thinking man still shudders to think what may follow when the golden outpouring ceases, as it must, unless we pass on into definite inflation with all its inevitable tragedies.

Huey Long declared that the total indebtedness of this country can never possibly be paid. Because of that he hoped to become the successful leader of the hosts of disillusionment, "the savior" from national disaster.

In October, 1929, Huey ran into Rudolph Hecht, president of the powerful Hibernian Bank of New Orleans and now head of the American Bankers Association. "The worst crash in history," cried Hecht, "has just occurred. It will be months before we will recover."

"It will take years," retorted Huey. "There will be no recovery until the wealth of the country is more equitably distributed." He made that belief the cornerstone of his political career.

And that was the strength of Long's appeal. He dared put his fingers into the real ulcer of social evil in American life. The Roosevelt administration has attempted constantly to conceal it, has prescribed nostrums for the secondary symptoms which daily reappear in different joints. Or, better stated, Roosevelt is an excellent physician curing the wrong disease. Thus he, not Huey Long, comes closer to being the quack, the medicine-man. Long was an excellent diagnostician. Was he a good doctor? In the long run only by providing a more valid cure could Huey's strength in the land have been diminished, though a sudden world war or a temporary return of prosperity would have greatly offset it.

If granted nation-wide powers, whether Huey carried out his program or not, he would, for reasons similar to those in Louisiana and perhaps through a repetition of his failure there, have been driven to increasing dictatorship. Only through dictatorial measures, however legally camouflaged, could he have beaten down the powerful resistance to his Share-Our-Wealth program. For the only way it could have been carried out was to have collectivized the means of production—a step to which Huey repeatedly expressed his unalterable opposition.

Similarly, if he had failed to fulfill his pledges in this hour of national crisis, he would, as Mussolini in Italy, as Hitler in Germany, as he himself had already done in Louisiana, have been obliged to betray the groups who rallied to his support and relied on his promises. He would have been obliged to substitute economic justice with an American version of Fascist dictatorship. By his death, we have at least been saved a skyscraper White House.

What will be the fate of his Share-Our-Wealth movement?

II—COTTOLENE AND BLACKSTONE

IN 1892 Huey Pierce Long, Senior, his wife Caledonia Tison, and their six children, moved from Tunica to a poor 320-acre farm in Winnfield, Winn Parish (county), Louisiana. There in a scraggly settlement among sparse pines on low red clay hills August 30, 1893, was born Huey Pierce Long, Junior. Like all true patriots he was born in a log cabin.

They and their neighbors—frontier people like those in the pine regions of Arkansas or east Texas—were descendants of the backwash of settlers that flowed over from Virginia and the Carolinas or down the Mississippi after the Louisiana Purchase, that later rushed across the plains to California—common sturdy folk who built the nation but have remained step-children of the prosperity they helped create, the forgotten men of the South.

All this folk—those not in the slave-holding aristocracy—had been shoved off upon marginal lands too worthless to be absorbed into big estates. For generations they had been out of touch with even provincial centers of civilization—lost souls in the folds of dismal low hills. Ignorant, superstitious, bigoted, inarticulate, they could not improve their lot or lift their swarms of progeny into the professional or business world. Their only outlets were sex, corn whiskey and religion. The Bible was their sole intellectual nourishment; they looked with dark suspicion on wider learning, rarely even read a newspaper. Mostly Baptists (southern Louisiana is Catholic), they were, like their obstinate red hills, their sun-baked fields and brittle corn-stalks, severe, dry, uncompromising men, who took life seriously and lived by Puritan morals, shaken at intervals by dark storms of incest, sexual monstrosities and social rebellion.

They had nothing in common with the light-hearted cruel

28

Creole aristocrats who had grown cotton with negroes under
the lash on rich alluvial plantations along the sluggish bayous
to the south or along the Mississippi levee. The backwoods
farmers had never had slaves. They tilled the sullen soil with
their own sweaty calloused hands and feared God. They bore
solid Anglo-Saxon names and spoke then and do still, piny
woods English, a homely colloquial utterance, not French
patois. Though Huey claims Dutch [German], Scotch, Welsh,
Irish and French descent, he was molded by the place and
people where he was raised.

Only men with brawn had opportunity; but those who lacked
the proper physical assets, because of neighborly generosity,
rarely went without. Huey was frequently sent by his parents
with food and clothing to some less fortunate family, among
them a Methodist preacher with small children but few parish-
ioners. Later one of the children, Huey declared, was "among
the foremost of the sinister-controlled members of the legislature" trying to ruin him as governor. Huey sent the self-
revealing message: "I'm still glad my folks didn't let you
starve." Others say they quarreled because the governor tried
to force him to perform a dishonorable act.

In 1900—Huey was seven then—the Arkansas Southern
Railroad was thrust from El Dorado into Winn Parish. Three
other railroads followed. Sawmills and lumber camps sprang
into life. Winnfield became a village, within ten years a town
of 3,000. A station was stuck up on the Long farm. Part of
their land became the main business section, part was cut up
for residences. "Some men got rich, others couldn't pay their
debts," remarks Huey. Homespun kindliness was soon modi-
fied by the new era of business.

The first sign he remembers "of a neighborhood where the
blessings of the Creator were shared with one another, being
transformed into a community yielding to commercial entice-
ments" was a sheriff's sale in 1902 on the courthouse steps.
The farmer "got right up on a little old crackerbox," and
pleading for his home for his children, asked folk not to bid.
Not a man did—except Huey's own cousin, who didn't even
need the place. The farmer was ruthlessly evicted. "I was

horrified. . . . It seemed criminal . . ." and he thought, "Something awful's going to happen to that cousin. And sure enough his wife died soon after and all sorts of misfortune overtook him."

It is not recorded, however, that such Jehovah vengeance restored the poor man his farm. But Winn Parish did not entirely depend upon divine retribution for social justice. Of all the parishes, it developed a tradition of rebellion. Strongly Populist in the boom days of Sockless Jerry, it stamped on to the Bryan band-wagon. It idolized Jeff Davis of Missouri and Carrie Nation of Kansas. Presently Gene Debs woke socialist echoes. A little later big Bill Haywood claimed many an aggressive I.W.W. convert among the sawmill workers. Huey's own father was something of a Socialist. Young Huey was exposed to these winds of doctrine.

2

The incoming sawmill workers were a rough and tumble crew. Along with gusts of proletarian revolt, the community was plagued by saloons, women, gambling. Huey's devout father feared for his offspring and bought another place ten miles back. During vacations or after school, Huey—plug of tobacco secreted in his jeans—used to ride out to the fields to help his father plow, cultivate and harvest. During "chopping-out" time he cut wood or hewed cross-ties for the railroad or drove a team of mules. Cotton-picking was paid by weight; at least once Huey was caught stuffing a watermelon into his lot to make it more hefty.

He hated farm work. Up before the sun, he had to toil far into the dark, after which there was nothing to do but eat supper, listen to the whippoorwills, and go to bed. The rows were long, the sun blistering, there was little companionship. Often he stopped to ease his aching back, mop his brow, and make resolutions to escape. Ever since, his sympathy has "gone out to those who toil."

His brother Julius, who became a bitter enemy, says harshly this is merely sob-stuff, that Huey never did an honest day's work in his life. Huey did make early attempts to run away from home, later sought more intelligent escapes from back-breaking toil. At thirteen he took up printer's work, a "well-paid" job, obtained through his boyhood friend, Harley Bozeman. He also auctioned off books and merchandise. Talking and trading were to become his two greatest political assets.

The only antidotes to small-town toil and boredom were religion and sandlot baseball. Huey later boasted he had played every position on the home team—presumably not all at the same time. He grew up in the shadow of Baptist holiness. At nine Sunday morning he had to go to Sunday School, then to church services; in the afternoon, the young folks' league, at night more services; Wednesday nights, prayer meeting. "We went to every funeral within ten miles. Most of us read the Scripture from cover to cover"—which explains why in later years, to the delight of just such narrow communities, Huey's political speeches were loaded down with Biblical references. At protracted revivals, held in the woods in pine-bough tabernacles, Huey and his friends, in itchy Sunday-best, sat open-mouthed under the spell of country-preacher oratory about brimstone and hell. In orgasms of emotional frenzy, people trekked up the sawdust trail to God; hillbillies hastened to ruin hard-earned Sunday meeting clothes by a dousing.

In such reunions, Huey saw the power of the spellbinder over the mob, the frail barrier most people have against the tumult of their own emotions, how crowds are swayed and controlled. The lure of the platform laid hold of Huey's soul; he visioned himself above the admiring crowd, the center of attention. He determined to be an orator.

At fifteen, sent from Winnfield High to the state debating rally at the university in Baton Rouge, he received honorable mention, next year won third place and a scholarship. For a time—he had been suspended—he paid his way at Shreveport High by selling patent medicines. During recesses, mounting an improvised soapbox, he harangued his fellow-students. He loved to recite Henley's "Invictus," learned in English class. "Master of my fate" and "captain of my soul" were to serve him in good stead during many political trounces when "his head was bloody but unbowed." He never lost an opportunity to speak in public.

Though brother Julius hastens to brand this tale as false, Huey brags that in 1907, only fourteen, he made his first sally into politics by managing the campaign, distributing hand-bills and making speeches, for a tick inspector candidate said to have no chance—everything for $2.50 down and $2.50 when elected. Needless to say, Huey collected the full amount.

3

Huey finished with Winnfield High in 1910, a hard year in town; and though six of the nine children, by dint of scraping, had been sent off to college, Huey, unable to secure any money for books and lodging, could not utilize his scholarship. Harley Bozeman (whom he later maligned) got him a job traveling for the N. K. Fairbanks Company, selling Gold Dust and Cottolene shortening. He journeyed through the countryside in horse and buggy, tacked up signs, distributed pie tins and cookbooks and held baking contests.

Huey made an excellent sales record. He would hitch his nag in front of the main grocery store, sell the merchant, then make the rounds for orders. Sticking his foot in the door, he would overwhelm the good housewives with talk and breezy humor. Before they knew it, he would be in the kitchen giving them a demonstration, not infrequently, perhaps, winning their hearts.

He flicked his whip over the ears of friend horse up and down the highways and byways, over the red hills, along clear swift streams, through pine woods, stopping at every country store, at every house door. He became intimately acquainted with the mental quirks of the ignorant, which he was to exploit so cleverly in years to come, learned how to take advantage of credulity and prejudice. He gained the gloomy opinion of Louisiana corduroy roads which later made him pour out so many dollars and buckets of cement to thread the state with highways.

In the summer of 1911, through faithful Bozeman, he secured employment with a packing company as a regular traveling salesman with salary and expense account. Now he could cock his hat on the back of his head and swagger in and out of the best hotels. A bed of ease. His head was turned. Convinced by other salesmen that if he reported good sales, he need not worry about his expense account or the regularity of his work, he ignored several warnings and was summarily discharged.

He went to Houston, Texas, to try to get reinstated. Unsuccessful, for several months he worked there at odd jobs, then left for Memphis, Tennessee. For several weeks he was on the bum completely, but in January, 1912, an appeal to friend Bozeman brought him the fare to Oklahoma City so he might attend the University at Norman. He got a job with the Dawson Produce Company, covering Norman and adjacent towns. With fifteen cents in his pocket, snow and sleet on the ground, he hoofed the eighteen miles to Norman against an icy wind. Reaching there about midnight, he warmed himself at an oil mill, then pounded the sidewalks until daybreak.

Bright and early he made the rounds and secured orders enough to make up a carload of potatoes. He had to hock his leather purse to phone in his order.

The company was out of potatoes!

Huey tells of his disillusionment. "I had walked; I had starved; I had disposed of everything of value I had on the face of the earth. . . ." But determined not to give up without one more effort, he went to the bank and tried to borrow twenty-five dollars. "At least the bank wasn't crazy."

About to walk the ties out of town, at the Santa Fe depot he told his tale to a well-groomed man, who unexpectedly loaned him five dollars and persuaded merchants to give him business and his store-keeper brother-in-law to let him have needed law books on credit.

Huey attended classes at the university from January to May, the happiest days of his whole life. He claims he was earning $100 a month. Brother Julius declares he was supported by brother Earl.

At the close of the term he secured a regular salesman's job with the Faultless Starch Company of Kansas City, and presently was located in Memphis at the famous old Gayoso Hotel in charge of other salesmen, covering nine states.

Since he was now helping others (as he claims) or because Earl could no longer send him money (as others say), in any event, to his "great grief and heartache" he was unable to return to the university.

4

During Christmas week, 1912, home on a month's vacation, he courted Rose McConnell in Shreveport, a lively small girl with black hair, forward teeth and pale Irish blue eyes. In one of his previous baking contests in that city, Huey had pinned the blue ribbon on the Bride Loaf Cake sent in by Rose. He delivered the prize in person.

Now Huey was arrested, charged with having shot at someone. Friend Bozeman furnished bail. At the time of the shooting, Huey had been in Rose's company at the Opera House hearing "Lohengrin." Fortunately she had kept the stubs. They located everyone near them at the show. Huey was cleared. Had it not been for Rose and the two stubs, his later political career might have been blasted. He was grateful —besides being in love—and the following year, borrowing ten bucks to pay the preacher, he married her in Memphis. Thus Cottolene not only laid the basis of his political career by promoting his persuasive powers, but—as Webster Smith has remarked—greased his way into matrimony.

Later summer, 1914—European war clouds had gathered —Huey, after spending a few weeks on the road for the Chattanooga Medicine Company selling Wine of Cardui, saved up $400, borrowed $400 more from Julius, and entered Tulane University in New Orleans as a law student.

He and Rose lived in a dingy apartment, and Huey, carrying the whole three years' course in one year, and going in for debating besides, studied from sixteen to twenty hours a day. His weight dropped to 112 pounds.

He passed all the exams the scholastic rules permitted— not enough to give him a diploma. His money gone, he faced the alternative of becoming a lawyer very quickly or abandoning the effort. He persuaded Justice A. Monroe and the bar committee to give him a special examination. May 15, 1915, at the age of twenty-one, he was sworn in as a full-fledged lawyer in the state of Louisiana.

5

Long tells how he went back to Winnfield and hung out his shingle, how his first month netted no returns, how he had to give up his office.

The truth is, says brother Julius (then prosecuting attorney), he took Huey into partnership and taught him how to handle a practice. But Huey insisted on defending cases Julius had to prosecute. Huey's insatiable need to dominate everyone did not sit so well with his elder brother. The partnership was dissolved. Subsequently Huey handled many such opposition cases, but according to Julius, lost all but one.

Without funds, Huey tried to get another job as traveling salesman. Unsuccessful, he made another stab at law. Over the bank of Winnfield—an uncle was president—he took on credit an eight by ten anteroom with no electric lights and but one window. He placed his three law books on a white pine table and had painted a fifty-cent tin sign. Even $4.00 a month rent was hard to get, the bank pressed him; but Rose was economical—no children yet—and they lived modestly. He picked up a little "chip and whetstone" practice, particularly workmen's compensation cases.

In 1916 this budding practice was threatened by a proposed law to limit employers' liability. Huey agitated widely against the measure and prepared an amendment which a friend, State Senator S. J. Harper, a director of the bank, agreed to present to the Committee on Capital and Labor.

In Baton Rouge, Huey was very disgusted at "the formali-

ties, mannerisms, kowtowing and easily discernible insinceri-
ties surrounding all the affairs of the session." To a chance
acquaintance, he remarked: "Everybody talks guarded, like he
was afraid to slip on something. . . ."

"You're fighting on a bad side. . . . Just as fast as you
can you are trying to fence yourself out of getting a pretty
good start as a lawyer. . . . Why do you think the Standard
Oil is located here?"

Attempting to speak to the Committee, Huey was rudely
squelched.

"Whom do you represent?"

"Several thousand common laborers."

"Are they paying you anything?"

"No."

"They seem to have good sense." Everyone guffawed.

About midnight a motion was made to adjourn. Huey leapt
to his feet—"For twenty years has the Louisiana Legislature
been dominated by the henchmen and attorneys of the interests. But, gentlemen . . . not until 1914 did they possess
the brazen audacity to command the General Assembly . . .
to pass unanimously a law by which a laborer's family should
not receive over an average sum of $300 for a life upon
whom they depended for education and support." The sacred
name of "justice" was being used with "fraud and deceit" by
those representing "the combined corporations."

After this first attempt at lobbying, Huey from then on
turned his hand to practical politics, back-stage manipulation
and vote-trading. He took an electoral suit to court and won it.

New legal opportunities presented themselves. Soon Huey's
practice was as large—he says so himself—as that of the
balance of the Winnfield lawyers together. He acquired a
library and a suitable office.

Suits against lumber companies brought him payment in
lumber. But how force the companies—their tram lines operated exclusively for their own output—to transport his timber
or else pay him a fair price? One concern was extending its
tracks into timber it thought it owned. Huey brought suit.

He won. To cross the land the company would have to de-

clare its railroad a common carrier. The president of the
concern called Huey. "Don't sue us any more. The next time
anyone comes to you with a claim, write me what you think
is a fair settlement, and I will send a check." Huey never had
to sue that company again. He had learned one of his first
important lessons in dealing with corporations.

6

Senator Harper had fought hard to keep America out of
the World War. His campaign booklet: *Issues of the Day—
Free Speech—Financial Slavery* got him indicted under the
Espionage Act. Huey defended him in court and in the press.
In the *Times Picayune* (February 22, 1928) Huey published
the whole germ of his later Share-Our-Wealth program:

"Senator Harper . . . announced that his platform was
solely one that this war . . . should be supported by a conscription of war profits and certain amounts of swollen fortunes, as well as conscription of men, or the country must
face financial slavery. . . . Two percent of the people . . .
own 70 percent of the wealth. . . ." Such ideas, in the enlightened year 1918, were unpatriotic, criminal. Huey almost
went to jail also.

But after tricky, pretended tampering with the jury panels,
which Huey himself has described in detail, he got Harper
acquitted. The importance of this trial was not its unusual
outcome during such bigoted moments, but that from Harper,
Huey got his *fixed idea* of sharing wealth. *Harper's little booklet contains all the ideas, much of the wording and statistics
which Huey has used from that day to this.*

Huey got himself draft-exempted as a notary public and
continued—dangerous those days—to broadcast his (Harper's) Share-Our-Wealth views. But having already learned
to conceal his left hand from his right, he also campaigned
in behalf of the Liberty Loan drive—in company with one
John H. Morgan, later exposed—and declared the war a just
war. On the other hand he was setting forth (*New Orleans
Item*, March 1, 1918) on the basis of President Wilson's 1916

Industrial Relations Commission report that between 1899 and 1910 "the wealth of the nation trebled, yet the masses owned less in 1910 than in 1890. . . . Wealth is fast accumulating in the hands of the few. . . ." Then the inevitable religious note: "There is not the opportunity for Christian uplift and education and cannot be until there is economic reform."

For seventeen years Huey's cry remained exactly the same! Huey used these identical statistics in his famous radio-broadcast reply to Hugh Johnson, March 5, 1935! They are found in nearly every speech. Will Irwin has remarked: "As Huey Long was at twenty-one, so perhaps he is today—the brilliant boy who never grew up." As a boy he protested against the "Wall Street money devil," the "predatory trusts and the grasping corporations," the old resentment of rural South and West—plus all youth's idealistic dream of a perfect and just world. "And the knight in shining armor," continues Irwin, "who was going to slay the corporation dragon was none other than the author, Huey P. Long." But always, too, from the very first, there was the same hard, vain, selfish, practical note.

Increasingly, Huey was called about the state to handle cases, always—he has often boasted he has never taken a suit against a poor man—"in behalf of the underdog." "But 'save the mark' when we ran into battle against one of these corporations before a state board! . . . We didn't have the chance of a snowball in a fire." Huey fought to reform their personnel and conduct. "In my youthful enthusiasm, I felt perfectly equal to the task. Had I known then the hill I had picked to climb, it is certain that my plan to free those departments from corporate influences would have been less ambitious. . . . The road to reform is usually strewn with the bones of martyrs." For a long time, Huey showed no intention of leaving *his* bones along that road and when he was finally killed he was far from being a martyr.

In the summer of 1918, twenty-four years old, determined to enter politics to change things (*also to protect his personal oil holdings*), he threw his hat into the ring against four other candidates in the North District for member of the Louisiana Railroad Commission. His brother Earl put up the required $125 filing deposit and covered the twenty-eight parishes of the district several times, tacking up Huey's picture (Huey has never given him credit). Julius (and to him Huey has given no credit) claims he wrote all the propaganda, got ten outstanding Winnfielders to work for him, and managed his campaign.

In Shreveport, Huey established headquarters in his father-in-law's residence. His wife (their first child was only a year old), relatives and neighbors mailed out the literature.

Soon dead broke, Huey got his Winnfield storekeeper friend, Tax-Assessor O. K. Allen, to negotiate his note at the bank for $500 and with part of the borrowed cash bought a car to continue campaigning. He worked day and night, tacked up signs with his own hands, canvassed the voters in person, often routing farmers out of bed at late hours—they remembered him. In all his speeches, he pointed out the inequitable distribution of wealth and swore he would make the corporations toe the mark.

Huey won a place on the final ballot, some two thousand votes behind the first man, but after still more vigorous campaigning nosed into victory by a scant 636 majority. At the age of twenty-five he had become Railroad Commissioner of the state of Louisiana.

7

Brother Julius at once persuaded Huey to set up a law office in Shreveport so they could practice together. But, busy promoting oil companies that later collapsed, Huey was not particularly interested in the drudgery of building up a law clientele. In two years, complains Julius, Huey made "no progress."

Julius then moved there, and once more they formed the partnership "Long and Long" at 318½ Merchant's Building. Their business grew rapidly, although, remarks Julius, "not as fast as Huey's head." Claiming credit for the whole practice, he refused to be questioned by Julius "about . . . money spent belonging to the partnership, nor about other important things." Suddenly, August 2, 1921, Huey sent Julius curt notice to dissolve partnership and ordered him out of their offices.

This lack of harmony may have prompted Julius's later sour-grapes remarks regarding Huey's participation on the Railroad Commission: "He was too young, too inexperienced, too egotistical, ever to know or appreciate . . . what a great effort we made to elect him. He thought it was all due to his own smartness. Soon he thought those who elected him were of no consequence."

III—CORPORATION BAITER

A FELLOW member of the Railroad Commission has stated that Huey was so proud of his new position he proposed that all the commissioners wear gold badges. But Huey soon gained fame for the many round whacks he gave "greedy corporations," especially the Standard Oil.

As pay for legal work for independent oil friends in Winnfield, Huey had taken stock in their companies, and from time to time bought additional shares. He, O. K. Allen, and J. B. Thompson (later parole officer with one of the biggest expense accounts in the state's history) organized the Banks Oil Company, the Red Bayou Oil Company, and the Claiborne Oil Company. They sold thousands of dollars of stock.

But the "Oil Trust," buying their oil at $1.55 a barrel, suddenly refused to take any at all from them or other independents. Huey went to sleep one night expecting ere long to be "mentioned among the millionaires"—apparently a very ardent desire—but woke up to discover that "nothing he had was of value" because "three pipe-line companies said so." The Standard Oil was the prime mover and to the Vice-President of that company Huey shouted in a Shreveport Chamber of Commerce conference: "And this is a free country. You've done this before and got away with it, but this time . . . see when you hear the last of it." He rampaged out and for years gave Standard plenty of headaches.

Brother Julius, however, has suggested that although those to whom Huey and his associates sold stock "lost what they paid," not until the latter part of 1920—*two years after he went on the Railroad Commission*—did Huey "and his crowd" play out in "the stock game." In 1921, then beaten by the large oil companies, Huey walked despondently along Broad-

41

way in New York. He drifted into the 44th Street Theatre. "A high-stepping chorus" broke into song:

> "If your troubles were double
> They would still be a bubble."

Remarked Huey, "I don't know who wrote that song, but I owe a lot to him. I came out of that theater happy." Huey had always been easily uplifted.

Some claim, however, that he was still heavily interested in Louisiana oil, that this explains certain apportioning of oil quotas and that this was behind his consistent effort to make Standard Oil take Louisiana oil for its refinery. April, 1935, I asked the Assistant Manager of the Baton Rouge Standard Oil plant if Huey were still in the oil business. Frightened, he refused to answer.

But in 1919, *still publicly in the oil business,* Huey pushed a law to bring the large oil companies before the Railroad Commission for regulation. Springing his proposals by surprise in the March 25, 1919, executive session of the Commission, he demanded that it back "remedial legislation" to "curb the nefarious practices of the Standard Oil Company and the pipe-line concerns."

He deplored the unnecessary wastage of Louisiana oil while Mexican petroleum, congesting storage facilities, was blocking relief to local operators. The Standard Oil was not really a Louisiana concern: 99.7 percent of its stock—all except 83 shares for dummy officials—was owned by the Standard Oil of New Jersey.

The Caddo field. Independents had developed it, whereupon the price was cut to forty cents a barrel until Standard acquired full control, then it rose to $2.25. The same had been true of the Vinton, Edgerly, Red River Creighton and Spindle Top fields. Independents were encouraged, then "at a suitable time, the . . . Standard Oil brought destruction to those whose ingenuity had uncovered the fields." The Pine Island independents were destroyed in December, 1918, by a ten days' notice of an embargo. "Oil was wasted on the earth in the bayous and rivers of the state by hundreds of thousands of barrels, and financial destruction was brought upon those interests who did not early retire." During that struggle, Standard offered Mexican oil at New Orleans for fifty cents—less than transportation charges—but when it gained control, boosted the price to $3.25.

On other occasions by buying up crude at very high prices, then selling the finished product below cost, the company likewise squeezed out independent refineries. The monopoly covered every side of the industry.

Under the domination of Standard, independent enterprise was "as unsafe . . . as is a solitary traveler in the hands of a bandit." That institution had "profited with every development," but had "never developed." It had capitalized on "the efforts of others," but "never" hazarded its own fortune.

For the protection of the American public, "the oil business in all its phases . . . must be recognized as a public necessity" and regulated so that oil should be "produced and transported, manufactured and sold freely and openly . . . without discrimination against the producer, the manufacturer, or the consumer. . . ."

One commissioner seemed willing to sign Huey's proposals, but Shelby Taylor, the chairman, hesitated. Huey pointed out the window of the capitol. "Look . . . Shelby. There now is a ship coming up the river loaded with Mexican crude to go into tanks where they will not let us put our oil."

Taylor took one look and reached for the pen. Huey had the secretary engross the document, then gave certified copies to the newspapers. Sensation swept through Baton Rouge. Next morning, Standard Oil lawyers—the then largest refinery and tank farm in the world was near Baton Rouge—swarmed into town to see what could be done.

Taylor, who practiced law in Baton Rouge, then wanted to withdraw the document. "I've been made a fool of!" he stormed.

Thus Standard Oil, which had long dominated state politics, became a campaign issue.

2

Huey issued his first blast at a rally July 4, 1919, at Hot Wells. "A sensation!" said one paper. His speech was "hot as this boiling water that bubbles up from Hot Wells at 116°. . . ." Huey called Standard Oil "an octopus . . . among the world's greatest criminals . . . thrown out of Texas following its raid on Spindle Top . . . ousted from Kansas . . . forced to terms in Oklahoma." He whacked the governor: "Weak-kneed Democrats like Pleasant" had driven men from the party.

The campaign dwindled to two candidates—Frank P. Stubbs and John M. Parker, an old-style plantation owner from Bayou Sara. When the latter publicly made promises on the oil question, Huey declared in his favor and at once had thousands of circulars distributed and took the stump for ninety days. Parker squeezed through in the north by 761 votes. He sent Huey thanks.

But long before inauguration, Huey was shelved. Exaggerating his then importance, he laments à la Julius: "Those of us zealous for reform hied back to our . . . neglected affairs. . . . Wiseacres, skilled at flattery . . . surrounded our newly elected governor. Soon he was convinced that his insurmountable virtue alone had wrought the victory; before long he was made to see how much bigger the majority might have been but for the 'hindrance' of such 'objectionables' as myself. . . . When the slaves of the campaign had the time to visit him, the elements we had expected to oust were needed to introduce us to our late candidate."

Parker soon announced a "gentleman's agreement" with the Standard Oil, and made his own program with the help of the company's lawyers. Later Huey, as governor, would make his own gentleman's agreement with them, but now, hot on the trail of reform, he was on the personal up-and-up. Defying Parker's agreement, he kept the oil issue alive every minute— to force the pipe lines to common-carrier status and increase the oil-severance tax. He denounced Parker viciously.

The governor angrily challenged Huey in public meeting

to explain his "slanderous" attacks. Huey cited Parker's unfulfilled campaign pledge. Parker, furious, in the March, 1921, constitutional convention, "to get" Long, introduced an ordinance to create a Public Service Commission to displace the existing Railroad Commission. Later Huey frequently resorted to the same trick to get rid of objectionables, but now he drew up amendments to save his job, and his attacks and those of others threw the convention into an uproar. Even ex-Governor Pleasant, Parker's delegate, finally denounced the members for allowing the Standard Oil lobbyists to dominate their official conduct. He disclosed that at a conference at the governor's mansion "practically everyone" favored writing the 3 percent oil severance tax into the constitution, but Governor Parker suddenly rang for the treasurer of the Standard Oil. When he peremptorily said his company "would not stand for the law," the governor "informed us that ended the matter."

Huey circularized the legislators at the special September session: "As a means of forcing upon the state, legislation injurious to the people but highly profitable . . . to the Standard Oil Trust . . . you have seen an administration trade in offices which belong to the people . . . in a manner unbecoming an ancient ruler of a Turkish domain. Better to have taken the gold hoarded in the Standard Oil vaults at 26 Broadway and deliberately purchase the votes with which the administration has ruled this state . . . than to have browbeaten, bulldozed and intimidated the legislature for the benefit of the corporate interests through the free use of the people's patronage."

The Shreveport sheriff phoned him. "The governor has issued warrants for your arrest for libel." Simultaneously a House caucus was called to consider impeaching him.

Huey got bail, then rushed to the night caucus. The air was reeking with tobacco smoke and bitterness. Huey immediately suggested that all three members of his commission resign and stand for re-election.

A legislator shouted: "But he's the only one that can be reelected." Others seized upon this as a just, quick solution. The administration forces split. Even Parker's floor-leader became disgusted. "I'm no Huey Long man, but apparently you are not willing to do anything here that is fair. I'm taking my hat and walking out of this damn' session."

Pandemonium reigned. A yell would result in general confusion. Someone yelled. That yell ended all impeachment effort against Huey for eight years—*when he again stepped on Standard Oil toes.*

Huey faced Parker's two libel charges in Judge Brunot's East Baton Rouge district court. His brother Julius, Judge James C. Palmer (who had already put up $5,000 bond and whom, then and there, Huey promised to support for governor), and another eminent lawyer defended him. Extenuated because of his "impulsiveness," Huey was given thirty days' suspended sentence, and on the second charge, $1.00 or one hour.

Blithely he continued to reiterate more violently than before all he had been saying about the Standard Oil and Parker.

Before the 1922 spring session met, Parker, released from the gentleman's agreement, permitted the 3 percent severance tax law to be reintroduced without his opposition. "But, lo and behold!" remarked Huey, "from out of the woods (to oppose the bill) came former governor J. Y. Sanders." Huey laid a multigraphed circular on the desk of every House member: "The bold and publicly discredited lobby of the Standard Oil Company and its . . . corporate allies have [sic] been compelled to flee from the floor of the State House. Its methods, its demands, and its plunder-grabbing policy which it forced upon the constitutional convention and the state administration during 1920 and 1921 so stirred this state that the people were about to rise in disgust and throw the institution from the border of our commonwealth. . . ." Sanders, himself "interested in oil properties," had made "a deal with the Ohio Oil Company, a subsidiary of the Standard Oil. . . . Mr. Sanders, purported to be . . . disinterested [is] . . . doing all he can to defeat the 3 percent severance tax, just as he did in the constitutional convention. Mr. J. Y. Sanders is the author of our newest . . . tax addition of more than $5,000,000 a year on wagons, trucks, vehicles, buggies, etc. . . . [of] every salary raise in the constitutional convention. Now after adding these burdens on the poor people, is he going to be allowed to . . . prevent taxes on the oil trust?"

Sanders issued a reply. Huey answered it. Sanders subsided. The severance tax bill passed both houses. The governor signed it. Huey won.

3

November 22, 1921, following the death of a member of the Public Service Commission, Huey became chairman. At once, he ordered the Standard Oil to produce its books and records. A Baton Rouge court issued an injunction to stop the hearings. Huey risked contempt and proceeded. He forced the company to organize a separate public carrier pipe-line corporation.

The new company demanded an immediate fixing of rates, but withheld from the Commission the necessary records. Huey flayed its inconsistency, and proceeded to "approximate" the proper capitalization and rate. Order 123, May 5, 1923, cut the capitalization to *one fifth* that demanded. To nullify its new common-carrier status, the company asked to be allowed to accept only 100,000 barrel shipments or more. Huey made the minimum 1,000 barrels and gave shippers forty-eight hours' free storage in Standard tanks at destination, low charges thereafter.

Again Huey had won, though court battles still had to be fought. Strangely enough Huey never pushed the matter to a decision. It dragged on unsettled for three years until in 1926 a new member, hostile to him, was elected to the Commission, and Huey was ejected from the chairmanship and the sessions. The very first act of the reorganized commission was to revoke Order 123 by Order 433, establishing the prohibitive 100,000-barrel minimum, destroying the 48-hour free storage provision, and tripling rates.

There is great irony in the whole rumpus. Huey merely provided us with the forlorn spectacle of reformers everywhere. What use were common carrier pipe lines if the com-

pany had already crushed out the independents, *and he had
unloaded his own holdings?* He had won the battle too late.
He himself never bothered to carry it to the higher courts.
After all this uproar, after all this expense to the taxpayer,
he won—even had his regulation not been set aside—absolutely nothing at all—except a name and a career for himself.

His Pyrrhic victory also points to another moral. Companies go on forever, but administrations change. What one
official takes away, another, once public excitement has died,
quietly gives back. As soon as Huey was out, what little
future benefit might have some day accrued from his regulation was swept aside. In spite of all, the company gained a
monopoly and recouped on the cost of fighting their case by
raising the price. They lost nothing.

Yet Huey considered this his greatest, most successful, fight
with the corporations.

4

During the earlier stages of the Standard Oil difficulties, a
blanket application with no particulars was made by the Cumberland Telephone and Telegraph Company for a heavy rate
increase. On the day set for the hearing (October 15, 1920),
Huey called on Chairman Shelby Taylor to ask what he knew
about the case.

"Seems like somebody else is being told more about it than
me," he exploded, and produced a country newspaper. "Here,
read this. That little paper has a big influence. They think this
whole application is an outrage."

Huey and Taylor agreed they would postpone the hearing.

The company lawyers, headed by Hunt Chipley of Atlanta
with "the distinguished look and bearing of an English duke,
a cigarette in a decorated holder nonchalantly poised between
his teeth," marched down the aisle.

Cannily Huey whispered to Taylor, "Look at that pompous
guy with that decorated holder—looks like he has taken
charge now."

Chipley spoke, "Your honors . . ."

Taylor broke in. "I am glad to find out who is supposed to hear this case. What are you asking for?"

"Why, your honor," Chipley responded politely, "we are asking for a fair rate in this state. . . ."

"That don't mean anything to us," replied Taylor. "We hear this fair rate business every day of our lives, with everybody starving to death except those birds . . . yelling, 'Fair rate! Fair rate!' "

Huey backed him up. "We would like to know something in dollars and cents. . . . Just how much do you propose to raise the rate in Winnfield?"

"We have the figures here."

The chairman ranted. "Yes, you have got the figures there, but you didn't put them in your application. How did you expect those poor devils to know how much you are asking to raise their telephone rates?"

Cannily Huey added: "Seems at least you might have informed the chairman of the Commission."

The Commission's own attorney broke in. "Well, Mr. Chairman, I have understood what they are asking for."

"You have, have you?" roared Taylor. "Then they'd a dad-gummed better sight have told somebody that has something to do with it. . . ."

In due time the telephone application was amended. Immediately the two other commissioners granted all demands. Huey dissented and issued a public protest. Taylor had been worried merely about his official dignity; Huey, in making capital for his political career. The others helped him.

When he himself became chairman of the Commission he at once set a new hearing within four days. The company counsel stepped forward with a motion "to recuse the new member," just elected on a platform to reduce telephone rates.

"Don't read the motion," Huey instructed. "We will not allow it. . . ."

"Let it be shown on the record," the company attorney instructed, "that the chairman overruled this motion without consulting the other members."

"Let nothing be shown on the record except what I say

will be shown. . . . You are going to jail if you infringe upon the Commission procedure another minute," roared Huey.

In a few days the Commission annulled the former rate increase. The company filed suit. Huey took charge of the defense. Staging his entrance into court dramatically, he flung his brief case on the counsel table and cited precedent after precedent without once referring to his notes. The court upheld him.

The company continued to fight, creating a complicated legal situation. But Huey pushed the matter along rapidly and won a complete decision which meant an annual million-dollar saving and obliged the company to refund $467,000 to phone users.

According to an associate on the Commission, Francis Williams, Huey, before the final settlement, suddenly tried frantically to cut the amount to be refunded to the phone users in half. Apparently the other commissioners blocked this. Tearfully General Manager Stair protested that Huey had broken faith with the company officials by putting out a more severe order than he had promised. Even with the lower rates, said one commissioner, the company would earn more than 8 percent on watered capitalization.

The press applauded Huey's victory. Even the *Baton Rouge State Times* (for Huey, "a Standard Oil rag") editorialized, November 23, 1922, that it wished to be fair: "There has been some unnecessary horn-tooting over who is to have the credit for reduction in telephone rates. But the credit . . . belongs to Huey P. Long. . . . It has been his fight from first to last."

Presently Huey, without proper legal authority, had the Commission collect from the company $20,000 for estimated costs of investigating the books, an investigation wholly in his hands, and the rates were quietly upped 50 percent, netting the company over $500,000 and taking away in a single year the rebate Huey had effected for the people. In the original fight for rate reduction, Huey demanded the very large fee (according to Mayor Lee Thomas, Klan mayor of Shreveport and the press) of $25,000 ("though a regular attorney would have done the work for, at most, $4,000").

Similarly, Huey had the Commission collect $10,000 from the Southwestern Gas and Electric Company (which later made heavy donations to Huey's campaign for governor), and though he gave a slight reduction in light rates (a saving of $135,000 annually) on which he harped the rest of his life, he heavily increased the gas rate.

Shreveport, where natural gas was bought by carbon black interests for 3 cents a thousand, asked for a reduction of threatened high rates to 38 cents. Huey replied with a loud oath. They first had to hire Mr. Mark Wolff, New York accountant, active in Huey's rate-fixing then and to the time of his death. According to Thomas, Wolff charged $65 a day and expenses and $25 and expenses for his assistant. To the city's surprise, Long suddenly—after getting the $10,000 from the company—called Wolff off, promising that only industrial, not domestic, rates would be increased. Shreveport demanded that the commission, since it had now charged the company for the investigation, should refund the unnecessary $5,000 Wolff had already collected.

Huey replied with another oath they wouldn't get a damn' cent, then raised *both industrial and domestic rates.* According to Thomas, though Wolff had not completed his investigation, he recommended an absurd raise to 48 cents. Huey then effected a bombastic fake compromise at 45 cents, 10 cents more than the city demanded, and thus, "by grace of Huey P. Long, the people of Shreveport are paying half a million more a year."

None of these large "investigation" funds, exacted from the companies, were ever turned into the state treasury, but were kept by the Commission. Huey also soon exhausted the legal $15,000 fund allowed for corporation supervision.

October 4, 1923, during a campaign, Thomas declared: "Any man who stands as a corporation 'bull-baiter' and yet whose record will show that practically every corporation is getting more today at the hands of the Public Service Commission than they ever received before, and that he has unlawfully collected $24,000 from them, which was not deposited in the state treasury, should be taken with a large grain of salt. . . ."

In the twelve years since Thomas spoke, public utility rates had been somewhat lowered by Huey, but nothing in proportion to his dramatics. With each reduction, behind the scenes he had usually canceled taxes or given other privileges to the company affected. Louisiana's 2,000,000 uncrowned kings still pay.

IV—"RISE UP AND SHINE"

WHATEVER his real record, Huey's dramatics had won him state-wide reputation as a friend of the people. He put out the customary I-will-I-won't feelers for the governorship. At once he was confronted with an issue that was to worry all candidates.

Through ignorant poltroonery, the Ku Klux Klan was rising to sheeted cowardly glory throughout the nation. Klan leaders plus politicians, aided by publicity, fear, bigotry, and the defenselessness of their victims, had made the Klan a power over and above the law.

In 1922 the famous Mer Rouge case, in which it was alleged organized Klansmen had dragged two citizens from their homes, tortured and murdered them, then had thrown their bodies into Lake Lafourche, disgraced Louisiana in the eyes of the nation and caused the Parker administration to pass a law providing no one should wear a mask in public at any time except during the annual Mardi gras.

Fires of suppressed religious intolerance threatened to burst into open conflagration. Driving at night along country roads, one could often see the crackling flames of a cross lighting some hilltop. Long before the elections, the voters were split wide on the virulent issue. Candidates were branded Klan or anti-Klan; there was no middle ground.

To decide was not easy. Louisiana has the same religious physiognomy as Ireland, with its Protestant Ulster in the north. In the Baptist-Methodist pro-Klan north Louisiana Huey had his main hold. But the south—and Huey had to have backing there—was Catholic. This sharp division was enough to tax the ingenuity of a far more seasoned politician. Huey flirted with the Independent Regulars of the south, a civic-action pseudo-reform group, led by Public Service Commissioner Francis Williams and his brother, a mortgage broker, Gus Williams—both ardent Catholics. But how reconcile the Klan and the Catholic Williams "twins"? But Huey achieved the phenomenal by also securing the endorsement of high Klan moguls, among them Swords Lee, an uncle.

Once having patched up his fences in both Catholic and Protestant, Klan and anti-Klan regions, Huey, with a blaze of publicity, on his birthday, August 30, formally announced his candidacy.

Four other candidates were in the race. Dudley L. Guilbeau was not important. Henry L. Fuqua, plantation owner, hardware merchant, head of the state penal system under Parker, was the Klan's favorite candidate. Hewitt Bouanchaud, New Roads attorney, was very anti-Klan. Lastly, Judge J. G. Palmer—Huey's friend during his slander indictment, whom he had promised to support. Instead Huey now attacked him viciously as a representative of "the special interests," a corporation lawyer for "the Sinclair Oil Trust." "Four years ago we put one millionaire into office. We have paid a sad and heavy price for our super-folly, and we don't want another one."

Palmer (who shortly withdrew from the race) replied that Sinclair Oil had withdrawn entirely from the state four years ago, that Huey himself had supported him two years ago for the Supreme Court.

2

Huey presented himself to the voters as an out and out radical reform candidate at a time when national and state politics had sunk to their most debased level. The corrupt Harding administration of Tea Pot Dome scandal was smearing its way across the months. Louisiana was in the hands of plantation Bourbons and the corporations, working hand in glove with the corrupt Martin Beherman Old Regulars and their criminal underworld tie-ups. In 1920, pseudo-reform Mayor McShane got a few of New Orleans' muddy streets paved but made no dent on the Old Ring's intrenched positions. In the state as a whole, oil companies had long run

Louisiana's high politics, had dictated laws and constitutions, had bought off—with jobs, if not otherwise—legislators, judges and governors. Governors Blanchard, Pleasant, Sanders, Parker and others had stepped from the august halls of state into fat legal jobs with these or other corporations. Pleasant, Standard Oil man in Shreveport, had helped freeze out the Pine Island independents.

Louisiana as a whole had never shared the prosperity of North and West. New Orleans, though become an imperial city, had—thanks to Old Ring graft—rotten public services, rotten drainage, rotten streets, rotten schools, alarming health statistics. Its venal politicians, like brigands of old, laid tribute on the great shipping that moved in and out and gave practically nothing in return. The hinterland participated even less in the port's monopolized prosperity.

Elsewhere, plantations, still feudal, were owned by a small aristocratic clique without culture. Modern machinery had merely intensified social abuses. Upstate, share-croppers persisted on an extremely low economic level. Poor clannish whites, condemned to poor soil, still eked out a poverty-stricken, sickly existence. Popular education had never acquired roots. Louisiana still remained a backward, ignorant, diseased, illiterate state. Cheap race prejudice, accentuated by the struggle for starvation jobs, manifesting itself in cowardly hysterical lynchings and other monstrosities, made the poor white cling pitifully to a doubtful race-superiority, hence to the semifeudal masters and industrialist bureaucracy that with little effort had ruled for half a century over this sodden mass of inert subjects and pushed them down and down.

Like Pitchfork Ben Tillman, that South Carolina "agricultural Moses and slacker" of a previous generation, Huey put himself at the head of a similar host of people "who expectorate on the floor, have not toothbrushes, and comb their hair with their fingers." Huey poured out all the invective at his command. And the farmers hearing him say in understandable lingo all the things they ached to say themselves, formulating thus all the anger and resentment bundled up in them, flocked to his support.

To sneer at this is to fall into class aspersion of democracy. Not democracy, but past denial and distortion of democracy, produced this distorted caricature of democracy. Such distortion always, everywhere, characterizes the struggle of the terribly exploited to free themselves. Huey was, in short, the product of the evils of the unjust system which those so long smugly ruling Louisiana promoted. Into the lower white layer of Louisiana Huey swept with a message the people were to feel and remember.

Knowing this folk don't read newspapers anyway, boldly he discarded all attempt to get the support of the press, which attacked him harshly. Instead he devised and perfected means of penetrating the Louisiana belt of ignorance. Having little organized support, he put out numerous circulars. These and propaganda leaflets were handed out at meetings. Mrs. Long and his children mailed them from his home; employees, from his Shreveport law offices. The press estimated that the mere cost of postage on the first 100,000 circulars sent out was not less than $2,000, and wondered at the source of his funds.

He was indefatigable. He tacked campaign posters up with his own hands, utilizing his expert sign-tacker experience gained during his Cottolene days. Driving his automobile close to the tall trees, from the top of the hood he reached up with a long hammer to peg them beyond the easy reach of any hand. He drove his car himself, loaded down with literature and buttons to be handed out at his meetings.

He waded into the administration generally and specifically, and with negroesque love of verbiage announced: "Our present state government has descended into one of deplorable misunderstood orgy of frequent corporation dictations, mingled with bewildering cataclysms of various criminations and recriminations against the personal satellites of the governor and the immense public plunder which he has dispensed."

He advocated near abolition of the Conservation Commission—"the coon-chasing and 'possum-watching brigade," which controlled the raccoons and the 'possums "by cruising around in a fine steamboat on the Gulf or the Mississippi." "I'll cut off the tail of the Conservation Commission right up

behind the ears." This went over big with the poor fishermen
and trappers of the south. At Lake Charles, Huey accused
the Commission of being a political debt club that cost $60,000
more than all the courts of the state, which were so "cramped
for funds" that justice was often delayed four or five years.

He barged into the Highway Commission, accused it of
graft, spending more than half a million dollars on clerical
work before spending a dollar on roads, passing out automobiles to employees—not "highwaymen," because they rode in
Packards. Sanders, after tiring of his job on the Commission,
"saw a Packard automobile, squatted in it, and rode off and
hasn't been seen since." But the people continued "to ride in
the mud, while paying taxes which mount into millions for
roads which they never see."

The Dock Board "supposedly taken out of politics" had
increased its debt from $11,000,000 to $42,000,000. The
penitentiary, "with thousands of acres of free Mississippi
Valley land, with thousands of free laborers, free implements,
free mules, and free from taxes of all kinds" had been so
operated by Fuqua as to lose over $2,500,000 (not true).
Huey promised to make it a profit-returning institution.

Everywhere Huey spoke of the Ferry Lake oil theft, property worth not less than sixty million dollars. (When Huey
became governor he did nothing to recover this alleged steal.)

He told the northern farmers he would give them free
textbooks, and attacked Governor Parker's new university,
built on a new site, as but "a wild dream" to throw away the
taxpayers' money. He falsely characterized it as chiefly an
agricultural project. "Show me a man who has ever gone to
an agricultural college and then gone home and made a living
off the farm, and I'll put him in Ringling Brothers' circus."
$9,000,000 (actually less than $3,000,000 was spent) had
been "wasted" merely as "an act of Executive vanity" for new
buildings. Huey wept crocodile tears over the old university
which now stood out "as ghost cities of the past," its fine old
buildings abandoned, "their halls haunted and the property
left to the ravages of time. . . . I remember to this day how

at the age of sixteen or seventeen, when I tramped the snows of Oklahoma, I harbored an ambition to attend the old L.S.U. Everybody in the state loved that college. . . . What are to become of those grounds, beautiful, splendid and magnificent? . . . If one fourth the money spent . . . had been spent to enlarge the old university, L.S.U. would be a standing monument to state pride."

Yet the ancient pre-Civil War buildings were in far worse shape than the governor's mansion which Huey himself later tore down as an unadulterated act of personal vanity.

With his tales of squandering public funds by past administrations he promised tax reduction.

3

He argued for criminal court reform. A suit over a $101 mule could be appealed, not the sentence of a man to be hung. District judges reversed one fourth the civil cases. Were one fourth the criminals convicted innocent? "To convict the innocent man . . . fortifies disrespect for all laws." A rather leaky syllogism. Huey also denounced anti-picketing injunctions by the courts. "Perpetually tying the hands of laborers and their representatives is unfair. . . ." He denounced the "prying around" of the federal authorities as "a menace" to life, liberty and constitutional processes. "A single appointed federal judge, holding office for life, accountable to nobody for his misdeeds . . . has more powers and more to do with preventing the lawful and orderly processes of government than the supreme court of the state elected by the people. In fact the state courts are at his mercy."

He whaled the "poisoned press." The *Times Picayune* was "bonded to Wall Street," was owned by a man named Clark in Wall Street and by Edmond Phelps, attorney for the Western Union and the Texas and Pacific Railroad. The *Item* owed nearly a million dollars in Wall Street.

The corporations he whacked over and over again. Corporate lobbyists should be restricted. "They are at present swarming the capital with all the devices known toward tainting the character of men. . . . Their lawyers should not be called in to write the laws of the people."

"The Standard Oil swarmed the state house during the constitutional convention of 1921, threatening this state with a political revolution heretofore unknown if the people's representatives could not be compelled to back down upon the 3 percent severance. . . . In the words of the governor himself, they demanded their pound of flesh." Huey told how "the Grandest Sultan of Turkey" had put on a *25 percent severance tax*. "Why favor the crescent over the believers in the cross of Moses?"

In Baton Rouge, September 22, 1923, he stated: "As a country yap, I put up $1,050 in oil stock. The company made a strike. . . . [Then] the big oil companies, led by the Standard Oil, issued notices that they would take no more oil from independent producers, and my oil stock wasn't worth forty cents, while oil went to waste. . . . Do you blame me for fighting the Standard Oil?"

His hearers could understand the fight put thus in terms of personal grudge.

Huey finally got under the skin of one high Standard official, Colonel C. K. Clarke, who denied his company was fighting Long's election, then indulged in a prolonged frothing of the mouth that belied his denial and played directly into Huey's hands:

"Your vaporings are usually of as much moment as the braying of an ass or the yelping of a locoed coyote and are generally not worthy of notice by intelligent men."

"They say," said Huey, after Clarke's outburst, "men are judged by their enemies. What higher tribute . . . could be given to any living man than the combined opposition and undying animosity of the kind of political corporate elements that are arrayed against me?

"In every past election in many years, the successful candidate has cost his friends at least $125,000," but his own funds would "not come from the Oil Trust, the telephone company or the railroads."

Yet hard as Huey hammered the special interests, he was

not averse, even at this early date, to take their money and aid if offered. He was backed by W. K. Henderson, the wealthiest man in Shreveport, owner of large foundries, a bitter open-shop man who had actually toured the United States fighting union labor and who placarded his plants with huge signs, "No Union Labor Allowed Here." Long was also supported, according to his brother Julius and his campaign manager Francis Williams, by the Southwestern Gas and Electric Company and "other interests." Julius has stated: "To this day he is going in with every special interest he can connect up with, at the same time howling loudly how he will 'stomp them into the dust.'"

Ex-Governor Pleasant (September 21, 1926) declared the general average of public service corporation rates higher than when Huey went into office. He attacked Huey's war record, called him a "chesty, loose-mouthed rattle-trap," threatened to beat up the "coward," if their paths crossed. Huey was a "red-mouthed, white-livered, yellow-backboned enemy of our country." It was amusing to hear him use such billingsgate and in the very next sentence the pompous hackneyed Southern phraseology with which he described Huey's treachery to Palmer— "Instead of inviting his friend into a fair field with the debonair courtesy of a chivalrous gentleman, he attacked him with the meanness of a poltroon."

Huey replied, "I am probably 100 pounds lighter than the gentleman and have had no military training at the expense of the state. Such bullies as he describes himself as being could have been more successfully employed in the war than attacking others because they did not go to war." It was more to the point to know that Pleasant had promised tax reductions, but had increased taxes 125 percent.

Huey's attacks kept the state so stirred up it scarcely noticed the remarkable events occurring elsewhere in the world. People did pause to wonder regarding Louisiana virility when eighty-year-old fireman Peter Helmstetter was stabbed in an altercation over a woman, and when a nineteen-year-old bride had to accuse a forty-five-year-old widow of kidnaping and holding her husband; but it paid little attention that the state department had promised protections to Americans in a Cuba in upheaval, or that Daugherty, tongue in cheek, planned legal action on sales of war supplies. Louisiana was slightly jolted sometime later by the Tokyo earthquake's toll of 100,000 lives. More significant—Lee Christmas, come back from Honduras, lay dying in Memphis. His mantle had fallen on Huey —colonialism come closer home.

Such events were drowned out in the blare of the campaign, growing more bitter and scurrilous. September 15, in Franklinton, Huey appeared in a gray suit, black bow-tie, white shoes and socks, and talked of the "downtrodden common people." Presently he tore off his tie and yanked open his collar, later unbuttoned his vest. His tight shoes hurt his feet— he joked about it, and developed a panther tread, cursed the corporations, and mimicked Sanders, corporation attorney, making a pompous speech. Huey, already a great showman, was drawing huge audiences everywhere. Even people who thought him cracked went to hear "this fellow Huey," and many "allowed," after hearing him, that "this Huey" had something, after all.

He was young, dynamic, his appearance unmarred by his later obesity. He had the common touch. He could speak to the farmers in their own lingo, with good salty epithets. He had the knack of arousing his audiences to great enthusiasm. "You tell 'em, Huey!" lanky creek farmers would shout. "Give 'em hell, Big Boy!" Huey did. With his famous windmill gesture, his whole body quivering with emotion, revival-fashion, he told them about the black-hearted corporations, the abuses of the administration and the sufferings of the poor —all in a frenzy of convincing sincerity—then would suddenly turn off the emotional spigot with satire that swept his hearers with unexpected gales of laughter.

He was, said his campaign supporter, Mrs. August Frank (Independent Regular), "the light for which the people have long groped in darkness."

Hamilton Basso, in *Harper's Magazine*, May, 1934, paints an engaging picture: "I remember one meeting in a little town in the Teche country. It was late fall, but the long bayou summer had lingered and the evening was hot and still. There were patches of perspiration on the blue shirts of the fishermen and the women stirred the air with slow palmetto fans. Huey, his shirt plastered to his back with sweat, was speaking from the rear seat of a Ford; pouring, as they say in that part of the world, acid in their eyes. He attacked the utilities and corporations and the New Orleans Ring. He promised us paved roads, free ferries and bridges, lower gas and electric rates, free school books—and most important of all—a government divorced from crookedness and graft. It was possible to believe what he said, to think that he was earnest and sincere, because as Public Service Commissioner, he had actually opposed the forces he was now baiting—winning, in several cases, victories for the people. He was young, too, and spoke American instead of bombast, and I liked his similes and metaphors derived from the barnyard and the cornfield. I liked the stories he told and I joined the others in laughing. They understood and liked him. I liked him too. . . . He was such a relief after the ignorant and dull-witted ringmasters in New Orleans."

Huey's quixotic personality and fabulous promises aroused the rural districts from end to end. But New Orleans was still mostly hostile.

His speech there on Armistice Day in historic Lafayette Square under the very windows of the Old Ring Choctaw Club was a bit too rural to go over.

"Now, ladies and gentlemen, gaze at my two opponents. . . . Both come from the political nest of John M. Parker. One of them has been put under the incubator of the New Orleans Ring, the other . . . in the nest of the Sullivan Ring. . . . One is supposed to breed a cross to lose the cackle of Parker and the other is supposed to breed a cross to lose the Parker strut. . . . From the hatch of these candidates you will have nothing but two men with the same cackle, cluck and strut as you had during the last four years." But New Year's, 1924, Huey and Williams made a new drive on the Crescent City, talking louder than ever. His strength was picking up even there. The bayou political treasure-hunters began to roll their eyes heavenwards: if it didn't rain Election Day, so folk could git to the polls, Huey would walk into office easily.

4

But all the time the pestiferous Ku Klux issue had grown more pressing, nationally and locally. In Perth Amboy the Klan had celebrated a meeting of 5,000 members. In New Jersey a mob had beaten up 500 of them. In Oklahoma they had committed unspeakable atrocities. In Louisiana, Huey's home town, Winnfield, which between emotional orgies over God and the pearly gates, had given its heart to Watson, Bryan and other saviors, had j'ined up with the sheeted "brethern." There, September 27, were held important conclaves. But in Jackson Parish, in mass meetings in Chatham and Eros, the Caucasian American League was formed to curb Klan activities. Blood would flow.

Huey said his stand was that of the Declaration of Independence and the Constitution—safe enough. He was first against, then for, a new anti-masking law. He said he was opposed to any secret super-government, Klan, labor, farmer or otherwise. He was silent where he could be, straddled when he could, but in general his position was that he would not be a party to throwing the state "into a rage of religious conflict." "I have a record," he shouted. "Without the Klan issue, the election would be mine by default." He accused the corporations of using the Klan issue as a smoke screen to divide the people so they could plunder the state.

Insistently it was rumored through the Eighth Congressional District (pro-Klan) that Huey himself was secretly a Klansman. The ignorant Klan sheet, *Dalton's Weekly,* editorialized: "Huey Long shakes hands with the Great Titan of Orleans Parish. That makes him the Klan candidate, don't it?" At the same time it threatened the Williams brothers, then suing the *Times Picayune* for cartooning them in the company of Huey and Klansmen, for $100,000, with tar and feathers. "The next governor," it said, referring to Huey, "will be a member of the K.K.K. I am telling you so you won't be surprised when it comes out."

The basis of this belief was apparently a secret document being circulated, purporting to be Huey's certificate of membership. The Fuquaites got hold of this and proved it a forgery by a sworn statement from those two "monsters of the sheeted unknown," C. P. Duncan, Grand Dragon of Louisiana, and H. K. Ramsay, Independent Kilgrap. On the morning of January 12, Huey held forth in an enormous crowd in Klan-center Alexandria to try to repair the damage and immediately left for New Orleans and his closing meeting and first radio address.

5

The skies, that night of January 14, were clear, the stars shining brightly. Country folk could "git" to the polls. Huey was as good as elected.

But during the night the weather changed. The 15th, election day, dawned through lowering rain clouds. The heavens opened. Floods descended all over the state. The vote, particularly in outlying districts, was light. That night rain-soaked crowds with umbrellas, coats, newspapers, gunnysacks over their heads, jammed before the newspaper offices in the cities watching returns.

When the first box was reported, someone said to Huey: "Have you heard of the Clay box, 61 votes . . . there, and you have 60 of them?"

"I'm beat," replied Huey. "There should have been 100 for me and one against me. Forty percent of my country vote is lost."

The Klan issue and the rain did beat Huey. The "great unwashed" couldn't get to the polls.

The next day the newspapers reported Bouanchaud and Fuqua practically tied with over 80,000 votes each, but Huey less than 10,000 behind. With the press and political rings solid against him, he had come close to getting on the final ballot. And despite rain and Klan issue he would have been

there but for the New Orleans vote. A remarkable showing!
What was more important—if before the campaign many a
country yokel had not yet heard of his new Messiah, now
everyone had.

Huey could bide his time. Philosophical in defeat, he sang:

> "Rise up and shine,
> Stand up and take it."

V—BETWEEN BATTLES

AFTER the election, Huey made a drive—with little hope of success—to gain control of the Democratic Party in the state by breaking the Old Ring Beherman-Sanders slate for the national convention. In the tumultuous nominating convention, the Long delegation at least produced the loudest shouter, Vermilion Parish bank president State Senator A. M. Smith, who did not confine his yelling to the morning hours; but the Old Ring provided a close rival—leather-lunged Sanders. More to the point, it controlled 536 votes to Huey's 180. But gaily Long announced: "Our convention fight . . . reflects a growing leaning for a discreet rule of the people soon to supplant the grab, carry-away and plunder policy of the present day."

Up at the Republican convention mobs were howling at La Follette's "radicals." Cuba was in upheaval; an American cruiser rushed south. The Klan began to disintegrate. In Alexandria Long-supporter Swords Lee took over the fragments; in Shreveport, his enemy, Judge W. C. Barnette. Livingston Parish fined two nurses $5.00 each for hitch-hiking through in knickers—the local long-eared Dracon thundered: "Law is supreme in Livingston." The fat matrons of the Choctaw Club put on war paint and feather headdresses to tra-la-la the praises of bearded Senator Joseph E. Ransdell come home with a multi-colored coat of corporation favoritism.

Huey's term as Public Service Commissioner expired. Governor-elect Fuqua fiercely opposed his re-election with an out-and-out corporation man. But Huey spent all his campaign efforts trying to worst his very bitter enemy, Mayor Thomas, now running for the United States Senate, against incumbent Ransdell. Huey's stump anecdotes may not have been elegant, but they made the yokels roar and run to vote for Ransdell. He described the "sugar-tit"—dry biscuit, butter and sugar tied in a rag—used by mothers to quiet children at summer revival camp-meetings. Once the fretful child dropped off to sleep, the sugar-tit was passed along to others. "But, ladies and gentlemen, at birth the 'sugar-tit' of the state of Louisiana landed in L. E. Thomas's mouth. It's been there ever since. He's worn out a dozen of 'em. Now he's grabbing for more."

Long also attacked Thomas for seeking negro support, particularly that of Walter L. Cohen, Hoover customs appointee—"inconceivable" that a white Democrat should seek such an alliance. Huey had used this contemptible "nigger"-fear device against opponents in nearly every campaign.

And so thanks to Huey, among others, reactionary moss-backed Ransdell was re-elected by a large majority. Huey himself was easily returned as Public Service Commissioner by an eight to one majority—"the backwoods are still filled with shouts for Huey," sneered Judge Barnette.

2

Huey now had a number of railroad cases before him—one, the Missouri Pacific and Gulf Coast lines merger. It was feared that after the merger the M.P. would ship directly to St. Louis over its own lines, thus eliminating Louisiana. Huey forced a rate compromise, continuing the more round-about route.

The Illinois Central wished to purchase the Vicksburg, Shreveport and Pacific, running across the northern part of the state. The merger would raise the local road's efficiency and better its service to northern points. But Huey saw it only as a chance for another anti-corporation fight to prevent "the stagnation of this country through the domination of a single transportation enterprise." All outlet would be "strangled by one gigantic monopoly" whereas "competition [which didn't exist anyway] was the absolute life of the country." Huey fought the merger blatantly, but fortunately the deal went through.

Rates discriminating against New Orleans in favor of Galveston were proposed to the Interstate Commerce Commission. Huey raised the cry of alarm and rushed off to Washington to argue the case. His pleading—his later enemy, Francis Williams, claims credit for the brief—won a preliminary stay for New Orleans.

Huey's active monopolization of Public Service Commission matters brought him constantly into sharper conflict with co-member Williams. Huey could not go to the Memphis fertilizer conference, but was too dog in the manger to let Williams go; the tariff was unjustly raised against Louisiana. "Because of jealousy" Huey would give no aid to the New Orleans union station project on which Williams was especially keen, and blue-penciled $200 proposed traveling expenses. By September 9, 1925, an open breach had occurred.

Making "an oil and water" alliance with Shelby Taylor, without consulting Williams, Huey summarily discharged Chief Inspector Cabiren, a protégé of Williams. "The first I knew about it," complained Williams, "was when Scott Assenheimer walked into my office and said he had the job." (Assenheimer was a Fourteenth Ward New Orleans boss who had come over to Huey in the campaign.)

Huey now yanked the union station project out of Williams' hands and to hasten action catered to the Old Ring. Williams threatened to "reveal" the "real reason" Huey had sidetracked him. Huey then refused to sign a $75 check for Williams' November clerical expenses. Furious, Williams threatened suit.

Huey chuckled impishly. Cleverly he had maneuvered Williams into a petty squabble over his own petty expense accounts. Calling it "tomfoolery" he recounted his own noble efforts—how he had traveled all Thanksgiving Day to get the Interstate Commerce decision on Galveston rates set aside.

Huey also (May 3, 1926) harassed brother Gus Williams, then Recorder of Mortgages, by sentencing him to a day in jail and a $1.00 fine for contempt of the Commission. (That day five million British workers went on general strike!) Williams had to fight this through clear to the Supreme Court to have Huey reversed.

Francis Williams next accused Long of not enforcing the bus law. "Not even a Philadelphia lawyer could do that," retorted Huey. If Williams had consulted a lawyer for $10 or $15 or even an ordinary justice of the peace, he would have avoided putting in unintelligible clauses.

And so Huey completed the break with the Independent Regulars. More powerful alliances were in the making. He was merely clearing the decks for the next gubernatorial election.

3

In June, 1925, Huey had rushed to Baton Rouge to fight an amendment to the Workmen's Compensation Act, which limited compensation, also attorneys' fees (to 20 percent), because Long had gotten "thousands of dollars from the blood of the workingman." Senator Huson of De Soto Parish, sponsoring the amendment, charged that the previous year, Huey, "the compensation King of the state," had made $40,000 out of workingmen. Loftily he called Huey "a whipped cur." He had seen "the vulture perched on the trail, trying to prevent passage of the measure," and had gone out "to give him an opportunity for personal discussion," whereupon Huey had "slunk away" and given out a newspaper interview in Shreveport, "250 miles distant!" (Oh, ye Louisiana statesmen!)

Huey's long-distance communiqué was to the effect that he had "never fought a workingman in any case. . . ." Out of the one third awarded him by the court from sums collected, he had had to pay the expenses of the case. "Why, last year one corporation offered me more to represent it than I made out of all my practice!"

Huey pitched into another fight to bring him popularity, also animosity from corrupt elements. New Orleans, the Crescent City—largely surrounded by water—urgently needed bridges. A 1918 constitutional amendment provided that a free bridge should be constructed by the state over Lake

Pontchartrain, north of New Orleans. But the Fuqua administration dominated by Sanders fought to adopt a toll-bridge
policy for the entire state. Sanders, attorney for four years
for the Highway Commission, had had a $5,000 survey made
for a state bridge, then, February 26, 1925, had turned it
over to the private company in which he himself was interested—the Watson-Williams syndicate contract—providing
for a toll bridge with a possible maximum for a car leaving
and returning of $8.40. A $1,500,000 bid had been made,
whereas the syndicate, to justify such high rates, placed the
estimated cost at from $7,500,000 to $8,500,000.

"Good as a Chinese wall about the city," railed Huey. As
Public Service Commissioner he issued a statement favoring
a free legal bridge. As a taxpayer he filed suit to annul the
franchise. Though his suit was lost, the Supreme Court did
uphold the right of the state to build a parallel free bridge.

But the franchise holders—now the Pontchartrain Bridge
Company—had faith, since they controlled politics, and Fuqua
had dissipated the free bridge fund, that nothing would be
done if they built promptly. They advertised bonds without
properly warning prospective buyers that the courts had upheld the right to build a free bridge.

"The toll-project," shouted Huey, was "bartering the people of New Orleans as galley slaves. . . . Go build the
bridge, and before you finish it, I will be elected governor
and you will have a free bridge right beside it. You are building the most expensive buzzard roost . . . ever . . . constructed in the United States."

To warn bond buyers, Huey drafted a commission order
declaring the proposed bridge a public utility and annulled
the franchise rates. The Supreme Court held that the Commission should take jurisdiction over the bridge, but only when
actually built.

On the slogan of free bridges, Huey took the stump in behalf of incumbent Edwin Broussard against toll-bridger Sanders, candidates for the United States Senate. July 4, 1926,
at St. Martinville, Huey called the Fuqua-Sanders administration "the darkest in history," more plundering than the

Pinchbeck carpetbag rule. "Concessions of land, roads, public rights, patronage, public funds, public contracts, grants of fur lands, carbon-black rights, immunity for certain interests and the like too numerous to itemize."

July 13 he attacked Irion of the Conservation Commission for its carbon-black grants in Caddo and De Soto Parishes— no permit was allowed until the companies retained the odious Sanders—such factories had burned up more gas the previous year than all the Shreveport area in twenty years. If it were not for "Ma" Fuqua and "Pa" Sanders natural gas could be easily piped into every town and the women relieved of household burdens. Sanders, he shouted, controlled votes by squandering state funds on useless jobs to legislators so they would pass the carbon-black and toll-bridge bills—for instance, R. L. Prophit of Monroe, given a job on the Conservation Commission. Huey himself had been taught to hate Judas, but Judas, after betraying the Master for thirty pieces of silver, had been man enough to go out and hang himself; but "they took seats in the Senate." Such improper patronage took away money appropriated for the blind, dumb and deaf. Sanders had lobbied against bills "to give the children fresh air." His labor record was bad; with the connivance of the attorney for the Great Southern Lumber Company, he had emasculated the Workmen's Compensation Law.

Huey and Broussard covered the state in twenty-one days. Huey spoke four to seven times a day for an hour or more each time, a kill-the-mule pace the sedate Broussard could not maintain; his voice and strength gave out. But Huey was fresher, if hoarser, than when they started. Broussard was elected by a 3,479 majority.

4

But an anti-Long candidate, Dudley LeBlanc (who had supported Broussard for the Senate), had slipped into the Public Service Commission. Within an hour of taking his seat, he voted with Francis Williams to remove Huey from the chairmanship. Inspector Cabiren was replaced, Assenheimer sent home, and all orders Huey had issued against the Standard Oil and many other interests were immediately annulled without hearing. Suits long pending were withdrawn.

Huey accepted the change good-humoredly. "I have skated on ice for six years to remain head of the Commission." He was "content" to resign after his successful fight against the phone company and the Standard Oil. He recited his accomplishments, low Pullman fares, low rail rates on commodities, particularly sand and gravel, better passenger trains, etc.

When Huey next went to the capital to attend a meeting of the Commission, Williams informed him that he and LeBlanc as a majority had voted to hold the hearings without the third member.

"As a member of the Commission, I'm not supposed to sit on it?"

"That's right," Williams answered.

The Commission, however, asked him to continue to push the Galveston rate case to a conclusion and to fight high interstate gravel rates, recently raised. Huey declined to handle the gravel matter. Thomas, of Shreveport, gravel importer, and Francis Williams both assailed him. He was drawing a $3,000 salary to tend to such things. By refusing he was losing the state $500,000 (Williams said $1,500,000). Why? Huey was now attorney for the Meriwether Supply Company, benefited by high outside rates. (Q. Did Thomas and Williams teach Long how later to fight Farley?)

Huey retorted he had saved the state $6,000,000 already. "Why doesn't Thomas buy his gravel in Louisiana and ship it at 3 cents?"

Huey had more time for private practice. Previously he had handled few big cases. Now he "stayed up nights to take care of all his opportunities." He successfully fought three suits involving from $100,000 to $300,000 each. Naturally he was now collecting juicy fees. He bought a $40,000 home in Shreveport for his wife and three children.

VI—THE GREAT CAMPAIGN

"HE has stolen Huey's clothes while he went in swimming," Long's enemies chuckled.

Huey replied, "I'll lay my plans on the front porch and never holler 'Stop, Thief!' when they make their getaway."

New Governor O. H. Simpson (Fuqua had died October 11, 1926), on assuming office, at once reorganized the Highway Commission with tried and true souls and let contracts for piers on which free bridges could be rested. He did this to steal Huey's thunder. For Simpson, whom chance had made chief executive, immediately schemed to become governor in the next elections in his own right, and the Winnfield boy was his strongest probable rival. Though for many years an humble House clerk, Simpson knew the political game and at once dished out political plums lavishly. The highway rolls swelled up like cornmeal in water—unusual brigades of laborers, "regiments of inspectors and companies of inspectors of inspectors." His ambitions, they say, cost the state a cool $1,000,000.

Corruption was the order of the day, locally and nationally. The Harding putridness, temporarily covered up by plunder prosperity, was working irrevocably toward the downfall of narrow Republican Toryism—a water-closet collapse into the corporation cesspool. In Louisiana, Irion's Conservation Commission came under fire for improper utilization of royalties and improper concessions: Huey was letting the world know about the stenches of state.

In New Orleans, after his break with the Williams twins, he had been dickering with the New Regulars, the gambling, race-track ring headed by John P. Sullivan, corporation attorney and National Past Grand Exalted Ruler of the Elks. Huey also wore antlers. Most important, with Sullivan was allied Colonel Robert E. Ewing, publisher of the *Daily States* of New Orleans and three out-of-town papers.

Four years previously, Huey had stated that Sullivan (New Ring) and Beherman (Old Ring) were both Wall Street tools. "Wall Street knows how to call them in and make them sleep in the same bed. If Beherman took a dose of laudanum, Sullivan would get sleepy in ten minutes." Now, to get Crescent City support, Huey wanted to lie down in the same bed, and did.

But his friends, particularly his campaign-manager, Harvey E. Ellis of Covington, thought he would lose more by taking Sullivan than he would gain getting Ewing's papers. But Huey arbitrarily decreed, "We'll get everybody we can."

Ellis resigned (May 28, 1927) with a blistering statement regarding Sullivan's vice-connections. In a private letter to Huey, he wrote: "You know my opinion of Sullivan. He stands for three things: racing, gambling and whiskey. Were I opposing you, Sullivan would be the issue . . . and I would win." Huey would "lose the respect and confidence of the people . . . worth more than a thousand governorships," would be unable to give "a clean, progressive, fearless, honest administration."

Huey replied that he had never seen a dog or horse race in his life, had never bet, had made "no promise to Colonel Sullivan to protect gambling." In contrast in the past "high and holy" Ellis—"an Old Ringman, anyway"—had shown no hesitancy in allying himself with Sullivan, Sanders, Beherman and Carbajal (the most unsavory names in Louisiana politics). Huey himself had never been, never would be, on the side of the Old Ring. Before a month was out, Huey chose Nicholas G. Carbajal as his temporary campaign manager.

2

Many years ago a mysterious murder in Lulu White's dive down on Basin Street in the bowels of New Orleans' red-light district—known to polite folk as "Storeyville"—sent many Old Ring bigwigs scurrying for cover. For a time a clean-up was threatened; the scandal threatened to destroy the gang's power.

The official respectable quarters of the Old Regular Democratic organization is the ancient two-story building on the corner of Lafayette Square, the Choctaw Club—a landmark, that building, with its slightly sagging balconies, white paint, green shutters and iron grill-work. Ever since the carpetbaggers and scalawags were run out of office after a pitched battle between the citizens' committee and the negro police, the Choctaw Club, embracing the so-called "better elements" of the city, has ruled, for the most part, with undisputed sway. At the present quarters distinguished visitors are entertained. There the fat matrons of a hot city bedeck themselves in chaplets of Indian feathers and rally behind Old Glory in memory of Iberville and Bienvenu, not with whoops, but in the way a Southern woman should always comport herself.

But Lulu White's brothel, which in time grew to a three-story brick building, was the informal rendezvous. There and in the corner saloon gangsters, criminals, ward-healers, were paid off; there over absinthe and mint-juleps the bosses divided the swag, whispered about contracts, new school sites, jobs. This was the sweet mire from which grew the white lily of political righteousness and made it possible for dignified politicians to put their hands into their frock coats and talk of Southern chivalry, the flag, the glorious future of New Orleans, Queen of the Gulf, Mistress of the Mississippi, Gateway of the World.

Almost any night up in the petit, gilded ballroom at Lulu's men influential in city politics could be seen, along with gay young dogs, frolicking and dancing with the free-legged white and octoroon girls sans undies, to the syncopated music of the baby grand, and waiting for the midnight "circus," famous half around the world.

Lulu did not own the place when the disastrous murder occurred. An ignorant black wench, she had started as an underworld maid, but when at the turn of this century her blonde bejeweled mistress fled suddenly for South America, she held the fort and never squealed. Through all the ordeal of police investigation, perhaps not too rigorously pushed, she kept her mouth shut. Some say this is why thereafter she prospered with full protection at little cost. In any event she had saved up enough from the generous tips tossed to her by the girls and by the patrons, who wanted no talking, to take the place over. The Basin Street dive, in "the city care forgot," flourished more than ever. Lulu, black as pitch, white teeth gleaming, ever was able to gather unto her three-hundred pounds of jelly-like flesh, floating bosom and ebony heart, a white paramour—usually the star entertainer who banged on the baby grand and sang in ribald alcoholic notes, while the crowd gamboled or shouted or guzzled and the smoke hung low in blue clouds.

In the midnight popping of champagne, Lulu would come quivering out into the middle of the floor, clapping her diamond-sparkling hands, "Come on, girls. Hurry! Hurry up, you all! Get ready for the circus." And a bawdy circus it was, of the lowest forms of sensuality, without even the grace of the naked quadroon balls celebrated by the negro-baiting young aristocracy during the pre-Civil War plantation prosperity. Lulu's circus was rather a symbol of degraded politics, corrupt morals and intrenched viciousness which ruled New Orleans then and rules it now. Three blocks away is the city business district; a few blocks off are central police headquarters. In its heyday the annual vice rake-off was said to be at least $2,000,000 a year. These and other rake-offs went mostly into the coffers of the local gang. For thirty years that swart clever bar-room statesman, Martin Beherman, sapped the city of virtue and gold. And there in Lulu's and Stuber's downstairs on the corner, the feathers were plucked off the good Pelican State.

Lulu traveled fast when the federal authorities closed up Storeyville during the war. She traveled again during the temporary McShane reform. The vacation cost her her cunning. On her return she played the races, lost all her money, her diamonds, finally her property, and a few years later was laid to rest in a pauper's grave. But her place went marching on.

And in near-by Stuber's Old Ring bosses still split what little swag is left to split.

Not so many months ago a second murder took place. Again there was a scattering. Again there was a pseudo-police clean-up. New Orleans is bankrupt morally and financially.

Such is the last stand of "gentleman" politics in Louisiana. Mayor T. Semmes Walmsley, not so long ago himself beclouded by bad investment of city school funds, is a silkstocking aristocrat from one of the old families gone partly to seed. The cavalier velvet-breeches tradition clinging to its seats through co-operation with gangster politics, is about gone. More than one such family in this generation has found one brother a successful politician and the other brothers passers of rubber-checks, stick-up men and rum-runners. The line between crime and politics for three decades has been thin, very thin, in Louisiana. But the issue is growing clearer now. The ward bosses now distrust even Walmsley, partly because he doesn't say "ain't" and "git" and "youse guys" and indulges in highbrow palaver. Besides, they have been scurrying for cover, seeking new berth and birth in the Long machine. After all, Huey spoke their language—or so they believed. With his death, of course, the old gang has been given a breathing space.

But the political lines are still in confusion as a result of the elements of vice alternately having been harassed by the Old Ring and the Longites, a punitive tactic to hold them in line or bring them into line. Recently, Mayor Walmsley, in a last desperate effort to save himself, drove the denizens of Storeyville from the old Basin quarter beyond the railroad tracks. They have taken refuge in the Vieux Carré, to compete there for tourist patronage with prim old maids in curio and tea shops exploiting dirt and romance in the name of a vanishing French tradition, but now merely a puerile and commercialized Bohemianism.

We are getting ahead of our story. In 1927-28 the Old Ring and the old vice crowd, their finances depleted by the two closings, were back in the saddle. But pickings were now leaner, the snarling over the bones louder. Their ranks were shattered—Independent Regulars, New Regulars, and Old Regulars, with a Paul Maloney Choctaw offshoot. Long, taking advantage of that division—not for nothing did Loyola University later compare him to Caesar—allied himself with Sullivan of the New Regulars.

3

Smelling possible disaster, the Old Ring got busy. July 3, 1927, they called a conclave in Alexandria, composed of all groups not supporting Simpson (Maloney Old Ring faction) but opposed to Huey. With considerable beating of tom-toms, headlines and barbecues, Riley J. Wilson, also from Winn Parish, a man "embalmed" in the House of Representatives for fourteen years, was dusted off to save the state from Longism.

About a month after Wilson's rally, Huey placarded the state with posters and banners bearing Bryan's famous words: EVERYMAN A KING, BUT NO MAN WEARS A CROWN, and called the hosts to crownless gathering and glory in the same Alexandria.

Things were also happening elsewhere in the world. The same day of Huey's meeting (August 3) Judge Fuller rejected the Sacco-Vanzetti plea and thereby added to the world's illustrious roll of martyrs and Pontius Pilates. Bilbo, Huey's fellow demagogue in Mississippi, was in the run-off for governor. But what was to prove of supreme importance to Huey, what was to shake his future political career, though he and no one else then realized it, was the famous LeBoeuf-Dreher murder case, scheduled to go to the jury the following day. Of this more anon.

To the Long rally at the Bolton high school in Alexandria came 600 men and women in a special train from New Orleans under the leadership of Sullivan, Carbajal, and Old Ring renegade State Senator John C. Davy, bringing job-holders, bosses and products of gangsterism and vice. At the meeting Dr. Paul N. Cyr, later to become a thorn in Huey's flesh, was formally announced as his running mate. A dentist from

Jeanerette, in the heart of the Creole Catholic district, Cyr made a perfect vote-getting combination for Huey, Baptist from the north.

Ku Klux Klanner, Colonel Swords Lee, opening the rally, described the previous Wilson meeting as a "handful of hand-picked bankers from New Orleans, plus Sanders' Old Ring men." Sullivan termed Wilson's gathering "a hothouse country wild flower," picked by Marshall Ballard of the *New Orleans Item,* just an "outside meddler" who lived and voted in Bay St. Louis, Mississippi, wasn't a Louisianian at all. Overton said Wilson's gathering had been a "rump convention" wherein "the dukes, earls, and lords of the state's politics had gathered to witness the heralded birth of the new Crown Prince to preside over the destinies of the Commonwealth." He pictured the political stork arriving, placing the political babe—Congressman Wilson—in the cradle, from which he was handed from dignitary to dignitary. Then in a skyrocket burst, he compared Long's candidacy to Lindbergh's flight—he hadn't waited for fair weather prophets.

The highlights of Long's speech were free textbooks, vocational training for the deaf, dumb and blind, free bridges, hard-surfaced highways, reformation or elimination of useless boards, abolition of patronage, upbuilding of agriculture and industry, better marketing facilities, inland waterways, the draining of marshes.

He would enforce real game preservation, strictly regulate natural gas in the manufacture of carbon-black and make it available all over the state. The penitentiary would be made self-sustaining. There would, he shouted, be a schoolhouse for "every child in the state. . . . Stamp out the curse of illiteracy." How could farmers—they earned an average of $627 a year—give their children a college education calling for an outlay of $700 a year? They must be given the opportunity.

His speech bristled with stock phrases: "the self-appointed rulers of money and politics," "plutocrats," "65 percent of the people own less than 5 percent of our wealth." Those who had long "plundered" the state had called him a force of "destruction and terror." He and his friends had "tasted the dust of defeat year in and year out," their ranks "badly shattered" but "never discredited." always enough of them remained and others joined "to preserve the courage to continue the fight."

4

August 19—the day Captain W. P. Erwin was lost on his Honolulu flight—Huey's opponents started the old line of billingsgate. Mrs. Augustus Frank, who four years before had called him "the light for which the people had long been groping," now called him "The Prince of Piffle with a pickled record." He was, said the Williams brothers, "a dishonest, disloyal and despicable hypocrite."

Huey replied: "We must fight the bears and lions (Old Ring), but the skunks and porcupines (Independent Regulars)" weren't worth bothering about. He too went back to his old swashbuckler line. August 28, at the Fair of the Holy Name in Port Allen, he whanged the money-squandering "coon-chasers and 'possum-watchers." "They are hiring men to watch coons on the streets of Shreveport and New Orleans," yet past administrations had been "unable to squeeze out a few hundred thousand dollars" adequately to care for the halt and the blind. "When I expose a fraud . . . they holler 'radical' and sometimes 'bloody murder,' and it will be bloody murder, too, because I intend to bring murder to that set of hounds . . . feeding at the trough."

September 21, at the Crowley rice carnival, an Association of Commerce meeting, with Wilson on the platform, Huey berated his rival's Old Ring connections and charged him with "carrying around with him blackguards . . . practicing back-alley politics and . . . defaming my name." Simpson claimed the right to be a candidate "because a man [Fuqua] died," Wilson because supported "by the lords, dukes, earls, nabobs, satraps, and rajas who journeyed [to Alexandria] in special trains."

Again war broke out between Huey and Mayor Thomas of Shreveport. The mayor accused Huey—according to the latter —"of every vice on the list." Actually Thomas accused him of taking campaign funds from Cumberland Gas after allowing a ruinous rate increase.

Huey retorted that "electric light rates" had been cut, and resorted to one of his yokel anecdotes: "Why, ladies and gentlemen, a Chinaman, a Fiji Islander and Thomas made a bet as to which one could stand to stay locked up the longest with a pole cat. The Chinaman . . . stayed in ten minutes. . . . He couldn't stand it any longer. . . . The Fiji Islander stayed fifteen minutes . . . and came out a very sick man. Thomas went in and stayed five minutes and the pole cat ran out."

Huey was so proud of this story he spun it at great length in his autobiography. Thomas, though, had Huey arrested for slander. Huey laughingly got the charge dismissed on a technicality.

But not always billingsgate. Under historic Evangeline Oak of Longfellow fame, Huey melted into lush sentimentalism. "Where are the schools that you have waited for your children to have, that have never come? Where are the . . . highways that you send your money to build. . . . ? Where are the institutions to care for the sick and disabled? Evangeline wept bitter tears . . . but it lasted through only one lifetime. Your tears in this country, around this oak, have lasted for generations. Give me the chance to dry the eyes of those who still weep here!"

5

Long campaign headquarters had been established in the Roosevelt Hotel in New Orleans. November 15, in the Venetian Room, Huey and hangers-on ran into ex-Governor J. Y. Sanders, an elderly man, whose personality and administration Huey had been attacking so harshly for many years.

According to the local press, Sanders hotly called Huey a liar. Two of Huey's friends clutched the irate ex-governor. Huey swung back at his jaw, missed, then turned and ran. He covered the block-long lobby in creditable time and ducked into an elevator, panting, perspiration cold on his forehead. "For God's sake, start up." But elderly Sanders, no mean sprinter himself, got through the door and "the battle of the century was on," with the elevator boy holding "the only ringside seat."

Huey's friends rescued him. He emerged with a torn shirt-sleeve and cuff-link, which that night at a political rally he waved as a token of victory. To the press he said it would have taken four men to have pried him off Sanders. He was fighting "with the abandon of a Bengal tiger." Sanders described Long as "crouching in the elevator like a terror-stricken kitten."

Times Picayune reporter, Dr. P. T. Bodkins, "disguised as a potted palm . . . practicing hangman's knots" in the lobby, said Long "fell on his knees and bit him [Sanders] on the ankle."

Hostile commentator John K. Fineran has given a bitter picture of Long in his Roosevelt suite those strenuous days. His "favorite relaxation" was to come in, "remove his coat and shirt, pour himself a drink, sit before a mirror, and with half a dozen awed yes-men for an audience . . . indulge in an orgy of boasting. . . . At intervals he would beckon one of his henchmen to his side, hold a whispered consultation and send him back to his seat across the room." He revealed always "the temperamental sensitivity of a prima donna. Only the most perfectly cooked food could satisfy his delicate palate; his beds must be of finest down. If anything displeased him there was a scene often accompanied by a torrent of . . . abusive language."

6

The only things that took people's minds momentarily off the campaign mud-slinging were baseball and the gala opening of the Sullivan race-track, where "the beauties" of New Orleans "vied with the thoroughbreds" and displayed "all the incongruous allurements of fur coats and chiffon stockings"— this year "the pony coat and beige stocking fad" was "dying out." The press did not mention the pimps, prostitutes, pick-pockets and plug-uglies present, part of the riffraff attracted each winter from northern cities to the races, or their open graft in the easiest pay-off city in America.

If Sullivan packed the race-track, he also helped pack Long's January 9 New Orleans rally with criminal-court clerks and employees—he was there in person busily checking up "to see if all his henchmen were present."

7

The day before elections—January 19—Huey scanned the heavens anxiously. "Fair and warmer" came the report. This meant a record farm vote.

Returns early showed the tide clearly going in his favor. Soon the final tabulation was swallowed up in a deafening jangle of jubilant cowbells, singing, shouts and blaring of horns. The wild young mustang from the Winn Parish hills had galloped into office tail flying. Huey the Crusader had won. But most of his parish and legislative tickets had floundered; the voters put a crown on his head, but hog-tied him hand and foot.

The marble-colonnaded lobby of the Roosevelt, littered with cigarette butts, cigar bands, scraps of paper, stained with unwonted expectoration, was jammed until long after midnight. When the last extras were called on the street, joyous pandemonium drowned out the final radio returns from Feliciana Parish. There was a rush to congratulate Huey P. Long, Governor-elect of Louisiana.

Among those who jammed in was Hamilton Basso, reporter for a anti-Long paper—Huey had not yet surrounded himself with armed guards to gang up on newspapers and camera men. Basso described Long talking to his lieutenants: "His face, naturally florid, was flushed a purplish red. His shirt was open at the throat, and his eyes, set deep in his fleshy face, were heavy and bloodshot. Tousled reddish curls tumbled upon his forehead. He held out his hands, clasping those of his comrades.

" 'Thank you, Gus. . . . Thank you, Oscar. You fellers stick by me. We're just getting started. . . . We'll show this New Orleans gang who is boss. . . . I'm gonna be President some day.' "

Basso, secret admirer of Huey, now was shocked by his "driving mania for power." Basso could not reconcile these words with those of "the ardent young reformer" he had once heard in the bayou country; he felt he had "somehow been betrayed."

A reformer to reform must have power. To get power he must compromise. If he compromises he grows corrupt, so when he does get power he lacks will and spirit to carry out his good intentions. Apparently Huey was on this road. His new obesity, heavy drinking, physical change, were in his case symptomatic of spiritual change.

His smashing victory was enough to turn any young candidate's head. Thirty thousand more voters had turned out than in any previous election. Huey had the biggest lead ever accorded a gubernatorial candidate: Long, 126,842; Wilson, 81,747; Simpson, 80,326. He had tapped a new rural voting layer. But in New Orleans he received fewer votes than he had without Sullivan's support. Ellis crowed, "What did I tell you!"

Despite promises to Wilson, the over-confident Simpsonites, stung by coming in third, climbed on the Huey Long bandwagon. Fuqua thereupon withdrew from the race. A run-off was not even necessary.

A few days later on a busy Saturday afternoon, Attorney L. W. Cockfield, a Simpsonite, was playing off a debt riding Constable Patrick McGill along crowded Canal Street in a wheelbarrow.

Enthusiasts petitioned that slices be cut off from Sabine, Natchitoches and Vernon Parishes to form the Huey P. Long Parish.

The business interests, even the toll-bridge people, also rallied around the man they despised. February 15 he was tendered a testimonial banquet of a thousand covers in the Tip Top Inn of the Roosevelt.

Federal Judge Foster, who shortly before had called Huey "out of his mind," said, "I first looked upon Huey Long as a bad boy making faces at authority, but later I learned he knew his cases and studied law."

E. V. Benjamin hysterically hailed "Huey the Hewer," and revealed his own innate sense of humor by saying he had met Mr. Long only two weeks ago and discovered "he had a sense of humor. . . . Anybody who has a sense of humor has brains, and I believe that Mr. Long, having a sense of humor, has in him the makings of a great man." (The Greeks had a name for it, even though Euclid did not.)

Compliments and gifts showered on Huey. Robert Maestri, millionaire realtor, gave him a $1,500 emerald stick-pin; the banqueters gave him a chest of engraved silver. Later he said: "I ain't much on this society stuff. Once they presented me and my wife with a chest of silver, and I didn't even know what half the things were for. I guess I'll have to form my own society."

But Huey's head was not turned by last-minute flattery and band-wagon climbing. Without waiting to be inaugurated, he had Governor Simpson immediately operate free ferries parallel to the toll bridge. The company went into bankruptcy. February 24 at the Democratic Central Committee meeting, Huey said: "No music ever sounded one half so refreshing as the whines and moans of the fat pie-eating politicians. I promised my people I would get this gang of bosses and plunderbund pie-eaters out of control of the Democratic Party. . . . Four years ago this old moss-back, ward-boss, pie-eating, coon-chasin' and trough-feeding brigade had control of the Democratic convention of the Baton Rouge. . . .

"Who is leadin' the whinin' an' groanin'? First, the honorable Harry Gamble [Simpson campaign manager]; no man is more reprehensible and more repudiated and rebuked by the people of this state than Harry Gamble. There isn't a ward in Louisiana where he would be elected Justice of the Peace. . . . Yet Mr. Gamble for twenty years has been the greatest recipient of public plunder and of the state's funds of any man we can recall to mind in Louisiana. I'm gonna dismiss him."

He did, and gave Gamble's job of inheritance tax attorney, a $15,000 plum—an office he had promised in the campaign to abolish—*to his own brother,* Earl.

VII—THE KINGFISH COMMANDS

MAY 21 in Hamburg, leaking gas asphyxiated 400 persons, warning the world Germany was already secretly preparing for new fray. In Nicaragua, liberty-loving marines were killing patriots. The same day reform-loving Huey was inaugurated before 15,000 visitors, the largest similar assemblage in the history of the state.

The Louisiana National Guard and a naval reserve corps paraded. Boy scouts trooped along behind boy bandsmen. Next came goose-stepping Sullivan's New Regulars—portent of job-holding. The governor's father and three uncles, all over sixty, occupied a car with the banner: "The Four Long Brothers." Three of Huey's brothers and two sisters occupied another car—portent also of job-holding. One of Huey's children waved a paper flag and shouted, "Hello, Daddy!"

Colonel Sullivan appropriately opened the ceremonies. Baptist Minister Dr. Roy C. Angel said blessing. Chief Justice O'Neill administered the oath. Washington Artillery fired a seventeen-gun salute. The crowd cheered. Huey was governor.

Seated in the weather-beaten pre-Civil War redbrick capitol on the Baton Rouge bluffs, Huey yanked off his coat and in effect spat tobacco juice on the walls. Aghast, Louisiana's "better elements," accustomed to the hollow dignity of the Southern Colonel tradition in office, before they could recover from one horror-stricken gasp at Huey's cursing, his laws, his queer habits, were given still stronger shocks. Before his political enemies could tack about, he had whipped the wind out of their sails. Confused, confounded, they were reduced to impotent rage.

The legislature had convened a week before inauguration. Mayor O'Keefe had rushed up the very first day to rally the

Old Ring members against Long. Though furious, Huey held out the olive branch, but without offering them anything important. He told them bluntly they had lost all patronage—"the spoils of war."

One arose. "We think we'll let you run this state for about a year."

"Sounds like you mean impeachment," said Huey.

"Brother, you said it." He waved his departure.

Huey faced a tough proposition. Of the 100 members of the House, only 18 were with him; of the 39 Senators, only 9. But surprisingly—at the first test, his candidates, John B. Fournet and "bell-cow" Phillip H. Gilbert, were elected to the Speakership of the House and Senate respectively. Huey thereupon seized everything.

May 19 (the day Bill Haywood, once on the rampage around Winn Parish, turned up his toes and died in Moscow) the *Times Picayune* declared, "The governor has taken control of the legislature and named every committeeman, doorkeeper and page." He was "a scorner of the people's rights . . . usurper . . . ruling with sinister hidden henchmen."

Huey expressed satisfaction over such "whines and groans" of the "old plundering element which cares as little for the welfare of the state as the course of the Amazon. . . . They announced they were coming to Baton Rouge and . . . wreck the administration. Blare and trumpets sounded their arrival. When a vote in the House . . . and in the Senate [went against them], they departed like the Arab, not near so much noise. . . . New Orleans today is being plundered by the O'Keefe squadron; nothing short of murder is being done to that city's growth and prosperity."

2

Huey proposed to raise additional funds for highways, schools, free textbooks, the blind, deaf and dumb, the two insane hospitals, and the two charity hospitals. He pointed out that the blind school was in an old building abandoned in the 'nineties as unfit for use as a public school; the insane were held in jail cells or locked beds, in the daytime chained to hoes and plow-stocks to work. The charity hospital was in wretched condition, the Commission hamstrung with five million dollars' debt. He further proposed to abolish the unpopular tobacco tax, increase the severance tax on oil, gas, timber and other natural resources, put a 4 cent tax on the manufacture of carbon-black, and submit a constitutional amendment for a bond issue to cover existing debts, pave highways and build free bridges.

At once the carbon-black and oil interests started a fierce campaign against free textbooks and improvement of charity institutions. Huey attacked Old Ring Senator Norris Williamson (who opposed tobacco tax repeal and had warned educators against free textbooks) as a spokesman for Sanders, carbon-black attorney. He hoped the tax would drive the pernicious carbon-black industry out of the state and thus permit the distribution of cheap gas to the people.

Senator Williamson hotly accused Battling Bozeman, Huey's bodyguard, of having threatened him with violence unless he ceased his opposition attacks. He accused Huey of "ruling the legislature with the will and dictatorship of a Mussolini, forcing through bills to give himself power, dictating appropriations for his own personal use, bluffing and bulldozing committees into hasty action . . . and finally daring to intimidate those who oppose him."

The Senate ordered Bozeman out of the capitol. He refused to leave. Baton Rouge secret police were called upon. Huey thereupon forced the Chief of Police to remove entirely his customary secret agents from the building.

Barron's Weekly and the *Wall Street Journal,* widely quoted locally, attacked Louisiana for "oppressing capital." "The gross immorality [of Long's severance taxes] . . . which cannot fail to drive desperately needed capital out of Louisiana, is on a par with the governor's course in the disgraceful betrayal of the Pontchartrain Bridge Company." Local organs took up the same song.

Along with such long-live-boodle cries, the Catholics howled against free texts. Though they paid taxes, their children would not be benefited. Their attitude struck at the basic principle of American government, but Huey could not afford to offend the dominant sect, so he evaded the Constitution, which expressly prohibits state donations to private or sectarian schools, by writing the law so as to give the books, not to schools, but to all children.

Such bickering blocked legislation. The calendar—both sides introduced scores of bills—was soon clogged; it became impossible to force consideration of important measures. Huey rolled up his sleeves and pitched in. He dashed up and down the corridors, into this committee and that, even out on the floor occasionally. Busily he lobbied, marshaled his forces, glared at his enemies, whispered to his pals. Once, angered by an oppositionist, he bellowed out across the chamber, "I am the Constitution." But all bills were blocked.

He called numbers of caucuses. No workable plan to extricate the pet administration measures could be devised. Suddenly a little French representative stammered out excitedly, "What would happen if you passed all those bills? . . . No man can complain because you pass his bill whether he speaks or not."

Huey saw the light. The following morning, the Speaker immediately recognized the floor-leader for each bill, who moved final passage. The opposition thus outmaneuvered, the calendar was cleared by noon.

Later Huey signed 297 bills, vetoed 21. All the fuss and feathers over, he got only ½ a cent tax on carbon-black and smaller severance taxes than he wanted. Among the vetoed bills was one for tuberculosis hospital funds (a cause he had campaigned for) because the institution was promoted by Mrs. Pleasant, wife of the ex-governor. "Spite work," she said succinctly. But from the beginning Huey never paid out one red penny that did not promote his machine power.

3

Huey could not carry out his campaign pledges against hostile boards. Besides, he needed to bestow all possible patronage. He sought to control them—the Highway Commission, the Board of Health, the New Orleans Charity Hospital, the Orleans Levee Board, later the Dock Board, the Conservation Commission, the Board of Pharmacy—all the agencies of government.

Mostly he was quickly successful, in the end had his way everywhere. In the face of bitter opposition of Old Ringer Williamson, Huey promptly started an investigation of the Highway Commission and had Attorney General Fred Odom prosecute its former head, Major Frank T. Payne, on criminal counts. He at once secured the resignation of all members, many employees, and most of the highway police, then moved in his own political followers. May 22, Williamson charged that the payrolls were growing again; salaries had been increased, new jobs created; once more the taxpayer was groaning.

The Levee Board. Huey shoved through a bill creating an entirely new five-member body with four-year terms, thus eliminating Orleans officials and Fuqua and Simpson appointees. He manned it with his own or Sullivan supporters, such as Abe Shushan (now indicted for income tax evasion), whose wholesale drygoods company was favored with much juicy business and who ere long had the board building the new Shushan Airport. By a false ruse, Huey got undated resignations from all five appointees, and one bright morning (after he broke with Sullivan) members W. D. Gardner and Waldo Pitkin suddenly read in a New Orleans paper that they had resigned. Charged with politicalizing the Board, Huey replied that the danger from the river made it necessary for that body and the governor (but apparently not New Orleans) to work in harmony.

Long next nibbled at the Board of Health. Its members called on him. He let them stand and shouted, "When do your commissions expire? . . . I must pass a law," then strode from the room. Immediately he began denouncing the board and its president hated Oscar Dowling who had survived five administrations, of wasting half a million dollars a year—not phenomenal then or since in Louisiana—and demanded his immediate resignation. The old Doc proved obstinate. Huey pushed through a bill creating a new board and ending Dowling's term in 1928 instead of 1932—precisely Governor Parker's attempted tactics to oust Long from the Railroad Commission. Soon sputtering Doctor Dowling was out.

Huey got hold of the penitentiary and boasted, January 25, 1929, he was saving $50,000 a year by buying "good heavy shoes." But in July, two months after claiming the institution, had a $22,000 surplus, he was obliged to ask $285,000 for it. During Long's first year—he had promised to make it a profit-making institution—it cost $407,000.. Two years after Long went in, a Senate investigation reported, June 13, 1930, that the institution had already cost over a million dollars, in addition had a $794,805 deficit. Favoritism in orders had been shown to friend Henderson of Shreveport and to Shushan Brothers. Proper bids had not been called for. Conditions were worse than under Fuqua. F. L. Cox, ex-chaplain, revealed how less-favored prisoners were maltreated. Liquor was manufactured and sold, wild parties staged among the favored prisoners. Long merely growled "Trouble-maker"—the usual bureaucratic cliché. Scandal arose over the beating to death of a negro.

Huey also tackled the Public Service Commission. Unsuccessful in patching up a temporary alliance with the Old Ring to block the re-election of hated Francis ("France-ass," Huey called him) Williams, Huey cut off practically all funds to that important body.

He removed election registrars wherever he was beaten at the polls.

The legislators balked when he tried to throw Dr. Leakes—whom Huey charged should be behind bars—out of the charity hospital. But by August, country politician Dr. Arthur Vidrine of Ville Platte had Leakes' job.

But Huey was definitely beaten on his judicial reform measure, which sought to increase the number of circuit appeal judges from nine to fifteen and raised Supreme Court salaries from $8,000 to $10,000.

In the main, however, he was successful in all measures to

expand his political control and patronage and build up his machine. April 10, 1929, the New York *Nation* commented: "Every proposal for legislation, every acceptance or rejection of a bill, every appointment to office, every public act of Mr. Long, has been destined to create for him a slavelike political machine to thwart the will of the people, mock the legislature and circumvent the laws. . . . The result has been to spread the weight of spoils politics everywhere."

Not Huey, but the political system, was to be blamed. Theoretically the various boards had previously been taken out of politics. But as a single party and a single machine had dominated Louisiana for decades, all governmental agencies were an integral part of the corrupt system. Non-politicalizing the boards in effect had merely permitted Ring henchmen to enjoy perfect job immunity, creating foci of permanent political power. Though not subject to the spoils system of each governor, the boards were all part of a complicated powerful régime of a vicious political clique tied up with large corporations and the underworld. *Huey had to do exactly what he did,* or else be another meek corporation and underworld puppet like his predecessors. Whether his purposes were genuine, whether the reforms he espoused were worthy and important, are separate questions entirely.

4

In both his campaigns—other governors made the same promise—Huey had sworn he would bring natural gas into New Orleans. He now proposed—he states in his autobiography—that the legislators create a franchise commission to force this step. After heated argument, Huey put on pressure and forced the concern controlling artificial gas distribution to terms. Then, despite the mild weather which discourages the use of gas for heating purposes, "the considerably lower rate" caused consumption to double. Huey harped on this success to the day of his death.

As a matter of fact, Long *was not responsible at all for that achievement.* To have brought natural gas from the distant

Caddo field to New Orleans, with its low consumption, would have proved little economy. But once piped down to Baton Rouge, a refining center, it could profitably be piped on south, and in 1927, a year before Huey became governor, the local subsidiary of the Electric Bond and Share Company was ready to turn natural gas into its mains. The city was merely holding the matter up until assured a proper rate. An independent concern had already offered to lay down new mains and provide natural gas for 65 cents a thousand, 40 cents lower than the artificial gas rate. As the existing company proved stubborn, Old Regular Senator Fernández, *not Huey at all,* introduced bills into the legislature to permit the city to open franchise bids to get cheap service. June 17, despite a powerful utility lobby, the bills were approved by the lower house. The company was thoroughly frightened.

Two days before his inauguration, Huey had declaimed: "The New Orleans Public Service Company has an old artificial gas plant down there upon which they are claiming a value of about $14,000,000. Today we can build a much better modern gas plant . . . at a cost of around $7,000,000. They want to guarantee a return on this antiquated plant on a basis of $14,000,000. A valuation of $7,000,000 would guarantee natural gas at about *70 cents a thousand or less, with double the heat value.* They are fiddling down there . . . like Nero fiddled with Rome burning."

Now, four weeks later, he blatantly called a rate conference for June 26 in New Orleans, and proceeded *to save the company at the expense of the consumers.*

"The politicians've been talkin' for twenty years 'bout gettin' natchal gas. Now I'm gonna give ya natchal gas an' I'm gonna fix the terms an' prices on which this gas is gonna be sold to the people."

In a blustering voice he demanded *90-cent gas,* 20 cents more than the maximum he himself had named a month before! A 15-cent reduction of the existing artificial gas rate, but 25 cents more than the rate necessary if the city put in new mains.

To Huey's discomfiture, Commissioner Klorer and the

Mayor demanded that the maximum rate should not be over 80 cents. It was apparent that out of flashy sensationalism or for other reasons, Huey was playing the company's game, even though their representatives made a false show of protest. Huey's good friend Rudolph Hecht, chairman of the directors of the Public Service Company, brazenly declared that to break even the company should charge $1.65 (!), but that it was willing to stand some loss during the development period. The 90-cent rate would impair earnings $1,320,000 annually.

With false dramatics Huey set a date for compliance by all parties. "I control the legislature like a deck of cards . . . and I will deal it to suit myself, an' if the city don't accept I'm gonna have those Fernández bills killed." (Loud applause from a trained claque.) *This would turn the city entirely over to the mercy of the company.* He continued, "An' if the Public Service Company don't accept my terms, I'm gonna have those Fernández bills passed." (Loud applause.)

Numerous civic organizations held angry protest meetings, and the city administration, still hoping for a reasonable rate, pushed the Fernández bills, but they could not be gotten out of committee because Huey broke up every quorum. Representative Dupré complained that whenever Long whispered to the members "they began disappearing like mist from the rising sun."

Long now argued that 80-cent gas—he had already forgotten his earlier remarks about overcapitalization—would give the company only 1.13 percent profit. "If you want a corporation to make only 1½ percent profit, then you are talking to the wrong person. Put the responsibility of 90-cent gas on me."

The Fernández bills were killed. The city had to pass a 90-cent ordinance. The company smiled up its sleeve. August 28, natural gas was turned into the mains with ceremonious speechmaking about progress.

Huey, contrary to the general assumption, did nothing to bring natural gas to New Orleans; he merely took false credit for something he didn't do and misrepresented the wrong he did do as a great achievement.

5

Nearly all Huey's new laws were contested before the courts. In every case he was sustained. But when the public schools were ready to open in the fall of 1928, his enemies, as companion litigation to annul carbon-black and oil taxes, filed suits to set aside the free textbook law. Unable to secure funds for the books awaiting delivery, Huey got the Board of Liquidation to authorize $500,000 until the contested taxes could be collected. But the bankers informed him coldly their attorneys doubted the legality of such a loan.

"All right," Huey bluffed, "I too will be guided by your attorneys' advice. The state owes you $935,000 on Board of Liquidation loans now. . . . It ain't gonna be paid. . . . If it's illegal to make them [loans] then it's illegal to pay them! We'll keep the $935,000 and buy the books and have $435,000 to spare under the ruling of your own lawyers."

Huey went to his hotel and nervously ordered a thin sandwich. In a few minutes one of the bankers entered and blurted out, "Let's stop this talk. We've voted to make you the loan."

To the waiter, Huey cried, "Take back your sandwich. Fry me a steak."

Only in Caddo Parish did the angered opposition, led by Huey's inveterate enemy, Mayor Thomas, still hold out. "This is a rich section of the state. We are not going to be humiliated by having it advertised that our children had to be given the books free." As a matter of fact, much of Caddo's population was and is too poor to afford schooling; with respect to negro education the parish is one of the most backward in the state. But their school board and public bodies— "the best people" of course—in their hatred for Huey, cried "corruption" and ordered suit. Even the state Baptist convention in Shreveport—Pope-baiting in the back of their heads —did the Lord's work by denouncing the law.

Huey brought the Caddo folk sharply to time. An army airport for the Third Attack Wing was scheduled to be built adjacent to Shreveport provided the state ceded, cost-free, eighty acres of land. Huey refused to make the deed. "You have decided that your children can't have free textbooks. People so well off don't need an airport." He also held up Caddo road work.

Helping poor children was one thing: promoting war and merchants' sales another. With one voice the newspapers howled. But Huey was adamant. The Caddo authorities finally capitulated.

Huey that first year had been blocked in some minor matters, nevertheless, despite the consistent opposition of political outs, corporate interests and a hostile legislature, he had come through on everything important with flying colors.

VIII—VICE AND VOTES

HUEY'S $30,000,000 bond issue was ratified five to one. He at once scanned the state to get the proper person to spend the money. Oscar K. Allen (storekeeper-friend, client and oil partner) promptly camped on the eggs, said he would take care of all the things "dead up that creek."

Years later, Huey stated, "No one ever came before the Highway Commission Advisory Board of business men with a single charge that contracts were irregular or that favoritism was shown anyone. . . . The Board was composed of men of high standing in the state, including several of my most vicious political enemies, none of whom ever registered a protest or dissent to the authorization and expenditure as the work progressed."

But criticisms were made, members and others did protest, and various scandals have come to light in connection with the $100,000,000 that went through the hands of Allen's commission. Shells were paid for at the rate of $2.00 or more per cubic yard, private individuals would have paid 67½ cents. The recent income tax trial of Huey's henchman, Joe Fisher, revealed fancy profits made on materials by him (shielded at times behind the name Schieffler) and other favorites. On over 50,000 cubic yards of clam shells taken from Fisher's Reef in Little Lake, the Highway Commission *paid him as clear profit and commission more than twice what the gross cost would have been in the open market.* In 1930 alone, he provided 22,022 cubic yards and received a total, above costs, of $31,901.80. For the various jobs his profits ran from 50 to 75 percent of the entire cost of the shells. F. D. Autremont, on oath, told the Senators the Highway Commission had paid Senator Jules Fisher (uncle of Joe and also under federal indictment) "$22,000 more for materials than was proper."

Will similar revelations appear in his trial and that of hench-man Abe Shushan (far more favored)? Battling Bozeman, Huey's own bodyguard, testified to serious thefts which neither Allen nor Long, though he told them repeatedly of them, stopped. It would also be interesting to count the number of private roads, driveways and yards in Louisiana that are bedded with shells.

Purchases without bids, and commissions to numerous intermediaries, were frequent. The Louisiana Sales Agency received 10 percent commission for transmitting orders. Overnight corporations, subscribed to by salesmen or close puppets, got juicy orders.

The cement bids were improperly opened. One critic, probably exaggerating, estimates a $1.25 barrel overcharge, a loss of millions. But Huey tells how he saved the state a cool million dollars; a few months later he decided the saving was $3,000,000.

In Long's home parish, a Winnfield quarry had been doing a desultory business in crushed rock. Road experts had declared it too soft; railways had rejected it for ballast. Long, Allen, and railway attorney Couch (according to Public Service Commissioner LeBlanc, Huey's brothers Julius and Earl, and others) developed this project as the Louisiana Quarry Company for sale of crushed rock to the state. The quarry was advanced half a million dollars to start business; in all, $1,250,000 for rock. The quarry charged the Highway Commission $1.65 instead of 62½ cents, and Julius charges that into "practically every carload . . . an enormous amount of water was poured" to increase the weight—very literal stock-watering indeed! The Commission sued the Public Service Commission to raise the rate for the hauling of such rock over a certain railroad. A concoction called amesite—apparently Winnfield soft rock and asphalt with a little mineral oil for black topping—was "invented." This product was then written into specifications and sold to the state at $7.00 a ton. Improper lease accounts are said to have cost the Commission over a million dollars. Huey's brother Julius summarizes: "That great fund of $100,000,000 has been used . . . to

control the politics of the state and fill the pockets of henchmen and fawning followers. Fat commissions were made on
the purchase of cement, gravel, motor trucks, road machinery,
crushed rock, asphalt, limousines, galvanized iron culverts, and
guard rails."

Under Fuqua's administration, the Commission had hired
one lawyer for $250 a month. Under the Long-Allen régime
eventually 26 were on the payroll, total salaries $150,000,
besides special high fees for special services. Yet when anything special came up, still other outside talent was often
paid for. Long and Cyr clashed over the $31,800 fee to the
William C. Dufour and John St. Paul, Jr., law firm for collecting $533,000 from the federal government, allotted the
commission for road flood damage in 1927, when a three-
cent stamp would have brought the money. The Commission
Advisory Board complained of high attorney contingent fees
of from 10 to 20 percent. "The contingent fees in my cases
never run that low," sneered Long.

Manufacturers' Record gives the surfacing cost of Huey's
highways at $25,000 a mile. Grading and filling would bring
this to $40,000, with overhead to $45,000 or $50,000—$10,-
000 to $15,000 above normal cost, double that for wider and
better concrete roads in at least one other Southern state—and
Louisiana is a flat country!

In 1932 the Commission was bankrupt. Contracts had been
let for many millions in excess of bonds sold. The law provided
the bonds had to be sold at par, and the market that terrible
year would not absorb them at that rate. Huey rushed back
from Washington, had the contractors turn over $15,000,000
of their outstanding work certificates and the state $15,000,-
000 of unsold bonds to the Pyramid Securities Company
(Huey's friends). The bonds were put up as collateral for a
$12,000,000 bank loan, which money was then turned over to
the contractors. The loss was shifted to the contractors. But
Huey announced grandiloquently he had "saved the state."

It all sounds like Chase Bank manipulations in Cuba under
dictator Machado. The Pyramid Securities affairs have never
been properly investigated, but it can be seen there was a

possible "legal" $6,000,000 leeway in the transaction, the state and contractors holding the bag.

In 1933 it was estimated that Louisiana had already disposed of $71,119,000 of highway bonds. The gas tax, bringing in $7,500,000, totaling in ten years $75,000,000, was alone sufficient to build nearly twice the concrete highway built. In addition, in ten years $40,000,000 was collected for road purposes on vehicle licenses. The United States government has contributed millions. Huey's fine roads have cost Louisiana a pretty penny—an unnecessary luxury in a poor backward state. Cheaper surfacing at $7,000 to $9,000 a mile, if accompanied by honesty and heavy-truck restrictions, would have built permanent highways on a satisfactory pay-as-you-go basis. Too much showy costliness in a state of starving people!

2

In Orleans and adjacent parishes gambling flourished. The dice were clicking merrily and the roulette wheels flashing round, day and night. In the Jai Alai Fronton and Arabai Club on Friscoville Avenue in St. Bernard Parish, women and girls were thick at the tables. Newspaper exposés appeared. Business organizations, including the Association of Commerce, sent Huey repeated appeals in behalf of legitimate trade. Huey merely told New Orleans, "Come into court first with clean hands," a polite reminder it had been niggardly with its votes for him. The municipal authorities staged a few raids on the Vieux Carré bright spots, such as the Old Gem Social Club, 127 Royal Street.

Huey then decided to act. Governor, commander-in-chief of the National Guard, he would call out the militia. The move satisfied his inordinate restlessness and desire to forge new political support—a spectacular play for the hillbillies. If he cleaned up the gilded dens, this would sidetrack accusations that because of Sullivan he was protecting wide-open gambling, would also whip vote-controlling vice elements into line. But ere acting, he mollified Sullivan by Levee Board and Jury Commission patronage.

Late Saturday night, August 11, Long reached New Orleans and imperiously ordered State Adjutant Ray Fleming to act. Colonel E. P. Roy, put in personal charge, rose to Caesarean eloquence. If ordered, the boys were to shoot "without hesitation." "We are to deal with most desperate men. Remember you are soldiers and that you are engaged in serious business for state and country. You are to enforce its laws [by breaking others]."

At 1:30 in the morning armed uniformed members of Headquarters Troop 108th Cavalry and Washington Artillery, Battery A, staged a sensational raid on the Jai Alai Fronton and Arabai Clubs.

The "desperate" man at the Arabai look-out cage, though holding a Springfield rifle, shotgun and revolver, merely trembled and tamely submitted to arrest. Inside, 500 patrons were swarming about the tables in a bedlam of babble. Ivory balls were whirling, red and black flashing; dice danced on baize, white-marked tables. Stony-faced dealers were dealing faro in stony contemplation. A tip-off. A shot. Scuffling at the door. "Cripes!" snapped a croupier. "I had a hunch!" The armed troopers crashed in. Women screamed. Men yelled. All stampeded, panic-stricken, to the exits. Guardsmen with rifles barred their departure. *Times Picayune* staff photographer, Neil Simes, was beaten up and had to be rushed to the Presbyterian Hospital.

More than $15,000 was found on the tables. All paraphernalia was taken over to Jackson barracks; about $7,500 worth was burned.

Long announced: "Gambling is halted in St. Bernard Parish. It's going to remain closed while I'm governor." For several weeks there was not even an echo of a croupier calling craps.

Long, fond of his new-found toy, the National Guard, in November—to take people's minds off more serious matters—after appointing Sullivan head of the New Orleans election supervisor—once more ordered out the khaki boys.

This time Battery B had its chance for glory. Forty guardsmen swooped down. Beverly Gardens patrons made hasty exits through the windows. Proprietor Tom Getz—the tables were not in use—swore there had been no gambling. At Metrairie Inn no games were found either. But gambling, with patrons in full evening dress, was flourishing at the Fargo Grocery Store. $12,000 was found. Again the troopers made a merry bonfire. The names of all patrons were taken, and they were released. Next morning, Huey made a deal with gambler Brophy to accept a blanket check for half the amounts of all checks seized from patrons, which were then returned, thus destroying evidence.

The following afternoon Huey rode triumphantly back to Baton Rouge in a new sage-green auto "given to him by friends and members of his staff."

The press criticized him more severely for using the militia without civil request. Attorney General Saint held star sessions with militia officers behind closed doors in the Civil Courts building, then accused Long of suppressing evidence against the check signers instead of suppressing gambling, thus preventing proper prosecution and "orderly investigation." There was "no excuse" for his "compromising" with the violators of the law. He was merely "playing to the galleries . . . a cheap boosting of cave-man methods."

"No one asked for his opinion," growled Long, and accused him of having sat supinely in his office for years without forcing five cents out of the dens "for all these criminal activities."

3

Difficulties soon developed between Huey and Colonels Ewing and Sullivan, partly over the raids. Sullivan scarcely liked to see Huey muscling in to underworld control. Huey tried to get Ewing to desert Sullivan. "You know and I know," Long told him, "the people of this city will not stand for Sullivan and his business as a gambler. We had to get him to get your help. . . . Had we not better . . . give him to understand that while we can help him, he should locate himself in something besides politics? He cannot help anybody, and can only hurt himself."

Ewing apparently agreed. Huey called Sullivan to his hotel and repeated the conversation.

Sullivan, Ewing also, thereupon tried to scuttle back to the Old Regulars. January 29, Long publicly denounced the merger. Ewing published a tart retort: Was Long Napoleon or Mussolini? "We await his excellency's return to normalcy." The rupture was almost complete.

4

In February, Huey returned to New Orleans. On the 8th and 13th the militia swooped down on the dens; on the 8th, among others, Rudy O'Dwyre's Original Shreveport Club. In one drive $25,000 was found.

The evening of the 13th Huey dined with friends, then went to a party in the Vieux Carré at the "studio" of Alfred Danziger, head of the Young Men's Business Club. Helen Clifford, among others, "danced the hula in a short crop of alfalfa." A girl present, it was later charged, tipped off the gamblers.

In his hotel, later that night, Huey kept posted on the progress of the raids by telephone. Angered that the gamblers had gotten under cover, he ordered every guest searched for chips or other evidence. Most—a few protested—submitted tamely, but Fred P. Kriss and wife flatly refused. By Huey's special order, they were held all night in Jackson barracks, then forcibly searched in the morning, Mrs. Kriss by three women, while—it was later charged—the privileged peeked. Both were as free from any incriminating evidence as the rest.

Next day New Orleans was in an uproar. The press wept crocodile tears over the outrages suffered by the patrons. One woman claimed a guardsman had stolen her $500 purse. Huey defended the honor of the National Guard and rejoiced that the state now had $10,000 for the schools and hospitals—"if it had only been more!"

The *Daily States* was particularly indignant. Colonel Ewing, standing by his bosom gambling friend Sullivan, published

Mr. and Mrs. Kriss's pictures, commiserated them on their
"martyrdom," and passionately called Huey, with scant attention to accuracy, "the boon companion of indicted criminals,
a chronic distorter of the facts, a habitual double-crosser, a
traducer of character, a beneficiary of funds contributed by
gamblers, a tyrant suffering from delusions of grandeur, and
the singing fool of the New Orleans cabarets." Suit was
threatened by those raided.

Huey retorted: "I welcome any court action any of the
gamblers . . . bring. . . . It will give us an opportunity to
get them on the witness stand." He demanded, since he had
given Ewing his post of Democratic Committeeman, that the
latter resign.

Ewing retorted he had made Long governor, not the other
way round, but would resign if Long would do likewise. "The
Prince of Ingrates and Knight of the Double Cross" was
merely "sore" because he wasn't allowed "to run a one-sided
city campaign" and become "dictator."

Long gave the press a police "mug" of Kriss and called
Ewing a spokesman of gamblers, a friend of murderers and of
habitués of rogues' galleries.

March 2, Ewing came back with affidavits of two women
entertainers at the Danziger party; that Huey was so hilarious while the floor-show was going on, he was dancing cup in
hand all by himself in the center of the room and had given
away the proposed gambling raids. The press chortled: Huey
had risen from "toying with a naked woman on his knee to
raid the gambling dens in the name of virtue."

Now there was no patching up the Long-Sullivan-Ewing
alliance. Huey promptly kicked Sullivan men out of their jobs
and Sullivan himself from the electoral Supervisor's Board.
A new line-up was in process. Previously Long had taken over
some Independent Regulars when he broke with the Williams
twins. Now he took over some New Regulars, a few Old
Regulars and made his own alliances with part of the underworld, a process of trading in connection with raids.

Some years later I went out to see Rudy O'Dwyre—new
raids were threatened—and got a peek at his home cluttered

with marble tops and gaudy gold, an atrocious *nouveaux riches* ensemble. I did not see O'Dwyre and was escorted off the premises by a polite negro servant and a scowling gunman. The following day I talked with a gambling lieutenant.

"I suppose you're closed up the last few days for fear Long will crack down on you."

"Now get this straight, buddy, we ain't got nothin' against the Senator. He gives us a square deal. He's a square shooter so far as we're concerned."

In April, 1935, I was out to the "Original Louisiana Keno Palace" on Marais and Mehle Streets in St. Bernard Parish, run by "Freddie" Rickerfor—a big-jowled swarthy guy under a Stetson hat, with a swanky stride—an old-time gambling type, "All winnin' bets'll be cashed on the barrel head." It was the 10:45 P.M. drawing of his daily lottery. Freddie swept with his retinue into a room filled mostly with negro lottery venders. At a side table the dice clicked, the croupier droned.

And in June, 1935—seven years had passed under the bridge since his first raid—Long was saying over the radio (Mayor Walmsley was then raiding dens and cribs to break underworld allegiance to Long): "Well, if you folk are all set to be gamblers an' nothin' 'll stop you, there ain't much I can do about it 'cept just let you go ahead an' gamble."

Huey swore in 1928 and 1929 that gambling would stay closed all the time he was running the state. Except for short periods, it has never stayed closed. His raids were all a fake show, motivated by dramatics and by the one aim at the root of all Huey's acts—to gain political power by building up a more iron-clad personal machine.

IX—THUNDER CLOUDS

IN the spring of 1929, the United States Supreme Court reversed the local court on the severance tax injunction—an "alarming" though "temporary" victory by the big oil companies—for the tax money was pressingly needed. Also, the opposition was encouraged to new resistance, and once more "soon blazed and turned to white heat."

Huey infuriated over "the persistence" with which the big companies resisted payment, would "show 'em," by ramming through still stiffer taxes. He secured a pledge of nearly two-thirds of both houses to impose a five cents a barrel tax on oil refined in the state—$1,500,000 more for the schools—and called a special session—his "gauge of battle to the Oil Trust."

For the Monday, March 18, opening, Chambers of Commerce, Boards of Trade, special correspondents, corporations lobbyists, all the ex-office holders of the New Orleans Ring, descended on the capital in full formation. Baton Rouge was swarming with strange faces. The corporate interests, through many people and organizations, flooded the legislators with telegrams, protests, letters, telephone calls, newspaper clippings, editorials. Remarks Huey, "The combined 'Oil and Gas Trusts' which had lashed at me with clubs . . . now struck with hammers of iron; pens of publications that had been dipped in gall . . . were now dipped in vitriol. . . . The apparent free use of money exceeded anything I had ever seen. Daily, weekly and monthly publications were not larded with unusual advertisements displaying popular brands. . . . The Oil Trust knew how to fight."

Almost immediately he began to lose backing. Supporter after supporter abandoned him. He was in for the battle of his life.

2

One had already done an about-face—Lieutenant Governor Cyr. During the 1928 session and oil fight, he had remained faithful. He then made some inquiry who would be the next governor, but not receiving much encouragement, he found an excuse to break with Huey over the Dreher-LeBoeuf murder case, tried before Huey came into office.

Dr. T. E. Dreher and Mrs. Ada LeBoeuf, of Morgan City in southern St. Mary Parish, were convicted of luring the latter's husband out at night, murdering him and sinking the body in a lake. Colonel Ewing's *Daily States* and other papers exploited every gruesome sordid detail; then when the two were convicted, stirred up sympathy to obtain executive clemency.

It was argued that small-town viciousness had influenced in their conviction. The evidence had circumstantial features. An attempt had been made to throw the guilt on a servant. No white woman had ever been hung in Louisiana. Dr. Dreher, a highly respected St. Mary's physician, was prominent in local church and social circles.

Dr. Cyr, dentist in neighboring Iberia Parish, jumped on the band-wagon of maudlin sentiment, false chivalry and plantation privilege. At first he had not dared, as member of the Board of Pardons, to vote to commute sentence, but now he took his stand with fine old family class-feeling and the folk shocked at hanging a white woman. Observing the clamor of the newspapers and the widespread misguided sentimentalism, he and many another political enemy of Huey saw the chance to unite good old Southern traditions and their own political pretensions. In a new Board of Pardons session, Cyr voted for commutation. The trial judge still objected. Huey, undoubtedly in good part because his political enemies were making capital out of the case and because the backwoodsers were really shocked at adultery plus murder, at once rejected the Board's revised recommendation. Cyr took his refusal as a personal rebuff, became furious. The more mob sentiment he detected behind him, the more furious he became.

Huey was not consistent. About this time he did commute the sentence of Pleasant Harris, underworld pimp, gunman, gambler and rum-runner. Huey contended that the woman whom he had murdered, Katherine Wilson, had shot at him several times and when she was finally killed, "the discharge of the gun was accidental." The judge "had made a mistake" in failing to notice this fact. Actually Harris himself had claimed this; there was no witness.

Another Southern chivalrous factor entered. The woman killed was a prostitute. For a white Southern man, whatever he might be himself, to die for such a type was improper. Besides, Harris, an underworld personage, had powerful financial and political backing. Katherine Wilson, who knew too much for the vice elements, politicians and police, had threatened to squeal.

Harris's "woman," Katherine, the "lovin'ist" on Tulane Avenue, was kept by a rich elderly "sugar daddy" who visited the "love-nest" only from time to time. Between his visits, Harris padded into the apartment, lured other men there to work the ancient badger game, and threw parties with the money Kate gave him.

One Saturday night in the midst of one of these drunken parties, a quarrel flared up between Harris and Katherine. Glassware crashed. He knocked her down and beat her.

Sheltering her head with her arms, she dashed barefoot in her crêpe de Chine pajamas into the street, Harris after her with drawn pistol. In her bare white feet with lacquered toenails, she fled screaming down Tulane Avenue toward police headquarters two blocks away. One o'clock in the morning, the street was empty, not a policeman in sight. A lone automobile. Katherine rushed toward it, shrieking for help. It slowed, stopped, but at sight of Harris and his gun whoever was in the car pushed her back into the street and raced away.

She knelt on the car tracks in the middle of the street and raised her arms while Harris beat her. He ended her screams with a pistol shot. She slumped there in her muddied crêpe de

Chine pajamas, her white feet smeared with the slime of the pavement.

Harris vanished down a dark side street and escaped to Nassau on a rum-runner's boat. Months after, he was arrested at a Canadian race-track.

He was defended by influential lawyers; whatever money was needed mysteriously appeared. But a fearless jury found him guilty. Pressure was transferred to the Board of Pardons and the honest country boy governor in Baton Rouge. Suddenly, at the very time LeBoeuf and Dreher were waiting news of their fate, Huey lifted the sentence of death on Harris. At Angola, the State Prison Farm, things were made easy for him. It is said he was promised eventual parole. But despite Cyr's importunity, in the other case Huey remained adamant.

Suddenly it was rumored Long had been kidnaped. Cyr rushed hopefully to Baton Rouge to become governor, telling the press (February 11, 1929), "I'd not only settle the LeBoeuf-Dreher case, but I would pardon the kidnapers. . . . It would be a good thing for someone to rid the state of Huey Long." He (Cyr) "would protect whoever did so."

Now he fought Huey tooth and nail on his oil tax measure and delivered a speech which the press hailed as "immortal."

3

Bombshell No. 1. When the legislature convened Monday, March 18, in the old turreted state house overlooking the Mississippi, young Rabbi Walter Piser, who knew or thought he knew on which side his bread was buttered, refused to offer the opening prayer: he could not "call down the blessings of God on such a governor."

The legislature opened without the pious rabbi's assistance. Huey, on hand in person to cajole and trade, soon had still more inkling of the rocky road he was to travel.

Bombshell No. 2. Representative Lavinius Williams suddenly rose up "like a Roman senator of old" and with a glare at Huey demanded the enforcement of House Rule 20, forbidding lobbying on the floor. Ten others rose to enforce the rule. "I want to serve notice," thundered Lavinius, "that every time the Executive comes into this House without invitation, I will be one of the group to try to put him out."

Bombshell No. 3. Huey's arch-enemy, J. Y. Sanders, Jr., introduced a measure condemning the governor for vote-trading.

But though ejected and condemned, behind scenes Huey continued laboring, arguing, offering jobs, trading bills. He even gave up his long fight on cattle tick eradication, to which hick farmers were opposed, but which the state so needed. If his own measures were sponsored and the occupational tax raised to six cents, he promised to give two cents of it for tick eradication. The deal fell through.

Bombshell No. 4. A vote to suspend rules so legislation could be handled expeditiously failed of the necessary two-thirds. Huey held a worried caucus. Representative Bennett (whom Huey afterwards said he had bought like a load of potatoes) moved adjournment until the following day. To the press, Huey—undaunted—stated: "While we have a substantial majority . . . apparently it is difficult to muster the two-thirds vote to suspend rules . . . [hence] legislation cannot be passed in six days." He called a new fifteen-day session.

March 20, less than two days after it had convened, the six-day session adjourned *sine die* and reconvened in the afternoon as a fifteen-day session.

Bombshell No. 5. That morning the *New Orleans Daily States* had published an interesting list of names—legislators drawing other state salaries—forbidden by the constitution. House Resolution No. 4 at once condemned the appointment of legislators and their relatives to such jobs. Harney Bogan of Caddo Parish quoted Matthew to "Sack of Potatoes" Bennett: "Where your treasure is, there will your heart be also." The galleries tittered. But Felix Delaune of St. Charles Parish, who had voted against the suspension of rules, suddenly changed his position. Barefacedly he admitted Governor Long had offered him a good Highway Commission job.

The legislature thereupon condemned any attempt by mem-

bers of the legislature or the governor "to influence the legislation either by promises or threats." Resolution No. 3 asked
the governor to withdraw his pet occupational tax.

In the galleries was a delegation led by State Superintendent
of Education, T. H. Harris, who had ordered the teachers to
come to Baton Rouge to support the oil tax on the ground the
money was for education. The House passed a resolution
censuring Harris for politicalizing the school system. The
Senate followed suit, nineteen to fourteen, giving the lie to
Huey's boast of a majority.

Senator Anderson, ex-Baptist minister, opposing the anti-
Harris resolution, recited the dire needs of the state institutions. Senator Huson of De Soto got in the counter-jab:
"Don't you think it would be well to take the $150,000 for
the governor's new mansion and use it for the epileptics?"

The governor's mansion was a sore point. An old Southern
pre-Civil War home, it did not come up to the new governor's
tastes. Claiming it to be infested with termites, he sent for
the Baton Rouge building inspector, who reported it would
have to be reconditioned. Huey then informed the Board of
Liquidation the building could not be repaired and had $150,-
000 appropriated, subject to legislative approval, for a new
mansion. But Huey, already aware of how fickle are legislators, flouted the attorney general's ruling and ordered the
old building torn down immediately. The new mansion, he
announced, would have White House features. The legislators
were furious.

Bombshell No. 6. Thursday, March 21, the *Baton Rouge
States Times* carried in the center of its first page:

THIS, GENTLEMEN, IS THE WAY YOUR GOVERNOR FIGHTS

Long had sent word to editor Charles Manship, who had
a brother (Douglas, in the East Louisiana Hospital under ob-
servation: "Tell Manship that if he don't lay off me, I'm
going to publish . . . the names of the people who are fighting me who have relatives in the insane asylum." The editor
ended with this dig: "My brother Douglas . . . about the

same age as the governor . . . was in France in 1918, wearing the uniform of a United States soldier, while Governor Long was campaigning for office." (Q. Was editor Manship more incensed with Huey than chagrined by any airing of his personal affairs?)

That same day Lieutenant Governor Cyr sensationally accused the Kingfish of having temporarily allowed the transfer of nine salt oil domes previously leased to the Louisiana Land and Exploration Company for $206,300 and ⅛ royalty to the Texas Oil Company for $1,800,000 and ¼ royalty. "The Tea Pot Dome scandal dealt with only one oil dome. In Louisiana we have seven [nine?] oil dome scandals. . . . If the good Lord will ever forgive me for supporting Long, it will take a great load off my conscience."

March 24, Huey replied that the leases in question had been legally made by previous governors, none under him. "As governor I had no alternative than to enter into the drilling contract."

"Not convincing," retorted Cyr. Long had signed no drilling permits, but had allowed the transfer of a contract, in which sub-leasing was specifically prohibited, involving speculation in mineral rights of $100,000,000 or more without getting a red cent for the state. "While the governor was giving out bombastic statements . . . about . . . alleged economy stunts . . . he was signing away the mineral rights of the state . . . worth more than enough to pay the then state debt of $11,000,000.

4

Late one night, Huey was called to the home of a member of the administration. Hiding in the kitchen was a terror-stricken assemblyman. "They are going to impeach you!"

"Well, that's news, sure enough! Are you going to vote for them to do it?"

"Every member of my family has been looked up. They have all come to me. Everyone of them loses his job now if I don't swing into line. The Standard Oil Company will fire them all. They cannot live without their jobs. . . . I want you to tell me what to do."

Huey told him he should vote with the opposition. "With all the folks you have I don't see how you can do anything else. . . . But . . . if I see your vote is material, can I have it?"

"If it will save you, I will give you the vote when you want it."

One understands why Huey *had to give jobs* to protect himself and those who stood by him. Huey now told him, "We've got to fight the devil with fire. They are using the bread and butter of your family to make you cast an improper vote. . . . Turn now and be vicious; don't ever pay me another compliment. When they say damn, you say double-damn. Just keep me lined up on the incidents. I will never expose you unless the time comes when your vote will save the day."

March 22, the *Shreveport Journal* demanded investigation of the charges against Long with a view to "impeachment." The press clamor became louder.

March 22. The Capitol. House roll call. Prayer by Reverend I. Boyd Wenger. Charles P. Manship's letter was presented, also a resolution by the West Baton Rouge School Board: "Resolved . . . the only salvation for Louisiana is the investment here of capital . . . which escape[s] . . . similar . . . taxation in our sister states . . . the levying of the slightest tax on manufacturing enterprises . . . will cause . . . withdrawal of investments now in Louisiana . . . paralyze the economic development of the state."

Great though the excitement, the House paused to adopt Mr. Thibodeaux's Concurrent Resolution No. 8, which regretted the death of Marshal Ferdinand Foch, "the greatest commander of the greatest army of all time." The Louisiana solons leave us nothing to do but agree with this remarkable declaration, even if there be a suspicion—this seems subtle for a Louisiana legislator—of an indirect slap at Huey's pacifist record.

March 23, still not realizing his full danger, still hoping to get something, Huey issued a supplementary call which let down the bars to any kind of legislation "to care for the schools and institutions." But to snag the Long program, Senator Holcombe introduced a resolution for a ten days' investigation of the dire straits of the eleemosynary institutions. "This plea for the lame and the halt and the blind is just a smoke screen to have us punish the Standard Oil." The Senate also adopted House Resolution condemning vote-trading by twenty-four to two. One dissenter cried out: "Have we sunk so low that we must remind ourselves to be honest?"

Huey now realized beyond all doubt that the special session was a Frankenstein monster. He could no longer shuffle his deck of cards. His strength had withered away until he could not command a majority on anything. "Rats began to leave the apparent sinking ship. I had to draw back to find out where I stood." By Sunday the legislature adjourned over the week-end. Huey was thoroughly frightened.

Monday, the 25th, Manship's paper, the *States Times,* told how a few days before, in the Heidelberg lobby, Huey had talked over with Dr. Roy O. Young of Youngsville, member of the University Board, the 1926 appointment (still unfilled) of Colonel Campbel B. Hodges—brother of an anti-Long politician—to the University Presidency.

"Hodges is not coming," snapped Huey. (He had Superintendent Harris in mind for the job.)

"Why isn't he coming?"

"Because I'm not going to let him come. He's a military man and unfit for the position."

Dr. Young drew himself up. "And I say that Hodges is going to come. . . . Unless you get enough votes on the Board you can't keep him from coming."

Huey grinned. "I get control of any Board I want and I do as I please." Harris's name came up. "He's my friend, and he can get anything he wants. . . . If he wants the Presidency . . . he has only to say so."

"How will he get it?"

Huey pounded his chest. "I will give it to him. . . . When you get back to Lafayette let them know we made it too hot for you."

News broke—supported by salesman B. L. Kiernan's affidavit—that Huey was supposed to have bought $20,000 worth of refrigerating machinery for Angola prison from his friend, campaign supporter and KWKH radio station owner, W. K. Henderson of the open-shop Henderson Iron Works in Shreveport, without advertising for bids as required by law. The newspapers also charged that, over the heads of the parole board, Huey had illegally paroled embezzler Elmer Dunnington, Convict 17,451.

Hot and fast, revelation trod the heels of revelation. The public gasped excitedly. Huey himself was dazed.

A showdown was coming. The storm-clouds were growing darker. That night the legislature was meeting. The explosion was due. The Baton Rougers bolted their dinners and swarmed toward the red-stone capitol.

One of the most amazing sessions in the history of parliaments took place.

X—STORM

BLOCKED in all his plans, facing charges, Huey's one thought now was to get rid of the troublesome hornets' nest by a *sine die* adjournment. That effort precipitated an amazing uproar.

To read the official record in the *Journal of Proceedings of the Fifth Extra Session* of 1929, one might imagine that it was the shortest, most uneventful session in history. Mr. Frugé moved *sine die* adjournment. Speaker Fournet then declared the House adjourned, 67 to 13. Mr. Spencer appealed from the ruling. Mr. Fournet vacated the chair, whereupon Mr. Spencer, acting as temporary chairman, polled the House, 71 to 9 against *sine die* adjournment. The body then adjourned until Tuesday, March 26.

To learn of the coup d'état that really occurred, one must consult eye-witnesses and newspaper accounts. The most brilliant is that of Hermann Deutsch, star correspondent of the *New Orleans Item*.

The galleries were jammed, the whole House seething. Roman Catholic priest Gassler finished his opening prayer. Pandemonium at once broke loose. Representative Cecil Morgan of Caddo Parish leapt to his feet, yelling, "Personal privilege!" Half a dozen others also clamored for recognition. Speaker Fournet ignored Morgan, recognized floor-leader Frugé, who offered a motion to adjourn *sine die,* which could not be heard because of the uproar.

"I am speaking," screamed Morgan, "and I will not yield the floor. I have in my hand an affidavit from a Baton Rouge citizen that the governor has tried to procure the assassination of a member of this House!"

Fournet's gavel whanged. "Mr. Sergeant at Arms," he shouted. "Seat the gentleman!"

Before the Sergeant at Arms got halfway up the aisle, several representatives, led by Harney Bogan of Shreveport and Lavinius Williams of New Orleans, tossed him and his assistant aside and, making a living shield, advanced with Morgan to the rostrum.

Bedlam. Maniacal screeches. Fournet banged his gavel savagely and continuously. Everybody yelled. Morgan yelled all the louder.

"A dastardly outrage!" he bellowed. "It is charged in this affidavit . . . not one of you shall shout me down! Not one, sir!"

Still guarded oy a dozen representatives, big George Perrault of Opelousas now at the head, Morgan continued to shout over the bang-bang of the gavel, the insane yawping and the madcap furor.

"It is charged here by Battling Bozeman that Governor Long wanted to hire him to assassinate J. Y. Sanders, Jr., and you dare not adjourn this House until I have had my say!"

Everyone was on his feet; as Huey described it: "The assemblage was like unto a few hundred highly intelligent animals temporarily bereft of reason and milling about. Blood and fire shone from every pair of eyes and the most trivial and untoward incident might have caused them to run amuck."

Finally the mob entered upon one of those brief calms so typical of mass hysteria. The Speaker seized the opportunity. "A motion to adjourn *sine die* is recognized." He called for the vote.

"No vote! No vote!" cried the mob. But everybody rushed to his desk to press the voting-machine button that would show a green light—"NO"—beside his name on the board above the Speaker's rostrum.

But lo! Red "Yes" lights flared out. Screaming redoubled. Howls of protest rose from the gallery. "The machine is fixed! the machine is fixed!"

"I voted 'No,' and it showed 'red.'"

"I haven't voted, but my red light is on."

Ignoring the seething, yelling members and shrieking gallery, Fournet declared the House adjourned *sine die*.

The volcano erupted. Rioting broke out in earnest. Ink-wells, paste-pots flew. Battles began. Noses were punched. Eyes were blackened. Clothes were torn.

Visitors rushed in a torrent on to the floor. Women, caught in the stampede toward the Speaker's table, screamed holy murder. Men cursed at the top of their lungs, shook their fists, tried to keep their clothes from being torn off.

The frantic anti-administration members kept shouting: "We are not adjourned! We are not adjourned!"

"Open that machine, you God damn' crook!"

One member, tears of rage coursing down his cheeks, kept shouting, "We must do something! Oh, God, don't let 'em get away with this! Oh, God, don't let 'em get away with this!"

Bogan vaulted over the press tables to the clerks' desk, from there to the Speaker's rostrum. He snatched the gavel from Fournet, now thoroughly frightened, and butted him aside. "When they steal the vote, we'll take the vote ourselves!" he shrieked. "The House will come to order."

But the House continued in insane turmoil, the noise more deafening than ever. Clinton Sayes of Avoyelles, jumping from desk to desk like a mountain goat, clawed up the ladder to the voting machine above the Speaker's chair. Bogan hurdled back to one of the press tables. Williams leapt to another, yelling vainly for attention. The hoodlum roar from the galleries was incessant.

Fournet, amid wild shouting, curses, threats, blows, tried to get back to his rostrum.

Sayes dropped like a wildcat, breakneck speed down the ladder from the voting-machine booth, one foot smack through correspondent Deutsch's straw hat, the other smashing the keys of his typewriter, and catapulted to Mahoney's desk. "The vote was fixed! The vote was fixed!" he yelled. "The operator didn't know what he was doing. It was a crooked vote!"

Jumping from desk to desk he carried his Garcia message through the whirling, bawling crowd. At the Speaker's dais, in the confusion, someone struck him. Instantly the pit was a mass of struggling men—worms in a fish-can. Bogan jumped over a number of heads to Sayes' assistance. A stick flashed. Someone slugged with brass knuckles. Sayes' forehead was laid open in two gashes. Powerful George Perrault "bucked the line for a ten-yard gain." He and Bogan got Sayes, badly hurt, back to his seat. Men all over the House, spectators included, were shedding their coats for a bigger and better battle. More bloodshed seemed inevitable.

Mason Spencer, another big fellow, shouldered forward. Climbing up to the rostrum between two press tables, he thundered: "Gentlemen, the Speaker has declared the House adjourned *sine die* and has vacated the chair." A semblance of order fell.

"Point of order!" shouted Representative Ginsberg of Rapides with an irony neither he nor anyone else appreciated at the moment. "A motion to adjourn *sine die* is unconstitutional. . . . No House can adjourn for more than three days without the consent of the other House."

"The point is well taken," replied Spencer. ". . . I want to appeal from the decision of the Chair." He turned to the Speaker's desk.

But in the previous uproar the Speaker had sneaked out.

"I call on the clerk to call the roll."

The clerk had sneaked out.

The tempest now subsided to a dramatic hush. Spencer continued. "Very well, with the permission of the Gentlemen of the House I myself will call the roll. . . . I appoint as tellers . . ." (He chose an anti-Long, an independent, and a pro-Long man.)

The pro-Long man declined to serve. "We ought to go home when such scenes as this are enacted." Boos, hisses, stomps, from the gallery.

"Very well, gentlemen," said Spencer, and instructed the other two to serve. In a ringing voice he called the roll.

Seventy-one were against *sine die* adjournment, nine in favor. "Sack of Potatoes" Bennett suddenly rose and yelled, "I did vote to adjourn *sine die,* but I want it understood that

I voted 'No' on the ruling of the chair." Cheers from the galleries.

Other Long adherents made similar statements. More cheers.

Temporary Chairman Spencer cried, "What we have done, we have done simply as citizens and to save the state. Let us not mar it." To show he had no personal motives in his seizure of the post, he proposed Ginsberg of Alexandria as Temporary Speaker.

So it was voted. Spencer handed Ginsberg the gavel. Yells of approval thundered from the galleries.

Ginsberg stridently called for order.

"Mr. Speaker!" called Spencer.

"The gentleman from Madison."

"The House," said Spencer, "is in no condition to transact business and in order to let cooler judgment . . . prevail, I now move that this House adjourn until eleven o'clock tomorrow morning."

At the first orderly roll-call in days, only three representatives voted nay. Thus ended the strangest, most disgraceful session in all the annals of Louisiana's history.

Cheers burst anew from the spectators. Crowds of visitors and members crushed about Spencer. Former Long members deserted like rats. They flocked to the press tables, anxious to have the reporters announce their changed status. One fought his way forward, shouting at the reporters, "They got my vote wrong! . . . Make them change my vote! I want to vote against Fournet."

Down in Mexico the Escobar revolt was shaking a nation. In Louisiana a bad voting machine had shaken a state.

2

Next morning the *Baton Rouge Morning Advocate* front-paged: GOVERNOR LONG'S TYRANNY OVER LOUISIANA SHOULD END. All newspapers demanded Fournet resign the speakership. Huey also came in for a hiding. Those who know the inside story declare that the queer conduct of the voting-machine (in charge of a nephew of Senator Ransdell, a political enemy of Huey) was all an accident due to failure in the tense excitement previously to clear the board properly.

In a deeply apologetic speech, Fournet who had no access whatever to the machine, explained that, not knowing it was working improperly, for some time did not realize the meaning of the uproar. His words, though listened to coldly, did calm spirits, but the opposition agreed that he had to go.

Huey at once had three loyal members suggest three opposition candidates. When these conflicting claims had been ironed out, Huey repeated the trick on three others. The opposition never was able to get together on a new Speaker, until there was actually a majority against Fournet's removal—one of the most brilliant political maneuverings in the face of overwhelming odds ever effected by any political leader.

That chastened morning of Fournet's apology, on the desk of each representative was a printed list of nineteen impeachment charges. There seemed a majority, perhaps a necessary two-thirds, eager to impeach. The fight was on in earnest.

The Long forces played for time to cool the situation.

"It was here," Huey writes, "that I felt the hand of fate in more ways than one." He lamented that his wealthy relative, friend, campaign contributor and most powerful supporter, Klansman Colonel Swords R. Lee of Alexandria, had died. Once, when many friends declared Huey had made a mistake, Lee shouted at them, "Damn it, this man don't need friends when he's right. He needs them when he's wrong."

"Only such help as I had previously had from him," mourned Huey "could have quelled the tide and ended the desertions that I was suffering."

3

The impeachment resolution had to be held over until the next day. The House went on with other business. It called on the governor to submit to the Senate for confirmation the names of all his appointees. It demanded within twenty-four hours an itemized list of expenditures for repairs to the state house and the governor's mansion, an accounting of $6,000 appropriated a few months previous for the entertainment of the national governors' conference in New Orleans, and a list of the members' entre-session votes on Board of Liquidation appropriations. No one really knew whether all loans and assignments of money had been properly approved or not. The resolution against the occupational tax was passed. A committee was appointed to investigate Battling Bozeman's murder charges.

In the afternoon, a Long man, Allen J. Ellender of Terrebone, rose to express his shame over the Monday night session and to move once more for *sine die* adjournment.

Bogan retorted that his heart "throbbed with pride" at what had been done Monday night—"pride at the manhood of this House that . . . put to rout the attempt to put over a fake vote." Clinton Sayes' blood had been shed "in the interest of freedom."

McClanahan urged adjournment because of the baselessness of the charges—every governor had promised jobs for support.

Pounding his desk with clenched fist, J. Y. Sanders, Jr., shouted, "If you have any charges against my father, speak them out."

McClanahan soothed him, whereupon Sanders said, "I am a Jacksonian Democrat, and I believe that the spoils should go to the victor . . . but . . . I resent any comparison between the administration of Long and my father."

"If the Augean stables need cleaning, then this House . . . should be the Hercules to do the job," shouted Ginsberg.

After an hour's angry debate, 55 to 38 voted against *sine die* adjournment. The Long forces were mostly on the run.

4

It had been another bad day for Huey.

In New York, 8,246,700 shares had changed hands in the second of the terrible market crashes. In Paris, 100,000 heads were bowed as Marshal Foch was laid to rest. In Louisiana, so his enemies thought, few heads would bow in reverence when Huey Long was laid to rest.

It was a bad evening for Huey.

The opposition held a mass-meeting in the Baton Rougé Community Club Pavilion to start the impeachment fireworks. *Times Picayune* headlines read:

6,000 AT MEETING CALLED FOR INQUIRY INTO LONG'S ACTS

From a near-by balcony, Huey, unseen, listened to his sentence by prominent business men and politicians. Some pictured him as a tyrant, some as "too weak and unlearned to give the courage and talent necessary to the Executive Department." The taxes to be levied on the corporations were described as "blood drawn from a sickening indigent." The meeting was provided with a sixty-piece band, but someone forgot to rub off "Stanacola Band" from the big drum. Ordinarily the Standard Oil band wore uniforms; this particular night its members "wore no master's collars."

The first, most prominent cause for urging impeachment by the mass-meeting was that "for the purpose of satisfying a personal grudge and getting personal revenge . . . and in pursuance of a boast often shamelessly publicly announced, he has . . . used the power of his great office to have enacted a so-called occupational tax on oil refineries and other manufacturing industries of the state," etc.

The meeting, calling for impeachment, resolved: "We condemn as . . . vicious, dangerous and utterly without merit any . . . tax, which directly or indirectly seeks to impose tax burdens on the industries within the state."

In other words he had dared to try to tax the Standard Oil Company!

"That," grieved Huey, "was the answer to my program to shift taxes from the small man to the flourishing corporate interests . . . so that the wealth gathered from the top might be used to build up citizenship from the bottom. . . ."

Tuesday, Huey had one bright ray. His New Orleans organization called over long-distance: the *Times Picayune* was coming out to denounce the whole "impeachment fiasco."

"The sooner the better," replied Huey. "I sure . . . need . . . a breath of life."

That night he slept better. He confessed he needed rest badly.

When he passed through the hotel lobby the following morning, a front-page editorial flared from the *Times Pica-yune.* "They rushed the matter up," he thought. "That will be a lifesaver."

For once he did not sneer at newspaper support. He bought a copy.

The flaring headlines demanded his impeachment. The paper would support any legitimate means of ousting him: "Cruel, political tyrant . . . he has used forms of individual and group bribery . . . objectionable bravado . . . strong-armed, callous, high-handed methods . . . intimidation of the courts . . . unfit to govern the manhood and womanhood of our state," were its violent and partisan words.

Huey read no further. "I had seen so many changes occur so mysteriously in favor of the big oil companies. . . . As in the other newspapers, the big advertisements of the 'Oil Trust' began in the *Times Picayune.* . . . This had not occurred be-fore the newspaper's change of attitude."

And he adds, "Only those who could resist the tom-toms of the mighty or the lure of their 'courtesies' came to me. My mail . . . was scant. Few callers knocked on my doors. At last I had the peace of quiet and solitude for which I had so often longed."

He felt lonely, beaten. He barricaded himself in his rooms at the Heidelberg Hotel. Some say he threw himself on the bed and wept. Outside his windows, the Mississippi raced by in rising flood. Huey knew the power of that mighty torrent. Was such a flood now descending on him?

But surely he would hear from some of the mighty ones remembering what he had done for them. "Where was Sen-ator Ransdell, to whose relief I had gone in 1928? Where was Senator Broussard, whose own organization conceded his defeat until I stemmed the tide? L. E. Thomas, who had opposed Ransdell, and J. Y. Sanders, who had opposed Broussard, were on the ground helping to direct my impeachment. I had gone to the aid of Ransdell and Broussard in their hours of distress against those men. There must be some mistake! I waited for some time and called for one of them. He could not be reached. I understood—

" 'That's gratitude!' "

XI—DOWN WITH THE GOVERNOR

THE main impeachment charges, as Huey described them himself, with distortions, twisted comment and omissions, were:

"1. That I had carried a pistol at times, particularly during the Dreher-LeBoeuf hanging; this, notwithstanding the fact that the laws and constitution of the state of Louisiana not only make the governor the chief peace officer of the state, but make him head of the National Guard. [Article 9 actually said he *"habitually* carried concealed weapons" in his office and in public places. No mention was made of the Dreher-LeBoeuf hanging.]

"2. That I had illegally paroled a convict . . . Elmer Dunnington; this in the face of the fact that the Attorney General, Percy Saint, and the Lieutenant Governor, Paul N. Cyr, my political enemies [of the Board of Pardons] had signed and recommended in writing the granting of the parole and it had passed through my office almost as a matter of form. [The governor could pardon, but had no power whatsoever to parole. Saint and Cyr were not members of the parole board. Their recommendation was purely personal, made because they admired embezzler Dunnington's heroism. The parole board at the time had protested against Huey's usurpation of authority. Impeachment charge No. 17 declared the prisoner "ineligible for parole at the time."]

"3. That as governor, I had bought some law books, to wit, Reports of the United States Supreme Court; Statutes of the United States and Reports of the Supreme Court of Louisiana and Revised Statutes of the State of Louisiana. It appeared to be the view that the governor need not consult the statutes. . . . [Article 4 originally stated he had "misused, misapplied and misappropriated funds and property." It was finally whittled down to the law-book charge—he had used funds appropriated for other purposes for a private purpose.]

"4. That I had torn down the old mansion; this, notwithstanding the fact that the Board of Liquidation, by unanimous vote, and the Legislature of the state, by overwhelming vote, had authorized the building of a new mansion on the old mansion site. [Article 15. The Attorney General had ruled that authority to build a new mansion did not authorize his tearing down the old building.]

"5. That in using the militia to raid gambling houses and to seize their funds and to otherwise maintain law and order, I had acted without authority. [In reality—Article 7—it was charged that in time of peace he had "subordinated the civil authorities to the military," and put the militia above the courts, "causing the said militia to loot and pillage private property."]

"6. That when the Legislature allowed me $6,000 to entertain the governors of the state, either all the money was not spent for entertainment or else that part of the same might have been spent for liquor; this, notwithstanding the fact that I had held a receipt for the expenditures made in the full amount from the member of the entertainment committee placed in charge of the matter, and that certain additional costs had been paid by friends and people anxious to have the best of entertainment. [Huey is slightly mistaken. The charge sent to the Senate was: "The expenses of the entertainment . . . amounted to less than . . . $6,000, *i.e.,* $4,000 or thereabouts. . . . The said Huey P. Long, governor of the state of Louisiana, did thereafter convert to his own use and use in a manner other than directed by law, the balance of the aforesaid . . . $6,000, *i.e.,* the sum of $2,000 or thereabouts. . . ." This money, it was sought to prove, Huey had used to buy a personal car which he blatantly had had painted "Not State Property."]

"7. That one Battling Bozeman had been asked by me to kill a member of the Legislature; on this charge the testimony of the said Bozeman was accepted without allowing any testimony to be introduced to the contrary. [Article 19.]

"8. That a publisher of a newspaper [Charles Manship] had a brother who was in the hospital for the mentally sick (which brother was subsequently cured), and that I had told the newspaper publisher that I was going to tell the public about it; this, notwithstanding the fact that all persons in public hospitals of the state are enrolled on several records subject to the public's general inspection. [Of course Huey, who published the fact over the radio, was merely playing a nasty trick on a man who had attacked him viciously. This charge—No. 14—included "an attempt to suppress the freedom of the press."]

"9. That during the Mardi-gras season in New Orleans, I had attended a Little Theatre where some actresses hired for the show danced scantily clad, and that some of the persons had taken a drink of liquor during the performance. [This was the Danziger studio party. The legislators sought to prove Huey had fondled one of the half-nude girls and was himself drunk. Actually the charge—No. 11—included: "in public places throughout the various parishes," he had deported himself in a "scandalous and ridiculous manner, thus holding up the state to ridicule and shame."]

"10. That I had fired some people and appointed others in their places, among whom was a telephone operator who failed to secure a telephone connection soon enough to satisfy my extreme haste. [Not one of the charges—though the manner in which he had cursed and had had discharged an elderly woman, sole support of her grandchild, was brought out in testimony. Article 10 dealt with "violent abuse."]

"11. That a cousin of mine had been hired and paid money to act as a chauffeur. [Not one of the original charges, but sent as a charge to the Senate. His cousin had been paid a large amount from the mansion repair fund, and supplied most of the automobile tires to the Highway Commission.]

"12. That I had walked into a committee of the Legislature and asked it to adjourn, and that upon the chairman refusing to do so, I persuaded the members to adjourn and leave anyway. [Article 12 states he had "usurped the powers of the Legislature" and had broken the quorums of many committees to stop legislation.]

"13. That I had undertaken to impose my views upon the Legislature, the condition being that the Legislature could operate better without the governor. [This and the previous one were part of Articles 2 and 18 of "improper coercion" and "bribery" of legislators and improper use of the executive power.]

"14. That I had recommended that the Highway Commission pay for some culverts which had been built, which some thought to be defective; this, notwithstanding the fact that the culverts had been paid for before I became governor of the state and the Highway Commission under me had held up some other money belonging to the contractors until they made some deductions on the same. The culverts are in use to this date. [He had forced the Highway Commission to pay $4,000. At one time certain culverts had been condemned by the engineers of the U. S. Bureau of Public Roads and the engineers of the Highway Commission. Not an original charge. Senate Article V.]

"15. The members of the Legislature who helped put through programs of the administration were favored by patronage, but that those who voted the other way were not favored so well. [The charges call this "bribery.]

"16. That when visitors from the City of Shreveport —where they had refused to hand out the free schoolbooks— called upon me I used some 'cuss' words in expressing the way I felt over their actions. [Article 8 declared that "he had attempted to force parish bodies to follow his dictation in matters of public litigation as the price of passage of legislation affecting such parishes."]

"The foregoing include a great many things upon which the House . . . did not vote impeachment. It likewise includes everything upon which they did vote to impeach me."

As a matter of fact, for instance, the House also voted to impeach Huey (he does not mention this) on a charge of having had issued an illegal subpoena. Huey in this account, as we have seen, was evasive, shifted the ground, omitted charges, whittled broader charges down to specific insignificant points, broadened specific points to vagueness, etc. He omitted:

1. (Art. 1.) "That he had used his appointive power . . . to influence the judiciary" and "had boasted" of it. (Anyone knowing the character of Louisianian judiciary can understand the reason for his boast.)

2. (Art. 3.) That "in violation of the constitution" he had demanded and obtained "as a condition to appointment" un-dated resignations, though the terms of office had been definitely fixed by law. [Not very sporting! Huey knew the turn-coat caliber of Louisiana politicians, and his own.]

3. (Art. 5.) That he had contracted "illegal loans."

4. (Art. 6.) That he had removed school officials for purely political purposes and had intimidated teachers and pupils in the educational institutions of the state, "suppressing free thought and free expression." Senate Article II read: "Thereafter, on February 1, 1929, the said Huey P. Long . . . by coercive measures . . . compelled the Board of Administrators of the State Colony and Training School to . . . terminate the employment of the said F. D. Richardson, the Secretary-Treasurer of said institution, and to elect one B. F. Eubanks (his cousin) to the said position. . . ." To accomplish this he "did pay to the said F. D. Richardson . . . in all . . . $5,400 . . . an unnecessary and wasteful payment of the funds of the . . . school. . . ."

5. (Art. 10.) "Violent abuse of officials . . . members of public boards . . . and private citizens visiting him upon public business."

6. (Art. 13.) That he had caused to be purchased the Henderson $20,000 ice-machine for the penitentiary without advertising for bids as the law required.

7. (Art. 16.) That he had disposed of and destroyed the furnishings in the mansion and state house without authority or accounting.

Under the Louisiana constitution, of course, a governor can be impeached for "high crimes and misdemeanors in office, incompetency, corruption, favoritism or oppression in office, or for gross misconduct or habitual drunkenness."

According to some standards, his favoritism certainly was flamboyant—but then every governor in Louisiana's history should have been impeached. His "gross misconduct" at a strictly private party turned out to have been not so gross, but his enemies played it up to the limit—to queer the strict moral backwoods vote. Certainly he made no pretense of being a teetotaler, even in his public speeches.

There was considerable justification in the humor of the *Memphis Commercial Appeal* which later, April 27, 1928, said: "The Lower House is still considering evidence and it may be that some legislator will discover that Governor Long has been guilty of the heinous offense of having at one time played the saxophone."

2

Wednesday, March 27, the House took up the impeachment resolution. Representative Delesdernier of Palquemines Parish, a comical fellow in gallused trousers, argued that the House could not legally vote on impeachment because such was not included in the governor's special session call. After considerable debate, this technicality was thrust aside. Twelve members were named from either faction to question witnesses.

April 2, swamped by pro- and anti-telegrams, the House again engaged in lengthy legality debate. Hearers were impatient, but the quibbling dragged on. Representative Morgan finally suggested obtaining an opinion from Attorney-General Saint. Aged Judge Gilbert Dupré of St. Landry, almost totally deaf, shook his finger in Morgan's face. "And will you be bound by his opinion?" he shrilled.

Morgan shook his head.

"Then what in hell do you want with his opinion?" Dupré growled. The gallery tittered.

That night Saint informed the House the proceedings were entirely constitutional.

Huey exploded: "Ever-ready-to-rule Saint . . . he ruled laws off the books and back on the books as fast as the occasion required. . . ."

On the morning of April 3, with the twelve cross-examiners seated in the well before the Speaker's stand, the House began hearing witnesses. The Senate had hurriedly passed two unimportant bills, then adjourned so the members could rush over to the House. Not admitted to the floor, they agitatedly trotted around the back of the packed galleries—people had even brought their lunches—looking in vain for standing room. A prominent visitor was Mrs. Huey P. Long, come down from Shreveport. The morning was hot, sultry, the air tense.

Charge No. 2, that Long had "bribed and attempted to bribe legislators" was taken up first. Representative Adolph Gueymard was called.

"Did he (the governor) offer you a job to vote for the tax?" asked Ginsberg of Rapides.

"Yes, he did. He asked me how much I owed the banks . . . how much it took me to do business. I told him about $25,000 a year. He told me I would not have to worry, as he controlled the bank examiner, and the banks were violating the law anyway. . . . He . . . would put me in a position where I would not need any bank's help. . . . The first position the governor offered me was that of manager of the penitentiary of St. Gabriel . . . then a position in the accountant's office . . . then . . . the Highway Commission."

"Do you feel your conversation . . . was in the nature of a bribe?"

"Yes, sir. I do."

At a later session Senator Schwing corroborated this evidence, though the "bribe" jobs he mentioned were different. Schwing had called on Huey at his hotel Sunday morning, March 24. "We had a few drinks. He told me he could give my brother, Charlie Schwing, a good job, and could give Mr. Gueymard the job of purchasing agent at the Louisiana State University. . . ."

"What were you drinking?"

"Good whiskey. Drug store whiskey. There's nothing unusual about that."

Representative Davis Richarme of St. James testified that on the second day of the special session, he and Representatives Felix Delaune and Cassagne from St. John were called to the governor's office.

"I want a job," said Delaune.

"How much education have you got?"

"I have very little, but I have some brains."

"Would $150 a month do you?"

"Yes, with expenses."

"All right. $150 and expenses goes. . . . You start on the payroll on the 24th of March. . . . Get right, that's all."

The governor then asked Cassagne what he wanted. Cassagne wished to name his registrar of voters and get ten highway employees appointed. "The governor called in his secretary and told her to remove the registrar of St. John Parish."

Testimony was taken on the Manship charge, then Sheriff C. H. Andrews of East Feliciana related that he was on a committee to request the governor that Manager West and Superintendent Perkins be retained in their positions at the East Louisiana Hospital for the Insane. Asked if Representative Bennett's name came up, Andrews chuckled, his plump bay window jiggled mirthfully. "The governor, he says, 'What about Bennett?' and we answered, 'We give Mr. Bennett to you.' And the Governor says, 'I bought and paid for Mr. Bennett . . . like you would a carload of potatoes.' "

"Did the governor smile, did he appear to be joking . . . ?"

"I took it that he meant it."

Bennett shouted an indignant denial.

After lunch C. C. Chapman, druggist and town councilor of Clinton (East Feliciana Parish seat) confirmed the sheriff's testimony. "To show you that I have paid for Mr. Bennett in full," Huey told them, "Mr. Bennett brought an ex-sheriff in here and asked me for a position for him, and I refused to give it to him." [Apparently Huey had a slight sense of humor.]

On the morning of the 4th the House was so packed, the gallery so shaky, the building inspector had the Sergeant at Arms clear out all those without seats.

Representative Bennett again branded the "load of potatoes" story as a "dirty libel"—but he resigned from the Highway Commission. The House then gave him a vote of confidence.

The administration forces tried to introduce rebuttal witnesses. After an hour and a half of debate, this was refused. Fair play was at a premium.

Testimony was given on the governor's entertainment fund that no accounting was ever given before or after. The State Auditor said Huey's secretary, Alice Lee Grosjean, had handed him $300 of it to entertain the National Association of State Auditors.

Seymore Weiss, Assistant Manager of the Roosevelt Hotel, testified Huey had given him carte blanche in the spending of the $6,000. He accounted for all but about $2,000, then balked. After much prodding, he said it was spent "on a party of such nature" he would not give details without first getting "permission." (Governors of various states later denied there was any such party.)

Old Judge Dupré said this was letting Weiss off too damn' easy and wanted him cited for "contempt." "Let us do our duty," he shrilled.

McClanahan said Weiss's testimony "would incriminate members of this House." Members immediately shouted protests from all over the floor.

3

The pro-Long members, few though they were, left no stone unturned. The hearings could not go beyond the fifteen-day session limit set in the governor's call unless at least one indictment were returned. They precipitated long acrimonious debates. If they could hold out only a few days more, Huey would be in the clear.

April 5, the more alert oppositionists woke up that the session would expire midnight next day—less than thirty hours away. One proposed immediate consideration of the impeachment resolutions. After an hour's dickering an agreement was reached: a final vote had to be taken on one or more of the counts not later than 8 P.M. the following night, April 6, and if passed, sent immediately to the Senate to insure the continued life of that body.

The rules were at once suspended (not allowed when it had been a question of getting through an oil tax) so as to expedite matters.

The House took up charge No. 10: Huey's alleged use of vile abusive language to state officials, boards and citizens. Mrs. J. W. Lumley, an elderly woman with a grandchild, for six years telephone operator for the Highway Commission, was sworn in. She asked not to be obliged to repeat Huey's vile language. "A call came in from Shreveport . . . for Mr. Allen. I asked who was calling [This was required of all operators.] . . . 'Governor Long. Connect me with Mr. Allen.'

"When Mr. Allen answered, Governor Long told him the first thing he could do was go out in the hall and fire that blankety-blank woman." She testified that the governor had often sworn at her and had cursed out the members of the Highway Commission.

H. H. Huckabay of Caddo Parish testified he had come down with a group from the Police Jury, of which he had been a member eighteen years, to see why maintenance funds for Caddo roads had not been forthcoming.

"We found him sitting in the anteroom talking to an insurance agent. 'Get the hell out of here!' he told the agent. 'I wouldn't give four thousand dollars for this building [evidently the governor's mansion] . . . and if anybody burns it down I won't prosecute him. . . .'"

The governor led them into his private office, opened up a box of cigars, took one and lit it. "This is a damned good six-cent cigar."

Mr. Ernest Bernstein, a friend and law-client of Long who had come with the delegation, suggested he pass the cigars around. Huckabay at once said he would like one. The governor said, "I didn't invite you."

Bernstein then handed the governor a statement regarding the maintenance road funds. The governor read a few lines . . . then threw it back. "Caddo Parish . . . will have to see that the severance tax and free schoolbook suits are withdrawn and that the Caddo representatives support me in every damn' thing." He demanded that the parish contribute to the Shreveport Hospital upkeep and treat the State Bureau of Identification right. The Commission explained they could not control the school board or the Ohio Oil Company . . . and couldn't get . . . [the suits] withdrawn.

" 'By God, you had better get it done if you want anything from me,' he answered, using language so obscene and profane that it would insult the sensibilities of you gentlemen [perhaps doubtful] and I would dislike to repeat it."

Huckabay quoted Huey as saying: "I'll learn you how to take off your hats and bow down when Governor Long comes by. . . ." "He was mad as a wet hen. . . . The sight of us . . . like waving a red flag in a bull's face."

Another Caddo Police Jury member, said Long demanded to know why the Parish didn't build a proper road (a private thoroughfare) to his friend W. K. Henderson's radio station. The parish engineer testified how Huey cursed and raved. He was asked to repeat Huey's exact language. McClanahan jumped up to protest, "a shame and disgrace to have it repeated with women in the gallery and women employees in the House. . . . My God, men, where is your Southern chivalry?"

The engineer, leaving out oaths, quoted Huey: "When people throw snowballs at me I throw brickbats at them. . . . Try to hold back taxes in Caddo; I'll send the militia up there and collect 'em."

Two weeks of argument, yet the House still did not recommend any one of the nineteen charges, but called members of the parole board and others for lengthy testimony regarding the illegal paroling of embezzler Dunnington.

The House then jumped back to the entertainment fund. The cashier of the Union Bank testified he had honored Huey's check, handing over the $6,000 *in twenty dollar bills* to his Secretary, Miss Grosjean.

An agent of the Barnes Buick Company told how late in November the governor had bought a Buick coupé. One of their salesmen told how he went to the governor's office to get the check; how Huey handed him $1,300 in *twenty dollar bills* and an extra twenty to buy a license.

One representative thereupon repeated Huey's famous words of July 4, 1928, when his automobile item was stricken from the appropriations bill: "You damn' suckers wouldn't give me ten thousand dollars for a car, but I'll get the car just the same."

The House shifted back to the Manship charge. This petty accusation had aroused more indignation than any other. They devoted most of the forenoon to bitter debate on it. "Any man," shouted a representative, "who will hold up for ridicule the afflictions of a man who has lost his mind . . . who is guilty of so reprehensible and brutal an act . . . is not fit to occupy the chair of chief executive officer of this state!"

Huey's Ellender rose to say that the constitution provided for impeachment for acts committed in *official capacity*. The governor was acting as an individual, whereupon Lavinius Williams shouted, "My friends, what a weak defense that is to hide behind." Was the governor acting in his "official capacity" when he summoned "a crowd of hoodlums here"?

"Mr. Speaker! Mr. Speaker!" yelled half a dozen members dashing forward. "Take that back!" they yelled. "Take that back!" "Sack of Potatoes" Bennett, with McClanahan at his heels, ran to within a few feet of Williams, shouting, "None of that! None of that! Several respectable citizens from my parish were in that delegation."

Lavinius withdrew his remark and sat down.

Old Dupré shrilled: "You talk about appropriating money for the halt, the sick and the blind, but you appropriated money for the governor to raise hell in brothels and everywhere else!"

Delesdernier unfolded his telescopic length and hitched up his galluses. "Bear with me in patience while I say what I have to say. The title of my speech will be: 'The Cross of Gold and with Shackles of Paper.'

"Nineteen hundred years ago there was a cross of wood erected and a Divine Creature of that time was nailed to the cross. This Divine Creature was going through the country relieving the sick and afflicted, curing the lame and the halt, aiding the deaf and the blind, and driving illiteracy from the country that surrounded Him by teaching salvation to man, woman and child. He was surrounded by a committee of twelve. There was a traitor in the ranks. Charges were preferred before a judge."

The Chamber surged to its feet again. "Blasphemy!" "Sacrilege!" came from all sides. Delesdernier continued:

"The Judge washed his hands of the charges . . . and the mob . . . not satisfied with the verdict of the judge, . . . took this Divine Creature and crucified Him by driving nails into His hands and feet. Today we have a creature among us who is relieving . . . [loud interruptions] the blind, aiding the lame and the halt, and trying to drive illiteracy from the state, and he is being shackled with paper to the cross. The cross was manufactured—one of the uprights—out of a saintly piece; the horizontal part of the cross is from the beams of the moon; and this divine creature is being shackled—I mean this creature of today—is being shackled with paper!"

Deafening protests burst out from all sides. Delesdernier raised his hand and screamed into the microphone: "Take my life, but spare me my privilege!" then collapsed on top of the official stenographer and slid off on to the floor.

Water was thrown in his face; he was carried to a window amid surprised gabble, and revived in time to vote. No more absurd address was ever heard this side of Timbuctoo, and not even in the Louisiana Legislature. An accomplishment in itself.

Another Long champion moved that Huey be only reprimanded publicly, but not impeached. Thereupon a tedious argument ensued over the previous night's agreement. After three hours of debate and despite every possible maneuver of the Long forces, the Manship charge, the flimsiest of all of them, came to a vote. Huey P. Long, governor of Louisiana, was indicted 58 to 40.

The galleries went wild. The House was in pandemonium. There were cheers, shouts, boos, hisses—a celebration. McClanahan, his voice unheard, pounded his desk and called his next-seat neighbor, Charley Woods, "a rat!" They began plugging at each other.

Order was restored. Solemnly the childish indictment was carried to the patiently waiting Senate and delivered augustly at 3:00 P.M.

Already the Senate had sent for Supreme Court Justice O'Neill to preside, per the Constitution. He arrived at five-thirty, a slight but austere man, and was escorted to the rostrum. Lieutenant-Governor Cyr thrust the gavel into his hand.

Flashlights boomed. The smoke eddied into the great dome of the state house. The stage was set.

The House committee entered. . . . The House clerk read the charge to the Senators and the Chief Justice.

The special oath was administered to the Chief Justice. . . . Next the Senators came forward in groups of ten to receive the oath: "Do you solemnly swear that in all things pertaining to the impeachment . . . you will do impartial justice . . . so help you God?"

After this purely rhetorical question, a committee of five was appointed to formulate rules. $100,000 was voted for the expense of the trial. The Senate adjourned until noon, Thursday, April 11.

XII—SINGING FOOL

LONG'S more conservative friends said his defense should be strictly judicial before the Senate, reliance upon cold facts, no propaganda—the typical lawyer attitude, an assumption that justice and honor, not politics, were guiding motives.

Huey had no intention of risking his fate on star-chamber proceedings. Friend O. K. Allen shouted: "Hell! You've got to fight fire with fire. . . . These Senators will do . . . anything they dare. . . . Start out over the country. Get those circulars going. You'll stick here and be ruined. Get up a mass-meeting. Get it up quick!"

Stick-pin friend Maestri asked: "Do you need money?"

"All the silver in India and all the tea in China!"

"How fast do you need it?"

"Just as fast as the printing office can turn out circulars and the government can sell the stamps."

Immediately they set to work. Through circulars Huey had repeatedly fought the organized politicians and newspapers. A system of hand-to-hand distribution had been perfected. Also, Huey now had Allen's Highway Commission—trucks, personnel, police—to help out. Alice Grosjean, his secretary, could call on volunteers to speed out immediately large bundles to central distributing points. A document prepared in the evening could be printed and placed on the porch of practically every home in Louisiana during the following morning.

A circular from Huey was an event. People read them avidly, passed them from hand to hand, discussed them. Thus were "the farmers at the forks of the creek, the merchants at the cross-roads, the laborers on the railroads and in the factories"—those whom Huey had visited during his Cotto-lene days—"brought into perfect coördination," and at the same time, remarked Huey, "taught not to believe what they

read in the daily press . . . the newspapers have been rendered powerless in the politics of Louisiana." No one has
taught the cross-roaders that Huey's circulars might have
lacunae. Nearly always he quoted the Bible, the clincher argument to people ignorantly believing that every "i" and every
"t" of that Book had been inspired by God.

Now Huey also got out a miniature newspaper. During the
March 30-31 week-end, while the rest of the town took a Good
Friday holiday, typewriters rattled night and day in the execu-
tive offices. Twenty-five stenos and clerks prepared copy.

Huey's first circular, his "Cross of Gold" declaration, was
blatant but effective:

THE SAME FIGHT AGAIN
THE STANDARD OIL COMPANY *vs.* HUEY P. LONG

*Has It Become a Crime for a Governor to Fight
for the School Children and the Cause of
Suffering and Destitute Humanity?*

"PEOPLE OF LOUISIANA:

"I had rather go down to a thousand impeachments than
to admit that I am the governor of the state that does not
dare to call the Standard Oil Company to account so that we
can educate our children and care for the destitute, sick and
afflicted. . . .

"Where they poured out hundreds in other fights, they have
poured out ten thousand in this one. They have covered their
newspapers, front, inside and out with every imaginable lie
and vilification; they have stormed the state house to where
the weakhearted feared even for the life and safety of my
supporters and myself. . . . They have been able to either
'take over, to beat over or to buy over' some in whom I re-
posed respect and confidence and for whom I yet indulge a
charity. . . ."

An all-day mass meeting was hurriedly set for April 7 in
hostile Baton Rouge. People were circularized in all parts of
the state: "Watch out for lying newspapers— They say that

this meeting will be called off or that the governor has resigned—Pay no attention to anything they say—Come to Baton Rouge—Don't take time to dress up—A man's a man."

The city was jammed, according to Huey, with farmers and laborers—"a determined set of people"; according to critic Smith, chiefly with highway employees, imported by the hundreds. Handbills were distributed: "The Press Swings the Bull Whip." One stanza read:

> "No pistols, perhaps, do they pack on their hip,
> But the newsies are certainly there with their whip;
> And this is their song, which they shout high and strong,
> 'Get out all your hammers and sock Huey Long.'"

John H. Overton, Gaston Porterie and Long addressed the gathering through loud-speakers. Said Overton: "As I see him there now with his rapier flashing, fencing off his enemies to the left, to the front, and to the right, when this smoke of battle shall have been cleared, as in the beginning, I will be standing or lying by the side of Huey P. Long."

Huey spoke vibrantly for more than two hours, giving the complete details of every public quarrel he had ever had, recounting the laws he had passed and tried to pass, and the need for revenues for the schools and other eleemosynary institutions. "What's all this about bribery? Yes, bribery so that the schoolchildren . . . might have free textbooks. . . .

"They . . . say I tried to have a little numbskull murdered. . . . Even my enemies have said they didn't believe it. . . .

"The buzzards have returned. They want to gloat and gulp at the expense of the poor and afflicted. The demons of hell couldn't gloat like they gloat. . . . I proposed a little tax on the sacred Standard Oil Company. They told me that if I put a little tax on oil they would impeach me. . . . If a man can't be governor of the state and advocate an oil tax, then take me out at the outset. . . ."

Never was his favorite Henley poem more appropriate. Huey roared it out with real feeling:

"Out of the night that covers me,
Black as the Pit from pole to pole . . .
I am the master of my fate;
I am the captain of my soul."

As a result of his speeches and circulars, soon messages, letters, telegrams, rolled in on the House. "Paid men here getting telegrams endorsing Long. . . ." "People elected you and him to represent them . . . not the Standard Oil." "Caldwell Parish . . . 90 percent behind Long. . . ." "Long is standing by the schoolchildren . . . the sick, the blind. . . ." "The whole thing is nothing but a desperate move of the Old Ring. . . ." "Must we close our polls and prepare to wear the stripes of our industrial master . . . bend the knee to the Trust Potentate?"

Huey described the battle graphically. "They have filled up the city with enough money to burn a wet mule. . . . They are laying their plans to try to ruin me. But we will have the entire state plastered with our literature before we are through. I have never rested since I became governor. I will not now."

2

Day after day the House continued taking evidence and considering more charges. April 9 it took up petty charges that the governor was guilty of using abusive language toward public officials. J. W. A. Jeter of Shreveport testified that Huey used abusive language to one of his close allies, Representative Ellender, uttering "hell," "damn," possibly put a "God" in front of it. Many a better man has done the same while shaving on a foggy morning. But old Judge Dupré rose slowly to his feet. "Mr. Ellender, I think you should certainly make some explanation of the governor's using such language toward you!"

Later Ellender explained Huey had phoned to him in Houma: the legislature was "a hell of a bunch of fellows to make him live in a dilapidated mansion"; he was "damned tired of living at the Heidelberg . . . a hell of a mess" for him to be "living as he was living."

F. D. Richardson (anti-Long), former Secretary-Treasurer of the state feebleminded colony at Alexandria, testified how Huey had persuaded him with over $5,000 advance pay to give up his job and take a specially created position as "building advisor" so his old job could be given to Huey's own cousin, B. F. Eubanks, son-in-law of Swords Lee.

"Must minor officials get the support of Governor Long before they get positions?" Sayes asked him.

"Yes, sir. . . . The new superintendent . . . told me to go . . . ask the cook if he voted for Mr. Long." Richardson told the cook if he had not voted for Long, he would be fired. "The cook said he voted for Mr. Long."

His testimony was corroborated by Dr. J. C. Willis, Vice-Chairman of the board of the same institution.

Dr. V. L. Roy, eighteen years president of the State Normal College at Natchitoches, testified re Long's politicalizing of educational institutions. "In February, 1928, word came . . . that as I had not voted for Mr. Long . . . he would have me ousted. . . . T. H. Harris, Superintendent of Education, called me and said I would not be ousted if I was 'easy.' "

"On election day," continued Roy, ". . . the governor called me on the telephone and told me that one of the ballot-boxes near the State Normal School 'wasn't going right . . . to go out and get busy.' . . . I was incensed. I never heard such a request being made of a college president. . . ."

Finally Roy was so harassed he took his resignation to the governor, who then made him sign a statement for the press about their "friendship." "I had been driven and beaten until I could stand no more. I could not think clearly. I signed that statement which now seems humorous to me. . . ."

Not so humorous. Huey had Roy appointed purchasing agent at L.S.U.—educator to lucrative job-holder.

Baptist Reverend J. V. Tinnen testified he had come to Baton Rouge, February 26, to see Long in Roy's behalf. "The governor . . . said he would rather talk about chorus girls and wild flowers. . . . The governor said he was going to remove Mr. Roy and put a Long man in."

". . . Have you ever seen a weapon on Governor Long?" asked Representative Morgan.

"In his hotel room here, there was a small revolver, what in the West we call a 'blood-poisoner.' He said . . . some Chicago gangsters were being brought down to get him. He put it in the inside pocket of his coat and left the hotel. . . ."

"Don't you know," asked McClanahan, "that the governor is commander-in-chief of the state militia?"

Judge Dupré struggled to his feet and trebled. "If you can find where that authorizes him to carry a concealed weapon, I'll buy you a new suit of clothes!"

After long bitter debate the charge covering Huey's attempt to bribe Gueymard and Delaune came up for a vote. The opposition won, 56 to 40. At last the governor had been indicted on a charge of some importance.

3

The House now took lengthy testimony on Charge No. 3 that by tricky misrepresentation Huey had exacted undated resignations in exchange for appointments to the New Orleans Levee Board, then had sawed the limb off under Waldo Pitkin and W. D. Gardiner, Sullivan men.

"You say your resignation evidently was accepted by the governor?" Pitkin was asked.

"It was—not 'evidently'—but accepted!" The House roared and went on to an attempt by Huey to have a subpoena issued illegally.

On another day, the chairman of the governors' entertainment committee testified that only a little over $4,000 of the $6,000 had been spent, leaving $1,935 to be accounted for by the governor. There was no wild party costing $1,500.

The supervisor of public accounts told the legislators that, contrary to the customary warrant system, Huey paid bills directly with checks drawn by himself.

He mentioned checks to W. O. Long (Huey's cousin),

$1,112.40 to the West Publishing Company for law books, several large checks totaling over $10,000, one of $200 to Joe Messina, successor to Battling Bozeman as Huey's bodyguard.

Huey had acquired a bodyguard soon after becoming governor. Enmity aroused in the previous session plus his militia attacks on the New Orleans underworld had made him take precautions. Ever since the previous hot August days, he had been constantly protected. "Dogs get rabies in such weather." Numerous gentlemen had threatened to punch his highness's nose. Many had already done so.

While fear had never stood in the way of Huey's doing or saying what he wished, he was not usually pictured as a man of physical courage. His optic had suffered many humiliating blackenings. Once, in January, 1926, R. T. Moore, chairman of the Commercial National Bank of Shreveport, held him by the throat against a wall and jiggled a knife threateningly over his heart. In June of that year, attorney James V. Galloway had given him an ugly trouncing. State Representative Robert Prophit, Jr., in retaliation for the exposé of his job-holding on the Conservation Commission, had, September 9, 1926, broken a heavy cane across Huey's head, shouting "yellow dog."

Battling Bozeman at first took care of any such contingencies; now after their falling out, Huey's bodyguard was Messina, tailor by trade. He testified to the House he had been hired by O. K. Allen on the Highway Commission "to check licenses," but was assigned to the governor's mansion —"just a personal attendant," salary $150 a month. He was quizzed about the allegedly illegal disposition of furniture and silverware from the mansion. Persistent questioning wormed out of him how it had been scattered about. Nothing very wrong was encountered. The House went back to the charge that the mansion had been illegally destroyed, jumped to another charge, then back to the silver and furniture, then to still another accusation.

Mr. Weiss, again put on the stand, refused to testify regarding the mysterious two thousand dollars, and left under Judge Dupré's shrill threats of prosecution for embezzlement.

Huey later rewarded Weiss with numerous juicy jobs. He became one of the biggest shots in his machine.

Attorney General Saint testified that despite his ruling, Long had destroyed the mansion without authority. He also had informed the governor and the State Adjutant General that it would be unlawful to call out the National Guard without first declaring martial law.

General Fleming, several gambling-hall check-room girls, and others told of the militia raids.

April 24, the House voted five more indictments: (1) Huey had improperly paid F. D. Richardson $5,400 to resign; (2) he had paid cousin W. O. Long $5,780 out of the mansion repair funds; (3) he had used $1,112 from the same fund to buy law books; (4) the defective culverts; (5) failure to account for the balance of the $6,000 governors' entertainment fund.

Bitter debate preceded. Dupré made the leading address: "Father, forgive him, he knows not what he does." He outlined the charges at length. Confirmation of embezzlement was "as strong as the Holy Writ." [No one on that messy occasion could do anything in Louisiana without pounding the Bible.] The old man ended in a burst of Confederate eloquence: "But by the graves of my ancestors, one of whom honored this state [family pride with a vengeance] as its chief executive, by my sire who distinguished himself as a member of the Confederate Congress, by my eldest brother who gave up his life for the Lost Cause, by the grave of my only son, for the love and dignity of this great state, for the rising generation and those who are to follow us, I ask you, I beseech you, I implore you to give him his just deserts and send him to the bar of the Senate which he has sought to corrupt in advance of trial, and let him defend himself there if he can do so. And I say this without malice, but under a supreme sense of duty I owe my people, my country, and my God!"

J. E. McClanahan was "ashamed of Louisiana." He read from a *New Republic* article: "When the impeachment process becomes a tool for persecution, it will have become one of the most vicious of political devices." He defended Huey's various financial operations. Not the Bible but Roman history provided his illuminating climax: "I want to remind you of the assassination of Caesar by Brutus. Brutus said he did not love Caesar less, but loved Rome more. . . . You know what happened to Brutus."

Harry Bogan stepped up to the microphone and characterized the *New Republic* as "a Socialist rag," and made insinuations about the source of the governor's money spent so recklessly in big bills. "Where does he get the money?" Ginsberg of Rapides charged that McClanahan had not read the beginning of the article in "that ultra pink magazine, the *New Republic*," and quoted: "Even the most partisan of Governor Long's friends do not completely exonerate him. Some of his actions certainly seem open to grave question, even though they do not justify the extreme measure now being taken against him. . . . He is not a kindly person. He is irascible and arrogant. His language, to put it mildly, is not gentle. Vindictiveness is one of his major traits."

Ellender cried, "What does it mean, this charge of the misuse of public funds? Add them up. It amounts to $19,000. Even if . . . all of that amount was misappropriated . . . the cost of this proceeding will be far in excess of the alleged embezzlement." Curious defense.

4

April 25, Alfred Danziger testified that his famous studio party on the night of the raids was attended "by the best people." Huey "had a glass in his hand most of the time he was there. . . . The idea was to have a jolly time. . . . I am not positive whether or not the governor sang, but I saw him take a few steps like a jig. . . . A chorus girl tried to sit in his lap, but Governor Long pushed her away. . . ."

"Was one of the features . . . a hula dance?"

"Yes, but there are different kinds of hula dancers. [The assembly pricked up its ears.] . . . The girls didn't make it too snappy."

"How was the hula dancer clad?" [The legislators leaned forward to drink in every word.]

"In the conventional, or unconventional, costume . . . a straw skirt and an arrangement about the chest. . . ."

"Did the woman have shoes and stockings on?"

"I think she danced barefooted."

"Aside from the regalia you mentioned, the upper part of her body was bare, wasn't it?"

"Yes, but she had the usual arrangement around the chest. . . ."

"Didn't the hula dancer circulate among the guests?"

"She came down off the stage . . . in between where the guests were sitting. . . ."

Long asked where the entertainers came from and Danziger told him, "from an agency."

"Didn't one of these dancers dance immediately in front of the governor?"

"I don't think she danced closer to the governor than to anybody else."

Hula dancer Helen Clifford said the governor had pushed her away, but pulled her back. She then sat on his lap, his arm about her neck. "Everybody was drunk and the governor had *plenty!*" She said the governor had spent most of his time on a settee with a woman who had called to him, "Come here, Huey!" "He played with her hair . . . was admiring it."

"Would you please tell us what costume you wore on that occasion?"

"I had on a straw skirt, no stockings and something around here—was bare between here and here." Miss Clifford gestured. . . .

"Did you see any drinking?"

"Yes . . . highballs. . . ."

"Did you see the governor drink?"

"I saw him drinking. . . . At the beginning he was very quiet, but later on he got very frisky. . . . I saw him walking across the floor with a glass in his hand and he wanted to dance with everybody."

"Were you presented to Governor Long?"

"Yes, someone asked us if we knew who that was, and one of the girls said, 'That's Huey Long,' and then I said, 'How do you know?' and she answered, 'By the dimple in his chin.' "

"Now, Miss Clifford, were you asked to pay any attention to the governor?"

"Yes."

"Did you sit on his lap?"

"He pulled me on his lap."

"How long did you stay there?"

"Only a few minutes. I got off when I had finished singing." McClanahan tried to show she had been employed by one of the raided gambling houses at the time she made her affidavit to the papers.

"Did you have any hesitancy in sitting on the governor's lap?"

"I couldn't help it; he pulled me onto his lap. Then he kind of pushed me off and pulled me back again."

"Now, little miss, aren't you accustomed to sitting on men's laps?"

"I am not."

"Have you ever sat on a man's lap?"

She demurred. Loud objections were raised all over the House. McClanahan insisted his question was relevant.

"Have you ever sat on a man's lap? I *insist* on an answer."

"Yes; I am married."

The House roared. One representative demanded the witness's address and telephone number. Miss Clifford objected, but nearly every man in the House insisted.

A statement by Harry James, owner and manager of "The Frolics" cabaret (padlocked), told how Huey had gotten his pre-Kingfish sobriquet, "The Singing Fool."

Each time Huey visited the club, James testified, he danced with the so-called hostesses, got drunk, mounted the platform to conduct the orchestra and sing to the patrons. Huey, he testified, wasn't much of a singer, but was much encored. "The patrons and guests, employees and hostesses . . . familiarly referred to the said governor, Huey P. Long, as 'The Singing Fool' of the cabaret."

5

The representatives went on to Battling Bozeman's charges that Huey had tried to have him assassinate Sanders. Long had first had him threaten Senator Williamson "if he didn't lay off the governor and me," which Bozeman had done, "letting Long make a goat of me by dictating a statement to Miss Grosjean . . . and having me sign the same."

Bozeman was peeved that Huey kept him busy ten to twenty hours a day, promising to pay him $250 a month, "but for the two months I was guarding his dirty hide, he never paid me anything but a promise. . . ." He told about highway graft.

Five or six weeks before this testimony, he had been called to the Heidelberg by Long.

"Bozeman, I'm the kaiser of this state; when I crack my whip whosoever disobeys my orders . . . I'll fire 'em; they won't last as long with me after disobeying one of my commands as a snowball in hell. Shut the door over there. Come over here and sit down by me."

The governor was "three-fourths drunk." On one occasion before, testified Bozeman, Huey had been so tipsy in the Heidelberg, he was wearing only his B.V.D.'s, one shoe and his hat, and but for Bozeman would actually have gone down to the lobby in such attire. Now Huey said:

"I'm going to call a special session of the Legislature, Bozeman, and this son-of-a-bitch, J. Y. Sanders, Jr., is going to fight all my measures. I want you to get him out of my way. I've chosen you to do away with this bastard."

A queer sensation hit the pit of Bozeman's stomach. "Governor, what do you mean?"

"I mean for you to kill the son-of-a-bitch! Leave him in a ditch where nobody'll know how or when he got there. I'm the governor of this state, and if you're found out, I'd give you a full pardon and many gold dollars."

Bozeman replied he wasn't a gangster. Huey told him to go back to New Orleans and think it over.

When Bozeman returned to Baton Rouge, he ran into the governor on the street, sober this time.

"Well," inquired Huey, "what about it?"

Bozeman wiggled uncomfortably. "Oh, everything's all right. I believe it's going to rain."

"Damn the rain! I mean, what about Sanders?"

"I told you before, governor, I ain't gonna do it."

"Very well," roared Huey, [and turned mad] "remember what I told you. I'm the boss!"

In a few days the Highway Commission fired Battling Bozeman "right now, not tomorrow."

He told highway heads O. K. Allen, Ames, and Nugent (Secretary, also Huey's cousin) that he was going to tell the world why he was fired, that, "If they were going to let me off for that reason and keep a bunch of drunkards and crooks that I thought they wasn't as decent as the crooks and drunkards."

His words threw the Long camp into "consternation." Huey sent for him, then refused to see him. Allen called him and hinted at a new job.

"I told them . . . I didn't care to have anything more to do with him or the governor either."

Huey then had Beasley and Nugent interview Bozeman at the Istrouna Hotel. "Well, how do you feel tonight?" Nugent inquired.

Bozeman was not softened. "You oughta know how I feel after you fired me like you did."

"Oh, that's all right—you don't know what I know!" Nugent said with coy mystery. . . . "The governor wants to see you. He'll give you a good job, but you want to keep it under your hat and not give anything to the newspapers."

Bozeman did not nibble; he said he was through.

Beasley asked Bozeman if he had a gun on him. Bozeman replied no. Why did Beasley want to know?

"Well, things don't look so good to me tonight," responded Beasley. "When Huey comes down out of his room, I want you to take a walk with us."

Bozeman didn't choose to walk.

The next morning Huey told him: "Bozeman, I want you

to go to work in the morning . . . a new raise. I'll give you four hundred a month and a new car to ride around in."

Bozeman, cautious now, inquired what his duties were.

Huey waved his hand airily. "Oh, the biggest job you'll have is to get your check every month."

Bozeman declined.

Examination brought out that Bozeman was just then out on bond on two separate libel charges, which slightly reflected on his veracity. The whole matter sounds like the disgruntled, frustrated comeback of a childish person with a grudge; but in any event, the story stands, for what it may be worth, on the records of the noble and sovereign state of Louisiana.

XIII—BUBBLE

MEANWHILE Huey worked day and night. He left not a single chance to fate. He propagandized, he pamphleteered, he rallied the backwoods, he spoke over the radio, he lobbied, he traded for votes. Seven speeches a day. The crowds were "enormous," a new kind of reception now; note this touching chip off the perfect chrysolite of demagogic sentimentalism: "Here and there a straggling child would bring me flowers which no hothouse or florist had ever seen. . . . We were at grips with the problem of the common people."

"The gang cannot get back into power by an election . . ." he shouted to his hearers, "so they now try to get twenty-six men in the Senate to . . . do what they know hundreds of thousands of people in the state will not do."

Ewing's *Shreveport Times* (April 16) said: "With one Senator absent, the anti-administrationists were, Monday night, within three senators of the sufficient number to impeach." At such remarks, Huey commented: "The opposition . . . made it known . . . that votes, not crimes committed or the law thereon, was all that it took to secure a man's impeachment. . . ."

He would pay them in the same coin. Besides, a quick move was necessary to hold his friends together. Fourteen Senate votes out of thirty-nine could prevent impeachment. Huey determined to be sure of them ahead of time [Julius claimed credit for conceiving and executing the plan, but Huey presented it entirely as his own] by having fourteen sign a secret pledge that "by reason of legal irregularities" they would not approve the impeachment proceedings or charges.

He telephoned fifteen senators—a car was at their door in the act to pick them up—to come to Baton Rouge.

Thirteen came. All—a few argued—signed. One more name

154

would give him more than the requisite one-third of the Senate membership.

A fourteenth reached his office shortly before midnight. But he refused to be convinced of the propriety of the round robin. "You are asking me to say here that regardless of what may be shown, I will not vote to impeach."

This, Huey insisted, was merely customary court-procedure in filing a demurrer. Even a guilty client should not be tried on a defective charge. On the practical side—he was exhausted, didn't have a dime. "The fight has cost me all I had; all I can rake and scrape and borrow. It is taking one thousand dollars a day to get the truth to the people. How long can we stand it?"

"Is all that effort necessary?"

"It is necessary for you," Huey answered. "For you to vote to free me from this impeachment would be dangerous unless your people have been given the facts." They argued back and forth hour after hour. Soon the sun would be up. The Senator asked to consult his law partner.

They phoned him in New Orleans. He left immediately for Baton Rouge and arrived just at daybreak. Again they went over the proposition. The senator and his partner went off, came back.

"Governor," said the partner, "this is the right thing to do."

Later in the day a fifteenth member signed. Huey had one more than necessary. He had his enemies bottled up.

2

On their side the impeachers, the Old Ring, the corporation lobbyists and the newspapers, Huey charged, continued scheming. The round-robin senators were approached. "The offers to them," according to Huey, "were immense."

Unexpectedly one round-robineer broke faith, disclosed the existence of the secret document, but wanted it understood he had not signed it. Huey refused to be smoked out to confess it existed, merely declared over the radio: "Thirteen senators have pledged their votes to impeach me . . . and they ain't heard a word of evidence!"

Presently Huey heard the renegade senator was in touch with a Shreveport business associate of a millionaire once sued by Huey on swindling charges and forced to disgorge enormous sums. His hate for Huey exceeded that of any other man in the state. Late one night, Huey paid the senator a surprise call. Sitting on the side of his bed, he quizzed him. "Weren't you in Shreveport today?"

The senator was evasive. "Mr. X [the business associate] is sick in Shreveport. He's an old friend . . . I . . . agreed to . . . go up there tomorrow to see him. . . ."

"All right, if you are going to Shreveport . . . speak there with me tomorrow night." The senator reluctantly promised. But he did not appear.

Over ice-machinery Henderson's KWKH station, April 12, Huey made a highly emotional appeal. "In four desperate weeks of misrepresentation the filthy newspapers of the state have failed to deceive anyone, and they would not dare face an election tomorrow. . . .

"Now they say I carried a pistol. I am not only commander-in-chief of the state militia, but in 1928 we passed a law which made the governor head of the Bureau of Criminal Identification." This gave him "the power to arrest any person." All of them voted for that bill and still "the jack-asses don't know they passed it! . . .

"They said I tore down the mansion. Well, what do you know about that? . . . One of our own citizens up there said that if our governors had lived in it since 1856 he could see why I couldn't live in it. It's like the old lady who said to a roomer when he complained of a dirty towel, 'Why, there's been a hundred men used that towel before you, and not one of them has complained. . . .'

"They [the Standard Oil Company] have turned Baton Rouge today into a lobby to fight the sick, the blind, the deaf, the dumb and the insane and every school child . . . who are victimized by the lobbyists parading the streets and the capitol and the financial agents . . . approaching members of the legislature for the Standard Oil. . . . Oh, you know what I mean, all you financial agents, you henchmen of the Standard Oil . . . who are listening to me. You know what I mean by the use of money in the city of Baton Rouge today . . . to defeat the will of the people . . . and browbeat and intimidate and beat down the lawful process of Louisiana. . . .

"Standard . . . says that if this tax is passed it is going back to Texas. You cannot go back to Texas, Standard Oil Company! You were driven out of . . . Texas, and you came to Louisiana. . . . You are in Louisiana, just like an exiled convict escaped from the penitentiary. . . ."

But his pointed charge was: "Certain gentlemen in this city have been calling senators to this town to pay them off to vote for my impeachment. I may give the names, the dates, and the places." Hot stuff!

The following morning in the House, Hamiter of Caddo Parish indignantly read extracts from Huey's speech dealing with the bill creating the Bureau of Criminal Identification, which, he claimed, gave the governor no authority to carry a pistol. "If I have made jackasses out of this legislature, . . . *I am the biggest jackass of them all.*"

Judge Dupré called on the East Baton Rouge district attorney to arrest Long forthwith and charge him with carrying concealed weapons.

Senator J. O. Fernández of Orleans Parish testified Huey had offered him a job on the Highway or Tax Commissions for his vote against impeachment. Both House and Senate went on record that their members had never been improperly approached by the Standard Oil or anyone else and called upon Long to disclose the names of the agents and the assemblymen he was accusing. Senator Huson commented:

"Our governor has been widely quoted as referring to the Legislature as a deck of cards dealt to suit himself. I don't know how this body ever swallowed that, but it did. But we can't swallow this . . . charge of corruption. The deck may have become a little old, but . . . the 'dirty deuce' will be thrown out."

Huey ignored the House resolution, but to the senators

replied that his information was confidential, but would be glad to submit the names of persons who could give direct testimony if the Legislature saw fit to name a committee.

The Senate did not name a committee!

J. L. Anderson, speaking at Winnsboro May 3, declared he could have sold his impeachment vote for $10,000 to $50,000. McConnel of New Orleans said he had been offered $8,000 to $10,000. Were these also intimations to Huey they considered their vote worth more than the sums indicated?

The senator suspect, who had not appeared at the Shreveport rally, issued various sharp rebukes of Huey. But his name was on the round robin—that would cause him plenty of crawfishing.

Huey heard he was spending the night in Baton Rouge. After delivering an address in Monroe, Huey went to his hotel room, pretended to retire, then slipped unnoticed out a side-door. He drove the entire night, 250 miles, crossing the Mississippi just at dawn.

This was ever Huey's tactic; while others were sleeping out their weariness, he would be out working, speaking, preparing circulars, making new plans, driving on through the dawn hours.

At Baton Rouge he went first to see Maestri, who had been working on the senator most of the night and had baldly accused him of trying to cash in on the impeachment. They went to the senator's room.

"Well," the senator confessed, "here's the situation. I was to go to New Orleans today to be paid off by Big John. I've tried to keep you off me. The more real I could make this, the better. I have thought every day I could bring you the money to blow the impeachment out of the water. But they have hesitated. Now shall I try further?"

They drew an affidavit that the senator was on his way to New Orleans to be paid the bribe money which he would publicly hand over for exposure.

That same night the senator returned. "The son-of-a-gun was white as a sheet. Someone tipped them off I saw you."

"We were never able to make a real exposure," mourned

Huey. Early one morning, Huey's friend in the Legislature, voting opposition, but who had promised to keep him informed, ran to him. "Huey, they're going to pull a fast one. . . . They're going to make Gilbert governor in order to get him," *i.e.,* secure his vote and support for impeachment.

In few men, as in Gilbert, did Huey place so much trust. "Run back. Get me the very latest you can."

Within less than an hour, the assemblyman ran into the room. "Gilbert's turned 'em down!" he shouted.

3

In Tangipahoa, Huey quoted Sholars of Monroe as saying, "They bought Representative Cutrer so cheap they felt like they had stolen him." Cutrer, a clergyman, erupted in the House in indignant denial. Sholars said he didn't even know Cutrer.

At Abbeyville, Huey said: "They've got some two-bit stuff about me cussing out somebody at some time or another and about me tearing down the mansion, but them ain't the real reasons for this impeachment business. . . . I fought the Standard Oil . . . and put them pie-eating members of the gang out of office. . . . Old J. Y. Sanders, old John P. Sullivan and old L. E. Thomas and other politicians whose pie-eating dates back to 1892 [a year before Huey was born] want to get control. . . . They say they want peace and quiet in this state. . . . Yes, oh, yes, they want peace; they want a piece of that thirty-million-dollar road pot! . . . I told you I'd kick the old gang of pie-eaters out of office. I kicked out all I could. I used a crowbar to pry some of 'em out, and now I'm using a corkscrew to take the rest out piece by piece. . . .

"They say I tried to get that numbskull, J. Y. Sanders, Jr., killed. Why, if J. Y. Sanders, Sr., had died twenty years ago I wouldn't be governor. If J. Y. Sanders, Jr., lives twenty more years I may be President of the United States. A Sanders is what I need to assure my political future."

At Opelousas: "They [in New Orleans] said I couldn't remove Dr. Leake, *whose father is the Standard Oil Company's lawyer,* from the Charity Hospital. . . . I came up here and got Dr. Vidrine for the job. . . . The country people can hold the big jobs as well as the city men. . . .

"The people of New Orleans didn't appreciate my getting the natural gas, my winning the Galveston rate case for them, and my work for the city. I am the victim of ingratitude. They told me they wanted the gambling dens closed, and you know I was damned fool enough to believe they meant it . . . !")

He claimed that old Dupré had voted for Fournet "to get a committee job for his nephew. . . . Some people claim to be honest just because they are deaf."

When the House convened Monday night, April 22, Dupré rose up with the wrath of all his seventy years. "The governor . . . went to my home town yesterday and wickedly and maliciously and deliberately slandered me and my good name! . . . Long is dancing over a volcano. He has slandered every member of the House and Senate. He has called us 'jackasses.' I do not understand this man. I certainly never before heard of a man who would ridicule another man's infirmity." He was "charitable enough" to believe the governor was "not mentally responsible." Long "had the wrong sow by the ear." He (Dupré himself) fought in the open, carried no concealed weapons—he lifted his coattails. "But I'll fight anyone at the drop of the hat . . . if he doesn't quit slandering me."

4

The House heard more testimony . . . and still more . . . about this charge and that charge, about Highway Commission extravagances, Huey's interference with the Parole Board which had caused two members to resign, etc., etc.

April 26, for three and a half hours it discussed sending up a charge of general incompetence, embracing also the exacting of undated resignations, the issuance of an illegal diploma, politicalizing of public schools, the abuse of officials and other persons, and the retention of O. B. Thompson (an old oil associate of Huey) as a parole officer not performing duties and not accounting for large expenditures.

"Why, they couldn't convict a nigger-foot chicken-thief on such evidence!" cried Fournet. "If you can't catch him on one charge, you think you can catch him on another."

Debate grew red-hot. Two fist-fighting representatives were separated. Representative Bogan entered the Chamber, face bleeding. Earl Long had asked Maestri in front of Bogan, "Why are you talking to this son-of-a-bitch?" Bogan had struck Earl. They clinched. Earl sank his teeth into Bogan's neck.

At three o'clock the omnibus resolution was passed 59 to 39.

Practically everyone in the whole state now thought Huey would surely be impeached. Lieutenant-Governor Cyr, trying not to look smug, treated besieging reporters with the air of the next chief executive. "All I want is privacy. I just want to answer this correspondence and get back to Jeanerette. . . . No, you can't get a story out of me. I'm just an ordinary citizen, like thousands of other citizens. . . . The one thing in life that pays big and consistent dividends is honesty." He waved the reporters away.

5

April 27, the Sergeant at Arms waited before the Senate rostrum to receive the voluminous impeachment summons ordering Huey to appear before the Senate to answer for "high crimes and misdemeanors." He took them and walked solemnly down the winding staircase to Huey's office and placed them in his hands at exactly 1:33 P.M.

Huey laughed.

6

May 15. The trial was on.

After the preliminary routine, Overton offered Huey's pleadings. All acts subsequent to the legal time set in the governor's proclamation, April 6, were invalid. Therefore Articles of Impeachment 2 to 8 had no more legal effect than if "pre-

pared by . . . a mass-meeting of citizens." Nor was such
activity included in the special call. Proper impeachment procedure, prescribed in the Revised Statutes, had been disre-
garded.

For the prosecution Representatives Perrault and J. Y.
Sanders, Jr., held that the House, once engaged in impeachment proceedings, was thereby transformed into a judiciary
branch. If because of the defense demurrer, testimony was
not heard on the last seven charges, it would result in "ac-
quittal of the governor of the state on charges which he
should legally face," an evasion tantamount to conviction. Try
the case on the facts, they argued.

Huey's demurrer was ruled out by the close vote of twenty
to nineteen. The last seven charges would have to be tried.

With regard to Impeachment Article 1 (the Manship incident), the only article passed before the legal April 6 limit,
Huey filed Demurer No. 2, that the charge did not denounce
"any act or offense impeachable under the Constitution." Not
committed in the discharge of any official duty, it was not
violative of any statute, was a personal matter between Long
and Manship. In any case, publicity of the names of insane in-
mates is authorized by Revised Statutes, Section 1765.

The defense quoted precedent after precedent, the prosecution as many contrary precedents. Twenty-one senators voted
to sustain the demurrer; eighteen were against it. Thus the
first charge, the only one, Huey claimed, which had any legal
formulation, was dismissed. The Senate had done exactly
what the Kingfish desired—not a hitch.

But those not in on his scheming considered the victory
against him completely won. Baton Rouge was thrown into a
furor. The hotels seethed like anthills. The wires were hot.
Extras were shouted.

7

But rumor grew and grew that Huey was going to spring a
grand surprise. The opposition suddenly realized they could
never swing enough votes to impeach. Whatever Huey's guilt,
they were beaten. They began to flee the capital—"rats leav-

ing another sinking ship." Quarters were vacated in the night-time.

The Long group prepared a condensed resolution along the lines of the round-robin. The same fifteen senators signed. At 10 A.M., May 16, Phillip H. Gilbert filed the document. "By reason of the unconstitutionality and invalidity of all impeachment charges remaining" against Long, they would not vote to convict. Further proceedings were therefore "ineffectual, vain" and would incur "useless cost" and would only "prolong turmoil and . . . disrupt the ordinary . . . businesses of our state." The Senate, it was resolved, should adjourn *sine die.*

The prosecution, disconcerted, threw the Senate into recess to caucus the remaining twenty-four senators. The twenty-four finally emerged with a declaration deploring the attitude of their fifteen colleagues but admitting the futility of proceeding. They moved *sine die* adjournment.

8

Mrs. Long left her seat in the gallery, rushed downstairs and threw her arms around Huey's neck. She seized the telephone and called their children in Shreveport to tell them the glad news. Huey, in an expansive mood, joyously clapped his friends on the back and shook hands. He was smeared but victorious.

After all the fuss and feathers, the up-state and down-state campaigning, the airing of petty scandals, screaming headlines, fist-fights in the august legislative sanctum, after all the screeching, dirty-trading, vile language, baseness of every sort, all in an atmosphere of corporate tools shouting vengeance in the fair name of a long-raped state, and cheap politicians on both sides beating their breasts and shouting "justice" and "honor," after weeks of greasy vilification in which the eyes of the whole nation had watched the curious antics of the noble representatives and people of that odd sovereign commonwealth, the great gaseous bubble of talk, passion, foulness and deceit was suddenly pricked. Huey, whatever his numerous sins—and they were no worse than most of the men attacking him—had the decided moral advantage. Whatever his ultimate purpose, however insincere, he had stood on the side of righteous if befuddled measures. In large part, not because of his many improper deeds plentifully aired, but precisely because of his worthy efforts, they turned on him; precisely because he was smashing up the crooked Old Ring, because he was now seizing the power, patronage and limelight himself. Few entities in the world have ever displayed such lamentably ignorant skulduggery all around as did Louisiana on this famous occasion.

Huey had won by patronage, astuteness, and appeals to the people. All told, his defense against the organized corrupt might of the whole state was brilliant; his campaigning, his maneuvering, his final denouement, a masterful piece of political ingenuity.

Once more he had carried his gospel to every hamlet. If his prestige had suffered heavily among the urban literate (never very great, anyway) so far as the common man went, especially in the countryside and small towns, he was by all odds the most popular leader in the state. People like a man apparently whipped who puts up a remarkable fight and wins. And he had become a national figure.

Huey's hard-earned knowledge that his political enemies would stop at nothing to get him, caused him more than ever to take steps to render them impotent. He set out to make them powerless to move a tiny finger against him. This effort set him more definitely than ever on the road to dictatorship. To destroy his unprincipled enemies, he had to destroy free government in Louisiana. To destroy his enemies, he had also to destroy the liberties of the people.

XIV—VENGEANCE FOR SNIPERS

A HOWL of frustrated rage went up against the fifteen "Robineer" senators—they had betrayed their solemn oath. Huey—no one bothered to point out the dirty politics involved —should have been found guilty or cleared.

A feeble effort to launch a recall movement against him died, but his enemies insisted that the impeachment charges remained in the Senate, subject to trial at any time. The *Times Picayune* was particularly hostile and gave publicity to a Tulane University professor's speech contending that the charges were still pending.

Angrily, Huey charged that the controlling political factor of the *Times Picayune* (founded as the official organ of the old Louisiana Lottery crowd, heritage of scalawag government), was (and is) "a railroad, telegraph and power company lawyer, Esmond Phelps, also head of the Board of Supervisors of Tulane University, on which sat others affiliated with such interests. The institution is largely supported by the Rockefeller Foundation." "Standard Oil" again!

Two other groups of enemies refused to bury the hatchet —the Pontchartrain bridge people, frantic at their loss, and the New Orleans Ring. June 11, 1929, an eight-column streamer in Ewing's *Daily States* heralded the formation of the Constitutional League, headed by ex-Governor Parker, "to save the state against Long" and "political lawlessness." Three hundred citizens from all over the state met at the Hotel St. Charles. One hundred thousand dollars was raised in less than fifteen minutes. The paper called it "the most representative gathering of citizens [mostly washed-up politicians and corporation lawyers] within a decade."

Huey, branding the new group as the "League of Notions," declared: "The backbone of the organization, as usual, was the Standard Oil Company and the old New Orleans Regular organization."

The Constitutional League pried into the records, brought charge after charge: misappropriation of highway funds, graft, inefficiency, and accused Huey of having twenty-four relatives on the state payroll (in addition to Otho Long's tire monopoly), drawing a combined salary of $75,849—so that he held the record of "pie-eaters and trough-feeders" of which he had so accused previous administrations.

Huey replied that some on the League's list he had never seen, that his relatives had spent more to elect him than they had ever gotten back in salaries. Curious logic! Anyway, he said, there were so many of his tribe in the state that they had only their fair share of jobs. He suggested the League of Notions investigate whether the penitentiary was not perchance feeding some of his relatives free of charge.

Leaving his old friend O. K. Allen to hold the fort in Baton Rouge, Huey loaded the governor's office on to a truck and moved to New Orleans to start an organization with which to fight back. The newspapers sarcastically labeled his administration: "The Government on wheels."

2

Huey picked up the pieces of his administration, put them together and went on. The debit side of his ledger: fifteen Robineer senators might block impeachment; they could not pass legislation. Fights would be made on all his appointments. The House was even worse out of hand. And he had lost the Board of Liquidation, which could cripple his power of allocating highways to his own advantage, refuse to approve contracts and block any borrowing.

At once he proceeded, and by one means or another largely succeeded, to remove all persons unfriendly during impeachment, not only on this board, but on others. He broke his enemies and lavishly rewarded his friends. Rapidly he rebuilt his fences bigger and better on all sides.

Patronage, the real fountain of power, was undamaged. Unspent millions of the first highway bond issue remained.

Highways. As in the case of Caddo Parish, he punished refractory communities and favored those whose representatives favored him. Instead of paving main thoroughfares such as Jefferson, Lone Star, Dixie Overland or the Camino Real, Huey doled out the pavement in little strips wherever they would do the most good politically. For a time the road map of Louisiana was a curious patchwork. A series of such maps would be a perfect index of the progress Huey made in controlling the entire state. A few dabs of roads started, star-shaped, out from loyal towns, stopped at state boundaries, skipped this and that town, where the way continued full of ruts, dust or mud. In time the whole state was covered with Huey's power and with fine paved highways and good gravel roads.

Also a few good roads doled out thus whetted the appetite of the state for more. Huey had in the back of his head the idea of putting over a still bigger bond issue.

Jobs. After the trial, May 29 (Lindbergh and Anne Morrow had just gone on their honeymoon), Huey took the fifteen Robineers, twenty-four representatives and others, on a week-end to Grand Isle, a remote hunting and fishing resort below New Orleans (mostly owned by Huey's friend of fiestas, Alfred Danziger) to blow off steam after the strenuous days. Shortly after the boat left the New Orleans docks with the party of "statesmen," some were soon gloriously drunk, shouting and singing and shooting pistols into the air.

Huey was held up on a chair by four men in answer to a cry from the natives for "Speech! Speech!" "What shall I say? What shall I tell 'em?" he kept asking in a thick voice.

"Promise 'em a road"—this was what Danziger was hopeful of. Huey promised a road.

Members of the party pushed the simple-minded islanders aside and seized their women to dance. Senator Gore reported of the fiesta, "I went to eat and I ate plenty."

On the way back, May 31, one of the cars turned over, seriously injuring several legislators.

At the fiesta some of the faithful at once received their rewards—appointments to juicy state jobs. A few months after the trial, the Robineers, many of their relatives, everyone who had supported him in the slightest way, except the labor people who had gotten behind him, had been lavishly taken care of. The newspapers never ceased calling attention to any jobs or favors granted the fifteen loyal senators: "Theirs is the earth and the fullness thereof," the papers proclaimed.

Curious appointment was that of E. L. Engerran, publisher of the pro-Long open-shop anti-labor paper, the *Bogalousa News,* a town controlled by the lumber barons, where five strikers had been killed by white guards. Engerran, irony of ironies, was made State Labor Commissioner.

During the trial ex-Governor O. H. Simpson had befriended Huey—a queer pair of bedfellows—and was made "Supervisor of Assessments" in New Orleans. At the same time Huey knifed his boyhood friend Harley Bozeman. Previously Huey had had to take Bozeman off the committee supervising purchase of gravel and crushed rock—Huey had his own ideas about supplying those materials; then Bozeman had, much to Huey's disgust, gone ahead and approved the Orleans assessment rolls, thus depriving him of an underhanded weapon he wanted to use against the assemblymen from there. Huey asked him to resign temporarily so other faithfuls could be quickly rewarded. Bozeman was out for good. When Bozeman testified in 1933 to the Senate Investigation, Huey screamed at him, "You damn' lying scoundrel of a thief."

3

No enemy was too petty not to get. Ben Badeaux, bridge tender in Plaquemines, was fired by Huey en route to the famous Grand Isle fiesta—the poor chap was a friend of his enemy C. K. Schwing. The ax fell right and left from janitors to senators. More Sullivan appointees were ejected from the Dock Board.

Every jobholder Huey could use, every resource at his

command, was put to work circulating petitions to recall the assemblymen who had been against him. Personally he took the stump against them.

First target was Representative C. A. Morvant of Thibodaux. Huey's men got up an impressive petition. Morvant immediately applied for an injunction to restrain the registrar from certifying the names on the ground that many were forgeries, duplications and secured through misrepresentation. July 2, Judge Butler ruled that Morvant had no right to assume the registrar was not going to correct the list before submitting it to the governor. Hardly had the judge's signature dried than the registrar sped it off by fast automobile to Baton Rouge.

Murphey I. Sylvest of Washington Parish, W. F. Calhoun, Sayes and Drouin from Avoyelles, Roberts of Lincoln, W. C. Hughes of Bossier, all filed suits to restrain the various registrars from certifying the signatures on the grounds of fraudulency, unpaid poll taxes, improper representations, duplications, use of state-owned cars, interference by Long officials, patronage, etc. Mostly they were upheld. June 20, four recall leaders in Bossier were arrested, charged with "knowingly and unlawfully" signing the name of X to the petition. In that parish Brossier threatened the registrar, a woman, with dismissal if she removed any names, though Judge Drew had ordered the withdrawal of over half the signatures.

To Arthur Edwards, leader in circulating petitions of the recall of Senator John Gamble in the Fourteenth District, Huey gave a $200 job as state fire-marshal. In Iberville, by manipulating the parish police jury (governing board), Huey dismissed Registrar W. P. Obier, law partner of enemy Senator Schwing, and appointed his own man, both to punish and recall Schwing and Gueymard.

In Tangipahoa, the editor of *Parish News* disclosed that he had been employed by the Highway Commission as a plainclothes detective with no duties, so his paper would support the recall movement. He photographed his $187.50 pay check, cashed it, returned the money to the general state fund, and thereby broke Huey's recall efforts in that parish.

Injunctions flew in all directions. The Secretary of State (affiliated with the Constitutional League) let judgment be be rendered against him so that no ballots could be printed or recall elections be promulgated. Finally three district judges handed down the decision that the legislators were not subject to recall.

In Webster Parish, July 10, Representative J. S. Bacon—even though highway police broke up his meetings and Highway Commission trucks transported Huey's voters—defeated his opponent. Huey's schemes for revamping the Legislature were largely wrecked. He won only one recall election. Not so good!

Later, in the Eighteenth Judicial District he backed Fred G. Claiborne against Hewitt Bouanchaud for District Attorney. When Claiborne was defeated, Huey postponed the general election to try to make new appointments to the board of election supervisors and get a court decision. Failing, he tried to throw the elections into next year so he could appoint Claiborne without a plebiscite. No such postponement was recalled in Louisiana's history and reminded people of Latin-American dictatorships. The local authorities declared they would hold the election on schedule, rifles in hand, if Huey sent in the militia as he threatened. Long announced this would be no more successful than "trying to elect the Pope of Rome or the Minister to Turkey." The election was held on time, and despite heavy rains, there was a record turn out. Long's man got only 19 votes. Not so good!

Failing in his recall efforts and fearing impeachment would really loom again, Huey made secret overtures for peace. July 20, a special committee of bankers and industrialists, headed by Harvey C. Couch, power and railroad man (with whom Huey was on excellent terms and had aided in rate questions, and whose brother, Peter Couch, was later to have a suite adjoining Huey's at the Roosevelt), appealed publicly to Huey in an open letter to "a political truce" to co-operate in the development of the state [1] They promised a $20,000,000

---

[1] Among those also signing were B. S. Atkinson, Vice President of the Louisiana and Arkansas Railway, Lynn Dinkins, President of the Interstate

chemical plant if plans to impose occupational taxes were withdrawn and the recall movements stopped. If Huey accepted, further efforts to impeach would be spiked and the administration's program would get support. The Standard Oil agreed not to oppose further the payment of the severance taxes.

Huey accepted. The recall efforts against Ginsberg were dropped August 6. He appointed three bankers to investigate charitable and educational needs!

Huey also made overtures to Parker of the Constitutional League and to the Old Ring. Appeased by this and the ending of recall efforts, though they did not cease attacks entirely, they softened their direct hostility.

And so, after all the fuss and feathers, the impeachment, the campaigning, the radio speech-making, the circularizing of the electorate, the mass rallies, the turmoil in House and Senate, the obstructing of all state business, the upsetting of all Louisiana with bitter elections and law suits, *Huey, instead of going down with flag flying, surrendered; he signed away what he had asked the people to stand by him for.*

4

His opposition was heavily supported by the New Orleans Dock Board, still out of his control. The Board was a menace in another way. Under preceding governors, chiefly Parker and Pleasant, bonds for over $42,000,000 had been issued against the Port, but as state obligations (this had been concealed) without proper provisions for redemption. His enemies were lying "in ambush" to denounce "the orgy of extravagance of Huey P. Long" as soon as the bonds defaulted.

Huey "exposed" the situation—maturities would become serious in 1930—to the people. Unfortunately for him a governor could not remove the Dock Board members. But in October he began gunning, particularly at Chairman Ed. S.

Trust and Banking Company, George E. Bouden, President of the Whitney Central Bank, Rudolph Hecht, banker and power trust man, and Alfred Danziger, head of the Association of Commerce.

Butler: Butler's private cotton warehouses in Texas ports, Huey charged, "competed unfairly with the New Orleans state warehouses"; the New Orleans tariff was $1.90 a bale compared to $1.38 in Houston and $1.29 in Galveston.

Presently the situation was ripe for Huey to act. The term of one member was expiring. Another member was friendly. One more member and Huey would have three out of five. He persuaded a hostile member to resign—he does not mention the inducement—and thus two new pro-Long appointees (Rene A. Stegler and E. A. Carrere of the American Bank and Trust Company; Huey conveniently forgot his campaign promise to appoint a labor man) were installed, and he had control.

But the Conservation Commission, which Huey had attacked most bitterly from 1923 to date, still eluded his control. The legislators, some of whom had sinecures there, had blocked all his efforts to get his finger into this pie. Huey, however, fired Dr. V. K. Irion, head of the commission, and declared him replaced by stick-pin Maestri. But Irion refused to budge, appealed to the courts. Early in December, 1929, the state supreme court finally denied Irion's right to appeal to the United States Supreme Court. Before he could make any further move, Huey mobilized the National Guard to eject him forcibly. Irion pled for time, but facing bayonets, resigned just in time to keep the peace. Senator Duke rushed into the besieged offices and told all the workers they were fired.

Besides the Dock Board and the Conservation Commission, Jule Carville was forced off the Tax Commission, and Huey was making passes at the State Board of Pharmacy and other still-uncontrolled jobs.

The process of forming a powerful state machine, despite the impeachment revolt, went on before, during and after that epic battle. Let them try to impeach him; he was getting absolute control of all the levers!

XV—THIS KING BUSINESS

CARNIVAL in New Orleans is a gay period from Twelfth Night to Mardi gras, the last day before Lent. The celebrations, growing ever more hilarious, climax on "Fat Tuesday" in parades, floats, balls, music, masked street-dancing. A composite of "the Tournament of Roses, David Belasco's *Mima* and the five o'clock New York subway rush," it brings a whole complex of mass-hysteria, commercial boosterism and social snobberies. Five exclusive organizations, membership in one of which represents the pinnacle of social achievement in Louisiana, the Krewe of Comus, the Twelfth Night Revelers, the Knights of Momus, the Atlanteans, and the Mystery Club, shade on down to dozens of others, including negro lodges, and now—since Mardi gras has degenerated into modern boosterism—the more recent business society known as "Rex." Besides the hoi polloi street-carnival, there are held a series of very select balls around which revolve all the social aspirations of the élite.

Huey, the previous year and this year, 1930, had made it very plain he wanted to participate in one or another of the major balls. But New Orleans society was—and so to the time of his death—obstinately deaf—the first governor since carpetbag days to whom a bid has not been sent. He had successfully maintained the same distinction as senator. But even a state dictator could scarcely suppress twenty aristocratic, law-abiding organizations or the street festivities so tied up with business ballyhoo. Though to date he had not founded the Krewe of the Kingfish, the previous year he put a crimp on general joviality by cracking down on gambling and vice—part of the wide-open tradition to attract tourists—and gathered in the major share of the season's publicity.

This season he began his onslaught in December by attacking Mardi gras at a Co-operative Club luncheon at the Roosevelt in caustic words reminiscent of Kemal Pasha's strictures to the Mohammedans of Constantinople not to waste time praying in the mosques. Said Long:

"It takes us until January 1 to get over the effects of Christmas, then we dance until spring, go to Europe until fall and return to get ready for Christmas and Mardi gras again." Instead of really creating prosperity, such "idleness" had permitted Houston and other ports to take away all New Orleans' business.

Again Huey provided his own stunt and walked away with the carnival publicity. Jovial Rex, the annual carnival ruler, arrives in his yacht, is saluted by the guns of a visiting war-vessel, is handed the keys of the city, is the center of all the fanfare. Huey wanted no monopolization of kingship and so dramatically thrust himself into the limelight that all else went unnoticed, including Rex. Huey also got his salute. Seventeen guns.

The German cruiser *Emden* was in port. On a Sunday morning, resplendent in full-dress uniform, Commander Lothar von Arnauld de la Perière, accompanied by German consul, Roff L. Jaeger, paid the proper call on the governor of Louisiana, whose ambulating office was still in New Orleans. Colonel Weiss escorted them into the gubernatorial suite at the Roosevelt.

Though previously notified, Huey had continued in deshabille, "reading the Scriptures." Hastily he threw a red and blue lounging robe over his green silk pajamas, slid into his blue bedroom slippers.

"Your Excellency," proclaimed the consul. "Commander Lothar von Arnauld de la Perière . . ." The consul stammered, aghast. The governor looked "like an explosion in a paint factory."

The consul readjusted his monocle. The group chatted.

Immediately after they left, the consul demanded, through Colonel Weiss, an apology for his commander and himself. The governor's attire was "an insult to the German government. . . . Otherwise—"

"What's the matter with 'em?" the governor asked Weiss. "I had on a pair of green pajamas, took the time to put on a pair of bedroom slippers, a $25 lounging robe given to me by the State Banking Department for Christmas—what more do they want?"

"But, governor," pleaded Weiss, "this is . . . serious . . . international . . ."

He brought in Herr Jaeger.

Again Huey stepped into the parlor—in pajamas. "I am much embarrassed . . . for having given you and the commander umbrage. . . . I have not been well. . . . I hope you will excuse my failure to properly bedeck myself. . . . You see, I come from Winnfield up in the hills. . . . I know little of diplomacy and exchanges . . . indulged in by nations. . . . I only happen to be governor of the state by accident. . . . There was no royal heritage . . . by chance. . . ." He promised to call Monday in person on the commander to apologize.

The governor and his aides spent the remainder of Sunday digging up the proper apparel. From Weiss, Huey borrowed a pair of pin-stripe trousers, from another friend, a gray four-in-hand morning tie; and, says Long, "I borrowed a pair of patent leather shoes from a fellow . . . in a barber shop, and I got a boiled shirt off a waiter at the hotel and a preacher up the avenue . . . from my own town lent me a swizzle-tail coat, and I got a collar so high I had to stand on a stool to spit over it."

Only a silk stovepipe hat was lacking. Someone remembered the hat Danziger had worn to call on King George in Buckingham Palace. He volunteered to produce it.

At sunup Monday the governor and his aides prepared for the forthcoming visit. At last impeccably arrayed, Huey grinned from his splendid toilette with his Puck-like quizzicalness. But no silk hat yet. Time wore on. It grew late. At last Danziger arrived breathless—without the hat. Huey grabbed up a gray fedora. "If this ain't right," he said, "I can keep it in my hand."

At the foot of Canal Street, they boarded the Hugh Mc-

Closkey launch. It buzzed out into the river, American flag whipping in the stern.

After a friendly chat, as the governor and his party stood at the head of the gangplank, seventeen guns boomed out. War between Louisiana and Germany had been averted.

2

Huey likewise averted war with Canada. The city delegate assigned to entertain the Canadian delegation had refused to drink a toast to the king. All was discord.

"Send 'em to me while I'm all dressed up," said Huey.

The Canadian party came in glory, led by Scottish bagpipers in full—or rather abbreviated—garb. Huey made a warm address of welcome. Alderman Wilkerson responded for the delegation. Compliments and greetings were fervently exchanged. War between Louisiana and Canada was averted.

3

A day or so later, nobility in the person of Countess de Topor Lakopolanski, a Polish lady, carnival-bent, came ardently to Huey's defense. "Most amusing, you know, the green pajama incident. . . . People take it too seriously. Mussolini and Primo de Rivera frequently received even royalty while wearing intimate garments."

Huey issued a jubilant press statement. "With the Countess de Topor Lakopolanski having asserted the propriety of my reception of the German celebrities, citing precedents of royalty . . . , it may come down . . . to . . . where we will . . . go back to the common starting point, maybe to old Uncle Noah, to find out what there is in this garb complication anyway."

And so Huey walked away with the Mardi gras publicity. So effective was his stunt that June 5, when General McCoy of the Fourth Corps area and aides (all in full dress) arrived, Huey at eleven o'clock in the morning received them in his underwear.

"If General McCoy is loath to believe that he had a narrow escape," said the Baton Rouge *State Times* [quoted by Smith], "and that the governor does not receive visitors in the nude, he is just not acquainted with our governor. . . . Early in his administration he received a Baton Rouge delegation minus B.V.D.'s."

To offset yokel ill-feeling about his wearing highfalutin silk pajamas, Huey later had his picture taken signing a bill in an old-fashioned nightgown. He persuaded his supporters those pajamas were a symbol of their governor's contempt for pomp and circumstance. Later, pajamas even adorned Kingfish campaign posters. Huey remarks:

"The enemy newspapers may have thought that all of . . . [this] propaganda . . . would do me less than good; on the contrary, it redounded to my advantage and greatly pleased the folk of both city and country."

4

Huey, still nervous about what might happen when the Legislature met again, still fearing revival of the impeachment charges, made more overtures to the Old Ring. Rebuffed, he started his own newspaper, the *Louisiana Progress* (printed in Mississippi). "Friends throughout the state voluntarily solicited subscriptions," declares Huey, though at the time, March, 1930, he was busy denying that public employees had been assessed 20 percent of their salaries. Old-time employees were discharged—not, of course, because they had refused to contribute.

The paper began to make life merry for Huey's enemies with Trist Wood cartoons, statistics, comparisons, and billingsgate, and it lambasted the other papers, particularly the *Times Picayune*. Its first issue carried a front-page cartoon of "Feather Duster" Ransdell, incumbent United States senator, whose place people suspected Huey intended trying to usurp.

The *Times Picayune* continued to charge Huey with nepotism, so Huey kicked Arthur Hammond, Esmond Phelps' brother-in-law, out of two state jobs, and *Louisiana Progress* flared with:

" 'TIMES PIC.' DICTATOR'S MAN PRIED FROM TWO SWILL TUBS"

". . . Double salary collected while *Times Picayune* held up hands aghast at dual office-holding—Governor Long, catching the spirit of the *Times Picayune* to job propaganda . . . finds the Mussolini of the *Times Picayune* has his relative modestly taking state pay . . . with both hands at the same time."

Shortly after this, Mrs. Hilda Phelps Hammond helped organize and headed the Woman's Committee, which has persistently fought Huey for years. Every week for years it sent a long petition to the Senate to oust Overton and investigate Long, and got women's organizations all over the country to do the same. Huey classified her as just one of the "pie-eating outs" from the corporation and aristocratic die-hards. *Louisiana Progress* published bovine caricatures of her. Over the radio, at her family, he slung such epithets as "tar-brush" and "nigger-baby."

Huey, wishing to keep the fire glowing under the patronage porridge pot, prepared a legislative program which included a new $75,000,000 bond issue to build more roads, free bridges, and a new state capitol; also, a one-cent gasoline tax to retire the New Orleans Port bonds and improve Lake Charles Port, and a tax on chain stores. Huey would rather be "caught coming from the home of a burglar" than from such an establishment. Promptly caught wearing a chain-store hat and accused of living in a chain-hotel, the Roosevelt, he gave his hat away to a bootblack.

He propagandized the state in favor of his projects, his enemies against them. Cyr, a constant thorn, called Long rather inconsistently "a raving maniac . . . falsifier, menace to a free people." Huey, too, redoubled his billingsgate. His enemies were "hoodlums . . . varmints and coyotes howling for their prey . . . pie-eating sons of buzzards . . . fools . . . knaves." In Monroe, assuring the voters the bond money would be honestly spent, he said he had wiped out all "stealing." On the very day of his inauguration, "while the brass band leading me to the inaugural stands played," the old Highway Commission "slipped to a Baton Rouge bank [all banks were closed that day]" and "drew out the last $6,000" of the Commission's funds. "That band played a nice tune, but it cost the state $6,000."

The *Times Picayune* played up a story that forty to fifty convicts had been illegally contracted on the private rice farm in Pointe Coupee of John P. Burgin, Sr., a Baton Rouge contractor, and father of Burgin, Jr., Superintendent of the Highway Commission, that Burgin, Sr., also got equipment, including nine tractors, pumps and tools and $10,000 cash.

This inhuman form of penal punishment had been abolished by the constitutional convention of 1898. Huey blustered, then blandly admitted it was all true, but that it was a good bargain for the state. When he had taken charge, the penitentiary was losing $1,000,000 a year [not true] "and I promised to stop the leak." The farm gave work to 42 convicts who otherwise would be idle, but this way returned "a profit of $30,000 to $40,000" to the institution. The work was healthful. "So now . . . the great exposure . . . falls flat as a pancake." It was far from flat as subsequent events showed. The men were abused, overworked, exposed to disease, lived in horrible quarters, and got bad food.

In May, to offset this unpleasant disclosure, Huey found time to pose as a farmer before the cameras (à la Mussolini). He urged the eating of cornbread, turnips and turnip greens, and plenty of potlikker, for rosy complexions—this in the hour of America's greatest depression!

A woman heckler cried, "Bet you'd never find any turnip greens on the governor's table. You can look at him to see he lives off the fat of the land."

"When I leave office," retorted Huey, "I'll be poorer than when I entered."

"Oh, yeah!"

5

The Legislature convened May 11. A desperate fight was made to remove Speaker Fournet, but the vote in his favor, 55 to 44, threw the opposition into consternation. In some mysterious way it had lost 20 votes since the previous session. In the Senate, Huey easily put in A. O. King as President pro tem to take the place of Gilbert, since rewarded with a judgeship.

Immediately Huey kicked off of responsible committees all those who had voted to remove Fournet and replaced them with tried and true henchmen. As Huey put it, "We gave those enemies—as mild-mannered men as ever scuttled ship or cut a throat—no quarter."

In a last frantic effort the Old Ring opposition called another Baton Rouge mass-meeting at the Community Pavilion for June 18, 1930, to be addressed by various mayors. Huey countered with one of his own the same night on the old L.S.U. campus. Special trains rolled out of New Orleans for both. The crowds of both mingled in Baton Rouge. Many fights occurred. Huey's campaign literature took fire on the state house grounds.

At the Old Ring gathering, ex-Governor Parker made sensational charges of graft, favoritism and mismanagement. Long attacked the New Orleans officials, former governors and newspapers as "gutter-snipes . . . alley rats . . . till-tappers . . . polecats . . . not a thief or safe-blower at Angola" (penitentiary) could "hold a candle" to Mayor Walmsley.

Despite his initial victory in the Legislature, Huey had to fight every inch. The Senate harassed him with demands to pass on his appointments. He had to apologize for his previous year's charges against Cutrer. The spearhead of opposition was, of course, the New Orleans delegation.

Huey decided to strike hard: he undertook to starve the city into submission, as a local paper put it, "to sandbag it," by preventing the banks' lending any more money and having them call in the millions of outstanding loans.

New Orleans operates on borrowed money the first half of the year, taxes not being collected until June. The total of loans had steadily increased. Huey now painted the situation as truly alarming; the city was paying an assessment of over $7,000,000, but had "to compel its employees to work for nothing." At the same time, through the Tax Commission, he held up the city's assessment rolls to embarrass tax-collections. In New Orleans, before an audience of 8,000, he damned the New Orleans authorities and the banks. "J. S. Brock, state bank examiner . . . went through the files of the . . . banks and found loans of $3,000,000 . . . on their face . . . illegal and unjustified." The city in no way could guarantee payment of the $9,000,000 now necessary to get it "out of the hole," and the condition of the banks was "none too good," to face any such loss. Huey demanded that State Supervisor of Public Accounts Conway be allowed to audit the books. Mayor Walmsley—"Old Turkeyhead," as Huey ever after called him—sought a court-restraining order, called upon "the people" to rebel against the governor's tyranny, and retaliated by having the State Highway Commission enjoined from using any of its millions to build or maintain highways and bridges until $246,532.24 owed the city for paving Claiborne Avenue was paid.

Huey had Emile Bienvenu demand, as an ordinary tax-payer, to examine the city's books. Granted May 29. June 2, however, he was ordered to desist on the grounds he was using the information for political purposes. His incomplete audit showed uncollected taxes inadequate to meet proposed loans. In these ways Huey prevented the banks' lending more money.

But wealthy citizens stepped forward and underwrote loans in New York. The *Baton Rouge State Times* commented: "Governor Long has failed to strike a mortal blow at . . . New Orleans. . . . The governor has frequently bragged that through the Banking Department he controlled the banks of the state, and the action of the great financial institutions . . . in lending aid to the governor to cut the throat of their own city lends color to his bragging words. . . .

"New Orleans never could be bluffed. It has a long and

heroic history. It has fought floods, plagues and panics; it
has had its homes invaded by alien soldiers, but it has never
lain down, and we know that a little sniveling demagogue from
Winn cannot blackmail its people into doing something they
do not think for the best interests of the state." In reality it
was all a vulgar fight for political power, slush funds and
patronage.

6

Step by step Huey gained legislative support. Though at
times the House was in a turmoil reminiscent of the impeachment sessions, though every move of the Long group was
greeted with "Steamroller! Steamroller!", though Sanders
charged Long was trying to cow the members by gunmen on
floor and gallery, though fist fights occurred and the galleries
had to be cleared time and again, he won out. Once he had to
leave the floor one jump ahead of the Sergeant at Arms, and
the scenes made anything worthy purely accidental, the result
of jockeying for power and control at which, of course, Huey
was past-master. In Europe such undignified scenes were invariably the prelude to revolution or dictatorship. They were
in Louisiana also.

When Huey had finally swung the two-thirds necessary to
submit the constitutional amendments, two members favoring them unexpectedly died. The newspapers gloated. Huey
made a quick shift in tactics—another proof of his great
parliamentarian resourcefulness. A bill was introduced providing for a constitutional convention. This required merely
a majority vote in both houses. The convention could then also
adopt his program by a simple majority vote.

"A damnable outrage!" one opponent cried. "A subterfuge
to have a majority vote do what it takes two-thirds to do."

Huey's floor-leader shot back. "You have taken . . . advantage [of] . : . the hand of Death. . . . The people
should have the right to decide. You have the newspapers; you
have the political rings. If you are right, the people will . . .
see your side. . . ."

Whatever the wishes of the people, Huey tried to make sure that he would control the convention—the bill allowed him to appoint 12 of the 128 proposed delegates. The question, finally put to a vote, though the provision allowing him to appoint delegates was stricken out, over a majority favored calling the convention.

In the Senate Huey's ground was not so firm. A filibuster, led by Cyr, continued for the sixty days' session and Huey's plan did not go through. Greatly puzzled that faithful members made no fight to put down the filibusterers, Huey—at least to his own satisfaction—discovered the sinister reason in an intercepted private letter (which he front-paged in three issues of *Louisiana Progress*), written by R. C. Watkins, Southern Pacific Railway manager ("for many years engaged in an effort to cause a return to private interests of valuable oil and gas lands of many acres now held by the state"), to another high Southern Pacific Vice-President:

"DEAR TALLICHET:

"I take pleasure in advising you that Governor Long's proposal for a constitutional convention failed before the state Senate. . . .

"You will be interested to know that the party you undertook to *reach,* though previously with the administration, came out strong for, and stood consistently with, the opposition until adjournment. . . ."

"Such," remarks Huey, "were the influences operating in the dark."

7

As usual Huey made those who fought him pay dearly. He passed the veto over three significant appropriation items: $6,400 for ("unnecessary") expenses of Lieutenant Governor Cyr. $28,980 for the office of Attorney General Saint ("counsel for the Constitutional League instead of for the governor and the state") and the $100,000 (already advanced by the banks whom Huey had warned) for the 1929 impeachment costs. (Later Huey secretly made payments on the $100,000

out of the general fund.) A squall went up from Cyr and
Saint. But as they had been constantly alleging "extravagances," their clamor met a "horse-laugh"—Huey's customary
feminine tactic of putting opponents on the defensive over
a petty issue.

XVI—FAMILY KIDNAPING

HUEY was in a fix. Without more money his political career might fizzle out. The Legislature had balked, but his machine was intact. He announced he would run for the United States Senate against 70-year-old "Feather Duster" Ransdell. If the people gave him their votes he would expect them to back up the bond issues and all administration plans. Otherwise he would immediately allow Cyr to take the post of governor. If he were elected, he would finish out his term. One of Louisiana's Senate seats would thus remain vacant a year and a half; but—Huey assured the voters—while Ransdell was there, it was vacant anyway.

A newspaper commented: "Long has piled all his chips on the table to bet on the throw of the dice. Win this time, and we are through with him."

Since March, Huey had been fixing fences. He patched up an alliance with the Paul Maloney faction of the Old Regulars. March 21, Maloney had headed a caucus of ward leaders in Long's office in the Whitney Bank Building. In return for support to Long it was reported there would be a quick delivery of dock-board jobs.

Long denied having attended the caucus, saying he was in Baton Rouge. Caught in a lie, he gave a yank to his lavender-spotted pajamas and admitted he had attended a caucus, but Wednesday, Thursday or some other night.

March 26, the *Louisiana Progress* made its first bow, caricaturing Ransdell, but not until July 16 did Huey formally announce his candidacy. July 24, Gus Williams, president of the Jefferson Democratic Club, charged that Huey had offered the organization for its support 150 jobs.

August 2, Huey formally opened his campaign at Martinville under the weeping Evangeline Oak in Bayou Teche. He accused Ransdell of being the tool of Wall Street. Now, "in behalf of the Old Ring," he had come back to Louisiana "to fight free textbooks and good roads."

August 30, in Abbeyville, Long promised he'd be "even less dignified than in the past. . . ." There was "too much sapsucker, hillbilly and Cajan blood" in him. He recalled the green pajama incident, when he had made a breach of international "eat-a-calf," and added, "I want all you people to keep on calling me 'Huey,' but those newspapers and ring politicians have got to call me 'Mister.'"

Ransdell, distinguished, bewhiskered, an old-school politician who for many years had warmed a Senate chair as a corporation yes-man, was unaware of the new forces in the Louisiana maelstrom—or anywhere else. He conducted his campaign with pompous serenity; an old dog, he wouldn't learn any new tricks. Huey, who heaped upon him such epithets as "Feather-Duster" and "Trashy Mouth" taught him some—but he learned too late.

First of all, August 8, Huey's machine "assessed" government employees" "voluntary" 10 percent of one month's salary campaign contribution. No checks—cash. Over $50,000 was collected. The *Times Picayune,* investigating the matter, found no case of refusal to donate.

Second, Huey used his very effective stunt of temporary dummy candidates, so as to control the election commissioners for each polling place. If any skulduggery went on in such precincts Election Day it would be Huey's.

Third, he added employees generously to the state payrolls, padding the Dock Board, the Levee Board, the Highway and Conservation Commissions. During the weeks prior to the election, some payrolls almost doubled. Four hundred employees were added to the Dock Board. Every added employee meant one vote plus those of three or four relatives. "Jobs! Jobs! The Simpson-Payne régime was nothing compared to the present wholesale hand-out of jobs by Huey Long," wailed Manship's *Baton Rouge State Times.*

Fourth, Highway Commission surveying parties went out in all directions, setting up rows of little flags over remote hillsides. The farmers roundabout were told Huey was getting ready to build them a road. If anyone wanted the flags located differently, they were obliged.

Fifth, Huey was aided by government employees, not merely with contributions. The resources of every department were called upon to the limit. Convicts painted his portrait on propaganda tire-covers; stenos addressed letters; highway trucks distributed literature and transported voters; every or any employee, from college president to dog-catcher, was given orders to carry water for the circus elephants, distribute literature, caucus, what not.

Sixth, his anti-impeachment efforts had led to a perfection of propaganda distribution. By now he had a card catalogue more complete than that of any political machine in the world. Every voter's record was known, also the name of every Long man in every community, just how many circulars he would personally distribute. Huey's secretary maintained an elaborate multigraphing office. In a single evening letters could be addressed to thousands of workers. One New Orleans printing establishment was especially equipped to handle Huey's work in a hurry. State employees and motor vehicles hastened the circulars out. Copies of *Louisiana Progress*, "to fight the unanimous press opposition," were printed (in Mississippi) by the hundred thousand, then by the quarter million, finally by as many as a million copies the issue.

Seventh, by this time Huey had developed a remarkable radio technique. "Hello, friends, this is Huey P. Long speaking, governor of Louisiana. And I have some very important disclosures to make. But before I begin I want you to do me a favor. I'm gonna talk along without saying anything special for four or five minutes, just to keep things going. While I'm doing that, I want you to go to the telephone and call up five of your friends and tell 'em Huey P. Long is on the air and has some very important revelations to make." While I was in Louisiana last April, he spoke for five hours over the radio, weaving argument, anecdote, special pleading. In Louisiana he didn't bother much about the dignity he put on elsewhere, but spoke abusive profanity. That particular evening he called new federal appointee Peterman, of whom everyone speaks highly, not merely a "rat but seventeen kinds of a rat."

2

If Ransdell was sedate, his supporters branded Long as "an impeached thief and scoundrel . . . a political freak, cringing coward and monumental liar." The papers refused to spell his name with caps, calling him "hueyplong." Pleasant denounced him over the radio as an "ultra Socialist" whose real views went "beyond Marx, Lenin and Trotsky." Angrily they charged him with secretly having put out Tom Heflin's anti-Catholic pamphlet in the Protestant north—*Shall Rum, Romanism and Ruin Rule?* Looney (a candidate who withdrew from the race) attacked Huey's "morality" for "living alone" at a hotel instead of with his family. Brother Earl was accused of criminal assault on a young girl. Stick-pin Maestri, head of the Conservation Commission, was called by Mayor Walmsley "the King of the Underworld," who made his fortune out of Red Light property, renting cribs and selling furniture at high prices to the painted girls of Storeyville.

Huey denied the charges in detail. "Bob Maestri put money in my hand when the ship was sinking, when the gold of Wall Street was trying to buy my impeachment. I have made many friends, but under the shining heaven I haven't got a friend I would offer up my life quicker for than Robert Maestri." Maestri had turned the Conservation Commission's $10,000 deficit into a $288,000 surplus.

Secretly enemies backed a negro widow, Georgia Rayner, to bring suit for $25,000 against Huey Long, Clay J. Dugas (general manager of the state penitentiary) and John P. Burgin, Sr., the Pointe Coupee rice plantation owner, for the slaying, August 25, 1930, of her convict husband, Curtis Riley alias Curtis Blackwell, during a strike because of bad food, terrible conditions, long hours and "cruel inhuman treatment." The body had been immediately interred adjoining the rice farm without notifying the widow, "thereby depriving her of the right and privilege of the burial of her husband." Long had "coerced Dugas" into making the improper and unconstitutional contract, *not in their official capacities, "but for their own personal profit and gain."*

Convicts lost their lives in other ways. Convict Joe Stimson was found murdered behind the levee five miles beyond Baton Rouge. Huey rushed agitatedly to the place his body was displayed, crying, "I know who did it! In twenty-four hours I will point to the murderer," which he never did; but it required some explaining about favored prisoners allowed to live in Baton Rouge in a state-owned building, dress in civilian clothes, drive state-owned autos, and stage wild parties.

Politics has never been on a high level in Louisiana, but it hit the nadir of indecency and frantic desperation during this campaign.

3

In Alexandria, August 25, C. W. Furnan, an aged man, stopped Huey in the hotel lobby to protest about the treatment given one of his relatives in the insane asylum. Huey angrily threatened to slap his face.

"You will not slap my face, governor," said Furnan.

Huey thereupon ordered bodyguards Messina and O. O. Lawrence to throw the old man out of the hotel.

W. B. Miller stepped between them. Messina and Lawrence backed off. Later, two city policemen entered Miller's hotel room to search for a gun. They found only two fingers of whiskey in a pint bottle and lodged charges of possession of liquor and disturbing the peace.

On the night of September 4 Huey spoke at a big mass-meeting in New Orleans. His highway police directed traffic. The city police objected. The two groups were soon in a free-for-all, fists and blackjacks flying. Huey stopped in his speech to denounce the city administration for the riot. He whaled the Old Regulars. In Baton Rouge he had already referred to them as that "gang of ballot-box stuffers who have been voting the St. Louis cemetery for the past forty years."

September 1, at an open-air meeting in Destrehan, just

north of Louisiana, Huey was much annoyed by automobile-honking when a driver blocked traffic to listen.

"Hey, you highway cops!" Huey bellowed. "Go out and stop that noise."

The noise stopped, presently started again.

"I want that noise stopped!" screamed Huey. "The next man that blows his horn, pull him out of his car!" To his companions he muttered, "They must all be for Ransdell."

Finally obtaining quiet, he assailed the editor of the *New Orleans Item,* "Hop-needle Marshal Ballard, king of the dope-fiends," who had "robbed the Dock Board." Elsewhere he attacked the golf-playing editors in general. [He played golf himself.] The *Times Picayune,* he said in Martinville, had "filched" between $150,000 to $250,000 a year of state funds before he became governor. Reporters were "lying low-down skunks"; he didn't see "why the state keeps men in the penitentiary when they are running around loose."

The newspapers were allowed free storage on newsprint for a certain length of time and very low rates thereafter in the Port Board cotton warehouse. Now Huey made the newspapers pay the piper for their opposition. Charging that if cotton instead of paper had been stored, the state would have received $185,000 more, he forced a material reduction in cotton storage rates, thus crowding facilities to capacity with cotton so newsprint could not be stored there. The *Times Picayune* evaded his accusation, distorted his statements and argued that in six years the Dock Board had received $235,-307.74 of newsprint storage business.

4

In Breaux, August 30, Huey said Ransdell had voted against the debenture plan to pay every farmer $10 extra for every bale of cotton he raised. "Why, it was just as if he put his hand in your pocket and took out a ten-dollar bill for every bale . . . you raised." The issue of the campaign was "whether the people are to have 3,000 miles of paved roads,

6,000 miles of farmers' gravel roads and free bridges without costing the people a cent."

Everywhere he had accused "Wall Street tool" Ransdell of having had American troops sent to Venezuela, Honduras and other countries "to help the interests." In New Orleans, repeating more fully this charge, he found the "sinister" element behind Ransdell and attacked Samuel Zemurray, a multimillionaire, now head of the United Fruit Company, then head of Cuyamel Fruit Company, who had "financed" several revolutions by General Lee Christmas and Guy Maloney. He issued a "sizzling" bulletin:

WHY THE ZEMURRAY MILLIONS SUPPORT THE RING

THE BLOOD OF AMERICAN SOLDIERS THAT IS SPILLED FOR ZEMURRAY

". . . Among the men who have made millions in Central America out of the work of the soldiers of this country is one Sam Zemurray of New Orleans. . . . Wherever he drove down his stob and laid claim to a few hundred miles of property, no matter what side of a revolution he bought from, he was able to make good his claim by the fact that the United States would send soldiers there to back him up. . . .

"Mr. Zemurray took in as an associate . . . a nephew of Senator Joe Ransdell, one Joe Montgomery, and this Zemurray and Ransdell's kinfolks' conbination made millions on top of millions that anybody else could have made if they had only been furnished with the United States army to back them up in their concessions and grants. . . .

"Many a mother's son lies in an unmarked grave in the tropics for the cause of Zemurray's millions and Senator Ransdell's nephew's good association with Zemurray. . . ."

While getting all this armed protection, Huey pointed out, Zemurray's concern registered its ships under a foreign flag to avoid taxes to the United States and to Louisiana.

"Zemurray and his millions, the blood of the American soldiers, the sacred judiciary of the state, a seat in the highest Congress of the land—all of these are traded in as part of the Ring boodle, along with the vituperation of the lying newspapers, against the welfare of the state.

"THEY SHALL NOT PASS!"

Ransdell made the childish defense that he had helped send marines to Nicaragua not to protect private interests but "to protect the right to build a canal across that country."

According to Huey this circular created "a storm," and won over much of the Old Ring rank and file, a way of explaining his deals with Maloney.

Attacked because of his own use of troops in gambling raids, Huey retorted that he had never used them to protect "rich" interests.

5

While Huey was campaigning, his enemies plotted. Attorney General Saint and his assistant, E. R. Schowalter, after examining Highway Commission chemist Sam Irby and other witnesses, September 3, called a special session of the East Baton Rouge Parish Grand Jury to investigate the Commission's affairs. Subpoenas were issued for auditor A. P. Tugwell, purchasing agent S. M. Beasley, and Huey's private secretary, Alice Lee Grosjean.

Right here the campaign sank to its lowest level of muck and gangsterism. The enemy was not merely trying to make pre-election scandal by investigating highway affairs, it was dragging forth Huey's private life.

Alice Lee Grosjean, from a poverty-stricken tribe down state, was a twenty-five-year-old sparkling baby-doll brunette, with a hard mouth rouged to Cupid's bow coyness, whom Huey had taken up as his private secretary and confidante, whom he was soon to make Secretary of State, and who is now head of the public accounts bureau, a position of great power in vindictive state politics. Alice, a girl who talks freely but reveals nothing, has been loyal to Huey, but stuck out for her own rights. Some say she cost Huey a pretty penny, but that he admired her for it; she handled many a confidential deal for him.

Sam Irby, an ignorant fellow, was the husband of Alice's aunt. Alice, who managed to get many relatives on the payroll, introduced Irby to Huey, and despite his lack of qualifications, the governor at once made him chief chemist for the Highway Commission. Immediately he engaged in shady maneuvers and was fired, though he claims because he put Miss Grosjean out of their house for having caused so much trouble and having threatened to destroy their home.

Schowalter took Irby to New Orleans to get Saint to call the Grand Jury investigation. There Irby found his wife had abandoned the home roof to go to Baton Rouge to join Alice. Irby claimed that Huey Long and O. K. Allen had persuaded her to leave by telling her scandalous tales about him.

He ganged up with James Terrell, none other than Alice's ex-husband, whom she had divorced after three years of married life, and both immediately set out by plane for Shreveport, Huey's legal domicile, announcing they intended filing $50,000 suits against him for slander, Terrell "against the person responsible for breaking up my home."

This and the highway investigation were but treacherous campaign tricks, for Irby and Terrell were met at the airport by local anti-Long politicians, among them Martian Hamilton, Ransdell's local campaign manager, a former House clerk squeezed out by Huey, who admitted it was "low-down politics."

That night Irby and Terrell were awakened by heavy knocks on the door of their hotel room—a delegation of Huey's State Bureau of Criminal Identification! Refusing to open, they hurriedly telephoned the Caddo Parish sheriff. Three city policemen hurried up to investigate. Irby and Terrell then opened the door.

The state officers, among whom were Dave McConnell, brother-in-law of Huey, and Wade Long, cousin, dismissed the three policemen and took the two men off for questioning on "the rifling of state papers."

The next day neither could be found. Rumors flew thick and fast. Had they been murdered? The newspapers clamored for the facts.

Senator Pike Hall of Shreveport announced that, as attorney for the two men engaged to file suit, he had telephoned a Baton Rouge attorney to direct habeas corpus proceedings against the superintendent of Angola penitentiary, where it was rumored the two men were being held. The reporters raced to the institution, but Irby and Terrell had never been seen there.

Huey, in New Orleans, told reporters that Hall did not represent the two men and had no authority to bring suit in their names, that they had no complaints to make against anybody. They had been arrested at the request of District Attorney Fleury of Jefferson Parish. "The attorney general has been having him an investigation and half the district attorneys in the state have been having them an investigation and there are investigations everywhere, so if John Fleury . . . wants to have *him* an investigation, it's perfectly all right with me."

He then read a letter from Fleury to the Bureau of Criminal Identification: "Sam Irby and a young fellow he is carrying about with him under different names [Huey didn't like to give the name of Alice's ex-husband.] have been engaged in unlawful activities, taking property of the state of Louisiana with which I understand Irby has been trying to blackjack some of the concerns dealing with the state department. . . . Take him into custody. . . ."

"As a matter of fact," said Long, "the district attorney . . . has been led to bark up a hollow tree. . . . There is nothing in these charges, but I am perfectly willing for Mr. Fleury to investigate, and those two men are tonight in Jefferson Parish." (Which was the truth!)

Huey also read telegrams he claimed to have received from Irby and Terrell that they were "just where they wanted to be," but so fast the reporters could scarcely catch the words. One to Pike Hall read: "I renounce your efforts to bring

any suit for me. It is unauthorized. (Signed) Jimmie Terrell.
"This also applies to me. (Signed) Sam Irby."

Huey also read one to the Shreveport district attorney:
"I understand Pike Hall is trying to bring a suit for me. I am
where I want to be. (Signed) Sam Irby."

Next Huey read a telegram to Mrs. Norman in El Dorado,
Arkansas, Terrell's mother: "I am O.K. Do not worry."
But her own son must have known that a few months before
she had married a third time and was now Mrs. Hasselroth.
Huey seemed to have pulled a boner.

"Here I am," complained Huey to the reporters, "trying
to run my campaign and build roads and run the state and
about nineteen lawsuits, and lo and behold! if I didn't see
in the papers where somebody had been kidnaped by some
relatives of mine or something, so that I had to drop everything this afternoon and go out and hustle to find out what'n
hell had become of these two men.

"Well, I found out, and when I tell you, you're going to
see that these newspapers are the laughing stock of the whole
world, and that nobody can believe anything they print.

"Now, I want to tell you that if some cousin of mine or
some brother of my wife's—and of course I gave my wife's
brother a job! I have to live with his sister! You would do it
too. But what I am getting at is this: I hope if some district
attorney decides to examine somebody in my employ about
stealing a chicken, he'll wait until after election, because I
haven't got time or the money to answer this kind of blackmail. But you needn't worry, those newspapers are going to
have a new blow tomorrow evening [afternoon] at two
o'clock."

Reporters asked to see and copy the documents. Huey cited
them at his office at 11 P.M., but an attendant there informed
them the governor had changed his mind about making them
public; and no "blow" was forthcoming next day at two.

In a public address, Friday, September 5, in McCarty
Square and over the radio, Huey Long said the two men were
being held in Jefferson Parish for questioning, and at the
municipal auditorium the following night said *it* had been

intended to produce them at the meeting, but *it* had been learned that the New Orleans police would arrest them on sight.

"The newspapers keep talking about the kidnaping of Irby . . . like a nigger in a graveyard whistling to keep his courage up." Huey said he was going to take "the newspapers, Walmsley, Sullivan and all of them," tie them together in a sack, "and drop them in the deepest part of the river."

Reporters failed to find any trace of the "kidnaped" in Jefferson Parish. The only State Bureau of Criminal Identification man involved who could be found was Wade Long, who facetiously refused any information. The persons in Shreveport to whom Huey had said telegrams had been sent denied receiving them. Terrell's brother brought habeas corpus proceedings. The whole state was in a fever of excitement.

6

Huey's opposition at a Saturday night rally made the most of the scabrous occurrence. Walmsley, exaggerating, called it "the most heinous public crime in the history of Louisiana." If Louisiana elected "slacker" Long, she might as well "abandon her constitutional rights and become annexed to Mexico or Russia."

Charges of kidnaping were then filed in the federal court against Long, Fleury and six other state officials (a fact Huey deliberately hides in his autobiography). Schowalter also filed a habeas corpus petition against Sheriff Frank Clancy of Jefferson Parish. Federal jurisdiction was asked in both cases on the grounds that the authorities had violated the United States Constitution.

Huey was in a bad jam. Only three days off was the primary election to determine his political fate. Probably he merely had wished to keep Irby and Terrell out of the clutches of his enemies so they would make no rash statements. But here scandal had broken in a rash on the front pages in Louisiana and in the whole nation. Once more his enemies seemed to have cornered him.

But he beat them all by a flamboyant stunt worthy of Hollywood itself.

Sunday night, September 7, Huey introduced Sam Irby over the radio from his Roosevelt suite!

Irby said he had asked to be spirited away. He had found $2,500 under his pillow in Shreveport Hotel and was afraid to be left alone with the money which he did not know whether was for something he had done or was expected to do, so he figured the best way to get out of town with the unexpected swag was to have the police abduct him! Now, tonight, he had telephoned the governor and had been advised to slip into the hotel.

Two reporters, and only two, were admitted to the governor's suite. Immediately after his tall yarn, Irby was swiftly escorted from the room by two men flourishing revolvers. One reporter followed them to the freight elevator, but when he tried to get in, someone else jerked him back so violently as to tear his coat. One escort again waved his pistol and ordered the operator to start down.

Long declared over the radio that Irby had turned over the $2,500 to him for the campaign—it was just then being counted; then a little later: Irby had "got away with the $2,500—crossed the line. Pardon me, I laugh."

Everybody concerned had suddenly transformed himself into a phony dime-novel character. Silly G-men film stuff never held a candle to it. Later, in a sensational vindictive pamphlet, *Kidnaped by the Kingfish,* Irby claimed that for several days he had been brutally tortured, that he spoke before the microphone with pistols digging into his sides, merely reciting the words on a sheet of paper held before him. The pistols, however—pardon me, I laugh—may have been "long green."

7

When subpoenaed Monday, September 8, Huey was with Maestri. The deputy serving him was accompanied by *Item* reporter William G. Wiegand, who contemptuously asked Huey if he had any statement to make.

Huey cursed out the New Orleans papers. "You son-of-a-bitch. . . ." He raised his arm.

Wiegand slugged Huey on the mouth, drawing blood. Huey's guards at once seized him. "You son-of-a-bitch . . ." repeated Huey.

The reporter tried to break loose, but the guards held him. "Arrest that man!" cried the governor. "He got in here under false pretenses! He impersonated a federal officer."

The reporter denied this. Huey slapped him in the face. Wiegand, arms pinioned, laughed and kidded Huey about his lack of punch.

"Search that man! See who he is," Huey roared.

"A hard-faced man with blue eyes and another who looked like him" went through Wiegand's pockets. The three conferred, then Long said, "It will not do any good to charge this man with impersonating a federal officer. Turn him loose." Huey then apologized. "I wouldn't call any man a son-of-a-bitch," but he warned Wiegand he had made a mistake coming into his rooms. "Why, you might have been shot and killed. I have armed men around me at all times."

The reporter went down the hall accompanied by O'Hara, one of the searchers, who also apologized for what had happened. Wiegand later published the incident in the form of an affidavit. Huey made no reply.

8

Huey asked Judge Borah to postpone the court appearance so he could fill speaking engagements. But Borah was adamant.

Accompanied by bruisers, highway police and a detachment of National Guard, to the music of the smashing of newspaper cameras, Huey made a sensational swaggering entry into court.

He and Sheriff Clancy evasively denied all knowledge, though Clancy admitted having signed a telegram to the Criminal Identification Bureau that he had complete control over Terrell who did not want to leave his parish. He said he just signed it to be convenient "to someone," and did not realize the gravity of his act. The two men, he believed, had been summoned by Deputy Sheriff Arthur Sardis for hearing next Wednesday (after the election) in Gretna across the river. Sardis, it was promptly discovered, had gone on a week-end fishing trip.

Huey could not remember in court having made any statements as to the whereabouts of the two men when he spoke at the McCarty Square rally and testified that the telegram sent to Terrell's mother and other messages had been brought to him by Sardis (who later indignantly denied this). "I haven't seen Terrell for more than a year, but Irby was up in my room . . . last night and spoke over the radio. Why, he told the people . . . I was the best friend he had in the world." Huey said that Irby had told him that the $2,500 had been given him by Schowalter and Eberhardt Deutsch to file the slander suits.

At his public rally Huey had announced the two men could be brought in at any time; now in the federal court he testified under oath he didn't know where they were—not necessarily a contradiction.

Judge Borah adjourned court until the following day to hear what Sardis had to say. This suited Huey to a "T"— next day was election day—the ballots would be well filled before the newspapers could circulate "any more lies."

Next day Sardis said he had served summons on Irby.

Huey and his henchmen promised Judge Borah they would bring the two men into court within twenty-four hours—*i.e.,* the day after election.

Huey banged into office in the primary with a majority of 40,000 votes. Even New Orleans had given Ransdell a mere 5,000 majority. St. Bernard Parish, Huey stronghold, had reported 4,000 votes, practically all for him, though the parish had only about 1,900 qualified voters. "The people there live in boats; the census taker doesn't find them all," quoth Huey cynically.

Thus vindicated at the polls, Long brought Irby into court. In high fettle, Irby swore he and Terrell had been on Grand Isle (Jefferson Parish), a remote hunting and fishing resort,

once the headquarters of Jean Lafitte and other pirates, meeting ground of the famous round-robin party. It could only be
reached by boat or plane—Danziger's road hadn't been built
yet—and had no telephone or telegraph lines. An admirable
hide-out. Irby now said he and Terrell had never intended
filing slander suits against Long—ridiculous.

Judge Borah dismissed the writ of habeas corpus. Irby was
rushed from the courtroom by Huey's guards. He and Terrell
temporarily disappeared from the state.

Huey's enemies had tried to use two unprincipled men
against him at the eleventh hour. He had outwitted them.
*One should ponder the use of state officials for gangster
purposes.*

9

The Wednesday following Huey's smashing victory at the
polls, the Constitutional League was announced deceased.
The press, from vituperation, turned to flattery. The old gang
flocked around him. Mayor Walmsley hastened up to his suite
to agree to his entire financial program for the city and the
division of the spoils. He was immediately tendered a large
banquet attended by all men prominent in political and civic affairs and presided over by federal judge Rufus E. Foster, who
a few years previous had called Huey "demented," and now
spoke of the "nothing but good" that held sway. The speakers
were: Danziger ("the most constructive program" for "city
and state . . . since the Civil War"), Overton (untruly saying that Huey was the first man to be governor and senator
at the same time), Superintendent Harris ("peace and good
will and constructive co-operation have taken the place of ill-
feeling, prejudice and hate"), F. H. Milner (his roads were
a greater monument "than the Appian Way"), Walmsley
("Let us forget all bickerings"), Banker Rudolph Hecht
("the governor's generosity"), and finally former Old Ring
John Klorer (with the invariable political cliché: "Anyone
who withholds his support of the governor now is not a true
friend of the state").

To all this shower of praise, Huey was thinking: "If all

the good could but be true." And later remarked, "At least why could not enough be remembered that one, thus so highly pictured, is not found to be an exact partner of Satan because he undertakes to spread the wealth of the land among the people." (But shades of Satan! What wealth had Huey ever spread among the people of Louisiana?)

At the banquet Huey told an amusing story of a dead man exceedingly praised by the minister delivering the funeral sermon, whose mother-in-law got up and gazed in prolonged amazement into the casket. To her the preacher turned and said: "Madam, I know you are grieved; what is there that the neighbors can do to soften your heartache on this sad occasion?"

The mother-in-law replied: "I just want to stand here, parson, to be sure the man you are talking about was my son-in-law."

And, said Huey, "I am still hoping it's me here tonight with all these former opponents as well as my friends." At least Huey was never pompous.

Later, he cynically remarked of this moment in his career: "When some people start finding out how great one is they know no limits."

It was all very amusing, this haste of the defeated to lie down with the victor. A spectacle wearisomely repeated in all times and climes. Peace—as when he was elected governor— would last just so long as he handed out "pie" to his humbled opponents.

Huey, the flush of victory on him, immediately called an extra session to put through his program and the bonds. The same night of the banquet he motored to Baton Rouge to fix up his lines slightly broken by the efforts of his brother Earl, who despite the fat job he had been given, was trying to block the building of a new state capitol.

Among the scattered support Earl collected was old deaf Judge Dupré. But one day Dupré came to Huey complaining his seat in the old building was under a leak, and demanding instant repairs. Huey wrote on his pad:

"Are you going to vote for the new capitol?"

"No!" he shouted.

Huey then wrote: "Die, damn you, in the faith!"

Huey soon checkmated Earl. Otherwise, as Huey touchingly put it: "The dove of peace not only perched on the extra session . . . of 1930, but its wings fluttered and feathers scattered throughout both halls of the Legislature for the five days of the session."

Despite this rather muddled metaphor, the extra session unanimously dismissed the impeachment charges and backed Huey in everything. "Thus," sang Huey, "the extra session . . . adjourned with Huey P. Long, governor and United States Senator-elect . . . successful in everything he had ever advocated." (But not in the occupational tax, not in reducing taxes, not in making the penitentiary self-sustaining, not in destroying "pie-eating patronage," not in promoting labor legislation, not in building markets and warehouses—the list of unfulfilled promises is long. But his victories were notable.)

XVII—SON OF LOYOLA

HUEY now made continuous efforts to improve the University of Louisiana—of which General William Tecumseh Sherman, before the Civil War, had been the first president. This consisted chiefly in making it a subservient part of his political machine and taking all the credit for the foundations laid by Governor Parker. It was given "A" rating by the Association of American Universities in November, 1928, something with which Huey had nothing whatever to do but for which he has taken all the credit. In a few years, thanks to patronage to obedient students, he did increase the enrollment from 1,600 to 4,000.

Also, Huey did build four new buildings, one the excellent medical center in New Orleans, this out of jealousy for Tulane University, of which the controlling personality has been Esmond Phelps of "hateful" *Times Picayune* fame.

But it was not until the appointment of a new puppet university president, November 7, 1930, following President Thomas Atkinson's retirement because of ill health, that Huey really set to work. He was then presented with a budget showing the needs of the institution. "Go ahead with your buildings," Huey told them. "Get your architect and start out. . . ."

"But . . . the money?"

"That will be . . . my job. . . . You have to dare a bit if you build this school."

Architects drew plans; contracts were let. When payment could be delayed no longer, Huey had the university sell part of its old grounds as a site for the new capitol for $350,000 and part to the Highway Commission for roads, permanent offices and garages for $1,800,000.

Clamor went up from Huey's enemies, and injunctions were

sought against his improperly diverting bond money, but by the time the matter had been fought out legally, Huey's new buildings were up; the court had to shrug its shoulders. When the $2,150,000 was played out, again Huey told the contractors: "Go ahead, I'll find the money." He got a federal R.F.C. loan of $1,770,000. President Smith blossomed out with a $5,500 Cadillac limousine. February 12, 1933, the School of Medicine was approved Class A by the American Medical Association.

But in all this was also a new move for ironclad political control and future student political support. It marked, despite Huey's physical improvements, the death of a free university. For more than anything else, he was interested in showiness, all the whoopla frills that curse the American university. Not only did he want the biggest of everything, he wanted a dashing football team and went out and paid for it.

At one of the games with Tulane, Long, in a costly tailored outfit, raced up and down the side lines, yelling orders to the L.S.U. quarterback. "Kill 'em, goddam 'em! Break their necks! Show the bastards how to fight!" Or squatting on the lines he would suddenly tear up handfuls of grass, leaping high into the air, while 35,000 spectators forgot the game to watch his antics. Tulane won.

Missouri University came down to play L.S.U. at Shreveport. At the end of the first half the score stood 6-0 in Missouri's favor. Huey reeled around the field, leading the cheers, shouting. He told the coach that if L.S.U. lost, he was fired; he told the boys if they didn't win they could go slap damn to hell. Get in and kill those fellows, he told them. If you win, I'll give every slap damn one of you a job on the Highway Commission. They won. But, a member of the Missouri team told me, they were the dirtiest players Missouri had ever come up against.

Presently Huey was silent at the Tulane games, saying, "That Esmond Phelps and the rest of his gang told the game official if I let out a yip on the side lines, they'd demand L.S.U. forfeit the game. That's Tulane sportsmanship! I got the —— afraid of me, anyway."

He took out his managerial eagerness in the dressing-room:
"Go in there next half and kill those bastards. What the hell
do you care if you break your legs while you're breaking their
necks?"

Coach Biff Jones resigned in a huff because of such interfering. At future meets Huey kept his fingers out. "I showed
the boys how to do it," he said. "They don't need me now."

One of Huey's great delights was playing around with the
band, leading it, making it play his music, buying it new uniforms, sticking in a new horn or flute. He conceived of himself as a composer, but in part these antics undoubtedly were
due to Huey's naïve desire to experience a side of university
life denied him in his youth. Also his vanity was pleased that
he could boss things highhandedly at the university he himself
was never able to attend. It appeased his educational inferi-
ority complex.

2

Huey had his own academic talents in another direction.
Seeking an LL.D., he was rebuffed by Tulane, but had it
granted by the Roman Catholic Jesuit institution, Loyola
University in New Orleans, on the basis of his public record
and his compilation of Louisiana constitutions, with court decision extracts, made up with the aid of subordinates and the
purloined law books.

The coveted honor was conferred with fulsome eulogy February 2, 1931, at "quite a demonstration" attended by the
justices of the state supreme court and other officials and professors from the state and elsewhere.

"The honorable gentleman, around whom are gathered tonight such representative citizens of our state and nation, has
been judged by the Board of Directors of Loyola University
as a true son of Columbia, a man of action, with ideas born
of outstanding vision, who dares to fight for the realization
of his ideals, watchfully waiting, working continually. In the
words of Lucan, describing the great Caesar, 'Nil Actum
credens, cum quid superesset agendum.' "

(Huey grinned puckishly at this belabored night-oil piffle,

the tassel of his mortarboard bobbing in one reddish eye. Nice to be compared to the great Caesar. That "watchfully waiting" was the bunk. You couldn't afford to wait; you had to climb up in the dark while everybody else was sleeping and paint your name on the water-tank. What the hell did the damn' Latin mean anyhow?)

Next his public achievements were set forth glowingly, with more Latin (Ha! Less than two years ago they had tried to stamp him into the dust, they had blackened his name, they had slung mud, and some of it had stuck. Now they were all nibbling out of his hand. Nice lads. All the bigwigs were fawning. That God-damn' Latin had a nice cleansing sound.).

The eulogy went on and on. His roads surpassed "Italy's renowned Via Appia, known as the Queen of Long Ways— *Longarum Regina Viarum*." (Jesus, you wouldn't think those sedate old robed boys would pun—in Latin at that! Now who built that damn' ancient wop road? Must a been a great guy, too. They'd built 'em with slaves, but Louisiana roads were built by great American free labor at ten cents an hour, dadgum it, and good soft rock from the Winnfield quarry, dingbust it. Wonder if the old-time wops got their fingers into the pie like the Louisiana boys do?)

Now they praised him for his *"vade mecum"* (glad they said what the hell it was)—"a manual of sure guidance for the legal profession," his "masterful Compilation of the Constitutions of the State of Louisiana."

(Just wait till they see what I'm gonna do with those constitutions! Ha!)

3

Hardly did Huey have time to get his diploma framed before he revealed his great worthiness in the field of scientific husbandry. February 27, he waxed poetic over "razor-back hogs" and "scrub cows"; they were "the key to agricultural prosperity in Louisiana." They were, unlike good northern cattle, immune to the blood-sucking tick. Northern cattle sickened and died. Huey had always been, despite the good record in neighboring states, "extremely doubtful" that ticks could be eradicated. "I will not put the state one nickel in debt for tick eradication. . . . Razor-back hogs root for their own food. You have to feed high-class stock high-class food." The work of tick eradication, besides requiring experts, was fairly costly yet gave little opportunity for patronage.

But Louisiana needed good cattle and hogs. It could be one of the richest grazing states in the world. Certainly it should not have to import beef and milk, of which at present there is a grave lack.

The year before Huey had finally bowed to public clamor and finally signed the tick eradication bill, saying: "I think this is a perfect piece of legislation," then treacherously refused to provide the moneys to make it effective; he also refused to grant the Dairy Commission funds to subject 50,000 head of cattle to the tuberculin test.

Thanks to Doctor Huey, Louisiana tick eradicators had a truly *Longarum Regina Viarum* before they finally got anywhere.

4

Huey next turned bank savior. Banks were closing all over the United States. In Louisiana, the Bank of Lafayette and Trust Company of the Acadian sugar section (sugar was shot to hell) telephoned that a dangerous run had developed.

Huey, in bed with fever, dressed, and motored to New Orleans, got a bankers' conference, which he overawed by his armed guards, secured funds, rushed on to Lafayette all night by car, and personally stopped a run. He saved other banks.

For a bank to fold up because of a run is stupid, but the basic work still had to be done. Huey's efforts were merely temporary tooth-filling while leaving the pus at the roots. When the banking débris in Louisiana was cleared away— there is plenty still—one of the things which contributed to permanent collapse of many local banks and even some branch banks which New York concerns gutted before tossing the picked bones to the depositors, was their being overloaded with state bonds at par which Huey had rammed down their throats—the very thing he had prohibited New Orleans from doing. Thus the depositors in the banks were among citizens paying four times over for Huey's famous concrete highways; twice their worth in taxes to pay off the bonds, twice again in loss of deposits. And as the state also had very large deposits in many of the banks that crashed, which were also lost, even the taxpayers' multiple outlay and loss were without any results. Such is the great gyp game everywhere of modern government-financing!

5

With people starving on every hand, Huey's bright remedy was for the good folk to raise gardens, though dispossessed share-croppers were tramping the highways with gaunt families. The farmers could "thus feed themselves and their children food products . . . they might not have the money to buy in days of stress."

Huey began a marvelous propaganda for the traditional food of the South's prolonged misery and poverty—potlikker and corn pone "which can be fed to a family for a few cents per week, and the whole family kept strong and healthy."

Yet Huey described the food of social salvation: "Potlikker is the juice that remains in a pot after greens or other vegetables boiled with . . . a piece of salt fat pork. . . . If a pot be partly filled with well-cleaned turnip greens and turnips . . . cut up . . . with a half-pound piece of the salt pork, and then with water, and boiled until the greens and turnips are cooked reasonably tender, then the juice remaining . . . is the delicious, invigorating, soul- and body-sustaining potlikker. . . .

"Corn pone is . . . simply . . . meal, mixed with a little salt and water, made into a patty and baked until . . . hard.

"It has always been the custom to eat corn pone with potlikker. Most people crumble the corn pone into the potlikker. The blend is an even-tasting food."

But even poverty should have its elegance. "But, with the progress of education, the coming of 'style,' and the change of the times, I concluded that refinement necessitated that corn pone be 'dunked' . . . rather than crumbled in the old-fashioned way. So I suggested that those sipping of potlikker should hold the corn pone in the left hand and the spoon in the right, sip of the spoon one time, then dip the corn pone into the potlikker and bite the end. . . ."

February 16, 1931, he sent a dispatch to this effect from Baton Rouge to the *Atlanta* (Georgia) *Constitution.* The paper insisted corn pone should be crumbled. Huey then sent an indignant telegram, signed "Huey P. Long, LL.D., Governor and Senator-elect." The question was put up to the Southern governors and to Governor Franklin D. Roosevelt of New York. Some straddled. Governor John G. Pollard of Virginia declined to be drawn into another "liquor" question. Alfalfa Bill Murray of Oklahoma, due, Huey decided, to Indian influences, asked for a truce until his favorite hog-jowl and poke salad could be investigated. Most of the governors were "crumblers," and when Roosevelt telegraphed, lining up with them, Huey says, "I compromised—I compromised with all foes that it would be a commendable pursuit to eat potlikker with corn pone whether it be done by crumbling or by dunking. . . ."

He praised the food properties, iron, manganese, etc., "needed for health and complexion, sound bodies and sound minds, and the 'perfect 36.' "

Thus Doctor Huey settled the great academic problem. It was all good Democratic waggishness prior to the campaign of the great depression to change America's destinies.

6

The depression, especially in the cotton industry, had hit Louisiana as severely as the rest of the country. Politics was the only flourishing enterprise. The cotton farmers were clamoring for legislative relief. Huey saw the chance to seize the laurel crown, not only locally, but on the wider national stage he had just entered with his "dunker" dagger.

August 16, 1931, he telegraphed the governors, senators, and congressmen of the cotton states, inviting them to meet

in New Orleans, August 21, to lay plans to prohibit "the raising of a single bale of cotton . . . during the year 1932"—
the "one and only way" to bring "prosperity" to the South.
"Enact a drop-a-crop law," he urged, and the farmers would
get "more money for this year's crop alone than . . . for this
and the next two crops they raise. Cotton would jump to
twenty cents in three weeks."

(And the penniless consumers! And who would feed the
cotton farmers with their crops pledged for debts seasons
back? And would Brazil and Argentina and India and Africa
quit growing cotton? Just pure ballyhoo!)

Listen to Huey's argument. "The Lord told us to lay off
raising crops one year out of every seven to let the people
have time to consume them. . . . Louisiana will pass this law
if the other states will join us." Thus, in Sir Galahad fashion,
he advocated the most extreme policy of restriction yet presented in the United States, a policy for which later he was
so ferociously to denounce the national government.

At the New Orleans meeting, considerable enthusiasm was
displayed. Texas, the largest producer of all the states, was
considering already limiting the 1932 crop to one half or one
third the actual acreage. Texas, therefore, had to take the
lead. "It must be an entire hundred percent [sic] prohibition
. . . or nothing," declared Huey. "We are only waiting on
Texas."

August 24, Governor Sterling of that state retorted: "It's
Governor Long's baby; let him wash it first."

Huey took up the challenge and called a special session.
The Legislature met at 10 P.M., August 25, in the old state
house. Huey, immaculate in white *cotton* suit, strode down
the central aisle to the microphone and harangued, and the
following day greased the committee wheels.

Judge Dupré, protesting that the presence in the committee
room of "that smart fellow, his excellency," was "disturbing"
him, raised his lone voice to attack the bill's constitutionality.
"Hell!" replied another member. "If the government can tell
a man what he can't drink, why can't he tell him what he can't
plant?"

After unanimous adoption, August 26, the bill was rushed to the executive mansion for Huey's signature. He had sent out for a white cotton nightshirt. Sitting up in bed in this, he signed the bill with photographers' flashlights booming. "Now!" he cried, "I can take this damn' thing off!" He backed out of it into his customary silk pajamas.

Huey sent a certified copy of the act to Governor Sterling by O. K. Allen, his announced candidate for governor, by plane at dawn. Sterling was in Houston, his home town. Allen flew there. Sterling met him at the airport: "Here is Governor Long's baby," said Allen, "all washed, powdered and wrapped up in a cotton dress. . . . You'll hear it cry, 'Daddy, take me up!' This baby of Governor Long's, if adopted by the state of Texas, will save the cotton farmers of the South. Nothing else can."

According to Huey (it was not true) Mississippi, Alabama, South Carolina, North Carolina and Arkansas would fall in line if Texas voted the plan. Huey was anxious to tour the South, particularly Texas; Dr. Cyr, ever so ready to pounce on the governor's chair, finally agreed to let Huey go for sixty hours, during which time he promised not to seize the post.

"Put that in writing," demanded Huey.

"My word is my bond."

Huey didn't trust him. "I have had that gentleman's word before," he said, and remained in Baton Rouge.

Sterling still delayed: Texas was "a little more democratic than Louisiana." Whereupon, September 2, Huey angrily radioed from Shreveport about Sterling's $35,000,000 personal fortune and how Texas farmers were starving.

A special session of the Texas Legislature convened early in September. Sterling, however, spoke of uninformed popular hysteria and mentioning a secret prior agreement, hinted he would veto Huey's measure.

"So he has reached a covenant with someone?" Long shouted back over Henderson's KWKH Shreveport station via remote control from the Baton Rouge mansion. (September 11.) "Not with the people. . . . Let's see with who . . .

then. Isaiah . . . 28th chapter and the 15th verse: 'We have made a covenant with death, and with hell are we at agreement.' "

Governor Sterling, with all any human being could desire, was "too contented with himself." He had said the people were hysterical. "It is not hysteria; it is men and women crying because they are hungry. . . . Every state has had a millionaire governor and only one." Long told how he had overthrown one in Louisiana and had kept one out in Mississippi. "Governor Sterling is fixing to give them [sic] a 50-50 law. . . . Yes, a law one-half ground rattler and one-half moccasin."

A few days later Huey shifted his attack to the Texas Legislature. The legislators had been "bought like a sack of corn to vote against the cotton prohibition plan . . . they have paid them off like a slot-machine." They were "under the blandishments of wine, women and money."

Angered, the Texas Senate and House paused to listen to Representative T. H. McGregor of Austin, who called Long "an arrogant jackass who brays from Louisiana . . . an ignoramus, a buffoon, a meddler and a liar who has the impudence and arrogance to . . . dictate to the people of Texas. . . . This liar, bully and braggart seeks to intimidate the Legislature of Texas with billingsgate . . . with slander." He compared Long to other men with "mediocre ability and towering ambitions," such as Nero of Rome and George III, "a maniac who ruled England. . . .

"Harriet Beecher Stowe, in her infamous book, told of a people called 'poor white trash' and predicted that one day this bottom rung might be the top. . . . This man Long is the first of this line. He stands politically like a mule—without pride of ancestry and without hope of posterity."

Crying "cheap politician, opportunist and rabble-rouser," Senator Clinton C. Small took up the cudgels, said Huey was playing a "political cinch," that when his plan was rejected, he would then be able to say that if it had been adopted "everything would have been all right."

Further to give the lie to Long's claims, the South Carolina

Senate voted down his bill 27 to 15, and Governor Gardiner of North Carolina telegraphed the Texas Legislature no session would even be called.

September 16, the Texas Senate took time to vote 21 to 7 that Long's charge of "bought" legislatures was "not only untrue but carries the vice of a lie and the venom of a liar . . . and its author is a consummate liar." Such were the dignified words scorched into the eternal sacred records of the Great Lone Star state. They proceeded to kill Huey's plan.

He then radioed that his bill had been defeated by "the vested interests, the scalawags of politicians, and men who have their feet on the throats of the Texas farmers." The speculators had fought his law so they would not have to pay Texas farmers $375,000,000 more, and the South as a whole, a billion more for the crop. Plenty of persons took exception to his skyrocket figures and showed how the share-cropper and others would on the contrary be utterly ruined.

(All agricultural restriction in a competitive system, with monopolized banking and distribution, is primarily a bankers' protective device, unless a government is willing to shoulder enormous loss, which other citizens must then pay in addition to higher prices. It benefits in the following order: (a) banks; (b) commission merchants and warehousers; (c) large plantation owners. It affects adversely in ascending order of severity: (a) small local business men; (b) small farmers; (c) day laborers; (d) share-croppers; (e) the consumer; (f) the taxpayer. And without an international agreement, it debilitates the national economy.)

After his rebuff, Huey fumed. The rest of the country need never look to Louisiana to help out in crop-restriction programs. He kept his word. Louisiana is the only state in the union which has increased rather than decreased its crop.

But probably, remarks a commentator, if the plan had been put over and *had* resulted in twenty-cent cotton, the Democratic Party might have nominated Huey Pierce Long at Chicago instead of Franklin Delano Roosevelt.

XVIII—RUBBER STAMP

JUNE 27, Huey definitely had announced he had selected
Oscar K. Allen, chairman of the Highway Commission, to
run for governor. Allen hailed from the poor "yan-side" elements of the Red River bayous beyond Winnfield. He had
been Huey's first client, had loaned Huey money for his first
campaign; they had been partners in oil, later in other business.
Life-time friends, Allen loved Huey beyond flesh and blood,
with dog-like devotion. Huey could have picked no more
obedient henchman.

But Huey, not sure just how the state would take his im-
posing a governor, was anxious. To be absolutely assured, he
needed the great voting power of New Orleans on his side.
This meant alliance with the Old Regulars, whom he had
damned from the beginning of his political career, with whom
he had sworn by all the gods he would never ally himself.

The Old Ring, since the pact reorganizing city finances, was
more friendly. A few of them had even backed Huey for senator. Now, March 7, at the Old Regular Third Ward caucus,
Huey got Sullivan kicked out, and Long, Walmsley, Joseph P.
Skelley, Ulic J. Burke, and W. Stanley Berhman agreed to
divide the local ticket and portion out local jobs between the
two organizations. The city council agreed to give the Louisiana highway police the same powers in New Orleans as local
cops.

Francis Williams at once attacked the merger as "horrible."
Long, fearing its effect on his upstate vote, denied the pact.
Other enemies took the occasion to pounce on him. Pleasant
said it would take twenty-five years to get the state out of
bankruptcy. "Scarcely a farmer, mechanic, merchant, clerk or
other person engaged in a beneficial occupation . . . is not
poorer today" than he was when that "spend-thrift tyrant"

went into office. State Treasurer H. B. Conner, in an open letter to Huey, declared that the state's financial situation was "appalling."

Long at once forced Conner to admit that his wife was drawing two state salaries, his daughter one, besides his own. Conner was merely trying to force the administration to support him for office by holding up payments of warrants to state institutions. Conner rejoined that "Huey has been so interested in golf and potlikker that he could not attend to the state's affairs." He had increased the debt to more than $93,000,000.

By July 3 it became fully apparent that the merger, though Long and Walmsley continued to deny it, was in working shape. Dudley LeBlanc, to become opposition candidate, declared in Abbeyville that apparently Long and the Old Regulars were "ashamed of each other."

Incidentally the merger benefited the city. July 30, Huey engineered an agreement with the railroads and everybody else concerned to unify terminal facilities and construct a bridge across the Mississippi. The merger also brought temporary support of Huey's consistent enemy, the *New Orleans Item Tribune* (co-owner James M. Thompson, son-in-law of Champ Clark, was promised a United States senatorship). Originally the *Item Tribune* had been a lukewarm reform paper, attacking the corrupt Martin Beherman Old Ring. But when Beherman made a show of boosting Genevieve Clark Thompson (James M.'s wife) for Congress, it switched. Since then, because of a vacillating policy, the paper had fallen into bad financial straits. Now it found salvation in supporting Huey's candidates. State employees found it convenient to give subscriptions; political pressure brought increased advertising; the paper prospered. But reporters who had consistently written violent attacks on Long and had been beaten up by his bodyguard, now had to swallow their pride and toot his horn.

This left only the *Times Picayune* (which had absorbed Ewing's *Daily States*) as the target of Huey's anti-press tirades. By November he was calling its editors "low-down, lying, lascivious murderers . . . a bunch of skunks."

As the campaign approached, Huey, puzzled by Senator Broussard's attitude, bearded him to try to make him declare his position. Broussard refused. Huey became impatient: "I have but one rule in politics for politicians . . . 'He that is not for me is against me.'"

July 26, eight-column headlines streamed across the newspapers: "BROUSSARD TO FIGHT LONG SLATE." The senator charged that Long was trying to elect a state government he could control by wire from Washington. Long should turn the governorship over to Cyr and tend to his business in the Senate.

Immediately Huey put out a circular:

"TO THE PEOPLE OF LOUISIANA:

"Broussard cannot make Mr. Cyr governor now, nor in one year from now, nor in ten years from now." He told how he had helped Broussard against Sanders when the latter controlled the state; now Broussard was praising Sanders and attacking Long "without cause."

Broussard's vote for a 30 cents a barrel tariff on cement had cost the Louisiana taxpayer $1,000,000 more for his roads. Huey told of the many accomplishments of his administration. "It may be that the senator . . . would rather go afoot than travel on Huey Long's concrete. . . ."

2

Besides Allen for governor, Huey put up faithful John B. Fournet for lieutenant-governor, and "a whole cold-deck ticket." There were five opposition candidates, W. L. Clark, Seth Guion, Dudley LeBlanc of the Public Service Commission, William C. Boone (Longite renegade), and Cyr, who later withdrew in favor of Guion. Only Guion and LeBlanc amounted to anything. LeBlanc (backed by the Williams brothers) ran negro insurance associations, which in the campaign Huey called a swindle. LeBlanc was at the same time a "nigger-lover" and a cheater of negroes. LeBlanc ought to be in the pen. ". . . Those T.B.A. and P.B.A. Associations operated by LeBlanc . . . why, he sent out cards asking the members to pay up in advance on 10 to 20 deaths at a time. He collected about $200,000 that way, and I will sign a deed to my home if he has a dime in the bank. . . ."

In addition, brother Earl, though Huey tried to dissuade him, insisted on running for governor, finally came out for lieutenant-governor. Huey at once made it clear he was ir- revocably committed to Fournet, was backing him "like he backed me." He retorted to a criticism, "I don't care if they run every brother and sister I've got, and my father, I'll stand by Fournet. . . . I have three brothers and five sisters, 5,000 cousins and three or four uncles. When I run a family ticket, I am going to run a full ticket, and not half a one."

Huey's brothers and sisters became very bitter and at- tacked Huey in vicious poor-white fashion. The newspapers amusedly whipped the family pettiness to white heat. During the campaign in Winnfield, Julius attacked Long harshly; one of the papers took delight in reporting that Huey P. Long, Senior, "stamped his feet in approval."

In the various family quarrels one cannot help sympathizing mostly with Huey, indifferent though he was to sentimental family obligations. If he had not directly helped his own father he had, at risk of his own prestige, given Earl the fat- test job in the state and had received in return what he con- sidered only ingratitude. The family as a whole, in view of its origins, had done well. After Winnfield boomed, they had constructed a ten-room house. An uncle (who had helped Huey start in law practice) was president of the First National Bank of Winnfield and reputedly worth $200,000 (Huey didn't bother to go to his funeral). Huey's numerous brothers and sisters had gotten an education and had come up in the world. Several brothers were lawyers, the third a Tulsa, Oklahoma, dentist. The girls were married comfortably to bankers, busi- ness men, and politicians.

What most infuriated them was that Huey was forever brazenly (as every good politician should) parading their early poverty and hillbilly origins. "He would even say he had negro blood if it meant votes," exploded Julius. In short, the family, grown middle-class, respectable, was sensitive about Huey's shouting at the corporations. The group in which they circulated thought Huey a monster. Embarrassed, they damned their own brother. Perhaps several also felt that they, not Huey, had the real ability in the family. It chagrined them to see the runaway, bum, drummer and black sheep getting on in the world faster than any of them. At the same time, possibly they felt he should do more for them than he did.

During the campaign, Julius got off the following twaddle: "Huey Long and Oscar Allen went by my poor father's house . . . at one-thirty in the morning and tried to browbeat that poor old man to fight the candidacy of Earl K. Long for lieutenant-governor. Huey begged his father to fight his own son. It was the first time that Huey Long had visited our honorable old father since he has been governor.

"I wrote the governor a letter and told him to invite my father to the mansion for a visit . . . and show the people that he had a grand old daddy. Several weeks later I heard from the governor, and not a word about inviting father down.

"I have let Huey Long lie enough, and if it is the last thing I do on earth, I am not going to let him ruin the Long family."

In Arcadia, November 16, Julius declared, more sensibly: "The Long family has done everything in its power to extricate Huey Long from the clutches of that powerful gang, composed of the old New Orleans Ring, the Union Indemnity Company, the cement trust, and bring him back to normalcy." On other occasions he called his own brother from the platform "Double-crosser . . . the greatest political burglar of modern times." In Gretna, Earl called him the "yellowest physical coward that God had ever let live. . . ." He insinuated that Huey had treated his wife abominably, and that even she would vote for Guion, not Allen.

It was all a very pathetic spectacle.

3

By November the Manchurian crisis was growing grave; and the Louisiana campaign was growing warm. As a campaign stunt to remind voters of the marvelous benefits of his administration, also with the typical self-eulogy hunger of self-made dictators, Huey started a move to have all schools put up bronze plaques eulogizing him for his free textbooks. December 11, the first plaque in New Orleans was presented to the Jackson school. The children marched by, saluting the plaque and singing *Louisiana*. On the plaque was inscribed:

Knowledge is Power

"This tablet is gratefully inscribed to that courageous and far-seeing citizen of Louisiana, Huey Pierce Long, lawgiver, governor, and United States Senator, in commemoration of his valiant efforts in making available free textbooks to all school-children of the state of Louisiana irrespective of color or creed. House Bill No. 90 put into effect by Act Number 100, Laws of 1928, originated, fostered and signed by the governor July 11, 1928. Placed by W. C. Ermon."

Already, in November, however, C. F. Ekchinger, manager of a local brass company, was complaining that the plaques had been manufactured outside of Louisiana; he hadn't been given a chance to bid.

In addition to such new publicity stunts, Huey also used all the old ones. The order went out that any highway employees discovered in Guion's or LeBlanc's meetings would be fired.

Allen was a pretty hard load to carry. Julius charged that Allen, when Long first told him he couldn't be governor, had "cried for days and nights," but that he couldn't even remember the jokes and speeches Huey wrote out for him. Julius said that Long said that Allen (they were painting the likeness on propaganda tire-covers at the state penitentiary) was the hardest man he had ever seen to make look as though he had ability. At Morgan City and Lafayette, November 29, Long, referring to a query as to whether he had ever been a

farmer, replied in Allen's presence: "I quit pulling and plowing corn as quick as I could. . . . Oscar Allen stayed at the
plow ten years longer than I did because he didn't have as
much sense as I did."

In any event Allen was probably brighter than his opponents. All told, it was a childish, stupid campaign. Nobody had
anything constructive to say. George Seth Guion, speaking at
Lake Charles, January 5, said he would bring suit to recover
the moneys spent on that "biggest scandal," the Winnfield
rock quarry. LeBlanc said the same. Property assessments,
for example, on the Roosevelt Hotel had been improperly
lowered, said Guion. LeBlanc said the same. Guion was going
to decapitate the Highway Commission lawyers; so was
LeBlanc. Both promised fair elections. Guion pictured this
pleasant prospect: "I will put a parish under martial law and
have the militia of this state count the ballots." Both charged
proposed election frauds by the Long-Old Ring machines.
They both would investigate such practices; they would both
trail down "every dirty dollar." LeBlanc promised free textbooks, but honestly bought. He would complete the road system; so would Huey, so would Guion, all of them honestly,
of course.

LeBlanc, at his closing meeting at the Tulane Theatre in
New Orleans, said he stood "for sobriety rather than drunkenness in our public officials from governor down," and invited his hearers to come next day to Lafayette, "and see
40,000 Frenchmen . . . and a barbecue for which 62 steers
had been killed."

Guion, at his closing rally in New Orleans at Canal Street
and Claiborne Avenue, asked whether the padded registration
lists in Jefferson Parish represented "men, women, muskrats,
minks or skunks?" Road favoritism: "In Huey Long's home
Parish of Winn, 53 miles of concrete have been laid, costing
. . . $8,700,000. You can go miles and not see a house. The
most important roads leading into New Orleans are in bad
condition, although you people have to pay one-third of the
taxes of the state." He said Long in Vermilion Parish was

supporting an exconvict for sheriff. He predicted Huey would take an aeroplane to Africa.

LeBlanc's most constructive note was that he would develop the $200,000,000 sulphur deposit at Lake Peigneur (it was a private concern) and use the money realized from it "to ease the tax-burden." Huey had been accused of making a deal with the Sulphur Trust to prevent exploitation of Louisiana sulphur.

Mostly it was good mud-slinging. At Monroe, January 7, Long said he had heard ex-Governor Parker had come out for Clark for governor, so the two could go into partnership on Parker's "snake farm to raise bull bats and exterminate all the mosquitoes in Louisiana." He declared, "You pronounce LeBlanc's name by trying to grunt like a hog and changing your mind when you're half way through."

This high note was maintained by Dr. Cyr, who at a Guion rally, January 17, said in reply: "I have eaten at the same table with Dudley LeBlanc, and I have no criticism whatever of his table manners. And I have eaten at the same family table with Huey Long many times and I want to tell you that he belongs to the hog family and the piny woods razor-back type at that."

LeBlanc stood "for ridding this state of Long and all his blood-sucking, tax-eating, bribe-giving and bribe-taking crowd . . . and New Orleans of the cursing blight of its present mayor. . . ."

Long had left the heritage to his children of having been "a cowardly slacker," but he (LeBlanc) had worn the uniform, was a member of the American Legion—that was "the proud heritage" he was leaving his children. "I now call upon those buddies who fought with me in the trenches for fourteen long months to go to the polls and vote for me next Tuesday."

Long, replying re this important theme, said that LeBlanc didn't enlist, he was drafted; his serial number being 4,157,-848, one of the last on the list; that he didn't go overseas, but stayed in Camp Hancock for four months and 12 days and wasn't "even kicked by a mule or bit by a horsefly. . . . A poor irresponsible fellow who was shell-shocked from staying 4,000 miles away from the guns."

The truly noble note was provided by ex-Governor Parker, supporting no one in particular, but attacking Long harshly and demanding fair elections. "The Siamese twins" (Walmsley and Long) had disgraced city and state and "had bowed the heads of our good men and women in shame. . . . Birds of a feather flock together." In the next breath he was saying what a mistake he himself had previously made in lining up with Walmsley. He warned the electors of the "abhorrent pair," especially that "pirate" Long. "We will not be ruled by the tenderloin undesirables and crooks of the Walmsley-Long gang. . . . Oh, men and women of Louisiana who love our state and family, our children and grandchildren, the time for action and vigorous action is here and now, and my earnest appeal and hope is that right-thinking men and women will unite in a determination for a fair, clean election."

To this rather lilac pomposity, Huey replied in rollicking form: "Mr. Parker said he made charges in 1929. . . . The only charge I remember is that Nugent, a member of the Highway Commission, sent to Washington on highway business, had a pair of pants pressed for 65 cents and charged it to the state. Parker spent $115,000, then $65,000, and then as president of the Constitutional League . . . $410,000 and during the Ransdell campaign . . . another $1,000,000 investigating, and he discovered that . . . Nugent ate a meal in Alexandria and was in Baton Rouge the same day. Well, it took 50 hours to get from Alexandria to Baton Rouge when Parker was governor . . . but since I have been governor . . . one hour and 40 minutes.

"All Parker can do is to lambast Huey Long because Huey Long accomplished things Parker couldn't do."

The following day Parker again spoke over the air. He was more tearful than the day before: "Do you intend by your votes to set the tiny feet of your children in the path that he has trod? Do you want to hold out to your boys that they must be as Long has been and is in order to succeed in life?"

He told of the padding, by a few hundred votes, of the

registration lists in the "Red Light Tenderloin District" and his voice quavered: "Great God! Are the pure women, the good mothers and the decent men of New Orleans to sit supinely by and let this fraudulent vote override the decent vote? If these women were legally registered to vote the Walmsley-Long dummy ticket, it would then be an outrage upon the pure women of the state."

"Parker is becoming a great moralist—of late," replied Huey.

In his closing campaign speech in the *New Orleans Athenaeum,* January 17, Huey said his enemies were the greatest bunch "of has-beens and never-was's ever assembled under one roof. . . . They are Has-Been R. G. Pleasant, Has-Been John P. Sullivan, Has-Been John M. Parker, Has-Been Harry F. Gamble, Has-Been Howard Warren, Has-Been J. Y. Sanders, Has-Been Ned Richtor, and Never-Was Joe Barksdale." They had all been trying to get their hands on the road money and public funds. They were shouting "peace, peace, peace—we want a piece of that $45,000,000." For thirty years that gang had been "sweeping everything into their pockets."

All told, it was as ignorant and meaningless a campaign as was ever staged in Louisiana history. Its results, though, were far from meaningless to the state and the nation. It taught two things: one was that the "has-been" opponents of Huey were mostly a crowd of pompous folk of the "flag and family" style of hollow oratory and that the inability of the old crowd to discover and propose any fundamental program of any sort is one of the chief secrets of its continued failure. The vapidity of LeBlanc and Guion explain much of Huey's success. Second, Huey was stronger than ever; in the first and only primary, Huey's ticket, "To Complete the Work of Huey P. Long," was swept in by a stupendous majority over all other candidates.

From now on Huey's rubber stamp would never get misplaced.

4

From March 21, 1928, when Huey became governor, he had not dared leave the state because Lieutenant-Governor Cyr was waiting to hop into his job. Bad enough to have Cyr lieutenant-governor—Huey told the people—without letting him become governor: "The place where he ought to go is back to plugging teeth in Jeanerette."

Clandestinely he did leave the state several times, but returned before Cyr woke up. Once Cyr learned Huey had made an overnight trip to Jackson, Mississippi; he rushed up from his home to Baton Rouge. But Huey got back just as Cyr drove up in front of the capitol. Both laughed sourly.

After Huey became senator, Cyr insisted the governorship had been automatically vacated and became more importunate than ever. Huey told a meeting: "I was coming down from Shreveport recently in an aeroplane, and at Angola the pilot started to cut across a corner of Mississippi to save three miles. 'Hold on there,' I told him. 'Get right back into Louisiana. Do you think I want Cyr to be governor while I'm 5,000 feet up in the air?'" Thus Huey had to forgo a trip with the L.S.U. football team to West Point, couldn't go harangue the Texans, couldn't attend a flood-control meeting in St. Louis. As some publications put it, Huey remained "a prisoner within the boundaries of Louisiana."

During the senatorial campaign, at Breau Bridge, August 30, Huey recalled how as a boy he had dreamed of sticks of red and white candy in his Xmas stocking, but woke up—times were hard—to find it empty. "That's just the fix Dr. Cyr is in. He's asleep and dreaming now, and he sees that red candy sticking out of the stocking, but he will wake up pretty soon, and the stocking will be empty. The Legislature voted $2,400 for Dr. Cyr's traveling expenses. I vetoed that because *he* ain't goin' anywhere." It had also vetoed Long's expenses as acting governor. "I vetoed that because *I* ain't goin' anywhere."

To each demand of his enemies and of Cyr that he go off to the Senate, Huey replied, "My work for the upbuilding of

Louisiana . . . is worth more. . . . It will be the garden spot of the Western Hemisphere in eighteen months. I can't leave this work."

One bright day, October 13, 1931, Cyr, infuriated at his inability to collect his expense account, suddenly took the oath as governor before the deputy clerk of the district court in Shreveport and announced he would file suit. "I want Huey Long to get out . . . as soon as possible, so I can go in and straighten up this state and . . . end this debauchery. . . ."

Huey, in New Orleans, hurried up to Baton Rouge. There the National Guard was already mobilizing on the Community Club grounds. Highway police roared in on motorcycles from all over the state. Cyr was ordered arrested. Cordons were thrown around the state house and executive mansion, and guards were put in the corridors of the Highway Commission offices in the Louisiana State Bank Building. Some vandal mutilated the newly finished murals of the governor's offices in the newly built state capitol, and a guard was also thrown about there. For some weeks the highway police carefully guarded the gates and south gap in the high cast-iron fence about the state house, apparently presuming Cyr had too much avoirdupois to climb over.

"Huey's scared," Cyr told the press. But strangely enough he did not appear at the head of any armed forces to do battle, merely proclaimed loudly that he was being "shadowed."

Huey took the offensive himself. "Taking the oath of office ends Dr. Cyr. He is no longer lieutenant-governor, and he is now nothing. . . . That rids the state of Paul Cyr." Huey called in Senate Speaker pro tem A. O. King of Lake Charles to take the office of lieutenant-governor. Cyr's salary was then paid to King. Thus Huey jockeyed Cyr out with neat dispatch.

It suddenly became the humorous fad in Louisiana for everybody to go to a notary and have himself sworn in as governor or lieutenant-governor. Cyr frothed at the mouth, but Huey had a lot of fun out of it, though he was careful that none of the upstart jokesters should get in to file their oath with secretary of state Alice Grosjean. When Governor Henry H. Horton of Tennessee invited him to attend the Tulane-

Vanderbilt football game as his guest, Huey declined on the ground that the other governors "might feel offended at not being asked also."

In November, Cyr's ouster suit came up for trial at Shreveport. The court declared itself without jurisdiction. Cyr went on to the Supreme Court. January 5, it listened to arguments all day. Huey left most of his defense to Danziger. Allotted two hours himself, he skimmed hurriedly through his brief and after forty-five minutes told the justices they could have the rest of his time to add to their lunch hour. He did not even appear in court in the afternoon. Cyr's attorney, Frank Looney, attacked Long's "flippant" attitude toward that august body. But the judges had evidently enjoyed their lunch. They, too, were "without jurisdiction."

At last Huey could go off to Washington. At once he had King sworn in as governor, and as farewell issued a lengthy self-flattering résumé of all his achievements during his administration.

XIX—FRESHMAN SENATOR

SATURDAY, January 23, 1932, highway police took their disagreeable posts in a driving rainstorm to guard the capitol, the executive mansion and new Governor King against Cyr, while Huey, resplendent in a flaring polka-dot tie, a swanky gray suit with enormous lapels and a gigantic white gladiola, took his place in a Pullman compartment in New Orleans, with his plump little wife, Rose McConnell, by his side. Leading henchmen made it the occasion of a gala trip to Washington. With him went pudgy, stubby-haired, balloon-chinned Abe Shushan of the Levee Board (now under an alias indictment for income-tax evasion); grinning Governor Allen; tight-lipped, bespectacled T. H. Harris, superintendent of education; "Turkeyhead" Mayor Walmsley; law partner Hugh Wilkinson; faithful Seymore Weiss; Highway Commission cousin K. M. Nugent; Fournet; Porterie and others.

Cyr news-released wryly: "If any person has business requiring executive attention, I will be found until further notice at Jeanerette."

In Washington, Monday the 25th, Huey at once received reporters in a replica of the green silk pajamas. Expansively and condescendingly, he spoke of the great presidential possibilities of floor-leader Robinson, Garner, Pat Harrison and Al Smith, but not favorably of Roosevelt. Apparently Long intended to be a stand-pat "Party" boy.

In the Senate lounge room, preparatory to taking the oath, Huey was sought out by his "old friend," Senator Broussard: "Huey, there is a rule here that a senator from one state should escort a new senator from that state when he takes the oath."

"Edwin, I will be glad to have you do that, but when . . . I reached here this morning I read in the newspapers . . .

227

that you had not decided whether you would or would not introduce me. . . . I made the statement that that was not a matter you were going to decide."

Broussard was angered. "I won't introduce you unless you ask me to."

"Don't hold your breath until I do, Edwin."

Broussard went off in a huff. Robinson tried to patch things up with Broussard, but came back and said to Huey, "I'll introduce you."

This was the first breaking of rules by the breaker of rules. Second, he ignored the ancient rule against smoking and marched up the aisle puffing on a Perfecto. Presented to Senator Borah, he embraced that dignified gentleman, to his thinly disguised astonishment, prodded mighty Jim Watson of Indiana in the ribs, and treated everyone as though they were just good Elks from back home. To Senator McReynolds of North Carolina, he cried, "I know you. You were running the skating rink at Baton Rouge when I was selling swamp-root." As the newspapers styled it, he "galloped about the Senate floor . . . like a colt turned out to pasture."

They just didn't know Huey. He was always a human grasshopper. His bustling energy never let him sit still a minute. Cerebration and action in him were Siamese twins.

Huey was given a freshman office on the far side of the capitol and a rear seat on the Democratic side next to Mrs. Hattie Caraway from Arkansas.

2

A few weeks later he had to rush back to the home grounds. Cyr, despite the Supreme Court again trying to become governor, had proclaimed the executive mansion and capitol—still heavily guarded—in the hands of insurrectionists and that the seat of government was now Room 443, the Heidelberg Hotel.

Huey phoned the owner. "Roy, what are you doing with the governor's headquarters there in your hotel?"

"I'm not having anything to do with the governor's office, Senator."

"You're not? You've got the Heidelberg Hotel advertised as the capitol. . . . I'd put the governor's office out of there, and do it quick, if I were in your place."

"It will be done right away," he answered.

Cyr, declaring he was evicted because the hotel's tax-assessments had been improperly lowered, proclaimed the seat of government to be Suite 312-14 at the Louisiana Hotel, three blocks further from the real capitol. Eventually he landed it at Jeanerette, one hundred miles away.

He sued Governor King and lost.

Long accomplished two other things this trip: he straightened out the fifteen-million-dollar deficit for the Highway Commission, via Pyramid Securities, and got control of the Democratic Central Committee of 104 members (he was already National Committeeman) to name himself and cronies as the delegation to the national convention coming off in Chicago, June 29. This procedure was at variance with the century-old custom in Louisiana—the delegates had always been named at a specially called state convention.

3

Back in the Senate, Huey Long made no effort to conceal his motives, viz., to gain control of the Democratic machine and leadership in that body and ultimately make himself dictator of the Party in the nation. At once he attacked floor-leader Robinson and cursed out his party for its treason in compromising with Hoover. Huey, however, gave nobler motives: "I had come to the United States Senate with only one project in mind, which was that . . . I might do something to spread the wealth of the land among all of the people. . . ." One of his first Senate speeches was against a seaman's protective law.

April 4 he gave his "Doom of America's Dream" speech: "Machines are created, making it possible to manufacture more in an hour than used to be manufactured in a month . . . but instead of bringing prosperity, ease and comfort, they [inventions and scientific achievements] have meant idleness

. . . starvation . . . pestilence; whereas they should have meant that hours of labor were shortened, . . . toil decreased, that more people would be able to consume, that they would have more time for pleasure. . . .

"The Bible tells us . . .

"God Almighty has warned against this condition. Thomas Jefferson, Andrew Jackson, Daniel Webster, Theodore Roosevelt, William Jennings Bryan and every religious teacher known to this earth . . .

"The gangsters have killed hundreds, maybe thousands, to carry out their nefarious rackets to extort money; but the hoarders of wealth have destroyed humanity by millions. . . ."

After getting into the headlines by having the Senate restaurant serve potlikker, April 12, he proposed a 65 percent surtax on incomes over $2,000,000 and a 65 percent levy on estates of over $20,000,000. April 27, he introduced as an amendment to the tax bills his $1,000,000-a-year income and an inheritance tax of 100 percent on all over $5,000,000.

Robinson scoffed, called Huey's bill confiscatory of wealth. Long jumped up and alternately waving his cerise handkerchief and a Bible, and throwing back his red-black curly locks, shouted: "I'm advocating what the Lord gave Moses." He smashed into the Democrats for taking orders from Big Business in writing the new tax bill and shouted his favorite statistics about wealth concentration. "What is a man going to do with more than $1,000,000?" he cried.

Robinson sat in the front row, scowling straight ahead.

Huey, his arms threshing the air, his face growing redder and redder, cried out that he'd vote for a Farmer-Laborite or a Republican if he advocated "reduction of swollen fortunes as God Almighty ordained." He beat the table with his fist and thundered out: "There has got to be another leadership responsible to the American people in the Democratic Party." The people couldn't get wealth redistribution through the Republicans, their "only salvation" was from the Democrats. "And here we have a Democratic leadership in the House and Senate that is coming out for the sales tax instead of laying taxes on Baruch, Rockefeller and the like." If these great properties were not turned back to the people, then you members "need not worry about Congress reassembling."

He sent up to the desk his resignation from every committee, the usual places given to freshmen senators, Commerce, Navy, Manufacturing, and Interoceanic Canals—he didn't want to be bothered about them anyway—and demanded more important posts.

Robinson called Huey's resignations "a comic opera gesture" to obtain notoriety and publicity. "It is easy to arouse class hatreds . . . but more difficult to find an adequate remedy."

Long gave out an interview that Robinson ought to be Hoover's running mate. Reminded about his former statement that Robinson would be a good Democratic candidate, Huey said he had changed his mind about him, Garner and Harrison. "I met myself coming back very quickly on that. I'm very discouraged and feel like I'm in a kind of maze. . . . If I nominated anybody this p.m., it would be George Norris of Nebraska." . . . Roosevelt. "No, he ain't got a chance."

May 6 he rushed back to Louisiana to the convening of the Legislature, returned to Washington, and May 12 again attacked Robinson and his corporation connections—he read into the record (May 3) a list of forty-six public utility and power concerns represented by Robinson's law firm. He became abusive. Vice-President Curtis ordered him to sit down. Liberal members protested. Long was allowed to continue if he would observe the rules against attacking the integrity of a fellow-senator. Shortly he was reseated amid a tense atmosphere.

The *Chicago Tribune* cartooned him in Russian costume, carrying a red flag and posters: "Soak the Rich," and "Confiscate Property," with Robinson portrayed in heroic mold, standing by a flagstaff from which the American flag floats. The cartoon was entitled: "Patriotism *versus* Communism— the real Issue in Washington."

They could not squelch him. Congress, striving valiantly to pass the necessary tax program and adjourn by June 10, Chairman Smoot of the Senate Finance Committee kept the Senate on the job at night in effort to clear up all amendments at one sitting. But at 7:20 P.M. Huey got the floor to favor the Connally amendment to fix income taxes at 4 and 8 percent and graduate surtaxes up to a 55 percent maximum on a million dollars and over, against the committee rates of 3, 7 and 45 percent. Huey's filibuster lasted two and a half hours.

He stood in the middle of the central aisle, near Smoot's desk. Now and then he ran his hand through his curly locks. Frequently his arm swept under the beet-sugar senator's nose. "Why, senators, this finance committee would tax even the little fellow who pays ten cents for his movie ticket!"

"The tax begins at eleven cents," protested Smoot.

"Oh, God bless the committee!" Huey exclaimed.

The stand-pat Democratic colleagues were red with rage, but he made them laugh in spite of themselves. Curtis repeatedly hammered his gavel to admonish the hilarious galleries.

Majority Leader Watson tried to check him, but the Kingfish remarked, "I am beginning to feel the logic of my argument. I feel the urge to talk." He particularly scored Pat Harrison (who handles tax problems for the Democrats) and veteran Senator Smoot. He mimicked the latter's mannerisms in announcing to the committee that Secretary of Treasury Ogden Mills should be sent to untangle the tax mess.

"I'll send for the Secretary of Treasury," Huey burlesqued Smoot's voice cleverly, and like him pounded the table. "I'll send for the Secretary of Treasury." The Senate was convulsed. He attacked the committee for letting Mills change their minds in favor of a treasury compromise: "It's very evident," Huey continued, "that the best minds of the Senate —and that means the best minds in the world [sic]—after three weeks of labor . . . changed their minds in thirty minutes." (Louisiana—two minutes.)

After a row with Democratic House leader Harry T. Rainey (Illinois) over oil and lumber taxes—"A little sassy talk from him, and the eight Louisiana Congressmen will yank him out"—Huey hurried back to set Louisiana in order again.

4

May 31, he was dictating to the Legislature and stifling opposition to his own tax plans. His previous reckless spending had plunged the state enormously into debt. The treasury reported a huge deficit. The Board of Liquidation had had to borrow millions. More revenues had to be secured.

The state would not stand for an additional real estate tax —Huey had boasted he would never raise that tax. Actually assessments themselves, through secret instructions to parish assessors, on smaller holdings and political opponents, had been greatly increased.

From the middle of May to the middle of June, both houses seethed with various schemes to raise money. A sales tax— given Huey's onslaught on Hoover's proposed bill—was quickly abandoned. A half cent tax on each newspaper sold was proposed, but also abandoned. Huey decided to ram through taxes on tobacco, soft drinks, electricity, corporate franchises, and insurance premiums. Two were taxes he had campaigned against.

Of course, ousted politicians didn't like his plan—they never liked anything he proposed. Also, a vitriolic attack was made on him by the Orleans Association of Commerce and the Louisiana Manufacturers Association. Long threatened to yank 300 state employees out of the Association of Commerce. Also there were many sincere taxpayers and whatnot, who looked with dismay on the new burdens on the poor. Thousands of protest telegrams rained in. Mass meetings picked delegates to go to Baton Rouge, but mostly—the old discredited political crowd.

Huey at once had his Old Regulars in New Orleans get on the job with a delegation. They entrained at once—twenty-one railway coaches full—for Baton Rouge. All state employees were ordered to knock off and repair to the new capitol.

On the day set for the hearing, protesting taxpayers left the old state house and marched out to the new capitol to present their case. Huey's cohorts arrived about the same time, with banners:

DONT LISTEN TO THE MUGWUMPS
WE MUST SAVE OUR STATE
WE CANNOT CLOSE OUR SCHOOLS

The large chocolate-colored lobby seethed with people. The Senate chamber called to order, veteran anti-Huey baiter, J. Y. Sanders, explained the measures his group (the corporations) was backing. Mrs. R. G. Pleasant, wife of the former governor, shrilled into the microphone: "Ladies and gentlemen of the payroll squad with your banners, I am [not] here . . . to make a political speech. We do not represent any political faction [sic]—we are taxpayers and human beings. . . ." She attacked Huey for being in Louisiana, usurping Allen's functions, instead of in Washington where he belonged. Her tax figures had been checked by a competent auditor, "not by any twenty-six-year-old girl [Alice Grosjean, now Supervisor of Public Accounts after Huey suddenly decided not to take her to Washington] who doesn't know the difference between single- and double-entry bookkeeping. . . .

"If these tax bills pass, it will be because the legislators bend their backs to Huey P. Long. When you follow the leadership of a paranoiac, you are in danger. . . ." Her father had put down carpetbag government in Louisiana, she was here "to help put down Longism, which has cost this state millions. . . . He curses the rich and taxes the poor. Any 'boob' knows that the corporations are not going to pay these new taxes, but will pass them on to the people."

Huey, seated near the Speaker's dais, paid no attention. When he finally took the floor, in thirty minutes he pulverized his attackers. He made salty references to Pleasant's administration. Repeatedly Mrs. Pleasant leapt to her feet, screaming "Untrue! Untrue!" Huey let her buzz, but when she shrieked, "Question! Will you yield . . ." he barked, "No! I will not yield to you or to anyone else. . . . The place for you to go holler about taxes is to the courthouse of your own parish."

The meeting broke up. The taxpayers went home, the payroll squad returned to their duties, and Sanders' opposition plan for the salvation of the state went quite properly into the garbage pail.

Huey now ran the Legislature with a high hand. No longer did he have to sneak out on the floor to beg a member to support such and such a bill, then leave one jump ahead of the Sergeant at Arms. Now he walked in and out freely, interrupted when he wished, and sat in the executive office and gave orders to Allen. One day he commanded Allen (Smith tells), "Oscar, go get me those goddam bills we was talking about." The offices were crowded, and Allen, embarrassed, affected not to hear his master's voice.

"Goddam you, Oscar," Huey screeched, "don't you stall around with me! I made you and I can break you! Get those goddam bills and get 'em quick."

He now had the Old Regulars on his side, 20 members of the House and 8 senators from Orleans Parish alone, and his formula was to tell the legislators there would be no money for jobs, and salaries would be cut if the bills weren't passed. This simple argument whipped the bills through both houses at a furious gallop. The arguments of the few remaining taxpayers were a cricket chirp in a storm.

A few days later, Mrs. Pleasant complained to the press that Huey had had his guards throw her out of the reception room of Alice Lee Grosjean when she went there to obtain information in connection with the university records. "R. L. Whitman, superintendent of the Louisiana State Board of Criminal Identification, seized me by the right arm. . . . Senator Long said, 'I can't have a drunken cursing woman in the capitol.' . . . With his hands cupped over his mouth, he 'booed' at me like a hoodlum.

"I told Senator Long I would not leave the office. He screamed at me, 'Stay in here, little one. But if she curses any more, put her out!' "

XX—CLEARING HATTIE'S NECK

DURING Huey's tax fight, he was confronted with unex-pected Party revolt. Prominent politicians, disgruntled en-emies, including three former governors, Pleasant, Sanders and Parker, also Francis Williams, Harry Gamble and others, all indignant over the freeze-out manner in which Huey's dele-gates had been hand-picked for the Chicago convention, called an assemblage in Shreveport for June 15 to denounce Huey, the state central committee, and name their own delegates.

Huey snorted contemptuously: "Just a bunch of 'ex's.' " For the next day, June 16, he called a burlesque convention in Baton Rouge under the chairmanship of jovial Pat McGrath of the New Orleans seventh ward. The payroll squad and the loyal legislators were ordered to foregather at noon in the House Chamber to name an "instructed" delegation.

A weird parade straggled down the main business street toward the capitol, brass band thumping, banners blazing:

> ON TO CHICAGO WITH PAT
> WE WANT OUR SWAG

The convention opened with Huey Long and Seymore Weiss standing in the back looking on. McGrath took the chair. Robert Brothers (a mysterious Kingfish hanger-on) was made permanent chairman.

Repeatedly the delegates stamped and shouted for more music from the band. Speeches, supposedly humorous, were made by former Lieutenant-Governor Ferdinand Mouton and Representative ("Uncle Dick") Wilds from Concordia. Jules Fisher, shrimp cannery king (now facing an income tax eva-sion trial), was nominated for President of the United States; for Vice-President, Huey's old pal George W. Delsdernier (author of the nit-wit "Cross of Gold" speech), who amid stamping and cheers announced he would bring back gin-fizzes. Pat McGrath was named national committeeman and Dorothy Dix (Mrs. E. M. Gilmer) of lovelorn fame, without her permission, national committeewoman. Amid clowning and band-blaring twenty legislators were named delegates to Chicago, whom Huey promised to introduce there, and did. Had his own delegation been thrown out, he might seriously have attempted to seat the Pat McGrath bunch of "fearless, independent and unterrified voters" by claiming for it as much right as for the Shreveporters.

Obliging the Legislature to work Saturdays and Sundays to finish up two weeks ahead of time, June 20, Huey headed his legitimate delegation to the national convention.

2

In his various suggestions about possible Democratic presidential candidates, Huey had invariably been doubtful about Roosevelt. But progressives of the Senate, particularly Norris and Wheeler, "the boldest, most courageous men" Huey had ever met, influenced him to cast his eyes in Roosevelt's direction.

Huey thereupon saw to it that Roosevelt knew of his own wealth-sharing views. "All the time, day by day," Roosevelt made commitments exactly "consistent" with Huey's "belief and understanding of correct government." Early in his candidacy in Atlanta, Roosevelt said: "The millions who are in want will not stand by silently forever while the things to satisfy their needs are within easy reach. . . ." Soon after, Huey received a letter from him: "You and I are alike for the rights in behalf of the common man of this country." With that, Huey was convinced Roosevelt was the white hope.

When the Massachusetts election went overwhelmingly against Roosevelt, Al Smith declared that a chunk had been put under the Roosevelt band wagon. Huey hurried to Norris's office. "Senator, I have wanted to declare publicly for Roosevelt when . . . it would do the most good. He has had a setback in Massachusetts that his opposition is going to play up to the utmost."

They agreed to declare simultaneously, and Huey, so as to make it appear he had dragged Norris on the band wagon, not the other way around, suggested that he himself would get off the train at Atlanta and hand Clark Howell of the *Atlanta Constitution*—"the best publicity from that source"—a statement announcing they were both supporting.

This was done. Jim Farley immediately telephoned Huey from New York, asking for help in lining up delegations. Huey set to work in various Southern states, particularly Mississippi, Arkansas and Oklahoma.

3

Now, in Chicago, June 21, a white-clad figure jumped from a train in the Grand Central station. A voice boomed. Two arms were tossed aloft in evangelistic pose. Shouting, gesticulating, exhorting, Senator Huey P. Long "bounced into town." He had arrived simultaneously with a political hurricane scandal in Louisiana: the Long-Wilkinson law firm was trying to get legislation to exempt the American Airways Corporation from paying the state gasoline tax.

To the Chicago reporters, Huey shouted: "I haven't drawn a dime out of that firm for a long time. They can't hook me up with any scandal."

To the reporters he repeatedly declined the Democratic nomination for president, three times in fact. "Roosevelt can serve the cause better than I. I do not wish the nomination." His interviewers became really convinced he did not want it.

"How about Vice-President?" someone asked.

The Senator gave him a withering look. "I wouldn't be a vice anything. I'd rather be the biggest man in a little village than the second biggest man in a great city. Huey Long stands second to nobody."

Reminded that his delegation was being contested, he replied, annoyed, in words of a true dictator. "They're always contesting down in Louisiana. Those fellows are like the Irishman who woke up drunk in the graveyard one morning and said, 'It's resurrection morning and I'm the first one to rise.' "

The Senator greeted his own joke with a burst of laughter and dug someone in the ribs. His audience smiled politely.

News soon came that the anti-Roosevelt elements would sponsor as many "favorite son" candidates as possible until Roosevelt's strength dwindled. Huey was up at daybreak trying to forestall this. Just as the first light was shimmering on the lake, he knocked on Alfalfa Bill Murray's hotel room door. "You are the farmers' candidate, aren't you? Most farmers are up this time of day."

Alfalfa Bill was "very gracious." Assuming Huey had already breakfasted, he telephoned for some food for himself. He dwelt upon all possible candidacies except that of Roosevelt and himself, even suggested Huey as a candidate.

Huey felt his bowels weakening. That would be ruinous— the very thing he was moving heaven and earth to keep down. His defection or that of anyone else, might have meant "a dangerous stampede in many directions." Fencing with Oklahoma Bill of Oklahoma, a past master at politics, was "time lost."

While Bill was shaving, Huey snatched off a good part of his waiting breakfast as a punishment, and departed.

The question of seating contested delegations arose. The chairman of the national committee, John J. Raskob, who, with Jouette Shouse, was the leader of the anti-Roosevelt forces, named a committee—three members to one against Roosevelt—to pass on doubtful delegations. Huey called a meeting in the Congress Hotel of the leaders of the regular, but contested, delegations from Minnesota, Puerto Rico and Louisiana, and they decided to refuse to present claims to the sub-committee. Thus everything had to come before the entire session of the national committee.

Huey entertained it for thirty minutes with jokes, presented the claims of his burlesque delegation, denounced the Shreveport crowd—because John P. Sullivan was representing the "Power Combine." (Huey in his 1923-24 campaign and in subsequent patronage hadn't worried about this.) Working himself up into revivalist frenzy, Huey shouted: "The Democratic Party in Louisiana? *I* am the Democratic Party in Louisiana! Who's got a better right to pick out a delegation? Every one of the Sanders bunch is a sorehead about the way he's been beaten by me. I beat them time and again. . . . They've been beat. Beat, beat, beat! Beat down there!"

His delegation was seated by a vote of 55 to 32. With regard to a protesting committee of Louisiana women, Huey shouted: "No bunch of damned skirts is gonna decide anything affecting me." But he sent an aeroplane to Louisiana for his wife and paraded her up and down on his arm, "to show these damned skirts I know how to treat a lady."

In the convention, the first session of which was held June 29 in the coliseum, Huey's delegation, after prolonged debate, was seated 638¾ to 514¼.

"It was a queer turn . . ." Huey later mourned. "After Roosevelt's election, my failure to support . . . legislation . . . to reduce the compensation to disabled veterans . . ." resulted in "the same persons who had appeared at Chicago to fight us, including the gambler and power-trust lawyer Sullivan . . . to be recognized for patronage in Louisiana."

4

Huey next cast his eyes upon the Arkansas Senatorial election, where Mrs. Hattie Caraway was running for re-election. She had voted for Long's motion to limit private fortunes. She had favored his general wealth-distribution plan. She disagreed with floor-leader Robinson of her own state even more than did the Kingfish. Washington, however, and even Arkansas, had never given her much limelight except for an occasional special article describing her as "a demure little woman who looks as though she ought to be sitting on a porch in a rocking chair, mending . . . socks."

But Huey would like to have her back rather than some unpleasant Robinson protégé.

Unfortunately, Hattie had no backing. She had been appointed on the death of her senator husband, as a temporary incumbent, largely as an accidental compromise because of jealousy among the Arkansas bigwigs, but on word of honor to the state bosses she would not be a candidate for re-election. But she was the second candidate to announce. The governor rushed to see her. "You promised not to run, Hattie. . . ."

"Oh, governor," she cooed demurely. "My sons wanted it, and I just couldn't go against their wishes."

The local political prognosticators said she couldn't come in better than fifth. Besides her, six men, jurisconsults, triumvirs and legionnaires, notable men all, had entered the primary contest. No one really gave her a second thought. As Hermann Deutsch wrote in the *Saturday Evening Post:* "A woman candidate for the United States Senate in the fundamentally—and fundamentalistically conservative heart of . . . the Bible belt? Don't be silly."

But Huey, though he didn't trust her a bit, wanted her support; and he hated Joe Robinson. He struck a sentimental pose: Six big *politicos* back in Arkansas campaigning against "one lone, little, defenseless woman" while she was working in Washington for the people—and against Joe. Monstrous! Long discovered that Hattie's home had actually been sold under a mortgage. "Get out the sound trucks," he ordered the Highway Commission—"I'm going to Arkansas to campaign for Hattie."

Circulars were prepared, cartoons drawn—Uncle Trustie pointing to six manikins: "We can't use Mrs. Caraway, because she voted for the people while the sheriff was selling her home. We've got to have one of these boys here." A special edition of the official American Federation of Labor paper, endorsing Hattie, was run off. Huey Long's "Doom of America's Dream" speech accompanied it—enough copies for every man, woman and child in the state.

On the way north with his trucks, Huey rushed over to Winnfield to visit his old father whom he had not bothered about for years—to pull off a little filial affection publicity. Writes Julius:

"Earl Long had provided the money to build the . . . home where Huey called on our father. It was in Earl's name.

Huey took a photographer with him, visited our father, cut a watermelon raised by Earl, and had his picture taken with our father eating Earl's watermelon on Earl's farm. Huey needed that picture to put in the newspapers of Arkansas to show he was a man who loved his father." Elsewhere Julius reported Huey as having said: "I have seen my mother cry because I did not have shoes to wear—" a remark that made Julius see red and indulge in lachrymose comment. "Nothing, nothing could be more wholly false. In the hope of appealing to the emotions of the people, he was willing to tell such a falsehood about his dead mother."

A day or so later, in Arkansas with his seven trucks and three or four automobiles, Huey announced: "I'm here to get a bunch of pot-bellied politicians off this little woman's neck." A whirlwind tour—a repetition of the Louisiana method of campaigning: a motley caravan that looked like a combination of old-time medicine show and revival meeting. Two of the trucks were specially designed by Huey with four amplifying horns, loud-speaker panels, battery units good for twelve hours' service if no electric current was available, an attachment for playing phonograph records, several folding chairs, a folding table, a pitcher and glasses, a battered copy of the Bible, and a throat-spray atomizer.

One small truck is an advance car; two men find sites for meetings, distribute handbills, drum up a local chairman. Four heavy vans transport tons of literature, wind-shield stickers, posters, printed matter.

Hermann Deutsch, brilliant feature-writer for the *New Orleans Item* and competent eye-witness of this whole Arkansas tour, describes the procedure: The first day's itinerary called for a meeting at Magnolia at 9 A.M.; another at El Dorado, forty miles away, at 11; Camden, thirty-one miles further on, 2:30 P.M.; Fordyce, twenty-nine miles, 4:30; and a big night rally in Pine Bluff, forty-four miles, at 8.

Long had passed the night in Shreveport. Before daybreak the two sound trucks, each with its convoy of two literature vans, rumbled northward. One went direct to Magnolia, the other to El Dorado. The light sound truck had already arranged where the sound truck was to be placed to obtain the best acoustics, etc. Connection was made with the city current. It began to play music, attracting the curious. The microphone was installed on the speaker's stand and tested. Meanwhile, two men from each of the two literature vans, with a hastily recruited corps of small boys, were distributing printed matter to early arrivals and offering each automobilist a gummed sticker: "Re-elect Senator Caraway."

When the meeting began, the four men from the literature van then acted as a squad to eject any obstreperous drunk, quell any fight, or soothe crying babies. If a baby cried, Long crooked his finger and one of the wide-shouldered track men jumped to the speaker's stand for a glass of water. Deftly the athletic young man would pick up the crying infant out of its mother's arms, give it a drink, pat it, hand it back. Huey would append a homily:

"Now I'm going to give you good ladies of Arkansas the benefit of what I've learned out of raising three children of my own and out of campaigning all over the country. . . . Ninety-nine times out of a hundred, when a baby cries, it's only thirsty, and if you give it a drink . . . it will go right to sleep. That's a good thing to know, when you're not so fixed that you can hire nurses . . . like the rich people do."

If all other resources failed, one or another of the tough-muscled experts, with a quick pleasant smile, picked up the baby and walked away with it, dandling it until the meeting was over.

While the Long-Caraway party spoke at El Dorado, the truck at Magnolia, and its two literature vans, was speeding on to Camden. During the Camden rally, the El Dorado unit moved on to Fordyce, and by nightfall both trucks had reached Pine Bluff and were set up in the ball park.

"Naturally," declares Deutsch, "Mrs. Caraway's six opponents, accustomed to the frock-coated school of campaigning for the office, with just a dash of baby-kissing, perhaps as a concession from Olympus to the humanities, were bewildered by this high-pressure disturbance which moved across the land [in Arkansas, of all places] with such clock-like regularity, military precision and devastating effect. By the time they had rallied their political faculties and begun to strike back, the damage had been done."

Huey took many a personal fall out of them. Of one candidate: "I ain't going to call his name because I wouldn't give him that much advertising in a big crowd; and besides, my parents taught me not to speak ill of the dead, even if they're only politically dead."

On another occasion: "One of the birds that's fighting Mrs. Caraway says he's for paying the soldiers' bonus right now. Why, that fellow's got no business in this race at all. He ought to be out supporting Mrs. Caraway, because she voted to pay the . . . bonus six months ago. And as for this great big war veteran that's saying he'll vote against the bonus . . . he might as well go home, too. Hoover'll see to it that the bonus ain't paid, so there's no need of you people electing somebody to help out on that job."

The main campaign issue for Huey was Wall Street and the Money Power *versus* The People. Mrs. Caraway caught the lingo quickly and developed from a timid speaker to a good campaigner.

"Think of it, my friends!" Huey would cry. "In 1930 there were 540 men in Wall Street who made $100,000,000 more than all the wheat farmers and all the cotton farmers and all the cane farmers of this country put together. . . . And you people wonder why your belly's flat up against your backbone! . . . Just think of it, my friends. Here I was actually proposing that a man had to live for a whole year of 365 days on one measly, lousy, slivery million dollars. That was awful! That meant that when one of these birds stopped under a shade tree . . . to cool off, he wouldn't be getting but about four dollars a minute while he was doing it. That meant that if he went to bathe and shave, he wouldn't be but about $500 richer when he got his clothes back on."

And the Arkansas audiences laughed and applauded and shouted delightedly: "Pour it on 'em, Huey!" The printed reproduction of fragmentary excerpts, remarks Deutsch, cannot convey "the unhalting rush of words, the quick haphazard gestures, and above all the rural intonation—'cain't' for 'can't,' 'pore' for 'poor,' the Southerner's easy slurring of consonants. . . . Huey Long is no orator; he is no professional silver-tongue dealing in sonorous rhetorical periods. He is a political revivalist; a Democratic gospel shouter who transmutes ponderous abstractions into the idiom of the people with a glib plausibility that is uncanny. The difference between one of his rapid-fire political broadsides and the customary campaign rodomontade is precisely the difference between the polished discourse of the curate of St. Somebody's church and an old-time Billy Sunday diatribe. . . . The curate of St. Somebody's may excite the admiration of his hearers, but Billy Sunday brought his, sweating and frantic, along the sawdust trail to the mourners' bench."

Listen to Huey's remedy: "Herbert Hoover is calling together boards and commissions to find out what he should do about it. The only dad-blamed thing on the living face of the earth that he needs to do is read his Bible. The Lord tells us in Chapters 24, 26, and 27 of Leviticus, in Chapter 5 of Nehemiah and Chapter 5 of James . . . that unless you redistribute the wealth of a country into the hands of the people every fifty years, your country's got to go to ruination. . . . Too many men running things that think they're smarter than the Lord."

Thereupon Huey recounted his own efforts, in the last session, to decentralize existing individual fortunes. After describing his own bill and giving as an example the cutting up of the Mellon fortune, enough "to run our government three or four years without anybody else paying a dime of taxes," he said: "So the Democratic leaders and the Republican leaders got together and they jumped on my little resolution with all four feet. Mrs. Caraway voted for it. I voted for it. But they killed it deader'n a doornail." There were a set of Democratic waiters and Republican waiters, but back in the kitchen was "only Wall Street, and no matter what set of waiters brings you the dish, it's only Wall Street that has cooked it up."

He continued his homely metaphors. He told of the patent medicine man selling High Popolarum and Low Popahirum, one made by taking the bark off the tree from the ground up and the other from the top down. The only difference between the two party leaders in Congress was that, "The Republican leaders are skinning the people from the ankle up and the Democratic leaders . . . from the ear down. Skin 'em up, or skin 'em down, but skin 'em. . . .

"Mr. Herbert Hoover, of London, England, was trying to balance his boodget—that's the way they pronounce it in England—and he was raising all kinds of special taxes on the people to balance the boodget. But we knocked so many taxes out one right after another, that he couldn't balance his boodget, and glory be! we brought 'em up to the lick log at last!"

They had to come out for the Connally amendment for 63 percent [sic] of all a man made over a million dollars a year. "That was the first big victory for the people. . . ." Huey was getting into his fighting revivalist swing. "They got 'em up a retail sales tax so that they could relieve the big boys at the top . . . by sweating it out of the little fellows at the bottom. But we fought 'em to a shirttail finish . . . and licked the everlasting stuffin' out of 'em." Mrs. Caraway helped kill that bill.

"With all the big-bellied politicians in Arkansas campaigning against this one little woman, she stood by you in spite of the fact that the sheriff was selling her home over her head . . . in spite of the fact that the big men politicians of her own state had their feet on her throat. Oh, we've pried a few of those birds loose already, and they'll all . . . get their big feet off her neck before we're through with 'em. If Wall Street can defeat for re-election a senator with a record like Senator Caraway, there's no use of . . . the rest of us ever trying to do anything for the people again. . . ."

He told of the preacher who came through his home town preaching fire and brimstone and so scared his wicked uncle he got baptized in the Dugdemona Creek. "And as the preacher led my uncle out into the waters of old Dugdemona, there floated out of my uncle's pocket the ace of spades, face up. And a couple of steps further, out came the king of spades, and the queen, and finally the jack and ten spot of spades following along behind.

"My aunt jumped up and flung out her arms and cried: 'Don't baptize him, parson! It's no use! He's lost! My husband's lost!'

"But their little boy cried, 'Pa ain't lost. If he can't win with that hand . . . he can't win at all.' And I'm here to tell you, my friends, that if we can't win with Mrs. Caraway's record of standing by you people through thick and thin, then we can't win at all, and we might just as well admit Wall Street is too strong for us."

Deutsch observes: "Unlike Bryan's 'Cross of Gold' oration, or Roosevelt's thunderous 'We stand at Armageddon and we battle for the Lord,' this speech was not delivered from the center of the nation's spotlight. But in the space of one short week it overturned the political structure of an entire state and became the focal point of as spectacular and bizarre a campaign as the annals of this generation are likely to record."

Hattie Caraway, not really considered a candidate up to a week before her election, received as many votes as all six of her opponents combined.

XXI—IMMORTAL POO-BAH

HUEY hurried down to Louisiana for a whirlwind windup with sound trucks in behalf of his old friend John Overton, candidate for the United States Senate against Broussard. Huey had supported Overton way back in 1918, when the Old Ring had knifed him just before election. Later Huey backed him as a candidate for representative from the Eighth Louisiana Congressional District. Overton had been the one politician of consequence in Louisiana who had stuck by Huey through thick and thin.

By August 20—the primary was the 13th of the following month—Huey was whanging through the state. Topping each handbill, poster and banner, were big letters: HUEY P. LONG; underneath in smaller type, "Speaking in behalf of John Overton." Many hicks got the idea Huey was running for still another office. As in Arkansas, as in all his speeches, Huey advocated wealth redistribution. Overton would support this.

"Turn out and beat Edwin Broussard . . . who dassn't blow his nose without orders from Wall Street. Edwin Broussard sits in his office about a block away from the Senate, and when it comes time to vote, they punch a bell, and . . . Edwin meets a feller in the hall, and the feller says, 'Vote no this time, Edwin,' and Edwin goes in and he votes no. . . . After a while the bell rings again, and . . . the feller in the hall says, 'Vote yes this time, Edwin,' and Edwin, he votes yes, and then goes back to his office.

"Once in a while they punch the bell, and they ain't no feller in the hall. . . . When that happens Ed just waits and watches how *I* vote, and then he votes the other way!"

From the old parade grounds near the new capitol Huey shouted: "They tell you that what you've got to do is tear up Longism in this state. All right, my friends—get you a bomb

248

or some dynamite and blow up that building yonder. [He points to the new capitol.] That's a good place to start. . . . Then go out and tear up the concrete roads I've built. Get your spades and shovels and scrape the gravel off them roads we graveled, and let a rain come on 'em. That'll put 'em back like they was before I come.

"Tear down the new buildings I've built at the university. . . . And when your child starts out to school tomorrow morning . . . snatch the free schoolbooks out of his hand that Huey Long give him. . . . Then you'll be rid of Longism in this state, my friends, and not until then."

By the day election rolled around, Huey had "cleaned that bird Broussard's plow" for good and all. Overton and all the other Long candidates went in—a walkaway.

Most important, he had put over Wade Martin to defeat LeBlanc for the Public Service Commission. Wadę Martin, a young chap, was no mean rabble-rouser himself. Taking no chances, Huey had put up nine dummy candidates so as to control the polling places. November 19, Huey appeared at the capitol, with Wade and his other man, Harvey Fields, and then and there reorganized the Commission, making Fields chairman. Chairman Francis Williams was reduced to an ordinary member. Dudley LeBlanc was out entirely three weeks ahead of his legal time. "He can't do that!" sputtered LeBlanc. But Huey did, and paid him and Williams back in their own coin for what they had done to him six years previously.

2

Right after the campaign, all state employees were asked for 10 percent of a month's salary toward expenses, $59,000 short. And right after, 2,000 convicts were released because of "lack of funds" to feed them. Political trade for votes? A reprieve was a better weapon than a pardon. The whole election smelled bad.

Broussard, complaining of the use of dummy candidates, with the help of the Honest Election League (Huey's old political enemies masquerading under a moralistic name) filed charges of fraud with the United States Senate, also started court action.

A sub-committee of Senators Tom Connally of Texas and Samuel G. Bratton of New Mexico were sent to New Orleans to investigate. Their hearings opened October 6.

"There are only 2,500 white people over the age of twenty in St. Bernard Parish," the League pointed out," . . . yet there were 3,189 votes in the parish, Overton receiving 3,176, Broussard 13." This and other charges pro and con whirled around the heads of the two senators.

Edward Rightor, becoming abusive, was barred as one of Broussard's attorneys in the hearings. Francis Williams was shut up as "an annoyance." Huey, acting as Overton's attorney, argued no allegations of fact and promising to file a written answer, left for the North to confer with the Democratic bigwigs. In Albany he told Roosevelt what he had done for Hattie and John Overton, and that he was going to campaign the Dakotas for him. He got out the sound trucks and banged forth, his "hopes for distressed humanity" rising to ever "greater heights."

3

Connally and Bratton reported many irregularities to the Senate, and $25,000 was voted to carry on a more serious investigation under elderly Senator Howell. The sessions, which began during the first days of February, 1933, soon became typical Louisiana camp-meetings. The Kingfish, barging in and out with armed guards, constantly interrupted proceedings with loud recriminations and Winnfield wit, or as brother Julius would have it, "his mouth all bulged out with wind." Sarcastic accusations spattered about. Spectators alternately cheered and booed.

The committee's aggressive counsel, General S. T. Ansell, World War adviser of Woodrow Wilson, clashed with Huey time and again. He grilled the candidate, his counsel, his managers, and everybody who could smear up Long, to whom he took a furious dislike. Long knew how to get under the general's skin. Once he charged him with taking "a lot of time" to make his job last long.

"We are here for a fair hearing, free from perjury and intimidation, and that is what we are going to have. The Senator knows I do not want a job nearly as much as he does."

"But I can be elected, and you can't," crowed the Kingfish.

"I have never run for office and never desire to run for office under your circumstances." The crowd cheered. The chairman rapped for order.

As a matter of fact, Ansell and the committee turned the investigation into a punitive attack on Long, pried into all his past and present activities, personal and otherwise. Ansell carried through with the air of an inquisitorial prosecutor rather than a true investigator. With much justification, Huey charged: "It is the law of every civilized place on earth (except before Howell and Ansell) that testimony be relevant to the case on trial."

Under oath, when filing his candidacy, Overton had designated himself as his own campaign manager, "the only person authorized to receive, expend, audit and disburse all monies . . . for the purpose of . . . promoting my nomination and election." Testimony soon brought out that Overton had paid out only a small amount for personal expenses, and he had no knowledge of what other amounts were expended. Huey, said Overton, had merely told him he was "as good as elected."

The actual, if not legal, managers were Allen J. Ellender and Harvey Peltier. But both declared that the actual payment of expenses was made by Weiss and Long.

"Your report says Mr. Long spent only $250," demanded Ansell. "Isn't that mighty small?"

"Well, he paid his own expenses."

"Yes, of course, he's the Kingfish. . . . Your letter says the sound trucks used . . . were owned by the Louisiana Democratic Association. And now I want to know more about this lodge of the Mystic Knights of the Sea, headed by the Kingfish . . . [which] has the lusty Kingfish, but also the simple-minded person of the Amos type. We have numerous of that type in the mystic lodge. You are familiar with 'Amos 'n' Andy'?"

In transcription, the general's wit seems a bit strained. And Peltier, perhaps an Amos, seemed puzzled. "Yes, but I am not a member of any such lodge."

Ansell sought to learn if state employees had been forced to contribute to the Overton campaign. Peltier knew nothing about it. Finally, calling the sphinxlike Peltier "an office boy," Ansell exploded. Didn't he know that Long had the "most high-powered system in the country?"

Unruffled, Peltier replied modestly. "He has been very successful."

The general, acting a bit childish, persisted. Peltier's invariable reply was, "Senator Long handled that."

Ellender took the stand. Just as Ansell was asking if he belonged to "the fish lodge," loud cheers rang through the hallways. Long stalked in, and from then on interrupted constantly.

Ansell turned back to Ellender. "Who chose you Overton's campaign manager?"

"I saw it announced by the newspapers which prompted me to believe I was it." (Laughter.)

"With the influence of the Long machine?" (As usual the general seemed to think he was making a political drive instead of an investigation.)

Ellender snapped back sharply, "I resent that. I am a respectable member of the state bar."

Long jumped in. "Go ahead, we are used to these insults which the chair has advised us we must accept."

"You are out of order," rapped Senator Howell.

"Senator Overton has testified he didn't know you were his manager," persisted Ansell.

"I did not say Mr. Overton chose me. He just understood as I did." Ellender raised his voice.

"Now don't get mad," pleaded the general.

"Are you trying to get funny?" snapped Huey. "If so, the

Dauphine Burlesque Theatre has an ad for a second-rate comedian."

"You should be there to take the job immediately," barked Ansell.

Long appealed to the chair. "The conduct of this hearing has become the laughing stock of the state bar."

Senator Howell squatted on his dignity. "The state bar is not conducting this hearing. I am. And I may not do it to your satisfaction, but I'll do it!"

Ansell, now hot to dig up all the dirt on Huey, called on his own two brothers, Earl and Julius, to testify to serious corporation deals: "An agent of the Electric Bond and Share Company [for whose subsidiary Huey had fixed the gas rate] slipped $10,000 in new bank notes into a bathrobe pocket. . . ." Agents of Rudolph Hecht's Union Indemnity Insurance, the $32,000,000 corporation that had just crashed, twice in the Roosevelt suite, "thrust into Huey Long's hands rolls of bank notes and Huey Long thrust them into his hip pockets—rolls so big they made his pockets bulge out and spoiled the fit."

Long's only reply had been, "In no campaign have I ever denied a charge they [my brothers] ever made, and in no campaign, public or private, have I ever made a charge against one of them. . . . I cannot attack my own blood. . . . But I had managed to keep newspapers from printing these canards. . . . When Ansell came down here, he brought my two brothers into the senatorial inquiry and he put them on the witness stand where they could tell the damnable tales they had been telling, so the newspapers could print them, and I was without the slightest opportunity to obtain any vindication of any kind."

The investigation went on. Weiss took the stand, "white-faced, hands trembling, his voice shrilling like a woman's." Despite threats of contempt, about all they got out of him was, "None of your business!"

4

Huey confronted the investigation with circulars:

KANGAROO COURT BY SENATOR HOWELL (FORMERLY CLOSE ASSOCIATE AND DEFENDER OF WALTER COHEN) [1]

"Howell and Ansell have already spent $25,000 of the people's money, collecting up this sort of tales from these scoundrels, when . . . all they had to do would have been to go to the newspapers with a pair of scissors and have clipped 2,000 columns of lies from these persons, and they would not have been out 25 cents to do it. But now Brother Howell wants $25,000 more of the people's money to spend like he did the last $25,000."

He compared the procedure with the Kangaroo courts of the carpetbag days of Kellogg, Pinchbeck, "and other scalawags."

The affidavits finally filed showed Overton's and Broussard's expenses both over $13,000 (of course they were much more); in both cases this was more than twice the $6,000 allowed by the Louisiana primary law. There was plenty of use of dummy candidates (by Broussard also), padded registration rolls, ballot-stuffing, intimidation, vote-buying, what not. But also there was little doubt but that Overton would have been elected in any case. There was no real contest. It was hard to go back of this *fait accompli*. Crookedness, of course, had been practiced by whatever clique was in power since the beginning.

The demand for more money to continue the useless investigations, already three vast tomes in length, brought on sharp debate in Congress. In slumgullion repartee the Kingfish had met an equal in General Ansell. Huey seized the opportunity to attack the general savagely from the floor—"liar, crook, scoundrel, forger, dog-faced son of the wolf."

North Carolina Democrat Josiah W. Bailey arose: "I have rarely heard anyone so vituperated and abused anywhere. . . .

---

[1] A Hoover negro customs appointee.

It is *ex parte*. It is by a senator under his privilege of immunity."

"I do not claim any privilege!" roared Huey.

Bailey made him repeat this four or five times. "No, sir," insisted Huey, "I do not claim any privilege from this scoundrel anywhere on earth under God's living sun."

General Ansell took Huey at his word and filed suit for $500,000 damages for slander.

Huey promptly scuttled back into senatorial immunity he so braggingly waived. "Kingfish Crawfishes," blared the Louisiana papers.

Ansell thereupon sued for damages on the Kangaroo Court circular and on headlines edited into Long's speech about him.

Long entered a plea for dismissal, was overruled. The case was still pending when he was shot.

"Fleas have a use," remarked Huey in *Liberty Magazine*. "They keep the dog awake."

In the Senate Huey warned his fellow-senators: "Never touch a porcupine unless you expect to get some feathers in you. That is a good rule to follow." And so the charges, after a little more debate, were shelved.

The *New York Sun* editorialized: "Not since the Emperor of Japan visited the town of Titipu and considered charges against the Lord High Executioner has any public servant been so happily and ingeniously exonerated. . . . Except for a libretto by Sir William Gilbert and music by Sir Arthur Sullivan nothing is wanting to justify placing the Committee's report among the foremost of public documents. The Committee finds that the election of Senator Overton was accomplished "by the use of fraud, coercion, intimidation and corruption." But . . . it received no probative evidence that Mr. Overton "personally participated in or instigated any fraud." "Immortal POO-BAH never achieved anything more subtle . . . The inference is . . . that Mr. Overton has a good title to a seat obtained through fraud, intimidation and corruption."

5

Following the failure of the Senate investigation, through March and April numerous Louisiana groups filed petitions in the Senate. Long had to combat many of these on the floor. Overton backed him up. One particularly aggressive petition was headed by the name of "France-ass" Williams. Ex-Governor Parker wired Vice-President Garner: "Senator Long knows neither truth, honesty nor decency. His black record is nationally known. Psychiatrists have said in my presence he is a dangerous paranoiac. The Senate should have him permanently incarcerated in Washington. He is the greatest menace to American decency and civilization."

Meanwhile the Dock Board workers were busy securing signatures for a counter-petition. Presently the Long machine began sending in wires defending Huey, attacking his enemies. Huey demanded a Senate investigation of those attacking him.

The longest, most detailed petition came in from the Louisiana Women's Committee led by Mrs. Hilda Phelps Hammond, husband of the ousted Dock Board employee, which continued barraging the Senate in a futile waste of time and effort up until the time of Long's death, demanding action against him and Overton. "Is the Senate afraid of Huey Long?" was their constant cry. Of course, it was.

The woman's organization was a spear-head for a lot of elements, business men, flat-tire politicians and others afraid, because of fear of tax-assessments, reprisals, what not to come out in the open. They used to pussy-foot up to the Committee's littered little office with its stacks of papers, old furniture, and ever-handy teapot, on the second floor of a rattletrap building on Royal Street in the Vieux Carré, to slip the good ladies advice and money—cash donations, no traceable checks. Very pathetic! And more so, because Mrs. Hammond is an honest, sincere woman, who did not know that the game had changed in Louisiana. Among the ramrods were Gladys Brezeale of the rump delegation denied seats at Chicago; Mrs. Charles Dunbar, wife of the law partner of Esmond Phelps; Mrs. Joseph Montgomery, wife of the young man taken into the Zemurray organization; Mrs. Roger T. Stone, daughter of Zemurray; Mrs. John M. Parker, daughter, daughters-in-law. The old-line corporation aristocrats had their long, long chance at ruining Louisiana and did a good job. The good ladies have been crying over spilt milk. Huey's death may give them a new lease of life—but not for long.

6

June 18, Huey had to rush back to Louisiana. Two thousand war-veterans (slightly ironical) greeted him at the station for his stand on the bonus. A new crisis had developed. The Senate might be cowed, or at least rendered speechless, by Long, but his local enemies were busier than bees. They had brought the election frauds before a Grand Jury on charges made by District Attorney Eugene Stanley, the Honest Election League, the Louisiana Bar Association, and the New Orleans Bar Association. But the Long-controlled Grand Jury brought in no bill. Judge Frank Echezebal discharged it. The charges were brought before a second Grand Jury. Attorney General Porterie ordered Stanley, himself facing investigation, to desist. The state bar association at once disqualified Porterie from practice. When the second Grand Jury, without even examining the ballot boxes, returned no bill, Judge Alex O'Donnell declared the jury disqualified, ordered Sheriff George E. Williams to eject them from their quarters and seize the ballots. The court heavily guarded, Judge O'Donnell proceeded to open and recheck the ballots. Glaring falsifications were encountered. In one box 300 false votes had been added to put over the highway bond issue. The *Times Picayune* (in which, Huey charged, the judge was a big stockholder) sent fans to the deputies to cool themselves while they thumbed over the stale ballots between sneezes, yawns and brow-mopping. Huey, twice in forty-eight hours, nervously mobilized the National Guard to protect election commissioners menaced with arrest.

An Allen circular—75,000 were printed—gave the history of the case and cited the clogged calendar. Why had not the case of the State against R. L. Browning, bondsman, father of Francis Williams, ever been taken up in two years? Why had the investigation against Stanley been consistently side-tracked? The court was merely playing dirty politics.

Huey issued statements, declaring the judge's action illegal. Now that the ballot boxes had passed through improper hands, they were no longer of legal importance.

It was all useless effort. The Senate would not act in any case.

At the next special session he rewrote the law so as to create an entirely new legal bar association of which he made Porterie the head (no elections). The old bar association petered out to a polite sewing club. Now Porterie could kick anyone out he pleased. This was exactly the same device used by Dictator Machado in Cuba to make the legal profession knuckle under.

And so the Overton election went into history—except for the weekly protest of the Women's Committee.

XXII—THE BATTLE OF SANDS POINT

EARLY in 1933, during the lame duck session, Huey jumped back into the headlines by his famous filibuster against the Glass Banking Bill. Good bankers' boy Glass later testified to an investigating committee that he was puzzled by it all. The new President of the Chase National Bank, Mr. Aldrich (son-in-law of John D. Rockefeller), who had taken the place of Albert Wiggin of such funereal fame, was now posing as an advocate of banking reform to ward off possible Senate investigations such as were to soon embarrass the House of Morgan and the National City Bank. Aldrich had urged Glass to put some very restrictive measures in the bill; then other Chase Bank officials, said Glass "were among those who came to Washington and violently opposed those provisions; and one of the officials [Mr. McCain] . . . [was] alleged to have been in constant communication with the man who has made the most vituperative and violent assault on those provisions of the law." Huey's filibuster—a filibuster on a banking bill always looks like a fight for the common people —was directed against the bill's most progressive features. Huey was finally silenced by the rarely used cloture rule, and announced that the bill was "as good as dead. . . . Take this carcass away. I am glad to say that it has no more chance of final passage than I have of becoming Pope of Rome, and I am a Baptist."

Long did not wait to vote on the measure, apparently not wishing to see a corpse brought back to life. Nor did he ever approach Pope-hood. According to Glass he had taken "the next train out of Washington for an interview with this official [Mr. McCain] of the Chase National Bank."

But, though few people knew what it was all about, Huey's name was on every tongue. Gripped in the depression, everyone was anxiously watching every move of Congress. Huey's activities gained him—according to the point of view, respective ignorance or knowledge—either admiration or disgust.

When Roosevelt became President, Huey again reintroduced in the first session his proposition to limit fortunes. The vote was 14 in favor to 50 against. Announced pairs would have given his proposition, in all, twenty votes.

In attempting to limit swollen fortunes, while coquetting with the bankers, Huey had anticipated personal hostility, but he soon found evidence, he declared, that efforts were being made, not only to cripple his political activities, but to injure Louisiana. January 17, 1933, the *Kansas City Star* stated that "Wall Street had furnished Louisiana about $50,000,000 since the Kingfish took hold down there," but was now showing signs of "growing weary of furnishing ammunition for Huey Long's War Chest." In denouncing Wall Street, Huey was merely "killing the goose that laid the golden egg. . . . Wall Street . . . Houses, previously identified with Louisiana financing, were definitely 'not interested' in the $5,000,000 issue scheduled for today." And January 23, 1933, the *Memphis Commercial Appeal* wrote: "A determined effort is being made to 'get' Senator Long. Whether the movement, which bears many earmarks of political persecution, is inspired by some of the powerful interests he has offended . . . or by his old enemies in Louisiana, or by the administration . . . secret service agents are investigating Senator Long's personal income tax over a period of several years . . . trying to find irregularities in a loan which he obtained from the Reconstruction Finance Corporation. . . . No stone is being left unturned. . . . Long's bank accounts everywhere are being scrutinized. When he made a trip to New Orleans during the Christmas holidays, he was shadowed by government agents, his telephone tapped and every movement watched."

Thus, remarked Huey, when his wealth reduction measure could attract twenty senatorial votes, the hostile publicity directed at him "took on organized form." He particularly cited the contradictory articles, previously favorable, now antagonistic in several national magazines "affiliated with the

House of J. P. Morgan and Company," particularly *Collier's Weekly*, which in December, 1929, had published a favorable article, but after his filibuster, in June, 1933, rewrote Huey's career, attributing to him "all the vices and crime in the catalogue of human sins. . . ." Both articles were written by Walter Davenport. In the first, Huey had "unconquerable confidence, cleaving to directness of purpose and speech, overflowing with an energy which flattens weaker beholders, ruthless as a machine-gun . . ." and in the second, "You would expect a picture of power, the intensity of a zealot, the burning eye of fanaticism, the uncompromising jaw of the crushing autocrat, the lean asceticism of the prophet, the austerity of a despot. But . . . he's pudgy. His cheeks are blotched, flabby. His uncertain nose is red. His face is weak, willful, and there is no discipline in it. But his eyes—soft, protruding robin's eggs—are nevertheless bold. Hit-and-run eyes that roll upward as he talks."

The first article told about his free textbooks, his able defense of state laws in the courts; the second called him "Hotcha Huey (Tell 'em nothing and make 'em like it), Get-'em-while-they're-hot Huey, Let's go Long, the hardest working demagogue in America." It threw reflections on his well-known lack of physical courage, how he slept behind a machine gun, how his slumbers were guarded "by such staunch lads as Joe Messina, Wheaton Stillson, Two-Gun Thompson and Squinch or Squinch-Eye McGee. There's a boy for you—Squinch. Listen, Mister, don't lay no hand on the Senator; just don't lay no hand on the Senator, pal, and you and me will be okay."

When the Senate Committee began inquiring into Morgan's affairs, Huey demanded of Thomas W. Lamont whether he was director of the concern publishing *Collier's Weekly*. The latter finally admitted that the "dummy" concern publishing *Collier's* is owned by the Crowell Publishing Company (which also owns the *American Magazine, Woman's Home Companion* and *Country Home*), affiliated with the House of Morgan. Huey demanded that he explain the contradictory articles. Lamont professed no knowledge, but admitted that at the time of this attack on the Kingfish, *Collier's* was publishing articles from Lamont's own pen extolling the various activities and personages of the House of Morgan.

2

February 3, 1933 (strangely enough the very day the senatorial investigations of the Overton-Broussard campaign reopened in New Orleans) Congressman Hamilton Fish made charges of "crookedness" in loans made by the Reconstruction Finance Commission to several companies, particularly Union Indemnity Company and the Union Title Guarantee, with the former of which Long was "closely associated."

Fish charged that R. S. Hecht, chairman of the regional advisory committee of the Reconstruction Finance Corporation, director of the Union Indemnity Company and president of the Hibernia Bank of New Orleans, had, though he knew of the impending collapse of Union Indemnity, used his influence with the R.F.C. to obtain a $1,000,000 loan for it, only a few days before it crashed, January 5, 1933, with loud reverberations after using the money loaned to pay back money owed Hecht's bank, the Hibernia.

At once a run developed on the bank. Panic gripped New Orleans. Collapse of the bank meant a major tragedy. Fish hastened to retract some statements and to express confidence in the integrity of Hibernia and Hecht.

Financial and political heads were put together. Frantically everyone sought for a good excuse to declare a holiday. Finally draft-exempt Long and Governor Allen issued the following pompous proclamation:

"Whereas, on the night of February 3 and 4, 1917, Woodrow Wilson, president of the United States, severed diplomatic relations with the Imperial German Government; and

"Whereas, more than sixteen years has intervened before the great American people have turned their eyes back to the lofty ideals of human uplift and new freedom as propounded by Woodrow Wilson . . . the illustrious Southerner who sought to break the fetters of mankind throughout the world;

"Now, therefore, I, Oscar Kelly Allen, governor of the

state of Louisiana, do hereby ordain that Saturday, the fourth day of February, 1933, . . . is hereby declared a holiday throughout the state of Louisiana."

It turned the trick. With the two-day delay, Huey got busy and, Sunday, secured for the Hibernia Bank a $20,000,000 R.F.C. loan. The bank also trucked in $4,000,000 more in cash. Monday morning few depositors came to take out their money. The crisis was over.

Once more, Huey took the credit of saving the state—from the consequences of the crash of the company with which he was so closely related. Just what Louisiana lost in that crash has never been revealed.

Union Indemnity (subsidiary of the Insurance Securities Company, organized to save it from disaster back in 1925) had had a virtual monopoly of Highway Commission bonding and state insurance. Huey's interest in it had prevented him from putting proper insurance and workmen's compensation laws on the statute books.

In 1934 a conspiracy suit was brought in the United States District Court of Louisiana, Monroe Division, by a Boston firm, "deceived into believing the stock valuable" against a long list of former Indemnity directors, among them the Brownells, Hecht, Felix F. Vaccaro, the fruit king (close to Huey). It was charged that the company "had been kept afloat by constant sale of new stock at high price, made possible by the illegal payment of dividends out of capital . . . a fraudulent stock-selling scheme on a large scale. . . ." Another sad story of paper-pyramiding during the great frenzy of our prosperity plunder era!

3

From March to June Huey laid down a smoke screen over these scabrous matters, by a constant barrage in the Senate. In grand style, he attacked the N.R.A., attacked recovery efforts and banking bills; he fought for the soldiers' bonus; he sailed into Glass time and again (once a fist fight was barely averted), into Eugene Meyer, chairman of the Federal Reserve Board (for not very holy reasons), six Americans who controlled the nation, Sweetness-and-Light Secretary of Treasury Woodin of Remington Arms, Locomotive and Cuban sugar and railway fame, Morgan, Lewis W. Douglas, Senator Ashhurst, and Roosevelt, Roosevelt, Roosevelt. Robinson quoted the Bible back at him. Down in Louisiana, Mrs. Rufus Pleasant brought a $250,000 slander suit against him.

4

In June he was back in Louisiana finishing up the fight on Stanley and the Honest Election League, and laying the basis for new campaigns. Through July a mass drive was made for subscriptions to revive the *Louisiana Progress* as the *American Progress,* a little more befitting the mouthpiece of a national figure. New Orleans ward leaders obliged all state employees to sign up. Rene Stegler, general agent of the Dock Board, busily solicited the steamship men for subscriptions. August 6, the *Times Picayune* came out with documentary evidence that state employees had been definitely ordered to subscribe.

Threatening an income tax evasion suit, the federal government also struck back at him by denying him patronage, throwing it to the hands of his political enemies. Edward Rightor, a Sullivan man, was appointed to handle Louisiana's share of the billions of the P.W.A. program. August 12, the rice job on the farmer adjustment administration was given to Charles D. Miller, brother-in-law of Senator Robinson. Long battled with Farley for a cut-in on favors, but got no satisfaction, and took out his spleen on poor reporters and cameramen, who were repeatedly smashed up by his guards. In every possible way the "ants were being put on him."

Every turn of publicity seemed to be unfavorable, and he couldn't keep out of the news. In August the whole nation laughed. On the 29th, at a party in the exclusive Long Island Sands Point Bath Club, Huey got into some sort of a jam and was punched in the eye.

The story, as usual, broke in the press. Blatantly he announced to the world that he had been beaten up by "a group of men" and accused the House of Morgan of trying "to get him." He burst into more bitter onslaughts than ever on the N.R.A., Wall Street, and the administration's reforestation plan. But for days the press all over the country preferred to give more attention to statements regarding the club incident and what really happened. The account of Jack Curley, wrestling promoter, differed considerably from Huey's. Ira L. Reeves challenged Huey to a return fight. A national magazine gleefully collected funds for a medal for the man who socked Long. The assailant was reported to be one of the four hundred. Newspapers at once published lists of persons who denied having hit him. Louisiana was used to such incidents, but elsewhere they were less known, though now bad manners connived to keep him in the headlines better than his attacks on Morgan. Again his guards roughhoused cameramen. A train conductor accused Huey of having thrown him bodily into the lap of two nuns.

But if well-mannered Easterners thought such unpleasant publicity would finish him, they were merely doing wishful thinking. The secret of political success is not the kind of publicity, but mass coverage. They themselves now talked about him constantly, something they had never done before. And they were unaware of cane-brake psychology. Down in the degenerate Red River bayous and similar God-loving and God-forsaken spots, the simple belief was that the House of Morgan really had tried to gang up on Huey, or else that the city slickers had tried to pull a fast one.

More actively than ever Huey broadcast his views on every and all subjects. Through August, he attacked the N.R.A., Roosevelt, Wall Street, banking and currency. "We ought to demonitize silver. . . ." He proposed inflation. "Give the people money enough for easy trade intercourse. That is one of the ways to help decentralize wealth and free people of debt."

"Back to the Constitution! Back to the Lord! Back to humanity!" he cried.

He talked about the enslavement of the Cuban people by

Wall Street and opposed American intervention. "There is no banditry against any American life in Cuba, Europe, Japan, or anywhere else like the slow starvation . . . practiced against them right here in the 'home of the free . . .' Let us, who cannot save ourselves, say to Cuba: 'Go free!'"

5

But he seemed to be slipping. The finances of his state were in dreadful condition. By October he was back trying to fix up a new tax program. Seven additional taxes—with much wrangling, fuming, bloodthirsty opposition mass meetings— were fought through. Sulphur and corporation franchise taxes were increased; a public utility tax was presented to the voters. An unpopular tax on railroad tickets caused the press to make much of the fact that Huey just at this time rode to Shreveport in the private car of Harvey Couch, head of the Louisiana and Arkansas Railway, and that since 1927 Huey had reduced assessments on that line 41.5 percent. But the poor traveler had to foot the bill.

Despite straitened finances, the same undiminished appropriations were made for the various state departments forming the payroll machine. All economy proposals were tossed in the garbage can.

The citizenry were angered. An irate mob pulled Long's name off the Red River bridge, in construction. Bigger Allen-Long signs were put up. Huey said he'd write his name on that bridge in steel. November 19, the sign declaring Long as the builder was burned on the Covington-Slidell highway. The Lafayette veterans dared him to repeat before them "that most men who served in the army were dragged in by the hair of the head." In Donaldsville he was booed; in Monroe heckled and called a "liar"; the meeting broke up in a riot. In Alexandria rotten eggs and stink bombs greeted him. At Baton Rouge the crowd cheered for the end of the Long régime. His popularity seemed definitely slipping.

The Sixth District Congressional election, where his enemy

Sanders, Jr., was a candidate, whom he wished to beat at all costs, grew bitter. Huey set a surprise date. The citizens were furious. Ballots had to be delivered secretly at night. In Amite citizens burned circulars, ballots, and tally sheets. Prominent men warned Governor Allen that if the National Guard were called out, it would precipitate a revolution. Guns blazed in Livingston Parish, as voters seized the ballots. Long, Allen and Judge Lee Ponder (Huey's man) were burned in effigy in Hammond. Other sections took up the effigy-burning craze. Long fumed, threatened reprisals. But the uproar continued all through December. When the elections were held, the local people went to the polls with their rifles draped over their arms. Sanders was elected.

The New Orleans mayoralty campaign was also getting hot. Sanders, Francis Williams, Walmsley, the Old Ring were determined to break Long then and there in the state. Amid a barrage of campaign vituperation on both sides, the local police began arresting men distributing Long circulars. Walmsley declined to heed Attorney General O'Conner's warnings to halt such abuses. Walmsley arrested Registrar of Voters Barnes and was denounced by Long, who reminded the electorate of the mayor's scandalous speculation with school funds. But when the smoke cleared up, the Old Ring had beaten Long again. Walmsley went back into office.

With this, the Sixth Congressional District defeat, the federal government putting on more and more heat, Long looked politically finished. But he in turn redoubled his blows in Washington. He made a sharp attack on the appointment of "sugar-hearted" Jefferson Caffery as Ambassador to Cuba (in truth a shameful thing) whose brother, a local sugar man, was against Huey; he lambasted other administration leaders and measures. Farley, over Long's repeated protests, merely continued to throw more and more patronage to the old anti-Long political gang. April 3, Huey bitterly attacked the throwing of patronage to "race-tracker" John Sullivan, and Colonel E. R. Bradley, whom he called an ex-gambling house owner— "the gang is picking the bones of the Home Owners' Loan

Corporation in Louisiana"; and he forced a Senate Committee to investigate the appointing of D. D. Moore as internal revenue collector.

But down in Louisiana it was becoming even profitable to be against Long.

XXIII—RABBITS

BUT neither renewed Old Ring victories nor federal patronage brought about Huey's demise. Those who expected his collapse were very short-sighted, wishful thinkers. For the most part, the Roosevelt federal patronage in Louisiana had been thrown to such lame-horse, flat-tire, corrupt and discredited political elements that for all the millions poured out, it failed to make a good-sized dent in Huey's power. And, except when allied with the Old Ring, he had never controlled New Orleans and Baton Rouge at all.

His defeats therefore were merely failures to make new conquests. The besieged held off the attack, but they made no sorties, and their food and ammunition were reduced. The failure to take the last citadels of the enemy was merely a stimulus to the Huey faithfuls to work harder. In any case the legislators and other henchmen who had ridden in on the triumphal surges of Longism in 1928, 1930 and 1932, still had at least two years to fatten on local patronage and preferments, and if they toed the mark and plugged hard, probably many more.

And just as Huey's Louisiana audience was beginning to yawn at his old song-and-dance acts, he dipped into the silk hat and pulled out what Oliver Carlson called two beautiful legislative rabbits: the Louisiana Debt Relief Law and the Homestead Exemption Law. The debt law, said Huey, "gave ease and the first peaceful night's rest many of our people have had for many months, because they did not know what night they would not have a roof above their heads. . . . So the Louisiana law I sponsored, somewhat based upon the law of the Bible, simply forbade one to oppress another for a debt he was in no shape to pay. . . . No law we have ever passed . . . has given the financiers more trouble. . . ."

Of course, as Oliver Carlson has pointed out, the Home Loan Corporation and other federal agencies were trying to do the same thing, but Huey's new law was shouted from the housetops in a loud chorus. As a matter of fact the greatest number of land foreclosures and bankruptcies had already taken place. From 1930 to the middle of 1933, poor folk in every part of Louisiana had already lost their homes and property. When they had really needed help no such law appeared on the horizon. As usual, Huey locked the door after the horse was stolen; and as usual his law had a joker.

State boards (more jobs to Long henchmen) receive the moratorium applications in a state where the motto is: "Give relief to those who support us, deny it to our enemies." Investigator Carlson could find no one at all who had received debt relief, nor was he granted any satisfactory figures. Actually, by fixing arbitrary partial payments on debts, the Board has become a coercive power which in certain instances has caused the loss of homes more quickly. One of the New Orleans daily papers recently carried fifty-four pages of homes being sold for taxes.

Despite such laws, despite his Share-Our-Wealth ballyhoo, concentration of wealth in Louisiana had proceeded more rapidly under the Long régime than at any time in the history of the state. In the fur industry, complete monopoly of trapping lands, trapping and distribution, had been effected in good part by several of Huey's very closest henchmen.

The Homestead Tax Exemption Law promised "ultimately to exempt all homes from parish and state taxes up to the first $2,000 of assessment." Huey told poor folk there would be "substantial relief" on 1935 taxes, that every year it would get better until the first $2,000 of a home will pay no taxes at all. But the enormous state debt created by Huey, the enormous yearly expenditures—doubled in ten years—amounting to $55,000,000, make tax-relief a silly hope. The minimum exemption at present ($800) is so low as to affect few homesteads, and the categories of beneficiaries have been so restricted as almost to nullify the law entirely—widows and orphans, for instance, are excluded.

In everything, with a weather eye on the September, 1934, primaries, the June-July special session of the Legislature, where Huey was lord of all the loaves and fishes, efficiently guillotined all opposition. Nineteen of the twenty-eight bills passed were aimed directly or indirectly at New Orleans. The attorney-general was empowered to supersede any local district attorney in any suit (no more embarrassing election investigations); he was empowered to name or discharge any of the local district attorney's legal assistants. No court could inquire into his actions. No New Orleans special officer or policeman or employee could carry arms without the governor's approval. The governor was allowed to call the militia out whenever he might see fit, and the courts were forbidden to interfere with it in any shape or form. No municipality or city or parish could impose, levy or collect any tax, license or excise without legislative authority, thus cutting off at one stroke a good deal of New Orleans' revenue. A tax on advertisements in papers of over 20,000 circulation (*i.e.,* the New Orleans papers) was imposed. The primary election law was changed regarding registration and allowed the appointment of special deputies to supersede regular sheriffs in delivering and collecting ballot boxes or policing the polls. There no local police were allowed to interfere, unless ordered (it was then compulsory) by the electoral commission. The office of the Monroe registrar of voters was abolished. No court could seize the records of any registrar of voters (a state-appointed official) or take away his authority, thus making him the absolute and final judge of the validity of all voters. Dissemination of racing track information was prohibited (federal patronage man Sullivan was hit) and heavy penalties put upon lottery operators—an attack on the Old Ring as well. Lastly, a legislative investigation of New Orleans was ordered.

Through these and a group of minor bills, Huey secured control of the city's election machinery and emerged, with special instruments at his disposal, as a holy crusader against vice and a savior of the people from the Old Ring.

2

Three weeks before election day, Huey moved, Hitler-like, upon New Orleans with his national guard. Guns surrounded his palatial New Orleans home, and the boys in mufti squatted in the office of the registrar of voters across the street from the city hall to prevent the city or the courts, despite the new law, from seizing the records—as Walmsley had done the last election. Huey threatened to put his militia in charge of the polling places. The guardsmen scowled across at the citadel of Old Ring power, at the regular and special city police, bivouacked there night and day.

Threat answered threat. The militant Old Ringers imported from Honduras soldier of fortune Guy Maloney, former Orleanian, to take charge of their armed forces. Huey called in more and more guardsmen. Bloodshed seemed imminent.

More loudly than ever Huey blared over the radio about the vicious moral and economic condition of New Orleans. His August 28 circular declared: "The New Orleans Ring now owes the banks in New Orleans about 7 million dollars. They will never owe them any less. We told those banks when we paid that Ring out of debt in 1930 (it was 5 million then) not to let them get into them again. But the special interests wanted to use the Ring to beat us."

Under special guard, his legislative committee began its vice investigation. The press and the public were barred, though the testimony was broadcast over the radio. As special prosecutor, Huey artistically besmirched the records of Old Ring candidates, the Supreme Court and the Public Service Commission, and all and sundry vice connections.

But the investigation, the scowling guns, were all *opéra bouffe*—a Chinese battle of bluff. A last-minute compromise kept both armed forces away from the polls, which meant that when the votes were counted, Huey's candidates were victorious, with majorities of from seven to fifteen thousand. When Huey seemed beaten, definitely on the decline, he turned around and captured the stronghold of his enemies.

In his eleventh-floor suite in the Roosevelt, weary but triumphant, he hilariously slapped the backs of a dozen of his boisterous cronies. "But don't celebrate now," he croaked, his voice hoarse from microphone shouting. "Go home and get some sleep. We won, but we ain't through yet. There's a lot to be done."

Even Huey was surprised at the convincing margin of his victory. What was its secret?

To defeat Huey Long in the First and Second Congressional Districts, a tremendous majority had to be rolled up in New Orleans itself to offset the votes from Long's subdictatorships in the border parishes: St. Bernard, Jefferson, St. Charles, St. James, Palquemines, and St. John, where he could pile in more votes than the total number of adult whites and blacks. In the old days the Old Ring counted itself in regardless of opposition. But Huey's monkey-wrench legislation had stripped the old cogs. The registration rolls were now his; Old Ring supervisory power over the polls was halved or worse. Whatever election thievery occurred, if any, would now be in Huey's favor.

At the same time his well-timed legislative investigation intimidated the vice crowd, including Red Light, race track and gambling elements, good for about 9,000 votes. While Huey was denouncing vice and its Old Ring connections, his ward heelers were promising the gang that if they got right, the investigation would be dropped right after the election, otherwise they would be mopped up to the last grease spot. Huey's colorful broadcasting was close enough to the truth to make many ardent reformers forget the political purposes behind Huey's crusading.

The Old Ring was hamstrung for funds. Besides the loss of the vice rake-off, the Legislature had cut off a million dollars' revenue, now had forbidden the city to collect license taxes not specifically named, had lowered assessments, had prevented the sending out of tax bills, and had added a mandatory burden of $650,000. On the other hand, Huey's powerful payroll organization in New Orleans had grown steadily stronger while that of the Old Ring was weakened. The previous January, when the Old Regulars and Long broke,

hundreds of shared political jobs became the exclusive right
of the state machine. Huey dumped out the old straphangers
at a moment when the Old Ring simply couldn't take care of
them. Naturally the job-voters flocked to Long.

The state-usurped power of assessment frightened big property holders into line, attracted smaller ones by promises of
relief.

Lastly, lack of leadership or planned action featured the
polyglot assortment of professional politicians and inflamed
independents fighting Long. All in all the Old Regulars barely
got an even break in New Orleans itself and were swamped
by the surrounding country vote.

Immediately after the election Mayor Walmsley announced
a clean-up campaign of his own. Thus the gamblers, lottery
venders, red-light women, and similar ilk were caught between two fires.

Huey didn't quite complete his domination—five of the
eight Louisiana Congressmen, all successful in the September
primaries, were still actively opposed to him, and anti-Long
dynamite still existed in the large and even some of the small
towns of the country parishes, but it had no cohesion and no
leadership. More than ever Huey had his enemies on the
run.

3

Victorious, Huey called his hip-flask legislature into its third
special session that year (December 16) in a new maneuver
to grab what little patronage was left in the state and also
to create a diversion from the new blow from Washington,
the federal indictment for income tax evasion of faithful Seymore Weiss and other intimate cronies.

The opening day, the lofty, fussily decorated chamber of
the House was noisy with talk, the galleries crowded. The
Long crowd was jubilant—hand-shaking, back-slapping, sly
genial conversations all over the lot. There was one strutting
ten gallon hat; most of the representatives were just good-
hearted, mediocre Main Street citizens, not even in the Bab-
bitt category, without much knowledge and less imagination.

Few knew what they were supposed to do—only a small clique of insiders, back from a caucus at the governor's mansion.

The gavel. Prayer, almost—as Swing says, as though these men really were there for the public good. Roll call. Again confusion, din of talking. Pages bring in refreshments while the titles of thirty-five bills were mumbled into the microphone.

Huey is there. Never before was the Legislature so entirely under his thumb. He is a dynamo, a jumping-jack, a self-motored ping-pong ball, one minute at this member's seat, whispering, now consulting the Speaker, now in the aisles, laughing, shouting, voice booming boisterously. A question was directed to him. He jumped up, grinning, waving his arms, bellowing reply with strut and grimace—half like a straw boss with a chain-gang, partly like an Elk on initiation night.

At last all the titles had been read. A few museum-piece oppositionists rose to ask questions. Nobody paid much attention to them. The thirty-five bills were referred, per custom, to the Ways and Means Committee to meet Monday at 9 A.M. on the tenth floor of the capitol tower.

Five minutes ahead of time, Huey, voice loud, face purple, banged in with his bruisers. "This is no way to run a legislature," he bellowed. "Nine o'clock and nobody here." One of the bodyguard slipped out; members scrambled in to take their places. Roll was called.

In a normal committee, bills would be studied, information sought, pros and cons aired, amendments made. Nothing of the sort here. The bills had come from the printer's only a few minutes before. No one had had time even to read them. And Long, with no right to be there except by invitation, stood by the chairman in full charge.

He spoke with unctuous humor. "Before I explain these bills, I want to hear any comments by opponents." The only one such on the committee, Williamson, never having seen them, scowled, muttered. Huey grinned. The chairman handed up the first bill. "This bill is just a formality." He explained its contents. A member moved a favorable report. The gavel banged. Approved.

Bill No. 2. An income tax measure. One sentence of explanation, one motion, no talk, one bang—approved. Bill No. 3, a patronage grab of thirty New Orleans tax-collectors. "This is a very charitable law." Huey grinned. "It gives the gentleman down in New Orleans [Mr. Montgomery, tax-collector] the advantage of the best talent." It "relieved" Montgomery's heart "of a heavy burden."

"Do you think he will like it?" asked oppositionist Williamson.

"He will have to like it." Bang.

And so through the list, mostly patronage grabbing, jobs shifted to the Long machine, even policemen and firemen. A new school of dentistry was planned to put that of Loyola University, which had restricted Huey's use of its radio during the last campaign, completely in the shade. Another bill prevented companies with pension schemes from discharging any employee just before his pension was due. Williamson remarked that the bill might cause all companies to abandon pension schemes.

"Anybody that does that admits he's a crook," retorted Huey. "Make the vote nineteen to one."

The previous campaign, Huey was rotten-egged in Alexandria. A bill gave him power to remove mayors; shortly, that of Alexandria was removed. The parish of East Baton Rouge, where most of the voters are Standard Oil employees, had always been against Huey. He had given it a long time "to get right." Now he subdued it by creating state control of the police jury (governing board), by the appointment of extra members and turning Baton Rouge into a miniature District of Columbia. Now the police jury, formerly nine to three against him, would be for him seventeen to nine. And at last on the Standard Oil was levied the five cents a barrel occupational tax for which Huey had been fighting since 1928— an increase of one to four million dollars a year in taxes. It was shoved through on the mean two-minute average before any Standard Oil attorney could smell it out and make trouble.

"This," remarks Swing, who has given us the most vivid account of this session, "is dictatorship," an object lesson in the "ease with which the form of democratic government can be twisted to serve the reality of one-man rule. The passing of bills had "no more merit than . . . if these men moved in hypnosis."

"Why," Swing asks, "do these committee members take it lying down? . . . How can they put up with his bullying, his unsavory, blasphemous, overbearing language. They do not seem to be afraid of him; they appear to like him. Psychology explains the dictators of Europe as appealing to the innate yearning for father-authority in most people. But Huey is no father-figure. He is a grown-up bad boy."

Revivalist Gerald K. Smith explained to Swing: "The surgeon is recognized as being in charge because he knows. Everyone defers to him for that reason only. The nurses and assistants do what he tells them, asking no questions. They jump at his commands. They are not servile; they believe in the surgeon. They realize he is working for the welfare of the patient."

A naïve explanation. Most of the legislators have extra state jobs, concessions, or their relatives have them. Huey got his; they got theirs. The only way they could get it was to swallow his bullying. If they didn't endure his bullying, life would probably bully most of them worse.

Swing concludes that Huey was "not a fascist with a philosophy of the state . . . expressing the individual. He is plain dictator."

He ruled, rewarded, punished. All who thwarted him were tracked down with relentless, efficient vengeance, frequently, however, flavored with good humor.

XXIV—SQUARE DEALERS

FURIOUS at the way Huey had sneaked over the long contested five cent occupational tax, the Standard Oil, as usual, threatened to close its Baton Rouge refinery and throw its 3,800 men out of work. Early in January, Huey came out with a counterblast circular: STANDARD OIL *versus* THE PEOPLE.

He accused them and other companies of running a pension swindle for many years. The employees, given a button for ten years of service, were invariably fired on the eve of qualifying for a pension. "The other day I wrote a law to provide against anyone firing a man . . . to keep from paying his pension. The law goes into effect January 10. Of course, the Standard Oil will fire the many it has had on the list before that law goes into effect. And, poor fools, they are making them shout for the Standard Oil, and ministers proclaim a fast for them . . . and in that way they . . . conceal the real reason why they are firing these men. . . . THE STANDARD OIL SHALL NOT RULE THIS STATE!"

Sure enough, Standard did fire 900 men, blaming Huey. And "the poor fools" reacted just as Huey had predicted. And Huey reacted exactly as usual. Four days after a circular announcing relentless undying battle against the company, January 22, he signed, with J. C. Hilton, manager, a public truce, terms not revealed. Once more secretly Huey had backed down by agreeing to call a special session within the month to reduce the tax to one cent a barrel. Employees, having lost their pension rights, were taken back.

Disgruntled—at Huey—they formed, in company with discharged state employees and Baton Rouge employees scheduled to get it in the neck, the Square Deal Association to fight him. January 19, right after Huey put out a harsh anti-

Standard Oil circular, 350 Square Dealers—many World War veterans—mobilized at the airport under Ernest J. Bourgeois, former L.S.U. student, fired from a Standard Oil construction job. Segregated according to wards, they were thrown into company organization to the notes of a bugle, a huge American flag billowing.

Mrs. J. S. Roussell, president of the women's division, a big-boned, little lady with a long face, large protruding teeth and fine marcelled hair, issued an appeal for money and support. "The women's organization of the Square Deal Association . . . calls . . . upon the red-blooded women of our state to help our cause." They distributed Square Deal buttons and gathered contributions.

Simultaneously resolutions of the Baton Rouge Chamber of Commerce asking for a repeal of the occupational tax were delivered at Governor Allen's office and mailed to all legislators—"enforcement of any detrimental legislation would seriously retard the development of industry."

The ranks of the Square Dealers grew rapidly. Two members (one was Sidney Songy, a Long spy) were arrested, charged with plotting to assassinate Long. As a protest for their arrest, January 25, 300 men armed with shotguns and rifles and plenty of ammunition seized the courthouse, defying Huey's dictatorship and demanding the two prisoners be released. They were aided with guns, transportation and advice by Park Commissioner Powers Higginbotham, whose elective job Long had announced would be (and was) legislated out of existence. One of Higginbotham's employees, Tobey LeBlanc, a fierce but "poorly dressed little fellow," later testified—somewhat with the air of a provocateur—that at the courthouse, shotgun and pistol in hand, he had made "a little speech": Any Square Dealer who deserted should be "shot down like a dog." His companions approved and chose him to carry out the proposal.

2

In New Orleans Huey denounced the "gun squads" over the radio and set out next morning for Baton Rouge. Governor Allen, following his instructions, had issued a general martial law decree for the entire parish, charging that "the officers and agents of the Standard Oil Company" were "the chief leaders of those exercising violence."

"Surely," protested manager J. C. Hilton, "the governor has been misinformed." Such charges were "incredible!"

Machine guns, trench mortars and tear gas guns soon bristled on the neatly landscaped lawn of the thirty-three story capitol, "Huey's silo." Armed guards patroled the approaches to the governor's mansion. Huey arrived just as his national guard began to appear in the streets and at once further accused the Standard Oil of responsibility—his "compromise" with the company was "off" unless it "stopped" the violence.

But he also gave another explanation for the courthouse raid: "Do you know why that bunch met down there? . . . A murder plot. . . . It was all fixed up . . . to block my car on the highway . . . force me in the ditch, and then fourteen or sixteen were going to come along in another car and kill me."

3

Despite martial law, the Square Dealers—who, after holding the courthouse for three hours and then hearing that Songy and his companion had been released, had dispersed— went ahead with a scheduled meeting that day in the airport. But they had become a frightened nervous bunch. When LeBlanc arrived at the airport, he was surprised that his pals, apparently forgetting all their World War experience, had made no provision for guarding the entrances; they just "stood around" and talked big about what they were going to do, till the troops deployed about the field with machine guns and army rifles which they trained on the little band.

"I'll get the officer first and you start picking off the soldiers," LeBlanc told a friend, and leveled his gun.

"Don't do that."

"Why not?"

"Because there ain't anybody here but us," his pal replied.

Looking over his shoulder, LeBlanc saw Bourgeois, their bold, bad chief, running away. He scaled the six-foot airport fence like a squirrel and fell into the swamp. He got up, fell again, got up. He shook his gun to see if mud had gotten into the barrel. It went off.

Square Dealer Alessi, a police juror of Independence, fell wounded. Later Alessi made an affidavit he had been shot by "two of Long's cossacks." Square Dealer James E. Mehaffey (later arrested) also said guardsmen had fired at him. "I was standing apart from the rest of the crowd on the edge of the woods. . . . I heard a crack and the whistle of a bullet near my head."

Adjutant General Ray Fleming emphatically denied that his soldiers had fired a single shot.

LeBlanc surrendered his shotgun to an officer, but retained his heavy revolver. Later, arrested for carrying arms, he languished in jail seven hours without any Square Dealers coming to his assistance. What he said of Bourgeois then "was not fit to repeat."

But apparently the doughty chief (both the authorities and his pals beat the woods for his body) had not stopped till he hit the state line. Days later, a laconic A.P. dispatch came through from McComb, Mississippi: "Ernest J. Bourgeois, president of the Square Deal Association of Louisiana, was reported to have left here tonight for an unreported destination."

Even in his absence some Square Dealers, especially outside of Baton Rouge, were still feeling militant. Secret angry drills, in the style of the old-time night-riding organizations, were carried on in half a dozen adjacent parishes.

Baton Rouge, hearing of these preparations, still remained fearful of armed violence. Sullenly the citizens watched the swank National Guard patrols moving through the streets and silently looked on while Governor Allen reviewed his "army" on the capitol grounds and had more severe martial law posters stuck up—more than two people "a crowd." Newspapers were forbidden to criticize the state administration.

4

Huey held an uproarious four-hour court session, given out over the radio, which sketched preliminary evidence regarding the murder plot. Among a number of witnesses, a stenographer testified to the time, place and date Huey was to be murdered.

Then, surrounded by burly guards, Huey hurried back to Washington. In his absence the Square Dealers gave out numerous flamboyant statements, and drilling continued in many parts of the state "to overthrow him." Mr. Lester, acting head, said, "God knows what will happen if Long dares to shove any more of his laws down the throats of our people."

So far, except for Bourgeois's cleaning his gun, it had been only a battle of words. January 31, Huey was on his way back "to end all nonsense in his state by doing away with even the semblance of local self-government." He arrived in New Orleans at 7:20 A.M., accompanied by an unusually heavy guard of highway police in civilian clothes.

Leon Trice, A.P. photographer, snapped his picture. One of Huey's bodyguard promptly struck Trice with his fist, smashing the camera to the pavement. Trice stooped to pick it up.

"Let him have it," Huey's husky protector was told.

At once Trice was again slugged over the head. Others seized the camera. Trice struggled to recover it, but it was smashed to bits. Trice, severely injured, was taken to the hospital, where the doctor said the blow, if it had landed a little lower, would have killed him.

Huey, bravely victorious in this battle of the pictures, sped on to Baton Rouge by motor, still surrounded by bodyguards and soldiers, to finish up the battle of words.

Baton Rouge had been as quiet as the Caribbean before a storm. In sharp contrast to the Senator's strong-arm return, was the simultaneous return of Gandhi-like fire-eating Bourgeois, his mustache shaved off, with a story of having been lost in the swamps. He said he was now back on the job and sentiment "was running high."

He was promptly arrested and accused of the injury to Alessi. Mrs. Roussell was detained forcibly in the Square Deal headquarters. She wired Roosevelt. "Plain-clothes men . . . threaten our women. Please act."

Up East, at the Hotel New Yorker, reporters swarmed around Mrs. Long, "a plump, dark-haired little woman with pale blue eyes," and her daughter, Rose, who resembled her. She declared they were just enjoying the city a few days while father was off to "the Louisiana civil war of words." Unfortunately the great war had interrupted work on his new book: "A Satire on Manners," also his efforts to found Share-Our-Wealth clubs. "But music is his real hobby," said Rose. "He can do everything, from composing words and the song to getting up and leading the Louisiana State University band."

From the Washington side, Long suffered a flank attack. To packed galleries representative Sanders (whom Huey was soon to try to implicate in the murder plot) hammered the Long machine with "dictatorship . . . coercion . . . intimidation. . . ." Baton Rouge who had "refused to bow the knee to Baal," thereupon found its citizens "stripped of their suffrage." Representative Fernández retorted: "Elections in Louisiana are fair and square." (Loud laughter.)

In Baton Rouge, Huey at once opened an *ex parte* investigation before District Judge Womack on the fourth floor of the capitol into the alleged murder plot, which his enemies said existed "only in his imagination," and was really "a build-up to destroy home-rule."

Highway police scoured the roads and by 7 o'clock had served 107 subpoenas. For the hearings soldiers with fixed bayonets patrolled the highways and every person who jammed into the court was searched for weapons.

". . . And God save the state and this honorable court . . ." read the clerk.

Long put into the record a confidential telegram sent, June 29, to Colonel McCormick, editor of the *Chicago Tribune* by the editor of the *Hammond Vindicator*, George B. Campbell, published in the home town of enemy representative Sanders: "Plans will be laid for the assassination of Huey Long upon his return from Washington Friday. . . . Determined citizenry vow to get revenge . . . bloodshed. . . . State-wide rebellion. . . . If Alessi dies, march on Baton Rouge inevitable. . . . 1,000 enraged citizens mobilizing. . . . Long's statement . . . that Standard Oil engineered Saturday's trouble, is denounced as damn lie over state. . . . God knows we need help of papers like *Tribune*."

Senator James A. Noe, a close Long follower, testified that spy Sidney Songy had been used to trap the conspirators. Taxicab drivers told of taking Songy to meetings with Standard Oil man, Fred O'Rourke, and deposed police deputy, Fred Parker.

Next Tobey LeBlanc took the stand. "Who am I talking to, anyway?" he asked familiarly.

"To me; my name's Long."

"I know of five Longs," said the witness, "Huey Long, Senator Long, Kingfish Long, Crawfish Long and Assistant Governor Long. . . ."

"This is Lawyer Long." The judge pounded his gavel.

LeBlanc testified about his participation in the courthouse and airport seizures. Numerous Standard Oil employees testified that for one reason or another they had taken armed part in the activities. E. L. McGee, courthouse custodian, identified Parker as the man who thrust his gun in his stomach and threw him out, that more than half the attackers were Standard Oil men.

Several witnesses named Dallas Gross, a secretary of representative Sanders, as a ringleader in the murder plot, but all efforts to subpoena him were fruitless. Fred O'Rourke, "chief of the Standard Oil Company's private police force," called by Long "the Standard Oil Company's chief agent," refused on constitutional grounds to testify.

Long said he had only one question: "Where do you work?"

"At the Standard Oil Company."

"Good as a confession," said Long gleefully.

Other witnesses testified they were in the citizens' army when it was dispersed at the airport. George Thompson, district agent of the federal Home Owners' Loan Corporation, testified that while in the courthouse he had appealed for additional arms and ammunition to a brother of sheriff Robert Pettit.

The hearing was adjourned until 10 A.M. and Long swept out preceded by a gas-gun and rifle squad and followed by his own bodyguard.

Up in New York, Mrs. Long and daughter were being escorted around Chinatown by Eddie Gong, secretary of the Hip Song tong. He pointed out half a dozen Chinamen named "Huey."

The evidence presented by the Senator the following morning in a tense crowded courtroom grew more dramatic. Former Baton Rouge deputy sheriff, George R. Davis ("Red"), confessed he had tried to kill Long on four or five separate occasions. He claimed he was egged on and accompanied by chief deputy Fred Parker, thrown out of his job on Huey's state Bureau of Criminal Identification.

Parker, a stout man, blue eyes blinking behind spectacles, took the stand smoking a cigarette, but refused to testify.

The sensation was Davis's testimony: Flatfootedly he said Parker had, last August 7, suggested he make some "easy money," $7,000 for each of them, by killing Long when he was engaged in his New Orleans row. "He said I was a good chauffeur and a good shot and it ought to be easy." The money would be payable thirty minutes after the fatal shot.

Soon after, while Huey was cracking his whip over the special legislative session, Parker summoned Davis, according to the latter, to the capitol. They reconnoitered the outside of the building, rifles in hand. Standing by a railing on the steps overlooking the governor's office, they took a bead on the chief executive's desk and waited for Long to seat himself there. Parker told him, "This is a perfect place to do the job." Finally, suspecting they were being watched, Parker called it off for the night.

Then when Long was getting in trim for the New Orleans

primary by sawing wood at the Maringouin camp in Iberville, Davis and Parker decided to assassinate him there. But on turning up the lane to the camp, Davis got cold feet. The Senator's assassination was postponed again.

"You don't know how lucky you were that you didn't come any further," remarked Long.

Another night Davis and Parker went to the levee along the Mississippi, intending to kill Long in his room at the Hotel Heidelberg. Parker pointed out the Senator's room. "I saw someone in the room, but I knew it was not you."

Long explained that the police had knowledge of the whole scheme and he had slept elsewhere. "If it had been Huey P. Long, what would you have done?"

"I don't know," Davis replied.

Becoming worried by the constant shadowing of Long's secret police, Davis began to tire of the proposition. Parker then told him the price had gone up—$10,000 for each. One night Parker and he went circling about the executive mansion where, they had been told, the Senator sometimes slept in a back bedroom. No opportunity presented itself.

Soon after Davis was fired from the sheriff's office. He received an extra month's pay and was told to get out. He left for Houston the very next day.

He learned later that Songy, Long's spy, had been taken on to carry out the mission of killing Long!

Huey tried to get Davis to implicate the Standard Oil. All Davis could say was that he had seen Parker and O'Rourke in frequent conversation.

Long permanently adjourned the investigation and never sought to punish anyone. Parker was brought up to Washington and given a job by Sanders. Later, in the Senate, Huey cried when criticized for putting Baton Rouge under martial law: "Why not martial law! . . . The Legislature votes a tax. They do not take it to the courts . . . [or] the people. . . . Men assembled with guns . . . to kill and murder. . . . Nearly all . . . were employees of one corporation. . . . Were we to sit there and have the laws . . . run with men armed with shotguns?"

But some people have declared the whole "plot," even the whole Square Deal movement, was a stool-pigeon plant by the Long forces themselves to provide a justification for the overthrow of local self-government in Baton Rouge. The murder plot, at the time seemed fantastic, almost as though Huey wished to pay Sanders off in his own coin for the Bozeman scandal in 1929.

Anti-Long citizens, appealing to Congress and the President to investigate "absolute dictatorship," declared "Long's charges of an assassination plot are recognized by every thinking citizen as an act of political showmanship and an attempt to intimidate by a frame-up those who oppose him, based solely on the perjured testimony of a well-known stool-pigeon."

If the Square Deal resistance was authentic, in any case their flash-in-the-pan, ignorant, half-selfish revolt, without any clear program, merely served to cook them crisper in their own fat. They played right into the hands of capable chef Huey from start to finish. But at any rate their revolt was not without its personal reward. O'Rourke, Parker, Higgenbotham and other Square Dealers have all been well recompensed by good federal jobs with F.E.R.A.

Baton Rouge was kept under martial law (still is) while Mayor Bynam Wade cleaned out anti-Long employees and the parish officials were changed.

Long did not use merely the mailed fist against Baton Rouge. Simultaneous to these maneuvers he announced that as special attorney of the Public Service Commission, he had secured sharp reductions in electricity rates to save consumers from 22 to 37 percent, about $52,700 a year.

Emitting another loud blast against the Standard Oil that he had changed his mind about the special session to reduce the tax to one cent, Huey went off to New Orleans, "to wait for overtures from the Standard Oil." His pudgy but mailed fist held an olive branch.

XXV—HUNTING ELEPHANTS

IN the Roosevelt Hotel, before a select audience, Huey spent his time gaily trying out campaign songs in preparation for the presidency. Tin Pan Alley. In a corner at a small piano a young woman played the proposed songs which were sung by a young night-club singer (whom I met later in Panamá). Huey's own composition *Everyman a King* was his favorite. Now and then the Kingfish suggested a change in tempo. "It was like a scene from *Of Thee I Sing,* but the Senator is no Throttlebottom."

An unfriendly portrait of him given shortly before this, pictures his "rumpled mop of red-brown curly hair, his puffy cheeks, thick grotesque pug nose, pale blue-gray shifty eyes, meaty hands, their backs matted with red hair, a raucous voice, less than medium height, a bulging belly . . . price of gross feeding, his periodic heavy drinking."

Now he had gone on the water wagon, for he was going places.

"Huey holding court in his green pajamas . . . in his bedroom, is the natural man," remarks Raymond Gram Swing. Green pajamas were his ordinary apparel for political duties at certain hours of the routine day. Sometimes he donned them in the middle of the afternoon, climbed into bed, and received a stream of visitors till late at night. In this garb and setting, he conferred with, or rather declaimed at, his henchmen. As excitement welled up in him, he leaped out barefoot, and giving his pajama pants a yank, paraded and ranted like an orator before a vast audience. Nothing mystic or trance-like (the only mysticism of the American is action), he would stand over his listener aggressively, shouting, waving his arms, prodding him with an emphatic finger, thumping him with his fist, whanging him on the shoulder, giving him a meaningful dig with his elbow as he turned away, leaving the other man's half-finished sentence dangling in mid-air, like a broken leaf in the sudden calm at the beginning of a tempest. Already Huey would be fusing all his talents to white heat on someone else. For he was a perpetual soap-boxer. He was a perpetual drummer, always selling something for a personal profit. The value of the wares was least important. He punctuated everything with cuss words and decided everything from a cow-pasture fence to the building of the town hall, from ticks to concrete for highways, from the pettiest patronage to major campaign strategy. He knew every parish better than its own corner grocery-store keeper. His mind riveted detail down to the wall of memory unshakable. And however insignificant any given issue, Huey paraded the carpet with bare feet, hitching at his pajamas, waving windmill arms, muscles bulging, eyes bulging, mouth bulging. Between verbal cyclonics, Huey climbed back into bed, muttering away half unintelligibly, until some other point was raised. Or some idea would strike, bolt from the blue. His mind would take fire; he would sit up, talk, hammer the spread, leap from bed, strut and stride and vociferate, aflame with declamation.

There was considerable order in it all, a core of cold logic running through all the apparent frenzy. After any conference, he turned on his henchmen and in rapid fire went over dozens of determined points, often as unconnected as a gravel road in Calcasieu Parish or an old document for the historical museum, and rattled off specific instructions to this one and that on this matter and that, jobs to be made, men to be appointed, contracts to be arranged, suits to be brought, wells to be dug, windmills to be erected.

Suddenly he crooked his finger at a husky but timid young fellow, a working type, who has been dangling his hat between his knees for two hours, ready to start up hopefully at the first sign of recognition from the Kingfish.

Now the young fellow bounced forward, bashfully, a bit awkwardly. "Say," Huey burst out, "who'n hell had those sound trucks painted yellow? People can't look at yellow sound trucks in this sunlight. It's too hard on the eyes. You gotta get 'em painted a dark color."

"Yes, sir, I'll attend to it."

"You ain't been paid since you went through South Carolina, have you? How much you got comin'?"

"It's $1,264.72, sir." He fumbled in his pocket, pulled out a much-creased smudgy paper. "I got everything down here, sir."

Huey waved him aside. "Now ain't that hell? I thought I'd have a little money to splurge around a bit this time, an' I gotta pay you off. Four months is a long time. How you been livin' all that time?" Huey had taken out a wad of bills and was fingering them.

"I borrowed the money, sir."

"You borrowed. Hell, anyone who can borrow money these days, don't need to get paid." The roll went back.

The young man grinned sheepishly, a bit alarmed.

"Well, here." Huey began peeling off the bills. "There's eight hundred for you. Get along."

"Yes, sir, yes, sir." He gulped. His eyes glowed. Before he could say anything, Huey was off to someone else. He went out with a happy expression.

"What do you make of that?" said one who didn't know the Senator well.

A pink-jowled politician twisted his cigar ceilingward. "Well, sonny, looks to me as though the Senator he done made him a deal."

2

Standard Oil came around—between encore and encore of *Every Man a King*. Better said, Huey came around. He agreed to call the special session to reduce the tax if Standard would fire every employee mixed up in the Square Deal movement and agree to keep out of politics. In other words Huey charged that Standard was responsible for his troubles, made them swallow the charge, then turned around and punished those he said were merely petty tools while giving Standard what it wanted. The "poor fools" of the Square Deal movement got it in the neck coming and going. But the federal government took care of the leaders.

This singularly unfair arrangement made, February 4, more secure than ever in his dictatorship, Long bade his people adieu over the radio and headed for Atlanta to tell the Georgia Legislature how he would save the country and make every man a king.

With him and his gunmen went Reverend Gerald K. Smith, a fourth generation preacher of the Disciples of Christ and revivalist of north Louisiana and southern Arkansas, who gave up his Shreveport pastorate to help the Senator spread the gospel of national salvation through the redistribution of wealth.

Smith is a very important cog. He is an attractive, heavy-set man, with a massive aquiline nose, blond boyish face, engaging innocent blue eyes, a winning smile and softly persuasive nature—most disarming. Not profound, a little slow on the uptake of ideas, not at all subtle, though clever at evading any real intellectual issue, he has built up a stock repartee for most platform and conversational contingencies. When smoked out of his stronghold, he is at a loss, tries to shove the conversation back to his set grooves. When cornered regarding less savory details of machine politics, he admits them with apparent laughing frankness.

But for all his good humor, there is concealed cunning and hardness about the eyes. When suddenly violently attacked for his position, he looks up quickly with sharp hostility, recovers, and a veil of ingenuous tolerance and humility drops over his expression.

He is an opportunist; complete, firm only in self-advantage, his consuming passion for power and more power. Dressed up in a uniform, Reverend Smith would look like a beefy New York cop or Goering. He has massive drive, is a bit bull-like, stolid, determined, shifty, but wearing the gauze of idealism, social adventure and kindliness.

He looks upon himself as a social dentist to pull the decayed teeth of social ills. No intelligent person should question his dentist. The patient should shut up and let "we," the inner claque of Longism—the personnel of which he will not reveal or the method of its selection—do the tooth-pulling. He fluctuates rapidly in his speech between the verbiage of simon-pure democracy to simon-pure dictatorship. Dictatorship can equally be the will of the people. He considered himself the third most powerful man in America—Roosevelt, Long, then Smith. Not even Huey was to be allowed to stand in the way of his Share-Our-Wealth movement, nor would he be permitted to betray it. "We decided Huey should make some money, so . . . We decided Huey should take this stand. . . . We decided . . ." The movement, of which Smith is the head, he presented even before the Senator's death as "bigger already than Huey." But Huey, as dictator, might have had a little trouble with Goering Smith. There might have been a purge some day.

Though less astute and less ready on the trigger than Huey, Smith is an even better rabble-raiser, a veritable Billy Sunday. In 1934 he addressed more than one million persons just in Louisiana alone. In South Carolina he probably did the same. He reckoned by February, 1935, that the Share-Our-Wealth Society had reached a membership of 4,500,000. July 15, 1935, he told me the membership had leapt to 7,000,000, which, even allowing for considerable exaggeration, represented the largest active political organization ever whipped together in this country. In 1934 he claimed that the public spent half a million dollars writing to Huey Long.

With the help of these clubs Smith and Long planned to whirlwind through South Carolina, and also to be able, with a week of campaigning in Mississippi and Arkansas respectively, to turn Senators Pat Harrison and Joseph Robinson out of office. Those gentlemen can now breathe more easily.

Let us look at the Disciple of Universal Kingship in a backwoods Louisiana village among the loblolly pines. The sun beats down on him and the five hundred listeners. An aide steps forth.

"Now all you niggahs quit crowdin' up here, stand back in the rear theah. Don't go takin' the place of no white folk. You all ah welcome to stay or you all can go on home jest as you likes. An' jes' don't sign none o' them Share-Our-Wealth cards. Them's fo' white folks."

The ex-reverend mounts the rostrum. Soon his stentorian voice, a warm embracing voice, rich-timbred, rolls forth. His reddish face grows redder. His invariable blue shirt grows wet with perspiration. His flailing outstretched arms are raised as in benediction. A side-swipe at the sweat on his face and again he whirls into action, his voice raised to a roar by the loud-speaker on the sound truck.

He virtually sobs. "All of you that ain't got *four* suits of clothes raise your two hands."

A thousand arms shoot skyward.

"I thought as much—I thought so, brethren. Now all of you that ain't got *three* suits of clothes, raise your hands."

Again a thousand arms.

"Just like I knew, brethren. Oh, blessed are the poor, but what a row they have to hoe. Now all of you that ain't got *two* suits of clothes, raise your hands."

For the third time all arms reach up convulsively, triumphantly.

"Not even two suits of clothes! Oh, my brethren, J. P. Morgan has two suits of clothes. He has a hundred times two suits of clothes. And that ain't all. Now all of you that ain't got even *one* suit of clothes—one single suit of clothes that the pants match the coat—raise your hands."

Once more a thousand arms are tossed aloft. A great shout, almost of thanksgiving, pours from the mass of ill-clad listeners.

And when pants-and-coats Smith concludes his two-hour diatribe against Wall Street and the money demons and the assorted enemies of Huey, he will have five hundred new members; five hundred gaunt, sheepish farmers and small-town rag tails will file up beside the sound truck and shove up their toil-worn paws to sign the cards that automatically make them members—no dues, no contributions.

3

Long now opened up his guns on the Washington bigwigs in earnest. February 11, on the Senate floor, he demanded that "Kingmaster" Farley resign as Postmaster General and as head of the Democratic National Committee, and introduced a resolution to investigate "general and specific charges of misconduct, irregularity, dishonesty and other activity" of the tamer of the spotted tiger clan. Huey's resolution alleged that Farley was implicated in a "wire service" leading into gambling houses throughout the country, that he had given $80,000 worth of new postage stamps to friends; that he had made improper contracts and purchases. It demanded that the investigation be provided with "any and all" reports dealing with contracts to the James Stewart Company for supplies furnished by the General Builders Supply Corporation of which Farley was formerly an officer (before turning over his post to his brother-in-law). Long based his demand on published charges that the Stewart Company, contractors for the $4,250,000 post-office annex and the $6,000,000 federal courts buildings in New York, received these contracts after bids had been rejected three times until theirs was lowest.

Farley was accused of using an R.F.C. $52,000,000 loan to coerce a railway president, John J. Cornwell of the Baltimore Ohio, to support Clem Shaver for the Senate from West Virginia; that when Cornwell conformed, the R.F.C. came across. Huey also charged that Farley had used his office to protect contributors to the Democratic Party from proper prosecution in the courts, that he had forced federal employees to put up political contributions.

"We can investigate Farley for a considerable less sum of money than was spent investigating me," Long shouted. "We ought to pass these investigations around. I don't want to hog the whole show."

Next day, hands in his pockets, red suspenders showing, Huey for more than two hours again attacked the "Generalissimo of the U. S. A." "I was called upon by the man living in the White House to go out and raise funds to put an end to this kind of slime, filth and rottenness in government. . . . What did we get? To get rid of the devil did we get a witch?"

February 15, administration leaders, hard-pressed by Long's attacks—for the first time they really hurt—decided to refer his resolution to McKellar's Post-office and Post-roads Committee, completely dominated by Farley, and give in to Huey's demand to call on Ickes for the records on Farley's business negotiations, though limiting the scope of the information demanded.

Expecting a stiff fight, Huey rose to speak, armed with clippings and documents. Among his clippings were several from the Scripps-Howard publications, which stumbled on to something that smelled bad in the building contracts. In its day that particular leak had been quickly stopped. A Scripps-Howard high up immediately found himself facing an income tax evasion charge. Of course we have no censorship in this country.

Again Long assailed Farley for his postage-stamp gifts and demanded to know why the little postmasters and postmistresses all over the country were being prosecuted for petty infractions and the Postmaster General was allowed to violate the law to the extent of many thousands. But before he got well started, his resolution was shunted into committee with instructions to call on Ickes, with a viva-voce majority.

Down in Sarasota, Florida, Farley, dedicating a new post office and vacationing, said curtly he was not taking Long's resolution seriously, but—apparently badly frightened—he shortened his Florida vacation and hurried North, arriving shortly before his mails delivered a broken glass chemical bomb at Huey's doorstep from some crank out West. The fifteen girls who wrestled with Huey's enormous correspondence were in the Senate lunch room; Huey was in New York; but a somewhat upset secretary, Earl Christenberry, laid it gingerly out in the hall.

For a long time it had been rumored around Washington that Louis R. Glavis of the Interior Department was prying into Farley's personal and public affairs. Shortly before the Long attack, Ickes had to apologize publicly to Farley for the circulation by his department of a reprint of a critical New York *Nation* article, issued (by mistake of course) from the office of the Bureau of Territories and Insular Possessions, headed by Dr. Ernest Gruening, ex-editor of *The Nation*. Despite this prior friction, Ickes (Progressive Republican) now made a firm united front with patronage dispenser Farley against Long. February 19 he flatly denied his department had ever investigated Farley or that Farley had ever sought to influence public works allotments. Asked whether he had sent the bomb to Huey, he punned, "That was just a hooey bomb to Huey Long."

February 21, Long appeared in the Senate with a bandaged hand ("a touch of athlete's foot," he explained) and held aloft a Farley speech marked "release, a.m. papers, Saturday, February 23." "I'm going to read from a speech Mr. Farley is making tomorrow night."

Gallery laughter was quelled. Robinson leapt angrily to his feet—"Unfair!"

"It's printed by the Democratic National Committee and I'm a member," Long retorted.

"But it's not released."

"Oh, it's released to me, and he's not going to use my money in that way," Long shouted back.

He accused Farley in his undelivered speech of trying to hide behind the President. "What I'll show in the next two or three days . . . will rock the capitol from center to circumference. I ain't begun to shoot from taw yet." He promised to show the Tennessee senators "something they didn't even know," and talked about "many bank violations." Reports were made by two government agents, showing 4,000 violations. Farley sent a man to Tennessee—

Senator McKellar interrupted. "The Senator is wholly misinformed. I advise him not to listen to any Tom, Dick and Harry."

They argued back and forth. Long shouted, "Let's have a showdown. Let's put the facts on the barrel head."

4

That same day Roosevelt suffered his second major defeat
at the hands of the Senate of the Seventy-fourth Congress
when it adopted 44 to 43 the McCarran "prevailing wage"
amendment to the $4,800,000 relief (slush fund) resolution.
And a Long coup did it!

The gag rule had been invoked to prevent proper consideration of the amendment. Nearly $5,000,000,000 of the people's
money for the Farley-Ickes-Roosevelt slush fund—and a gag
rule!

During the balloting the atmosphere was tenser than at any
time since the roll call on the World Court protocols a few
weeks previous. Now the count stood 43 to 43—a tie and defeat for the amendment. Long rushed across the chamber,
shouting that Mrs. Caraway, absent, would vote "aye."

Robinson challenged the right of anyone to say how Mrs.
Caraway would vote. Long replied he had just called her
secretary on the phone. Robinson, red-faced, annoyed,
dropped back into his seat.

Chief spokesman for the measure was bankers' boy Glass.
He denounced any doubt of the President's great purposes,
which should not be questioned. And so the fate of thirty
million Americans was put into Roosevelt's hands. How did
he respond to that faith? By putting great masses of them
on the insulting wage of $19 a month for honest labor on pub-
lic works, thus branding them as Chinese coolies and holding
their misery up to the derision of every Central American
banana picker. Union scales were cut in New York as much
as 75 percent. Even worse than Huey had done in Louisiana!

5

Long rushed back to Baton Rouge. With National Guards
enforcing martial law and swarms of plain-clothes men and
state police in the city, Huey—heavily guarded—snapped out
orders and gavels pounded in both houses for a fourth extraor-

dinary session. Just before the call for the session, Governor Allen filled seven legislative vacancies *by appointment*.

Eighty-six laws, sixty dealing with repeal of local liquor laws, the rest chiefly new taxes, started toward rapid-fire passage. One bill put out of employment Commissioner of Parks and Streets and Square Dealer, Powers Higginbotham. His duties and those of his seventy employees were put into the hands of a Long-appointed city councilor. February 27, the House Ways and Means Committee approved twenty-two bills in an hour. New Orleans was stripped of more prerogatives and the compromise entered into with Standard Oil for rebating the disputed tax to one cent (at the governor's discretion) was made effective. New state-appointed boards were to take over the police and fire departments of New Orleans, but the city's three-mill fire and police tax was ordered segregated to pay them. Huey's machine functioned without a hitch. The slender minority opposition was swept aside like chaff.

As a climax to the session, the Senator strode across the chamber and declared he was pleased with Louisiana, that he intended to run for governor. "Anybody ought to envy being governor of a state like this. Why, we've got $1,500,000 clear in the bank right now. I think I will be a candidate for governor in 1936. I will be a candidate."

"How about the presidency?"

"That comes later."

6

Back in Washington, Huey blithely announced Farley was going to resign and be replaced by Frank Murphy, governor of the Philippines—information from the highest authority.

Robinson at once jumped on him. He had information from *the* highest authority to the contrary.

Huey grinned. He'd had information from there himself once or twice—just whom did Robinson mean?

Robinson lifted his arm and crashed his fist down on his desk. "The President of the United States," he roared.

"The President is sometimes mistaken," said Huey, grinning still more.

He denounced Ickes' delay in sending the required information about Farley to the Senate—"something dead up that creek."

"A foul insinuation," retorted Robinson, infuriated.

But at last Huey had smoked the administration partly out into the open. Apparently it now decided on an attack on him from all quarters. Farley, Ickes, Hugh Johnson, Robinson, and others, all rushed to throw up a breastwork of loose-word sand-bags against the rising flood of Longism and a smoke screen to cover up Farley.

XXVI—PIED PIPERS

MARCH 4, Farley sent a 1,500 word denial of all Long's charges to Senator McKellar—a four-column spread in the daily press. The giving away of postage stamps was a practice of seventy years' standing. Ickes again declared his department had never ordered an investigation of Farley and that there was no data against him.

Next meat-ax General Hugh Johnson, dutiful mess-room phrase-monger, sprang into the breach by a speech at a Waldorf-Astoria banquet, tendered by that great organ of American culture, *Red Book*. Certainly no lamer duck could have been picked to ruin the administration's case and boost Huey further into the limelight. After a general résumé of the economic and political situation and many sweet bouquets to himself, Johnson spilled over in exuberant praise of Roosevelt and his "long-pull plan," but admitted ruefully that the drive was stopped; hoped-for benefits had "faded." Johnson's remarkable sociological explanation was that "the spontaneous co-operation of a freed people" had been "broken up into selfish warring groups by the deliberate design of business and political guerrillas." [Why?] More bouquets to himself and invented slap-me-on-the-back statistics, then he attacked the "economic kibitzers . . . sniping at the president . . . playing ball with dynamite."

Roosevelt was sane, but Johnson fired broadsides at the two "lunatic" fringes, the "Old Guard" trying to keep the government "in a cast-iron mold . . . a challenge to revolt" and the lunatic revolters with "emotions rather than beliefs . . . harp-of-the-winds upon which any breeze can play a tune," who did not "care a hoot about the essence of any government that blocks their desires." Huey Long and Father Coughlin, "enticing bums" were rapidly appearing as the leaders of the emotional fringe of "about eighty million abused babies . . . ready to strike back at disaster in any way that is shown them." These Pied Pipers were "piping out of the City gates with more and more abused babies at their heels. . . ."

For want of work this group "sits idly before its receiving sets, while there is pumped into it daily two ingredients—red pepper for its emotions, and for its hope enticing promises of money miracle—manna in the wilderness of despair—'like the coriander seed, white; and the taste of it like wafers made with honey—of which he that gathereth much shall have nothing over and he that gathereth little shall have no lack.' "

Long and Coughlin promised the impossible to abolish poverty. The final word on the matter was that of the Master —"the poor ye have with ye alway." (What would politicians do without the Bible to provide their economics?) And thus having glibly consigned Americans to perpetual un-American poverty, Hughie now burst into Jeremiah poetry:

"They ask us to go with them gaily down pathways by them called new, but that, in truth, have been trodden time and again in the world's history—but never to the rainbow's end they promise . . . [but] to chaos and destruction." After much meaningless rhetoric, Hughie called Huey and Coughlin "rash and murderous" tinkers, trying "a surgical operation on the human heart." He mocked Huey's $5,000-a-year-for-everybody proposal (the wrong figure, Hughie!). Next versatile Hughie, mimicking Huey's mimicking abilities, mimicked Huey: "Ahm not against the Constitution. Ahm not against p'ivate p'ope'ty. Ahm fo' p'ivate p'ope'ty. All mah plan says is tax 'em down—till nobody has mo' dan six million dollahs' income. Six million dollahs' capital an' one million dollahs' income is enough fo' any man!" (Again Hughie gets the figures wrong!) "Can you beat it . . . one million . . . enough for any man? But try and get it! . . ." After knocking down a few straw men and telling a "nigger" story, after some childish economics, Hughie warned that we are dealing with "a couple of Catilines. . . . These two patriots have been reading last summer's lurid story about an American Hitler riding into Washington at the head of troops. That would be definite enough to Huey because he knows what part of a horse he can be." (Humor.)

Already Huey was "the Hitler of one of our sovereign states . . . curious mixture of incredible mumbo-jumbo."

What was to be done? This is Hughie's brilliant answer: "Finish what we started and give democratic leadership, adjusted to crisis, something of a chance." That goes for everybody. "Bankers, businessmen, the unemployed and those burdened with debt and losses." The starving, bravely remarks starving Hughie, should "carry on patiently for just a little longer." They should tell off "the Father Longs and Huey Coughlins" and take "their religion from their church and their political leadership from their statesmen [such as "Sitting Bull" Hugh Johnson], and that they are not in the market for any shoes made by a milliner or hats by a cobbler or magic financial hair tonic put up by partnership of a priest and Punchinello guaranteed to grow economic whiskers on a billiard ball overnight." (Humor.)

Johnson might have added: "or their economics from a loud father-confessor saber rattling in a too big holder no longer attached to a uniform," but self-righteously he preferred to close with this drivel:

"Let us take our benefits with our burdens—the bitter with the sweet and—keeping our feet on the middle path between these two mad extremes—let us try to restore to the company something of the faith and spontaneous co-operation of a free people that led the whole world in the great war, from the darkness of disaster and defeat to the sudden glory of complete victory [what a victory!] and that started us so hopefully on our path to prosperity in 1933."

All hope, he ended, rests in the President. Then with the clap-trap jargon of a civilian general, he branded as "traitors" those "unable and unwilling to accept each situation as we find it." And so ended Hughie Johnson's famous discourse—a narrow Fascist mind arrogantly talking of preserving a democracy which he would be the first to betray. The difference between Huey and Hughie seemed to be that Hughie was not even a Pied Piper or a medicine man, but a big voice in the marsh fog—a very sad spectacle for the administration and a grand opening for Long.

2

The next morning Long took up the cudgels in the Senate against the man "retired from the army first and the N.R.A. next." His waistcoat unbuttoned, showing his pink shirt, and obviously playing to the galleries, hurling "ain'ts," dropping "g's," Long spoke of the "scourge of Baruch and Johnson." Johnson was the "hired hand" of the Barnard M. Baruch firm, the motto of which is "Presidents: you make 'em. We break 'em." (Laughter.) "He [Johnson] came from Baruch to Wilson and went from Wilson back to Baruch. He came from Baruch to Hoover and he went from Hoover back to Baruch. He came from Baruch to Roosevelt, and he went from Roosevelt back to Baruch. . . . We thought we were swapping from Hoover to Roosevelt, and we were swapping from Baruch to Baruch," a man who produced nothing, was just "a market rigger and a market operator."

Huey took up an article by Baruch in the June, 1929, *American Magazine,* "the Wall Street magazine of J. P. Morgan and Company," where Baruch said that the Liberty Loan campaigns had taught the people to invest, "first in Liberty bonds, then in municipal and railroad bonds, and then in securities of the corporations. . . . Instead of fighting the big corporations, the people now own them and enjoy the fruits of their growth." Huey exclaimed, "Oh, they do, do they? Now ain't that fine." (Laughter.)

And so Baruch, Huey continued, "this sagacious supplier of underlings to the departments of the government," says, " 'Don't fight the corporations.' " Johnson had been sent down by Baruch to get up the N.R.A., "a terrible sell-out." "And now they put Hugh on the radio to talk to us. . . . Is there no one left to speak well of what now stands other than those branded by itself as incompetent? . . . Is this the present predicament of this maligned order [sic], at the head of which I paraded with band and tom-tom the day of enlightenment, when I thought the Savior of humanity had at last arrived? . . . It . . . does dishonor to every cause I ever espoused to see the malefactors themselves called upon as the only persons capable to defame those who have undertaken to call back to sanity this administration."

"Where are we after two years?" cried Huey. "How many unemployed? . . . Eleven and a half millions . . . 54 percent less income of the agricultural people in 1933 than in 1929 . . . 19½ million people . . . on the dole. . . . The professional man, the doctor, the lawyer, the candlestick maker, who is not listed in the unemployee class because . . . never on anybody's payroll, stalks the streets today practically as idle as though . . . dismissed from the service of an industrial or agricultural employer."

Huey turned on Robinson: "No man shall go out of this Senate without a warning from me," he cried, advancing toward him. "Beware! Beware! If things go on like they've been going on, you won't be here."

Making a quick humorous finish he left the chamber in a gale of laughter.

Robinson leapt to his feet to attack Huey's demonstration "of egotism, of arrogance, of ignorance . . ." He himself preferred to back "to oblivion" than to depend on Long's approval. "He may come to an end which he prophesies for others." Robinson next rapturously defended his friend Baruch (on whose estate he usually spends his vacation) and also Baruch's economics, "not Long economics," but the "economics as we know it in the textbooks and as we know it in our own thoughts." (In short, as Huey pointed out, "market-rigging" economics.) With unconscious humor Robinson continued hotly that Huey's declarations that Baruch had been running the past three administrations and was running this administration was "another evidence of the accuracy of thought and speech of the present Senator from Louisiana." A comparison of Baruch's and Long's services to the government would "diminish the arrogance and the insolence" of Long's assertions. Rather childishly he demanded, "What right has the Senator from Louisiana to denounce his former friend, the President of the United States, in language like that? . . . Has he no sense of responsibility? . . . The manhood in the Senate," he averred, "should assert itself." (How many times in the old days in Louisiana had Long heard that faint note of defunct Southern chivalry!)

"Innuendos," continued Robinson, "insinuations and threats cannot prevail in the Senate of the United States unless we have descended to the level of mediocre degenerates. . . . Why pay any attention to the ravings of one who anywhere else than in the Senate would be called a madman?" (Sic! Sic! Sic!)

Senator Long came back. He denied having said anything "personal" about Robinson, denied he had broken Senate rules the way Robinson had, but didn't take offense. A politician, he had heard these things "many times on the hustings." He compared Louisiana at the expense of Arkansas. Robinson had indulged in "calumnies," saw "some nefarious motive in my undertaking to provide for the people in my state when people in surrounding states have not been provided for."

Huey twitted Robinson about his (Long's) power in Arkansas. Long voters were "loyal to principle," couldn't be "bought." (Loud gallery laughter.) Why didn't Robinson call him a dictator in Arkansas where he won the Caraway election, because the people's will was the source of his influence there as in Louisiana. Robinson nourished "a grudge" because Huey had exposed his corporation business. "Where your treasure is, there is your heart."

But out in the wide-open spaces the people knew what was going on in Washington and were not going to stand for it. "Take my word for it!" he cried, waving his hand toward the rear.

Senator Bailey rose slowly. "I am not willing to take your word for that or anything else."

Huey's face turned crimson. "The senator thinks that's smart. . . . Well, I bet you don't come back here; you ain't coming back," Long yelled. He said Bailey had hurled an uncalled-for insult at him. Bailey replied that Long had pointed "his index finger at him," and he had merely made an honest utterance. (What bright Senate boys!)

Repeating his prophecy about Bailey, Huey remarked, "You cannot keep these people starving to death . . . as has been done these last two years."

Jumping from his seat, Senator Dietrich tried to have Long suppressed for accusing the Senate of being guilty of "starving people to death."

Declaiming further about starving people and denying he had insulted the Senate or anyone else, Huey yelled, "Don't think I'm going to take anything off'n anybody! . . . Let the Senate go on. Let the senator from Arkansas insult everybody who dares to come here and point out the wreckage of Baruchism under Hoover is the wreckage of Baruchism under Roosevelt. . . . My voice will be the same as it has been. Patronage will not change it. Fear will not change it. Prosecution will not change it. It cannot be changed while people suffer. The only way it can be changed is to make the lives of these people decent and respectable. No one will ever hear political opposition out of me when that is done."

After some interchange with Robinson, Huey demanded to know if he had any relatives on the Arkansas payroll. (Long had plenty himself in Louisiana.) Robinson said he had, but called this inquiry an example of Long's mental capacities. He had never, as Long had done, sought to install a "puppet governor." He omitted to say that he himself is, in part, the puppet of the Arkansas machine; and he fell into Huey's trap. Huey at once reminded the Senate of the appointment of Robinson's brother-in-law over Huey's protests to the job of vice administrator in Louisiana. He kept his own in-laws at home. "But I am going to Arkansas next year, and I am going to ask for some of that pie in Arkansas. . . ." (Robinson has built up rich patronage there; Long apparently meant what he said quite literally.)

"Who goes around the capital with an armed guard?" next snapped Robinson. "It's a disgrace."

Long shouted back: "What about this thug [Fred Parker] you've got here in Congress? . . . Witnesses have said he

was coming here to kill me. . . . You want me to say I must
be murdered here?"

Sergeant at Arms Jurney approached him. "No, I haven't,"
he snapped angrily. Next Mr. Jurney searched the mysterious
Robert Brothers, always in the gallery, a gratuitous insult, for
he was known not to be Huey's bodyguard.

3

The following afternoon, between bitter personal clashes
with Robinson, Huey amplified the charges against Farley,
and said his own witnesses had been "hounded," their telephones "tapped . . . every device and scare cloud used to
browbeat and intimidate them." He went into detail about
Farley's supposed suppression of the prosecution of Paul N.
and Norman Davis (the latter, a relative of Roosevelt, now
Ambassador at Large in Europe, and with a not too savory
record of bond floating, etc., in Cuba) and others in which
the American National Company in Tennessee, the American
National Bank of Nashville and other concerns, after "hundreds of forgeries, erasures, false statements" had blown up
in smoke "with terrible loss to everybody except the Davis
brothers and their inside associates."

He would pry into the doings of the twenty odd concerns,
including six holding companies, "organized, combined and
affiliated for practically the sole purpose of transacting . . .
matters with which the United States government is identified
for the purpose of making private profit, a large part of which
inures to James A. Farley, in violation of four criminal statutes."

Senator McKellar, supposed to be investigating Huey's
resolution, and Farley tried to sidetrack the detailing of these
charges by denouncing Long for comparing Hoover with
Roosevelt. Long shot back: "Roosevelt has only a few millions more unemployed and only nine billions more debt than
Hoover."

Robinson said that if he had to listen to Long day after
day as he had, "criticizing and condemning everyone who does

not agree with him" (why not!), he preferred to get out of the Senate.

Long grinned. "I did not know whether I would run for governor . . . or for the Senate, but now announce that I will run for re-election to the Senate."

"God save the Senate," responded Robinson.

4

The whole country was on its toes waiting to hear Huey's piquant onslaught on Johnson. But with typical unexpected sidestep, instead of lambasting Johnson—"the late and lamented, the pampered ex-crown prince . . . one of those satellites loaned by Wall Street to run the government," astutely he seized the opportunity to present in detail his program for the nation—to probably the largest radio audience in the history of America.

Telling a black mammy anecdote about the defunct N.R.A. and "de wife of dese remains [Hugh Johnson]," he continued: "What is the trouble with this administration of Mr. Roosevelt, Mr. Johnson, Mr. Farley, Mr. Astor, and all their spoilers and spellbinders? They think that Huey Long is the cause of all their worry. They go gunning for me. . . . They are like old Davy Crockett who 'fired and fired' at a possum only to discover 'that it was not a possum he saw at all in the top of the tree, but a louse in his own eyebrow. . . .'"

Hoover and Roosevelt had both had the same projects of destroying cotton, corn, wheat, hogs and cattle while people starved, but Roosevelt had had his way, for two years "allowed to set up or knock down anything and everybody." "So . . . while millions have starved and gone naked . . . while babies have cried and died for milk, while people have begged for meat and bread, Mr. Roosevelt's administration sailed merrily along plowing under and destroying the things to eat and wear, with tear-dimmed eyes and hungry souls made to chant for this New Deal so that even their starvation dole is not taken away, and meanwhile the food and clothes craved by their bodies and souls goes for destruction and ruin. . . .

Is it government? . . . It looks more like St. Vitus's
dance. . . ."

He threw back the accusation of Fascist. "Let us look at
this N.R.A. . . . They had parades and Fascist signs just
like Hitler and Mussolini. They started a dictatorship here to
regiment business and labor much more than anyone did in
Germany or Italy. . . . Italy's sign of the Fascist was a black
shirt. Germany's . . . a swastika. So in America they sidetracked the Stars and Stripes and the sign of the Blue Eagle
was used instead. . . ."

He told how the little fellows were persecuted under it for
petty violations of the multitudinous rules. He ridiculed the
whole alphabet soup and again painted a tragic picture of the
country. "God save us two more years of the disaster we have
had under that gang."

His own plan was nothing more than "the exact provisions
of the contract of the Pilgrim Fathers in the year 1620 . . .
that they should have an equal division of the wealth every
seven years." He cited a long list of fellow wealth-sharing
philosophers from Socrates to Pope Pius XI and Theodore
Roosevelt.

He set forth his doctrine of restricting income by a capital
levy tax to a million dollars' maximum and a $2,000 or $2,500
minimum, and everyone would have a $5,000 patrimony. He
described cutting up "the two billion dollars" of the stock of
the Ford Motor Company, leaving $4,000,000 to Mr. Ford.
In such ways "the government of the United States would
come into the possession of about ⅖ of its wealth . . . say
$165,000,000,000 [slightly exaggerated]. Every family would
have a homestead, a radio and an automobile, not to be sold
except for replacement. About $100,000,000,000 would be
used up thus," and child labor and unemployment automatically abolished.

With the $65,000,000,000 remaining he would, first,
guarantee every person a college education. This "should appeal to General Johnson, who says I am a smart man, since,
had I enjoyed the learning . . . which my plan would provide
for others, I might not have fallen into . . . the dangerous

menace and demagogue that he has now found me to be. . . .
The billingsgate of all of the Farleys and Johnsons in America can't prevent the light of truth from hurling itself in understandable letters against the dark canopy of the sky."

He took Brisbane and Johnson to task for bearing "false witness," one that he proposed to give every person (not every family) $15,000 (instead of $5,000), the other for saying he proposed a $5,000 income instead of not over half that.

The country would have unheard-of prosperity if they could buy all they needed, and everything needed would be readily produced. When enough for a year or more had been stored up in advance, the population would tend to public works. Old age pensions would be provided "not from a sales tax or taxes placed on the common run of people" but "from the taxes levied on those with big incomes. . . ." The obligations owed the veterans would be discharged without stint. It was "unfair . . . for a country to begin its economy while big fortunes exist by inflicting misery on those who have borne the burden of national defense."

This Share-Our-Wealth program was approved "by the law of the Divine Maker." Leviticus, King Solomon, the teachings of Christ . . . Quotations. "Organize a Share-Our-Wealth Society in your committee tonight or tomorrow to place this plan into law."

In an interview the following day, Huey amplified his plan by saying wealth would not be distributed merely in cash, but in various other forms: automobiles, houses, non-voting stock, etc., etc.—just as soon as he "had driven the crooks out of government." He continued enthusiastically, "No, sir, money is not all of it by a jugful. We are going to redistribute in kind so the poor devil who needs a house can get one from some rich bird who has too many houses; so the man who needs a bedstead can get one from the man who has more than he will ever need. . . . As to the recipients of this redistributed wealth, they would file petitions . . . setting out their financial conditions and their wants and needs. Their cases would be passed upon individually. [This could scarcely be done under 240,000,000 work hours. Figure out the bureaucratic cost; also the gray hair and beards grown while this was going on amid chaos.] Communism? Communism? Hell, no! This plan is the only defense this country's got against Communism."

5

Such then was Huey Long's blueprint of utopia. The juggling of such astronomical figures sounds like the weird dream of a plantation darky. There are probably at least 30 million instead of 20 million families (as Huey estimated) which have less than $5,000. Crediting what little property some of them do have, at least $125,000,000,000 would be required. Examination of income tax figures indicates that the confiscation of all estates, say, over $3,000,000, would not return more than $50,000,000,000, *i.e.*, $75,000,000,000 less than the amount required. Thus wealth even on paper cannot be "shared" without far more drastic measures than those he proposes. To provide the $5,000 minimum in 1929 would have required the confiscation of all property in excess of $500,000, in 1933 of all in excess of $50,000, with attendant complete disruption and collapse of our economic system.

It should be noted that much of our total wealth is in purely latent resources, not exploitable for a long time to come. This and the 24 billions in warships, museums, churches, libraries, schools, public buildings, etc., can scarcely be distributed, nor the billions invested in highways, bridges, ports, dams, parks, etc. Taking out this wealth from the total, practically no one could then possess more than the $5,000 minimum, and even that might be hard to find for him. By what magic are railways, factories, mines, forests, highways, schools, oil wells, battleships, etc., to be converted into a house and lot, an automobile and a radio, and a bank account for any family in the nation? A levy on excess capital would not turn the trick.

How about distribution of income? If Huey appropriated all the income above one million—and once he had distributed the $5,000 patrimony there would be no such incomes—this would have given him in 1929 about $700,000,000. This divided equally among the 20,000,000 families that year who received less than $2,500, would have given each the splendid sum of $35. In 1933, he would have combed in $35,000,000 and distributed less than $1.50 per family! If the whole income of the nation, without allowing anything for reserves or for industrial expansion, had been distributed with mathematical equality in 1929, each family would have received around $2,700. Even at the height of prosperity, he would have had to confiscate all incomes over $4,000 to bring all up to the minimum. In 1933 such equal distribution would have given each family less than $1,400. He would that year have had to boost the national income from $40,000,000,000 to $75,000,000,000.

It looks as though Huey merely had a turnip on the end of the stick in front of about 7,000,000 people in this country to keep them hopefully plugging for him. His Share-Our-Wealth plan is either demagogic hypocrisy or else economic ignorance so abysmal as to inspire awe, a monstrous and tragic joke, which can only bring disillusion and defeat and stave off the real achievement of economic justice.

The first Kingfish in Louisiana was John Law, a Scotchman, who persuaded Louis XV to appoint him King of Louisiana and Duke of Arkansas (No Lady Caraway appears in the record) who organized the Louisiana Company and went about preaching that all men should be kings and that wealth should be shared. When the Louisiana Company became the Mississippi Bubble, 20,000,000 French would-be kings lost $600,000,000 and it took France a hundred years to recover.

Neither Huey Long nor anybody else can divide up wealth generally in this country or in any country that has passed beyond a purely simple primitive agrarianism. We need more wealth, not its dissipation or even its redistribution. We need distribution of economic power. We need the socialization of the basic means of production.

Or if we desire to preserve, if it be possible, capitalist economy and capitalist democracy instead of proceeding as we are into monopolistic capitalist feudalism with corresponding industrial serfdom and political military tyranny, we must rigorously control for social ends all monopoly wherever it appears, strictly limiting its profits; we must re-establish the right of labor to organize and fight its battle for shorter hours and higher wages; we shall have to socialize banking power and go in for social taxation, and we shall have to devise some means of taxing labor-saving machinery, without destroying the incentive for more efficient improvements, so as to take care of abrupt unemployment; and we shall have to indulge in certain other general reforms, such as making large unemployment impossible through effective social insurance.

6

Of course as vote-getting bait for a power mechanism, a cat-skinning process, nothing more astute than Huey's plan was ever invented. He was leading into a marsh by the dream of untroubled joy there to get our throats cut. Most people are dissatisfied but at the same time afraid of change. They want to have their cake and eat it too. Huey did just that— on paper. The social evils would be corrected and the capitalist system saved. Actually it would put a knife into capitalism so as to pick the watch off the corpse. But this component dissatisfaction plus fear of change brought him many adherents —a cure-all medicine when the patient needs the scalpel but is too cowardly to undergo the operation. As his plan could not be made effective, and the attempt to do so would merely have plunged us into chaos, he would have been forced by dictatorial methods, as has happened on a small scale in Louisiana, to push us more rapidly into feudal military capitalism, which has also happened on a small scale in Louisiana. Certainly many of the rich—Huey has numerous supporters among them—would rather take their chances with a purely power-seeking group, which invariably involves great corruption, as has also been proved in Louisiana, than on any liberal reformist tendencies, and much less on a social revolution.

And of course, Huey's plan hooks up the vague emotions, longing, frustrations and sympathies of the ignorant unemployed, the poor, the wage-earner, the farmer, the precarious lower middle class.

The demagogy of Huey's Bible arguments is diabolical. They are not legitimate literary references. Over half the adult people in the United States are members of churches. A large portion of them still ignorantly believe that the Bible is a book directly inspired by God, instead of being a Jewish-sacerdotal anthology. Even more of those righteous folk have never learned to distinguish between religion and economics, emotion and thought. To use the Bible, with its composite viewpoints built up over many centuries by a tribal folk, is treacherous for its effect on ignorant people and childish as an argument. I can prove Mr. Hoover's case by the Bible and I can prove Mr. Long's case. I can prove Hitler's case and King George's case or Lenin's case. To apply doctrines established for a primitive tribal people as a solution for the complexities of American life is too absurd to need refutation. But it gets votes.

Also, the vagueness of Huey's plan, and vague it was despite its dazzling use of astronomical figures in a beggar's bank account, has the further advantage that, not being specific, it permits of political trading with other groups. Originally Huey advocated a $30 old age pension plan; this now reads "an adequate old age pension." Reverend Smith told me, "We discovered that we were running foul of $40 pension advocates and $100 pension advocates and the Townsend $200 advocates, so we decided to put in the word 'adequate' *and let every man name his own figure.* This attracted a lot of Townsendites to us."

Also, looking at the matter with respect to the present administration, Huey had a permanent cudgel. The Roosevelt-Farley-Ickes-Johnson group have been merely supplying many demagogies instead of one vast demagogy. Unlike them, Huey presented a thoroughgoing diagnosis of our social ills. Having hitched this to an unattainable program, his program would have remained good for all the time he remained in politics and didn't get into power. No one else could meet it. And that is partly why Huey walked away with the de-

bating club show. After long indecision, though seeing in
Huey a force that might split the Democratic Party and
jeopardize Roosevelt's re-election, not knowing whether to
placate, pretend to ignore or fight openly, the administration
finally grew so nervous over the ticklish Farley matter, it
became so necessary to conceal that morass with a dust cloud,
that it stampeded into a cavalry charge led by the long-
sabered leader of the blundering six hundreds, Hugh Johnson.
Long mowed them down delightedly. They showed themselves
up far more than they did Huey. But in any event they kept
the spotlight off of Farley.

In such tactics Huey was by far the better trapeze artist.
Robinson is an old-style corporation machine politician of false
Southern dignity of just the type Long had learned to make
a monkey of in his home bailiwick. And Long was also a far
better machine ringmaster than Farley; locally he made fewer
mistakes. Besides, Huey welded machine politics with principles and a trend, while Farley has crassly confused the
whole trend of the administration, and today stands as a
living lie to all of Roosevelt's presumably good intentions.

Furthermore Huey was far quicker than his adversaries in
climbing down off the trapeze, smearing off the fake smile
and the polka dot grease paint, and talking—however much
the seasoned economist may sneer—what millions thought to
be good sense; for he was demanding, however impossible his
instruments, that economic justice and diffusion of purchasing
power which more staid economists—attempting vainly to
devise excuses and rationalizations for intolerable abuses—
have found no means of suggesting. Whatever his solution,
he—not the administration people—struck directly at the
major problem of our time. Long was therefore perfectly entitled to hand back the epithet of medicine-man to them. They
were more evasive than he. What Long said about the administration was mostly true; what they said about him. was true;
both were attacking the demagogy of the other; but in neither
case was the whole truth being told. But they held the breast-
works and that was a great advantage.

And when the war of words died away, there came forth

another thin voice. Renowned neither for verbal restraint nor wisdom, Anna Eleanor Roosevelt, cast back over Franklin Delano's two years for its most outstanding accomplishment and reported to the world: "The big achievement of the past two years is the great change in the thinking of the country."

She may be right.

HUEY'S nuisance value continued unabated. March 8, after reading into the record an affidavit on Tennessee bank irregularities, he started a filibuster against the War Department appropriations bill in order to prevent consideration of the President's work relief resolution until Monday, in the hope that support might be developed over the week-end for the McCarran "prevailing wage" amendment—being reconsidered—and thus upset Roosevelt's plan again. Shouting for recognition, he cried:

"I see by the newspapers that some votes are being switched on the prevailing wage amendment. Now, Mr. President, I don't like for them to go 'round here trying to switch votes without asking me about it. I might be in the market myself. . . . It is true, Mr. President, that I tell my people down in Louisiana that I won't take a bribe. But I have never been offered $100,000,000, as some of the other Senators [a thrust at La Follette] have been offered, for their state. I might weaken." He suggested an amendment to the Nira to set up a code to regulate the shifting of votes. "I'm a party man, I am— [Loud laughter from floor and galleries.] I don't know what party I am in right now, but I'm a party man, and I think we should have a code—"

Senator Duffey broke in. "Would the Senator accept an amendment to his code limiting the Senator from Louisiana to one speech a day? . . ."

". . . If I got what I wanted."

While in the midst of his short-lived filibuster, the Senate committee investigating the Farley matter filed in, headed by McKellar, to present an adverse report on Huey's resolution. After detailing the lack of concrete evidence and reiterating Ickes' whitewash, the committee branded Long's charges as "hearsay" and "muckraking." The committee particularly tried to defend Farley on the Tennessee banking scandal charge. But, all told, McKellar's language was that of a heated partisan, not the least that of a serious committee seriously interested in the truth. He left the definite impression that there was something very rotten in Denmark he was frantically trying to cover up.

Before Long could reply, Robinson moved adjournment.

2

For a brief spell Huey left the Senate in peace. March 26 he breezed into South Carolina. There, Gerald Smith and other organizers had been barnstorming with Huey's sound-trucks to roll up a local 40,000 Share-Our-Wealth membership. Before they finished, the whole state was eating out of their hand, and Huey arrived to head the final rally in the capital at the south end of the courthouse with two trucks to amplify the speaking. The governor sat on the courthouse steps to listen.

H. C. Godfrey, House member from Spartansburg, "leader of the textile operatives of the state," led in prayer (in the North politicians must have the Constitution and the flag on their side; in the South it is wiser to have God also). The platform thus properly sanctified, the Mayor—"100 percent Roosevelt"—gave the address of welcome:

Long was exciting "more wonder than any man in America. . . . He has gone the great Commoner, William Jennings Bryan, one better. His ideas, policies and theories are far deeper set on the minds of the people of this country."

Someone shouted, "What about Huey fighting Roosevelt?"

"Go to hell!" snapped the mayor.

At once Huey sensed he was addressing a pro-Roosevelt crowd. Directly out from the speaker's stand was a huge banner with Roosevelt's picture: "We love our president."

"Just bring that banner right up to the platform so everybody can see it and hear," cried Long. "I love our president, too. I got him his nomination. But for me he wouldn't be

President . . . and I'll stand by the party so long as it does not come between me and the people. . . . I may be contrary to what Roosevelt is doing, but not what he said he'd do. . . . I understand down here, in a Democratic state, you get about $13 a head [for relief]. Up in Michigan where they are Republicans, they get $283." He closed his customary concentration-of-wealth share-our-wealth argument with Goldsmith's lines: "Ill fares the land to hastening ills a prey, when wealth accumulates and men decay."

Huey went back to Washington, fought the New Orleans rate case all over before the Interstate Commerce Commission, compared Hoover to a hoot owl and Roosevelt to a scrooch owl, and headed for the bayous.

"A hoot owl," he explained, "bangs into the roost and knocks the hen clean off, and catches her while she's falling. But a scrooch owl slips into the roost and scrooches up to the hen and talks softly to her. And the hen just falls in love with him, and the next thing you know there ain't no hen!"

Down in Louisiana (Coughlin, April 1, was continuing his long-winded reply to Johnson) Huey began a new punitive drive against New Orleans to counteract the temporary independence it had just achieved through federal support. Huey had financial control of the city in his pocket. But one of the New Deal laws provides that the federal government may, upon application of the elected authorities and 51 per cent of the creditors, administer the finances of any city. Sunday, January 13, the city fathers and the bankers gathered all day in secret groups. At 8 A.M. Monday the application was made; at 9 A.M. Judge Wayne Borah signed the required order. Now he was handing down his decision on the proper settlement of the bankrupt city's financial obligations. He dismissed the intervention of the state and denied the application of the city firemen for a priority payment of $650,000 back pay from 1930 to 1934, but naturally allowed banking claims of over $7,000,000 (God bless our courts!). Huey for his part— and in this at any rate Borah's order helped him—was fighting for final control of the police and firemen of the city.

As usual, he thought in symbols of force. Toward the end of March he mobilized all officers and members of the State Bureau of Criminal Identification (the "cossacks") in Baton Rouge for gambling raids in Orleans and adjacent parishes. Four places were raided, including the Original New Orleans Lottery Company and the Turf Inn. Roulette wheels, a press for printing lottery tickets and other equipment were destroyed. Other raids followed in April. These raids, coinciding with various court struggles, were part of a new effort to further cut off all source of revenue to the local government and the Ring and frustrate Borah's supervision, and seize various functions of the local government.

The city was battling for an injunction to stop Huey from taking over the police and fire boards. "I'll fight with every power known to man, physical or otherwise, to retain control," cried Mayor "Turkeyhead" Walmsley on the stand in Judge Caige's court." . . . Grave consequences would result if the state appointive boards sought to wrest control of the departments from the present city boards."

"What would happen?"

"Chaos," barked the mayor.

But Police Superintendent Reyer (going pro-Long) cheerfully contradicted his pessimism. Efficiency would be continued under state control.

"Your Honor," federal patronage boy Edward Rightor argued for the city, in ignorant Southern verbiage, "this . . . case . . . can't [be gotten] . . . out of lawbooks. It boils down to a question of manhood. Just as the nigger government of this state in '68 attempted to repeal the home rule provisions of the city government of New Orleans, so we now find these white attorney generals coming in here to this court again and again and trying the same thing. . . . It is the intention of the state government to destroy the local government of New Orleans and leave the mayor of this city sitting up at the city hall like a dummy."

Assistant Attorney General George Wallace, thus subtly called "a nigger," said Louisiana hadn't yet come to a secret O.G.P.U., but that the Bureau of Criminal Identification would put its representatives into every police department in the state. "I don't care if New Orleans likes it or not; I don't even care if Winnfield likes it, the state police are going to have the power of approving police chiefs in this state."

Judge Caige, a bitter negro-baiting Old Ring judge, gave the city its injunction, but Huey's supreme court, a few days later, knocked it out. "Yes," Walmsley remarked, when told, "I heard Senator Long was down there writing the ruling last night."

Huey at once put faithfuls on the two boards, among others Stick-pin Maestri on the police board and Seymore Weiss on the fire board. He demanded the segregation of city funds— the city administration was living on borrowed money—to pay for the two departments. Walmsley refused. "Won't pay, huh?" exploded Huey. "Well, he may not be paying his own salary very much longer. He's just about done, and we'll probably take him out pretty soon. There ain't a business man in New Orleans wants him any longer."

Walmsley finally reluctantly had to advise his underlings that the new state law provided a penalty of $250 to $1,000 fine for any city employee who failed to segregate the city tax funds allocated for the two boards.

But Huey did not merely try to bludgeon the city. As in the case of Baton Rouge, he accompanied his punitive tactics with rate reductions—28 percent on light, 20 percent on telephones. In rare good humor, Huey appeared at the light-rate hearings in a natty gray suit, straw hat, and black and white sports shoes, and pouring himself a glass of water from the chairman's desk, perched on top of a table. The company demanded a rate base on $40,000,000. Long suggested $28,000,000 as fair. "But we are paying taxes on $33,000,000," protested the company counsel.

Huey reduced rates, reduced company taxes, patted himself on the back for his 90 cent gas rate of years before, then cut off $45,000 more revenue from the city by forbidding it to collect from the company for auditing, engineering and meter inspection.

3

The Kingfish also finished mopping up Baton Rouge. He refused to release last year's assessment rolls, thus forcing it into default on the parish school board loan of $73,850 and interest to the National City Bank. Police jury defaults went above the $100,000 mark. And by April 10 Huey's supreme court ordered the East Baton Rouge parish officials to seat Huey's appointed police jurors and turn over all funds and records to the new body.

4

Huey had other cards up his sleeve to block federal interference in Louisiana, but for the moment he hurried up to Washington to lambast Roosevelt, the New Deal, the Old Guard Republicans and some of the Progressives, including La Follette, for charging on the McCarran prevailing wage amendment.

"Cowardly Congress—Cowardly Congress!" he cried. "Get up, get up and legislate. Legislate on labor, legislate on the many things that are wrong. . . . Let's get this great wealth distributed."

Various senators jibed him about the Louisiana Legislature. He shot back, "Oh, Mr. President, when we pass a law in Louisiana the people know what it's all about. We write a law and say when a man kills another man that is murder, and he shall be hung. When this Congress passes a law, it says that when a man kills another and the President finds out about it, he shall refer the matter to somebody else who shall determine whether anything shall be done about it and if this adviser thinks so, then the President may decide to hang him."

Percy L. Gassaway, "six-foot Percy" with an extra "s" in his name, Oklahoma's cowboy elderly representative who cooks eggs on the capitol steps, called "militiaized dictator" Huey Long just "white trash born in the dark of the moon," a "tom-tit," *i.e.*, a very small bird that "tries to imitate the woodpecker" and attacks the "biggest tree in the forest [Roosevelt]."

Following his denunciation, Huey told Universal Service that his speech was his "opening gun for the presidency," and hied back to Louisiana.

5

With Baton Rouge still under martial law and National Guardsmen in the capitol, the governor issued a call for an extra session. In front of reporters in the executive offices, Huey shouted at Allen jovially, "What do you mean by calling this special session? When is it going to be held?" And to the boys, in raucous side whisper, said, "Do you know what the real purpose of this session is? It's to give the boys some money for Easter."

Simultaneous with the opening of the Legislature, state troopers dispersed a courthouse meeting of the still recalcitrant nine anti-Long members of the parish police jury. And during the session, Norman Bauer, anti-administrationist from St. Mary, introduced a facetious resolution demanding that the Legislature abide by the governor's martial law decree— National Guardsmen stood at the doors with automatic rifles —and petition for permission to meet.

The special session had been paved by a typical verbose Huey Long handbill alleging that the national administration intended to spend $170,000,000 in Louisiana, from relief funds for anti-Long political purposes. "TAKE THE MONEY AND VOTE AS YOU PLEASE."

The Legislature convened at 10 A.M. April 15. A few minutes later Long strode in. Spectators were ordered out.

Among the first acts was the kicking out of his seat of Senator Frank H. Peterman, formerly ejected by Huey from the speakership, and now one of his bitterest enemies in the state. He was replaced, like other legislators recently, by a governor's appointee! This was part answer to Hopkins's appointment of Peterman as Federal Relief Administrator in Louisiana.

The rest of Huey's answer to attempted federal politics-playing in Louisiana was found in many of the titles, which were now read, of the twenty-eight proposed bills. Huey was empowering his state agencies to supervise the expenditure of relief and P.W.A. moneys spent in the state on the grounds of enforcing honesty and protecting the credit and good name of the state. He threatened to jail Peterman if he didn't knuckle under.

At the same time Governor Allen brought suit to impound the $1,800,000 of P.W.A. funds just given to the New Orleans sewerage and water board commission, since then taken over as a state board, for sewerage and drainage construction. A restraining order to Allen was granted by Judge Prevosty.

The Legislature now created a special bond and tax board for the purpose of supervising the incurring of debt, issuing of bonds, the pledging of taxes and revenues by parishes and cities (Bill No. 5).

"We've got to stop them from piling up debts," Long explained next day to the Ways and Means Committee. "We paid 'em off once and we don't want to have to pay 'em off again. . . . We have got a lot of federal money. . . . If it is to be used for a good purpose it is all right, but if they are just borrowing it to spend it and throw it away, then it is a poor business."

Bill No. 8 provided for the supervision and state approval by the highway advisory board of contracts for the expenditure of money, funds and credit which may be obtained or borrowed from the United States government or anywhere else.

When it came up for final consideration, Rupert Peyton, Caddo anti-administrationist, declared facetiously, "This bill is harmless. All it does is to declare war on the United States."

"Wasn't the war declared first on the other side?" asked Wimberly.

"Did you ever see a dogfight?" replied Peyton. "Well, you can never tell which dog started it." He continued facetiously that he objected to the Louisiana people being contaminated by federal money. "The last time we fought the United States the damn Yankees whipped us. We didn't have any leader then but Robert E. Lee—now we have a leader and an army."

Long entered the chamber.

"About time you were getting here, Kingfish!" Peyton cried.

Huey grinned. He explained that the bill, which sought a measure of control over the proposed $170,000,000, was "just co-operating with the federal authorities."

Bill No. 2 required state sanction on all readjustment of finances of municipalities and other administrative subdivisions, and directly forbade the filing of any petition of any federal court for confirmation of any readjustment plan. This would put an end to the financial "secession" of New Orleans —the Walmsley-Borah arrangements—and was also a blow at P.W.A. control loans.

"We can't interfere with the federal courts," protested oppositionist Williamson.

He was told that the state authorities had a perfect right to prevent the cities and parishes declaring themselves bankrupt. And as for New Orleans, said Long, "We don't want that bunch of highbinders down there not to pay their debts and interfere with the credit of that state. Let that bunch of highbinders get out and we will put some in that will pay the debts. We have some highway bonds that haven't been sold and we want to protect the credit of the state."

The rest of the bills were to perfect Huey's control of the state and of elections, to squeeze New Orleans—a caucus was held to consider addressing Walmsley out of office—and to grab more patronage. Huey acquired power to hire and fire every employee in the state, including those in local governments.

As for New Orleans, the bankrupt government, April 12, had begun collecting 1935 taxes in advance by offering a 2 percent discount on all paid before April 22. As a result, the city, which long had had its employees on half pay or none at all, resumed full payment, except to the police and fire departments. Huey ran in a last-minute bill (No. 29) deferring tax collections until October 1. Expecting to take over the whole government there, he wanted funds with which to make a showing.

Bill No. 3 eliminated drawing the names of commissioners and watchers in primary elections by lot, and provided for their appointment, thus giving Long final absolute control over the counting of the ballots.

With a perfectly straight face Long declared that this made the new election boards nonpartisan because the governor couldn't re-elect himself; there was no reason for him to put "political friends" at the polls.

Bill No. 4 replaced the elected sheriff of Orleans on the board of election supervisors by a governor's appointee. Bill No. 1, further to break the Old Ring alliance with vice and cut off revenues, defined vagrancy so as to bring prostitutes and gambling elements in Orleans into the state criminal district courts.

"Why not extend it to cover gambling in St. Bernard and other parishes?" asked Williamson.

"Do you know of any gambling?" Long asked. (It was wide open in his parishes.)

"Well, I have seen the picture of it on the front pages of the newspapers."

"You had better quit believing the things you see in the newspapers."

Bills 17 and 18 formally did away with civil service for Dock Board employees, throwing the rest of them into the patronage hopper. It would only affect some twenty employees. "What will happen to them?" asked Williamson.

"If they are your friends," Long shot back ironically, "we won't fire them."

Before the Ways and Means Committee, Huey threatened to impeach Chief Justice Charles A. O'Neill of the Supreme Court, and Associate Justices Fred M. Odom and Wynne G. Rogers, if they monkeyed with his legislation. This came in connection with the discussion of Bill 15 designed to require the district courts to hand down revenue decisions in forty-eight hours.

"We need the money quickly," Huey explained. "It used to

be that acts of the Legislature were constitutional . . . until that crooked-legged Chief Justice came along and said they were not constitutional until they are held to be so." The office of the Chief Justice was a political outfit. "Three birds on the Supreme Court and three rotten Ring judges down here in New Orleans have got to be removed." The following day a general caucus issued a statement upholding Long and threatening impeachment if the Justices continued "such glaring disrespect of its laws and of the people's mandates."

Now that the insurance companies in which Huey was interested had gone down to shameful ruin, he permitted a bill regulating fly-by-night companies (Bill No. 20). He said sarcastically this would help his enemy insurance head, Dudley LeBlanc.

Huey rushed all bills rapidly through the Ways and Means Committee. One that did not meet his approval, he had laid over until Monday, two days after the end of the session, telling the members sarcastically to take it home and study it carefully over the week-end. One bill was adopted specifically to protect a forger friend of Huey.

The bills were all reported back to the House as a formality at 8 o'clock the same night. Some zest was given by the forcible ejection from the chamber of Square Dealer Mrs. J. S. Roussell, led out by the Sergeant at Arms as she waved a small American flag and sang *My Country 'Tis of Thee.* She shouted, "I'll be back." Similarly Representative Malcom S. Dougherty was thrown out of the governor's office. He was typing a resolution which Long had told him he didn't want introduced or passed. Long, coming in unexpectedly, strode over to the machine and yanked the paper out. "We only type things in here for our friends. Get out!"

Two guards at once seized Dougherty from behind. Struggling as he was yanked out, Dougherty shouted at Huey, "I'll knock hell out of you any time or any place I can get that close."

At the following morning session—Huey was present—all bills were rushed through rapidly. Huey snapped out whatever order occurred to him. Oppositionists had little chance to speak; nobody bothered much to reply to them. Mason Spencer did get wrought up about the iron-clad election bill, which he claimed disenfranchised the white people of Louisiana. In over-eloquent words which now sound prophetic, he declaimed, "I see a spot on the moon. But when you ride this thing through it will travel with the white horse of death. White men have made poor slaves . . . I know what has happened to men who have cried, 'Hail Caesar!' . . . The gravestones in a thousand battlefields will tell you that you haven't the right to sell the birthright of another white man."

And so Huey pegged up a few bricks more to seal up the tomb of democracy. And so did he carry on the war, not against the United States, but on Ickes and Farley and Roosevelt.

6

Huey's laws precipitated irritated explosion in Washington. Harold Ickes blew up. "We are certainly not going to give work relief funds to build up Senator Long's machine."

Yet he had given it to help Walmsley's Old Ring machine in New Orleans and without strings. The federal government had consistently given its money in Louisiana precisely to build up the broken-down old machine against Long.

Continued Ickes: "The Emperor of Louisiana is creating a situation down there where all allotments might have to be canceled." He said he would take back the $1,800,000 given to the New Orleans sewerage and water board. "Of course, it means keeping a lot of people out of work. Apparently the Senator is in favor of sharing wealth, but not sharing work." (It would seem, rather, that Ickes was keeping the people out of work.) And Ickes said, irrelevantly, "Perhaps the Senator knows how to produce wealth without work, and perhaps we'll have a profound economic and political theory announced after the Longislature has been in session some time."

In Louisiana, Long shouted back: "Ickes can go slap-damn to hell. When he sees what this legislation is, he'll have to apologize to us. We are trying to protect their money. If he had any sense, which of course he hasn't, or he wouldn't be in the cabinet, he would praise this legislation. There's one sovereign state left in America run by the people who don't give a damn about the combination between Stalin and the Nourmahal." He said he would answer the cabinet ministers and senators on the Senate floor Monday. As for Ickes, he would "nail his ears back."

As for the money given the sewerage and water board, "The court very properly recognized our men as that board. How is Ickes going to get the money out? When he starts that, we'll show him what a smart man he ain't." (Of course Ickes made no such attempt.)

Long added that "if Ickes and the balance of the brain-trust cabinet hold their breath until we send for them, there'll be several corpses. We are tired of these Washington messages. We are doing the United States government a compliment when we let them do business with us. We have a solvent state down here. We never allow a maturity date to pass for principle or interest on an obligation. We have revenues for more than we ever incur in obligations.

"We don't want the federal funds to be used here in Louisiana for political purposes, either for or against us! Neither do we want them dissipated through graft and corruption."

Senator Ickes came back childishly that Long was suffering from "halitosis of the intellect. That's presuming Emperor Long has an intellect." And he scratched $648,000 immediately pending for Louisiana off his list.

Huey won the argument, but Ickes had the power. What it all amounted to was the Roosevelt-Farley machine *versus* the local Long machine. The up-stage wisecracking on both sides merely concealed the unfortunate plight of the poor beings who urgently needed relief regardless of who granted it; they were the only sufferers from the feud.

As a matter of fact federal appointments and federal funds everywhere have been given to promote the Roosevelt machine —the greatest victor-spoils set-up in the history of America. And to many states where Roosevelt has been assured of support, money has, as in Wisconsin, been granted to be administered by state authorities with practically no strings.

In Louisiana, federal money from start to finish has meant dirty politics of the worst sort and its expenditure with the grossest sort of favoritism. The federal moneys and jobs in Louisiana have been mostly handed out to discredited political elements, gangster-types, vicious racketeers, race-track men, leaders in vice and shady business deals. Such is the New Deal as expressed in Louisiana. Its efforts, first and last, have been directed primarily in a political drive, utilizing vile and improper elements to accomplish the ruin of Huey, and, naturally, failing, despite its dizzy expenditures.

At the hearings in Washington on the D. D. Moore case, John P. Sullivan, John M. Parker, and Edward Rightor testified under oath that Sullivan and Rightor had been selected as federal patronage dispensers in Louisiana.

And, remarked Huey, "That testimony definitely put the New Deal's stamp of approval on the New Orleans vice ring as safeguarders of the people." Not a single Farley-Roosevelt appointment had ever been ratified by the Senate. When the confirmation of Rene Viosco as federal District Attorney came up, the Judicial committee voted unanimously for rejection. "Viosco was attorney for the Lake Pontchartrain Bridge Company, which sold millions of dollars of worthless bonds throughout the United States." *But Roosevelt gave Viosco a recess appointment.*

Huey charged that a principal realty interest in the Red Light district was the Queens Realty Company. The secretary and treasurer "is listed as Edward J. Pritz, who for years has been a lawyer in the offices of John P. Sullivan. . . . New Orleans' self-established dictator and . . . vice-king. The listed vice-president of the same company that rents the cribs is Abraham Burglass, who is in the furniture business. . . . John P. Sullivan was an associate of the "Queens Realty Company." He is the recipient of most federal patronage.

Thus down in Louisiana Huey's *American Progress* was saying: "And so a high-heeled 'rest' was prepared on the *Nourmahal* where Mr. Roosevelt fished and ordered the Share-Our-Wealth movement . . . blasted." The paper gave the connections of Vincent Astor, owner of the yacht, partner of the Rockefellers, big shot in the International Mercantile Marine, which company has mail contracts with Farley's Post Office Department, getting as much as $5,000, "to carry one letter to foreigin countries for which the postage is only 3 cents."

And so Roosevelt went fishing. "Poor field hands near and about Florida, some given a hand-out and some given nothing, were gladdened by the blare of Astor royalty." F. D.'s Delaware and Hudson railway stock "stood well in the market . . . another one of Roosevelt's sons showed up as a high-salaried lobbyist to skim off the treasury cream for a few clients."

Note the virulent and by no means truthful language:

"Roosevelt . . . having already installed a set of crooks to run federal work in Louisiana, who raked down as much as three-quarters of the Home Loan money on some of the loans made in New Orleans, a crook of that sort was needed for the relief work . . . H. J. Early . . . was removed and a tinhorn railroad lawyer, Frank Peterman, lately forced to submit his resignation as president pro tem of the Senate to avoid public exposure (really because of opposition to Long), was installed for that work."

Note the following twisted and, in some cases, unproven accusations:

"So the crowd is complete: Gambler Sullivan of the crooked wire-service; Paul Habans, operator of the crooked Home Loan outfit; Frank Peterman, the self-confessed resigner to avoid exposure; Arthur Hammond, caught drawing two state salaries and fired from both; J. Y. Sanders, who put over the $8.40 toll bridge that was swept aside with a free bridge; E. R. Rightor, in business with Sullivan in Red Light district properties closed by the militia, the concern known as the 'Queen Realty Company'—all now blessed into a covenant with 'Turkeyhead' Walmsley, and this clique forms the Roosevelt Boodle Brigade in Louisiana."

What all this really meant was that Mr. Farley and others were playing politics against Long with elements largely discredited politically.

But up in Washington, Roosevelt said solemnly, "Politics, so far as we are concerned, is out. If anybody asks you to discriminate because of politics you can tell them that the President of the United States gave direct orders that there is not to be any such discrimination. . . ."

7

Washington. The Senate. Long replying to Ickes. 5,000 persons, more than in bonus marching days, clamoring for admission.

Long strode in, banging the swinging glass doors back, and tossed his sailor-type straw hat to a page, to face a dense expectant gallery. He was a sartorial aurora borealis in a light tan silk poplin suit, a tie of mottled red and green, brown and white shoes and a lavender shirt with a check pattern.

Digging out a bristling array of adjectives from the depths of his explosive vocabulary, he hurled them at his administration critics and listed the prominent figures "in the third year of our reigning empire of St. Vitus's dance." (1) Prime Minister James Aloysius Farley, the Nabob of New York. (2) High Lord Chamberlain, Harold Ickes, the chinch bug of Chicago [this epithet was lifted from Jeff Davis, rabble-rouser dictator of Missouri twenty-five years back during Huey's youth]. (3) The Expired and Lamented Royal Block, Hugh Sitting Bull Johnson . . . the new oo-la-la of Oklahoma. (4) The Honorable Lord Destroyer, Hugh Almighty Wallace, the ignoramus of Iowa.

Shouting and waving his arms and rolling his head, Huey rampaged on to criticize the officials named for relief and other government work in Louisiana. The state would not "surrender its sovereignty into hands reeking with confessions [sic], fraud, graft and corruption." He described his new laws. And now the pronouncement from Washington "by the President through his Lord High Chamberlain, Harold L. Ickes, is that Louisiana dares not say to its own creature, 'There shall be propriety, honesty and integrity in the expenditure of this money.' That is the ultimatum."

He threatened another "Boston Tea Party" if Louisiana kept on paying federal taxes and got no benefit.

"And so the Chinese generals fought and the people lost their crops, their homes, and mayhap in some cases their daughters."

XXVIII—SOAK THE RICH

JANUARY 13, 1932, Francis Williams, still a member of the Public Service Commission, charged that Long had blocked development by a Louisiana company which had already spent half a million dollars on exploration work of the Lake Peigneur deposits, estimated to contain $200,000,000 worth of sulphur, in order "to curry favor with the gigantic sulphur trust of this country and to get more Wall Street money for his dummy candidates for governor and other state offices.

"The Texas companies—the Freeport and Texas Sulphur Companies—control 90 percent of the sulphur business of the world. They own or lease properties in Texas with an estimated total production of 84,000,000 tons. The annual world consumption of sulphur will not exceed 2,500,000 tons. At the present rate of consumption the sulphur trust has enough sulphur to supply the needs of the world for 34 years.

"One sulphur company netted $16,000,000 in profits in 1929.

"Is it any wonder the sulphur trust wants to stop development of the 250,000,000 tons of state sulphur at Lake Peigneur?

"Huey P. Long gives the people the headlines and the corporations the profits."

According to Huey's own campaign manager, Southwestern Gas and Electric contributed not less than $10,000 to his campaign expenses in the gubernatorial contest in 1924.

But if we are to judge by Long's radio speeches, his principal occupation in life has been that of making the "money masters" of Louisiana disgorge their wealth for the people. Yet strangely enough, in 1930, while 80 percent of the members of the Association of Commerce, representing all the powerful interests in the state, were against Long, Oliver

Carlson reports, recently "less than 50 percent are against him." In any case, he always had a power-drag there; its former president, Alfred Danziger, for years was one of the intimate counselors and friends of Huey.

Despite all the hue and cry raised by the utility interests, the banana and oil companies, the banks, there has been no concrete move on the part of any of them to pull up stakes in Louisiana. They are there stronger than ever. Huey's various occupational, franchise and rather mild corporation income taxes rather have been designed and imposed to force political allegiance than to establish "social taxation." Danziger easily got the manufacturer's tax postponed for eight months in New Orleans and hoped it would never be imposed.

The state income tax is nominal—it begins on $25 a week incomes and does not rise sharply in the upper brackets—a four-point spread, smaller than any such tax in the Union. No "confiscation" or "Sharing of Wealth" here. The inheritance tax, too, is low, and is in no way confiscatory to large holders of wealth.

We have already observed Huey's shadow-boxing with Standard Oil. Reductions of assessments on their properties have probably taken up most of his slight increase in oil taxes. A. D. St. Amant of Baton Rouge, in the June 25, 1934, issue of his paper, *Freedom,* declares:

"In East Baton Rouge Parish in 1928 the assessed valuation of the Standard Oil Company was $44,662,150. In 1932 this was reduced to $36,931,000 and in 1933, by a further reduction, to $34,191,000. In other words, a reduction of about $10,000,000 from 1928 to 1933 in East Baton Rouge alone. The total reduction to all property values in the entire parish between those years amounts to less than the reduction on Standard Oil property alone. But the average man's property was raised in value."

Within the same period, assessments on railroad property in Louisiana were reduced by $36,000,000. There have been various other reductions in public service assessments. We have already seen how in Shreveport, Huey at one and the same time from the Southwestern Gas and Electric Company secured a small reduction in the electric light rate and allowed a 38 percent increase in the gas rates.

Chief among his supporters have been the powerful cotton interests organized in the New Orleans Cotton Exchange, and directly linked with the New York Cotton Exchange. Taxes on the exchange have been reduced to an illusory amount.

Who were Huey's intimate associates among the wealthy and the heads of corporations whose property he proposed to "share" but who did not seem to fear him?

Locally, he largely owed his political start to W. K. Henderson, the bitter anti-labor iron-monger of Shreveport, who has placarded his factory NO UNION LABOR EMPLOYED HERE and toured the country, giving open-shop talks. At the same time he bitterly fought Greer, the head of the state A. F. of L.

Jules Fisher, the shrimp king of Barataria, known as the worst exploiter of labor, in his canning factories, of any man in the state, was an associate of Steinberg in monopolizing, with Huey's aid, 60 percent of the fur lands of the state. He put over, with Huey's consent, a vicious trespassing law which made it possible to wipe out the independent trapper, and he also killed the 8-hour bill for women in 1932—with Huey's consent. He is under indictment for income tax evasion.

Seymore Weiss, manager of the Roosevelt Hotel, Jewish colonel of the Fuehrer's staff, head of the Dock Board, member of the Fire Board. LeBlanc charged that assessments on the Roosevelt Hotel owned by the scandalously bankrupt Union Indemnity Company had been lowered, that Huey pardoned half a million dollars owed the state so that the hotel could pay off millions of bank loans. Weiss also is under indictment for income tax evasion.

Robert Maestri who, Mayor Walmsley charged, made a fortune from property in the notorious New Orleans Red Light district. Maestri is a member of the Conservation Commission, in charge of all the natural resources of the state, and under whose administration the fur lands were monopolized. Member of the New Orleans Police Board. He contributed thousands of dollars "to save" Huey, who said he would lay down his life for him.

Abe Shushan, New Orleans merchant, who became wealthy while supplying merchandise to state institutions. He is president of the Dock Board. A huge new airport in New Orleans is named after this distinguished citizen. He also is indicted for income tax evasion.

Luca Vaccaro, president of the Standard Fruit and Steamship Company, Vaccaro Steamship Lines, part owner of the Roosevelt Hotel, New Orleans (one of the largest in the South); and director of banks and other corporations.

In addition, his machine had the active support of numerous wealthy oil-men, lumber men, natural gas and carbon-black magnates.

2

How about the Power Trust?

For a time, as we have seen, he was allied with the power-trust lawyer and race-track man, John Sullivan. Shortly he made closer, better, and more personal relations with those seated near the throne.

1. Mr. Harry Abel, with whom Huey played golf, is the real head of the New Orleans Public Service Company, and a vice-president of the Electric Bond and Share Company. During the 90 cent gas hearings, he engaged in dramatic opposition to Huey, but the company got what it wanted. Whenever Huey has touched the rates of this and affiliated companies (still higher than in most places) he has given lowered assessments or other valuable concessions.

2. Rudolph Hecht—president of the Hibernia Bank, local official of the Public Service Company, director of the Electric Bond and Share Company, and president of the American Bankers Association—was an officer of the bankrupt Union Indemnity Company. Huey saved Hecht's bank, and saved him from worse things than the collapse of his bank. Hecht also participated in the 90 cent gas and other public utility rate hearings.

It is even said that Huey Long "imposed" Hecht as president of the A.B.A. There was great opposition to Hecht's taking over the presidency. His banking affairs had raised national scandal. He had come under fire in the senatorial investigations. Also, he is a Jew. Besides, there are dog-eat-dog splits even in the banking fraternity. A group of banks, two of the most powerful institutions in New York and one of the most powerful Middle West banks, were gunning against him. One of those banks, which treats its employees more ferociously than almost any enterprise in the country, was the fountain-head of Nazi propaganda in this country and started the short-lived Jew-baiting crusade in New York. Another opposition to Hecht came from the House of Morgan. The country was flooded with propaganda against Hecht. The newspapers were provided with photostatic material of very serious import.

The story is persistently told that Huey walked in on the banker opponents of Mr. Hecht, hammered the table and threatened to open his guns in the Senate against the House of Morgan and the others unless Hecht went in as president. In any case the propaganda against Hecht was suddenly soft-pedaled and he received the coveted post without further ado.

3. Mr. Harvey Couch, in whose private car Huey frequently rode. Cameramen who have tried to take their picture together have been smashed up. Couch has been frequently called "the Insull of the South," for he is a dominating figure in the power interests throughout the Southern states. Also, he is president of the Louisiana, Arkansas and Texas Railroad, which received reductions in tax assessments from Huey, and whose branch line from Angola is operated by convicts receiving no pay. According to LeBlanc and others, Allen, Long and Couch were business associates in the Winnfield Rock Quarry. His brother, Peter Couch, also close to Huey, lived in the adjacent suite in the Roosevelt Hotel. Harvey Couch was a Hoover appointee to the R.F.C. which saved Hecht's bank.

Couch and Long were very close to the Chase National Bank, particularly through Charles S. McCain. Huey's relations with McCain, as indicated by Senator Glass, apparently accounted for Huey's filibuster on the 1933 banking bill. Mr. Pecora, in the Banking and Currency Investigations of the

73rd Congress, brought out that Dillon Read & Co., H. C. Couch and McCain received a loan of $2,975,000 from the Chase National, of which Couch received $1,650,000—more than half.

Down in New Orleans, the Canal Bank Building, an affiliate of Chase National, had its assessments cut from a little over $6,000,000 to $3,870,000, or 37 percent, as opposed to the general ad valorem average reduction of 14 percent in the state. On that day Huey refused to hear the demands of a delegation of 5,000 workers asking for relief. Couch is said to have been one of the principal financial backers of Long.

How do these men explain their recent associations with Long? If Long had come into power, would he have confiscated their wealth? Were they going to get their throats cut or were poor folk backing him going to get theirs cut?

XXIX—FLESH AND BLOOD

ONE of Huey's stock accusations against Roosevelt was that he alone was responsible—having had his way in everything—for any failures. For six years, in Louisiana, Huey had iron-clad control over the destinies of the state—to do whatever he willed however he willed. By his own argument he should, despite the depression, have been able to show us a very tangible elimination—given his doctrines—of misery and poverty in Louisiana.

Obviously a single ruler cannot, beyond a certain point, run counter to the dominant economic forces of his community unless he smashes them. Louisiana is a monopoly capitalist and feudal enterprise. The standard of living there is approximately 60 percent lower than that in the Northern states; the percentage is perhaps even worse for the poorer wage levels. Culturally and economically, Louisiana is closer to Perú than to Wisconsin or Indiana. Its people live on a low Balkan standard, in some places are as badly off as Chinese coolies. Its population has never done anything important to emancipate itself.

But Huey did nothing important to change the economic set-up. What did he do within its frame? In 1930 he prophesied: "An unabated wave of prosperity will sweep over Louisiana. Growth will be almost magic. By the end of the year, I expect to see the whole state thriving and booming in every line. . . ." Nothing of the sort happened. Amid such frequent Hooveresque ballyhoo about the return of prosperity, the ranks of the unemployed continued to swell. Thus, before Long, nearly all longshoremen were employed; for years now 75 percent of them have been unemployed. Everything has gotten a little bit worse than in most places. Thus New Orleans, once the second port of the nation, by 1932 had dropped to twelfth place and is now tenth, exceeded for a while by Norfolk, Baltimore and Buffalo, and at present by such ports as Beaumont and Toledo, a patent absurdity, even for depression days.

His personality shines out in showy undertakings, but it cannot be said that he did anything whatsoever of a fundamental nature to improve, or attempt to improve, the general conditions of poverty and backwardness of the state. The record of his opponents, of course, was equally bad, though depression had not made this so apparent.

Louisiana certainly was a great field for Huey to till with his doctrines. Instead of that, monopoly concentration increased, workers' standards grew steadily lower; in some cases those able to earn an independent living a few years ago have been reduced to semi-serfdom.

Recently W. L. Donnells, editor of *The Federationist*, official A. F. of L. paper, addressed Long an open letter: "We are trying to get you to realize that thousands of people in . . . Louisiana are on the verge of starvation. . . . This condition has grown steadily worse since you became governor, and . . . you have done nothing to relieve it."

Child labor. In agriculture, in percentage of child laborers, Louisiana apparently ranks ninth; in nonagricultural occupations, it is near the top. Huey has talked overtime about the right of children to an education, but in few states are so many children denied education through having to toil in field and factory. In 1932 nonattendance of school children was higher than in any other state; the slight improvement since then, now being lost again, did not change Louisiana's relative position.

Early in 1935 Oliver Carlson investigated child labor conditions for the *New York Post*, especially in the strawberry industry about Hammond, and found no limits to the hours worked during the picking season. Child labor conditions there, within an hour's drive from the new skyscraper capitol, rivaled the worst in the country. Approximately the same conditions existed in the rice and cotton areas during the picking season. These children have been given free textbooks, but nothing has been done to take them out of their back-breaking toil.

The Association of Commerce of New Orleans puts in its bulletin on cotton (March 6, 1934) : "The picking scenes are delightful, too—negroes: men, women and children, with big bags slung under their shoulders, moving through the fields." Writes a recent observer: "I have seen the children on the great plantations from daylight till dusk. From late September until Christmas the women and children walk or crawl along the endless rows . . . a back-breaking task. At times they are ready to drop from the scorching heat. . . . At other times, late in the season, they have to work in the bitter cold winds that sweep down the Mississippi from the North."

It is legally forbidden in the cities to hire children under fourteen. This is evaded. No attempt at enforcement is made. Children, even of tender age, are employed in the cotton mills, clothing plants, laundries, factories, sweatshops.

Exploitation of female labor is severe. The laundry combine forced the minimum down even before the codes went out from 27 to 14 cents an hour, and this was violated. Regular workers get around $6 a week; wages as low as $4 are reported. The code minimum of 25 cents for restaurant workers had already been forced down to 16 cents with violations. In practice, few women get over $7 or $8 a week at most. In factories and sweatshops, as low as 7 cents an hour has been encountered. The condition of women workers in New Orleans, the best-paid city, is lower than at any time in history: wages cut, hours lengthened.

Likewise the exploitation of industrial workers and share-croppers has never been more abusive. Nearly every issue of *The Federationist* complains bitterly about lengthening of hours and slashing of wages. The Master Builders have seen their wage drop from $27 down to $13.20 a week. The Bakers' Union is practically smashed and wages as low as $10 are found. In the last two years the typographical union has seen approximately a 40 percent cut in wages, with few closed shops left.

The New Orleans Association of Commerce Bulletin, which

long invited capital to Louisiana because the wages there were lower than anywhere else in the Union, in its issue *Louisiana in Brief,* by Dinwiddie, states: "Louisiana forest laws are as complete and efficient as can be found in the nation." Actually semifeudal labor conditions, with armed guards, have long existed in the industry. This last year it was the most pathetic sight in the world to see whole families, kicked out of company houses, living in tin-can lean-tos, and virtually starving. The companies were wrecking their former shacks and selling them at $16, for scrap lumber. At the same time F.E.R.A. could not keep up with necessary building; it was, as a matter of fact, more interested in building $18 outhouses, often better than the leaky houses of the share-croppers they were given to; it had found no way of providing sufficient houses for people utterly dispossessed.

2

The Louisiana fur industry provides one of the most tragic situations in America today. The state averages more pelts than all the rest of the United States together, more than Canada or Siberia, over ten years, 4,000,000 annually. Nearly 150,000 people have been dependent upon the industry for a living. Formerly a trapper, by paying his $2 license fee to the state, could make $2,000; in rare cases, as high as $4,000 each ninety-day trapping season.

In a few short years, largely by the aid of several of Huey's intimate henchmen, they have been reduced from a free sturdy people to a frightful system of feudal exploitation. The trapper's life at best is one of excessive hardship in the bayou marshes. They are exposed to malaria, pneumonia, pernicious anemia, typhoid, floods, often freezing weather from November to February. During the season they have to live a hermit-like life. Only a trained "marsh-walker" can penetrate the swamps, loaded to the breaking point with 150 steel traps or furs, without sinking out of sight in the bottomless depths of fluid, gray, icy ooze.

In 1930 in west Louisiana, Morris Steinberg—a business

associate of State Senator Jules Fisher, a hand in glove man of Huey Long—began to acquire more bayou acreage, until his company probably controls 60 percent of the best trapping lands of Louisiana. In St. Bernard Parish, District Attorney Leander Pérez, a prominent Huey Long man, conceived the idea of organizing the trappers and charging them for the privilege of trapping, first $10 a year, then $50, finally $250 a year, ostensibly to buy lands. Instead, there was organized the Violet Trapping Company, incorporated in Delaware, behind which are the Mirandona brothers. Vast stretches were also secured through various means by Leander Pérez in a vast area from Pointe à la Hache to Delacroix Island, and the American Land and Fur Company formed. Another great landholding company tied up with Huey Long's henchmen, which started with trappers' contributions, is the Delacroix Corporation. The state lands, despite the protests of the trappers, were leased out to the Violet Company, and the game preserves were leased out by the state as a soft graft for politicians.

Thus all the trapping area in Louisiana has been tied up, and is now leased out on a fifty-fifty basis, with compulsory buying at company stores. The trapper also must sell his share of furs to the companies for 35 percent or more below market price and accept a lower grading, so that he loses about 60 percent of their value.

This situation, which the trappers did not accept tamely, led to violent and armed battles; trappers have been railroaded to jail and other abuses committed, and the company properties now operate under armed guards. An iron-clad control has been set up in the entire trapping region—about 7,000,000 acres. By means of a vicious trespassing law—put over by Jules Fisher in special session, Bill No. 78, with Huey's consent—the companies can practically keep everyone even off bayous, which are state property. This vast region has been divided up into three or four petty armed kingdoms ruled by guns.

Albert González, president of the Trappers' and Fishermen's Union, was railroaded to jail. *The Federationist* tells its readers to ask Huey Long "why his henchman, Sheriff Mereaux, agreed to get González out of jail if the union would make a compromise agreement with the land owners" surrendering lands; why Leander Pérez tried "to bribe González with a job"? etc., etc.

The imported scab trappers have no bed of roses. They do not derive much benefit from the betrayal of their fellows. Contracted for by the season on a fifty-fifty basis, they are taken out to company camps in company boats. They must pay back transportation. They have no boats, cannot escape if there is a flood. Often they and their families will have to live for weeks in water above their ankles. Into flimsy shacks, big as a small hotel room, are dumped three or four families: men, women and children. For the rent of these holes the trapper must pay $25 to $30 a season. For a dugout to get to his traps, $10 or $12 a season. A sack of sugar which sells in a store for $4.80 will cost him $8.00, plus 10 percent for delivery. Traps worth $2.75 a dozen are sold to him for $6.00 a dozen. I talked with one company trapper who had brought in four thousand furs, worth at least $2,000. At the end of the season he was $90 in debt to the company. A wizard of a trapper can now clear only about $100 a year.

If the trapper turns to fishing during the six months' open season, he can make at most fifty cents a day. A few cut broom straw at $22 a ton (requiring two days to cut, then drying, baling, and possible ruination from rain) and from this sum must be paid freight and commission charges. At Shell Beach we found trappers actually starving. Last year the Red Cross saved the Delacroix trappers from hunger. Many of them have been carried by the local storekeepers, but this credit is now cut off.

3

Long did not bring utopia or ordinary prosperity to Louisiana. He did not "share" wealth. He did not manage to maintain even the living standards existent when he came into office. Did he, however, ever help union labor fight for better conditions?

The answer is sad. Louisiana is little organized. The A. F. of L. holds the field, but has done little work, and has few unions except in New Orleans, Shreveport and a few scattered points. In New Orleans it claims 60,000 members, a peak figure, and probably does not have over 10,000 at the present moment.

New Orleans labor leadership has often been corrupt. The leaders have played politics with the New Orleans Ring or the Sullivan race-track faction, a few with the Williams independents. These first two foul alliances have not created confidence. For a good many labor leaders, Long certainly was justified in having less respect than for a good ward boss. Gradually, most of the A. F. of L. bosses went over to him. This is understandable. For instance Huey's most bitter enemy in New Orleans was the *Times Picayune,* which is not only open shop, but under the wing of which is run a strike-breaking organization for the whole country. This alone would have thrown union support in Huey's direction.

The A. F. of L. has also been debilitated as a bargaining institution by its cheap chauvinism toward the negroes. "Ask him [Huey Long] why he built the capitol with scab *nigger* carpenters?" demands *The Federationist.* Or—"We have tried to get you to realize the lockout of the longshoremen by the steamship agents was an effort to eliminate all *white* workers on the docks." This attitude helps explain precisely why in a depression crisis the organization has been so hard hit by scab negro labor.

In Washington, Huey fought for the McCarran prevailing wage amendment. *He thereby asked the federal government to do something he steadfastly refused to do in Louisiana.* Recently a delegation of organized labor called on Long to get future specifications for public works to carry a prevailing wage clause. Senator Long replied, "Why, I am surprised at you men. You should be glad to get work at any price in times like this! Do you think I am going to spend a million dollars for work I can get done for half a million? The

prevailing wage for me is what we can get men to work for."
That proved to be for ordinary labor 10 cents an hour. Only
a few jobs utilized union labor, and those were done by national contractors.

Nor did Huey put up one red cent for relief; he even had
jailed those who came to ask for it. At last, threatened by
loss of federal relief if he did not contribute something, he
allowed the cities and parishes certain new taxes for that purpose. But federal relief in Louisiana was never less than 98
percent of the total, and it has been entirely inadequate.

4

If no direct aid has been given to labor, in fact quite the
contrary, how about proper social and labor legislation?

In his earlier campaigns Huey had railed against federal
and state anti-picketing injunctions against labor; it was unfair
to tie the hands of labor in that fashion. This was not changed
when he secured full control over the state courts. In his first
legislative program in 1928, he promised adequate labor laws:
"it was as necessary to advance and safeguard the flesh and
blood of the state as . . . to promote its capital."

But ever since he got the legislature in his pocket, he passed
no labor law, no social legislation, no law regarding working
hours, minimum wages, child labor, women's labor. Instead,
he killed many good laws; for instance at the behest of canner
Jules Fisher, the eight-hour law for women. He fought old
age pensions which he demanded in his national program. He
was charged by the A. F. of L. with having ruined the compensation laws and made employment difficult by legislation
favoring the insurance companies. He killed the equivalent of
the 7a section of the N.R.A. He defeated the child labor
amendment when it came up for approval. He sidetracked the
full-crew railroad bill to cut down hours on railroads and help
prevent accidents.

There have been no inspection funds available for the state
Commissioner of Labor, who complains in every report that
to ascertain the truth about child labor, he is obliged to depend

upon federal surveys of his own state. Existing laws require that a child between fourteen and sixteen shall not be permitted to do night work between 7 P.M. and 6 A.M.; a child under sixteen cannot be worked more than 48 hours a week; no minor is permitted to clean machinery in motion—meager protection. The Workmen's Compensation Law does not even provide for the reporting of industrial accidents to state agencies, and Louisiana and West Virginia are the only two states in the Union whose laws specifically exclude all minors illegally employed from any compensation in case of injury. Louisiana is the worst of all. It excludes also those legally employed from compensation. Much criticism of this law has been expressed, even in Louisiana, but Huey Long never did anything about it; he passed no laws unless he was forced to, which did not in some way advance the political power of himself, his friends, and his machine.

Costa Rica, Mexico, Peru, Argentina, have more enlightened social and labor legislation than Huey Long's Louisiana. It is, in fact, in this respect, one of the most backward spots anywhere in the world. For anything similar one would have to go to the tyrannical lands of Venezuela or Japan.

XXX—BLACK UTOPIA

THE so-called civilization of Louisiana rests on a black cushion. The submergence and exploitation of the negro conditions all social phenomena, shapes all institutions and determines Southern reaction to significant problems.

The Louisianian does little thinking about race relations. It is impossible to "discuss" the negro with him. He has a few set clichés: "The White must rule. . . . The negro is all right in his place," phrases which mean nothing whatsoever in terms of social analysis. Pressed beyond defensive trite remarks, the Southerner grows angered, his neck muscles swell, his face becomes red, his violent passions are aroused. . . . And he lives in fear.

The negroes also have fear; but, being closer to economic misery, they are not so able to indulge that emotion. It is mostly consumed in the sordid struggle for survival. Strangely enough, despite negro poverty, the negro in Louisiana seems more alert, lively, significant, than the white. He carries himself better; he reacts in a more genuine manner.

The white is slothful, torpid; he drags his feet along the pavements; he is dull-witted; and his ignorance, being coupled with feelings of race-superiority, is a disgusting phenomenon. Ignorance, to be gracious, should be that of the natural man; in the exercise of such ignorance, the black in the south is far superior to the white.

Fear, if not always the product of not thinking, contributes to the abdication of thought. And in Louisiana, fear and kindred passions, which flare into violence, do so in a fashion more primitive than that of most primitive societies. Perhaps the introduction of human sacrifice à la Aztecs would be helpful.

Religion is an ignorant approach to solving social problems, but it does discipline passions. Religion, or rather religions, in the South, not really an indigenous growth, have, of course, bowed completely to the existing social and racial conditions. Thus, cowardly and contemptible as was the Ku Klux Klan movement, while it temporarily increased race violence, it marked the emergence at last of an authentic Southern religion, hence was the first sign in those parts of spiritual and social advance since Civil War decay. In other words the baiting and killing of negroes was beginning to become ritualized, and ritual is a species of law. Ritual breeds robes and hocus-pocus, and consumes passions, such as fear and hate, for its own mystic purposes. In another century, I thought, the South, with reference to the race question (though the nightgown is far from an esthetic robe) might finally reach the civilized level of the ancient Aztecs, with their ritualistic sacrifice of war-victims. Unfortunately the religious sentiment which leavened the Ku Klux Klan was obscured by its being a periodic wave of subtle fear rising into growing hysteria which finally reached a crest and crashed with the weight of its own insanity.

In Louisiana the negro is an exploited human being. He gets the raw deal in everything, from the worst beds in the charity hospital to the worst schools, the worst centers of entertainment. And his life at any given moment hangs on the possibility of the white losing his emotional stability.

Here then is the perfect tinder for a Southern Nazi or Fascist movement with its concomitants of race brutality, prejudice and violence. Unfortunately for any budding Fuehrer, the negro is not a privileged economic group as was the Jew in Germany. There is no race competition for jobs except on the lowest economic levels; the spheres have been delineated.

The real Naziism of the South occurred when the carpetbaggers were driven out. The South has been living under an American version of Naziism ever since.

This strains the terminology. The traditional system, prior to the depression, was, on the economic side, somewhat breaking down; Louisiana and other Southern states, for example, were like Cuba. There the importation of blacks from Jamaica and Haiti was gradually pushing the native white Cuban worker out of the cane fields and out of jobs. Because of his exploitation, the negro was becoming more and more a social strike-breaker, a lowerer of wage scales and living standards. Unlike Cuba, Louisiana had plenty of black workers without importing more, but the process going on was the same. In a free labor market the cheapest labor wins. Bad money drives out good money.

The Rooseveltian New Deal temporarily halted this process and buttressed up the neo-Confederate system. The slight raising of wages in the South by the N.R.A. codes turned the tide the other way. The poor whites, because of the arbitrary wage scales, were everywhere favored, under the Roosevelt New Deal, more than the blacks. And in this way the old cushion of black enslavement took the shocks of the depression. Thus if Huey, in Louisiana, was able to evade giving relief, it was because the depression, in its worst phases, has been a "black" depression.

However, Huey Long's program ran counter to that of Roosevelt. Huey's public works provided a great deal of relief for the suffering black, because Huey cut through the code wages, cut through the prevailing wage to get labor for the lowest sum possible. Thus the negro got more jobs with Huey's road building and other public works than did the white. Huey, in order to carve his name on bridges, roads and public buildings, and make his showing as ostentatious as possible, exploited human labor to the ultimate; he exploited the negro to the ultimate, and thereby perhaps gave the negro in Louisiana an alternative to lying down and dying.

Huey never used much white chauvinism and racial hatreds to feather his political nest, because it was not necessary; later, when it might have been convenient, he had his eyes set on the White House and had to cater to negro votes in the North. This tempered his whole attitude on the negro question.

Huey was not from the black belt of Louisiana, hence was without the passionate virulence of certain white chauvinists

of his state, but he did have certain typical poor-white prejudices.

If in the North he whooped up some black following, it
was in part because "the most bitter New Deal failures have
been in the use of differentials against negro labor." But Huey
did make some blunders on the national scene. In his answer
to Johnson, he made the bad break of saying he had received
a letter from an old "niggah."

Soon after this, Heywood Broun saw the Senator in Washington. When the latter paused for breath after a rather long
glorification of the personality and objectives of Huey Long,
Broun interrupted to say, "Senator, I met a man this afternoon who did not agree with you. In the diner coming down
from New York I got into a conversation with a negro waiter
who said, 'Don't you pay any attention to that Senator Long.
He is no radical; he is just a Fascist.' "

Huey Long sputtered for 30 seconds and grew profane,
commenting on ignorant people who couldn't possibly understand him. Heywood then asked, "Where is the negro going
to fit into your share the wealth plan?" "Oh, he will get the
minimum, all right." And that, remarks Broun subtly, "is one
pledge which Long of Louisiana is not likely to break."

Among the barbarous Aztecs where slavery was in vogue
centuries ago, no one could be born a slave, regardless of the
civil condition of his parents. In Louisiana, less than 75 years
ago, the Civil Code still declared every child of a married or
unmarried negress to be the property of her owner. When
the good master was in need of money, he often sold or mort-
gaged the child even before it left the womb.

Today, too, the negro child in Huey's feudal domain is
born with the cards similarly stacked against it. From the time
he leaves his dilapidated cradle, improvised out of an abandoned crate, until he is hidden away in his bare pine coffin,
the Louisiana negro, victim of a system of peonage and social
oppression equaled in only a few other Southern states, stum-
bles through life like a hunted trespasser, his gaze fixed on
two glaring warnings: "For Whites" and "For Colored." In
every walk of social, economic and political activity, from the

separate holy water basins in Catholic churches to the workings of the state's educational system and the various branches of private industry and agriculture, he is confronted with racial discrimination and hatred overleaping all pathological bounds. Here was where the bitter political differences between Huey Long and his old and new opponents vanished. Whenever the dreaded question of negro rights arose, Huey Long and his followers were good pat Southerners.

"There is no racial discrimination in my program at all," stated Long in an interview granted the editor of a New York negro magazine, but the briefest survey of social, political and economic conditions in Louisiana show that the direct opposite was true.

2

The full degeneracy of Louisiana is demonstrated in race-relations. Let us pick 1933—any year would be somewhat similar: *January:* Fell Jenkins (Aycock), charged with trespassing, beaten to death; three negro fishermen (Tavernia), no charge, hacked to death; *February:* Robert Richardson (Baton Rouge), charged with annoying a white woman (unnamed), shot; Nelson Nash (Ringgold), no charge, hanged. Let us skip six months. *September:* John White, charged with attacking a white woman, shot; Freddie Moore (Labadieville), charged with murder (the real murderer, a white man, later confessed, but was not lynched), tortured and hanged.

These cases got into the national records. They do not include dozens of cases that never see the light of the press. They do not include the record of negroes shot at from ambush while peacefully working in the fields or on the roads. They do not include the petty thefts of property, the intimidation and the brutal maltreatment that negroes receive in rural regions, of which nothing is ever told. They do not include the depredations committed by Saturday night larks, when the customary sport is for a gang of celebrating drunks to go into "nigger" town and "shoot it up," break up negro restaurants and cafés, insult black women, and commit any brutalities that come into their heads.

We have already considered the ill-treatment accorded negroes in the Charity Hospital; the obstetrics ward would be a disgrace to a Quechua Indian village. Consider the negro in jail. The following incident is unusual only for being extreme!

Saturday, May 5, 1928, a negress, sent to jail for thirty days by Recorder Paul LeBlanc for having no visible means of support, had to be taken to charity hospital with a fractured skull. As often customary, the daily paper reporting it gave the name of neither the abusive white nor of the black victim. "A short, bald-headed policeman heard her crying in the cell, entered it, knocked her down, threw water on her face, beat her on the head with a bucket and then kicked her in the stomach. Four deputies went to get sentenced woman, found her lying unconscious on the cell floor."

August 10, 1934, in Bastrop, a mob of 3,000 stormed the Morehouse Parish jail and dragged out Andrew McCloud, a twenty-six-year-old negro, suspected of attempting to assault a white girl (name unknown). Blood gushing from a knife wound in his neck, his body crumpled from a beating, in the public square his inert form was hoisted to the top of an automobile, a rope tied about his neck, and the car driven from under.

The jail was undefended. Chief of Police B. C. Walton was "out of town." Sheriff Carpenter said he failed to recognize any of the mob.

October 11, the merchants and land-owners and an official of Labadieville and the surrounding country lynched Freddie Moore and Norman Thibodeaux, on the charge of having murdered a white girl. Moore is dead. Thibodeaux is one of the few negroes ever to escape alive from a lynching. Thibodeaux was yanked out of bed, tortured, and hung alongside of the already dead Moore from the railroad bridge. After Thibodeaux was cut down at the behest of two white railway workers, he was taken out into the country and shot down, and, sure he was dead, his assailants left him lying in the cane field.

Thibodeaux made his way to the home of negroes he knew.

They feared to dress his fearful wounds. They feared even to let him stay in the house.

"The sheriff will come and hang us all if we keep you here," they told him.

Thibodeaux made his way to New Orleans where he went to Flint-Goodridge Hospital, a negro institution attached to Dillard University.

The New Orleans police held Thibodeaux five days, waiting for the lynchers of Labadieville to take him back and string him up again.

But the stepfather of the murdered girl by that time had confessed to the murder.

Thibodeaux was born and lived in Thibodaux, a little village where he says "people live in old wooden houses filled with holes in the roof and their walls are papered inside of the house to keep them from freezing to death. They work for small wages in the field. The white people's houses are very miserable too. Some live better than others. But they have a hard time to keep on going, trying to live too.

"The owners of the land work their people hard and give them little money. Not enough to live on. Some of them work hungry till they fall out."

As a youth, he drifted around at odd jobs: "After I got tired of going over the country and seeing the people that are against the workers, I came back after being away thirteen months and got a job working on the river front carrying bananas. It was hard work. I quit that job and started working for a paving contractor. It was rolling concrete all day long for three dollars and a half a week. I stood it for a long time, then I quit and went to see my grandmother that lived seventy miles from New Orleans. It was a place where they raised sugar cane. People worked hard there. They get up at four o'clock in the morning to go to work and work till night for a little bit of money, and they are afraid to say anything about it. They have no other work, so they are forced to take the hardship and danger that's put upon them, and if one of them quit, his whole family would starve, because they have to work for what they get.

"I can never forget that terrible night, October 11, in which that mob took Freddie Moore's life, and nearly took mine. The men who forced their way into my grandmother's house, they whip me with their guns and fists and torture me. That night will be long remembered for what they did to me. I think of it every day, dream of it every night. It never gets off my mind. Looks like I can see that poor boy hanging by his neck—killed for a crime he did not commit—murdered. . . ."

Early in January of this year a gang of eight men entered the Washington Parish jail where negro Jerome Wilson, convicted, with mob duress on the jury, of shooting a sheriff with a shot-gun (the evidence showed a pistol wound) was waiting the appeal of his case. The men began sawing the lock on the cell. Jerome started screaming. The lynchers straightway riddled him with bullets. Once in the cell, one man beat the prisoner over the head with a hammer until he was lifeless.

After the lynching, Sheriff J. L. Brock stated:

"There wasn't any lynching. There were just about six or eight men who were going about their business."

Following the lynching, the following telegram was sent to Huey Long:

"You have opportunity now to make good on your statement in the Senate last spring when Costigan-Wagner federal anti-lynching bill was being discussed that you could control lynching in Louisiana and that you believed the states could wipe out this crime. Stop. National Association for Advancement of Colored People calls upon you as the real head of government in the state of Louisiana to run down and punish lynchers of Jerome Wilson."

Huey did not reply and in February, 1935, Roy Wilkins, editor of *The Crisis*, interviewed him on the case. Long said:

"This one slipped up. I can't do nothing about it. No, sir. Can't do the dead niggah no good. Why, if I tried to go after those lynchers it might cause a hundred more niggahs to be killed.

". . . There are some things even Huey Long can't get

away with. We'll just have to watch out for the next one. Anyway, that niggah was guilty of cold-blooded murder.

". . . Sure we got a law which allows a reversal on technical points. This niggah got hold of a smart lawyer somewhere and proved a technicality. He was guilty as hell."

3

September 8, 1924, Manchuria declared war on Pekin. In Louisiana the papers told of a negro accidentally shot, who when taken to the Charity Hospital said he was glad for the bullet, as it gave him something to eat.

Never since the days of chattel slavery have the conditions of the negro share-croppers been worse than they are today in the state of Louisiana. Share-croppers have been forced to become day laborers on hundreds of plantations, getting 65 cents for a 12-hour day, working from "dark to dark."

Cash is not paid to the share-cropper, and he is compelled to buy what food the planter allots him on credit at the plantation. This includes only the barest of necessities at exorbitant prices, and tobacco, movies, books, recreation, etc., are entirely out of the question.

Wages of negroes in Louisiana are even more pitifully low than for whites. It is difficult and dangerous to try to obtain exact information. Only recently a Chicago negro newspaper man was threatened with death in the timber section if he did not cease questioning negroes regarding hours, wages and living conditions in the saw mills, where 60 percent of the workers are black. (Louisiana has the largest sawmill in the world, and the output of the state is exceeded only by that of Oregon and Washington.)

The bulk of domestic help in New Orleans is negro—an average wage of less than $4.00 a week.

He is even discriminated against by his white working comrades. Negro labor is practically unorganized, the strongest union being that of the Independent Longshoremen's Association of New Orleans, a company affair. At one time negroes in New Orleans had their own central trades and labor council affiliated with the A. F. of L. But no negro delegates can attend the meetings of the white Central Trades and Labor Council.

Last year a study of 523 negro households was made by the Social Service Department of the Flint-Goodridge Hospital and graduate students and faculty members of Tulane University. In the district surveyed—typical of negro residence districts in New Orleans—the streets, except for the main thoroughfare, were unpaved, with such deep ruts transit was impossible. The report adds: "The city street department at various times seeks to remedy this by dumping on the roads trash, garbage and tin cans. The trash is often stacked 3 to 4 feet deep, and although it is supposed to have been put through incinerators, unburned garbage and dead animals are often uncovered." Elongated one- and two-story tenement buildings are the common type of dwelling with such names as The Pepper, The Yellow Dog, Lizard, The Ark, The Red Devil. A typical one is divided into 36 rooms. Most families rent only one room. There are four toilets in the front yard for all occupants. On the lower gallery are six sinks with running cold water. There is no electricity or gas. Thirty-six buildings in this district had been condemned, but only eight were actually removed.

4

Illiteracy. The 1920 census showed that Louisiana had the highest percentage of illiteracy, both white and negro, in the United States. Negro illiteracy was 38.5 percent. In the 1930 census negro illiteracy had dropped to 23.3 percent. Declining school facilities make it doubtful whether this gain will be maintained. Most of the improvement, incidentally, occurred before Long took office. South Carolina, by that year, was then worse than Louisiana. Though Louisiana's black population represents 36.9 percent of the whole, negro illiteracy is over 300 percent higher than that of the whites.

According to the 1932-33 Louisiana State School Board report an average of $44.98 was spent for each white pupil and $7.88 for each black pupil, though the constitution states an equal amount shall be spent upon both races; the minimum expenditure set per pupil is $12. During 1932-33, average number days taught in white schools was 156 (a decline of 20 days over the previous year) and in negro schools 100. Whereas $50,384.88 was spent on material and supplies for teaching in white schools, negro schools received $6,116.58. In hundreds of negro schools throughout Louisiana there are no desks, the pupils writing on their laps. Teachers also complain about the constant shortage of paper and pencils. Few negro schools have toilet facilities in the building. White teachers' salary averaged $622 per annum, black teachers', $219.

School libraries in white schools got $30,560.89; negro schools $818.20. Huey was always talking of how he provided busses to take negro children to school, which, owing to the unfavorable location of schools for negroes, are much more necessary than for white children. In 1932-33, 3,388 busses transported 113,377 white children, including (this is anti-constitutional) 3,328 children of private, mostly sectarian, schools to and from schools. Nine busses in the whole state transported 305 negro children. $1,521,604.34 was spent to transport white children; $2,549.65 for negro children.

"Negro educational facilities are abundantly taken care of in New Orleans," says an *Association of Commerce Bulletin* (May 30, 1934). But if conditions in negro schools in the rural parishes are appalling, they are little better in New Orleans. That city, with 130,000 negroes, boasts one four-year high school. And what a school! "McDonogh 35"—an old brick structure considered unsafe for white children, gloomy rooms, the wooden walls creaky, but the corridors are packed with negro youth hungry for knowledge.

The J. W. Hoffman Junior High School for negroes has 1,250 children enrolled, with 26 teachers. There are 21 rooms. The principal, L. D. Crocker, reported, at risk of his job:

"There is no phase of our school which is as constant a source of dismay to us as is the physical plant itself. . . . Somehow, in some way, we must have relief. . . . Insecurely fastened doors, except when locked, due to the rotted condition of the wood, are generally without panes, broken from

the slamming of the doors; the roof leaks like a sieve. . . .
The flooring in many rooms is badly rotted, large holes being
in evidence. . . . It is a constant fear that some child will
fall through and break a limb." Even desks or chairs to sit
on were lacking.

The grammar schools are worse, badly located, many children have to walk through the Red Light district. Thus in
the J. P. Benjamin School district, a survey last December
showed that although 1,292 children live in the district as
opposed to 77 white children, the only school was for whites.
At Lafon School inadequate police protection is provided,
undesirables are allowed to "hang around" and dope fiends
harassing the neighborhoods with their trade, go after the
children.

In various negro schools one teacher takes care of from
124 to 150 children. Accidents are common from collapse of
parts of buildings. Last year 8 children were seriously injured
when the stairs and fire escape at the Arthur P. Williams
School collapsed. This school is surrounded by brothels.

Not a single vocational or trade school for negroes is found
in New Orleans. Negroes pay taxes for the white public commercial schools, but must themselves pay tuition to private
commercial schools where they must also purchase their own
books. New Orleans negroes cannot boast a single park worthy
the name, no swimming pool, no gymnasium. Their taxes help
sustain the main park, City Park, but no negro is allowed in
it. Their only gathering place, by custom, not legal fiat, is a
dreary two-blocks square Shakespeare Park in the heart of
the negro section. The only negro playground in use is that
at Lafon, badly in need of equipment. Similarly, negroes,
though they pay taxes for it, are mostly banned from the
New Orleans Municipal Auditorium. When they have been
sold some of the poorest seats, as during the visit of the
European Passion Players, horrified white protests have gone
up. Whenever the negroes have sought to lease the auditorium,
the price has been made prohibitive.

In school the negro children are required to sing the state
anthem:

"My Louisiana, dear Louisiana,
Down where the roses ever bloom."

5

In his campaign speeches Huey frequently resorted to the cheap practice of low-grade politicians of casting slurs on the negroes and implying that his opponent was a "nigger lover."

When he was supporting Ransdell for the Senate against Mayor L. E. Thomas, he got off the following ill-mannered falsity:

"For the first time in many years, Mr. Thomas furnishes us with the example of a native white Louisianian who would like to go to the United States Senate on help furnished by a negro Republican. He has made a most serious blunder in forming his alliance with Walter L. Cohen.

"For many months our senators fought the appointment and confirmation of this negro as comptroller of customs in New Orleans. Finally the negro emerged the victor and so long as we have a Republican president, *our senators must write letters to Cohen and call him Mister.* . . .

". . . Regardless of whether Thomas was to win or lose this fight, we never thought he wanted to get to the Senate as a result of assistance rendered him by Walter L. Cohen. I held Thomas in esteem higher than to believe that he would ever openly accept a negro's political help against a white Democrat."

In 1930 Long violently threatened the owner of the Crescent Theatre, erected by a white theater owner from Jackson, Mississippi, just scheduled to open for negroes, and incited the populace to lynch fever. ". . . The people ought to wait 12 hours to give these foreign interests a chance to be heard from, and I mean only one chance. That is enough. If they don't do something to avert this catastrophe, they will be hearing from me in twenty-four hours afterward.

"With New Orleans' biggest church on one side, its biggest bank on another corner, a department store on a third corner, and one of the biggest theaters in the city on another corner, it is nothing short of an outrage to consider permitting a negro theater to run in the location considered."

In his senatorial campaign, he constantly spoke of LeBlanc and his nigger lodge brothers, of his "coffin club and skingame." "LeBlanc ain't got time to be governor, because he's got to get back to be secretary-treasurer of that nigger lodge." He spoke against old age pensions on these grounds. "It will cost $20,000,000 a year to pay the nigger pensions alone, and you white people will be working the year around to pay pensions to niggers."

In an interview to Roy Williams in *The Crisis,* February, 1935, he said: ". . . Why, down in Louisiana . . . the whites have decided niggahs have got to have public health care. Got to give 'em clinics and good hospitals. Got to keep 'em healthy. That's fair and it's good sense. I said to them: 'You wouldn't want a colored woman watching over your children if she had pyorrhea, would you?' They see the point. The same goes for other diseases. We got hospitals and clinics down there to care for niggahs just like everybody else. . . ." (Their treatment in public clinics is infamous. Note the psychology—they were to receive treatment merely to protect the whites.)

Huey, in his radio speech, March 21, 1935, denied that he had done anything to give the negroes civil rights, or that doing away with the poll tax would give the negroes the right to vote, though he gave that impression—in the North. Speaking as the most ignorant and prejudiced of his fellows, he said:

"Some of our newspapers and politicians come speaking the rumor all around the country that there was a terrible clash coming in the city of New Orleans and in Louisiana between the white people and the black people because there was so many colored people registering and voting and so forth. And they undertook to prejudice up the minds of the people with this ignorant kind of prejudicial argument. I was supplied the figures on it yesterday by Mr. Gregory, who informs me that out of 40,000 people who registered to vote that only 594 are colored, about as few as there's ever been at this time of the year or any other time, and so all of this calamity you constantly hear you can put the pin down on it that it has about the same dadgum truth as the balance of the canard they continue to spread and think to fool somebody, but in fact fool no one. . . ."

And he said to the press, "The free poll tax will not affect the status of the nigger. Negroes can pay and do pay their poll taxes now, but that doesn't give them any better chance to vote. It is the registration law and the white primary that keeps the negro out of our elections."

Huey's sectional racial prejudice was about average. He could, if necessary, submerge it—in a political sense, he had no prejudices at all. His acts and utterances reveal that this, as much as anything else, would have stuck a spoke into his scheme of building a state on any ideals of equality of opportunity.

Louisiana was built, first, on exploitation of the Indian, then of the negro. Even in earliest days the abuse of the negroes became so pronounced that Bienville issued his famous "Black Code," which detailed the manner in which slave owners should discipline and manage their slaves.

That abuse, continued to the present day, has chained Louisiana to backwardness, has narrowed the minds of its white citizens and brutalized their conduct. It has demoralized and prostituted the subnormal of city and country and profaned the history of Louisiana and the nation. Even the famed virtues and purity of the Louisianian woman is attained, not so much through personal worth, as through the debasement of her black sister.

XXXI—DICTATORSHIP

ALL opposition was giving its last gasp in Louisiana when Long's life was snuffed out. Huey had riveted his power absolutely. What is the secret? How was his power obtained? How did it function? He had built a régime such as never was in this country. "From the shaggiest muskrat swamp on Barataria Bay to the last cotton row in Caddo Parish," his word was supreme. How did he acquire this position? The answer, of course, has been implicit in the preceding chapters. Let us pull the threads together. It is important to realize, and in the future, defend ourselves against this type of undermining of our political institutions.

Before all else, of course, one must consider the scene where he operated, the slothful laxity of the climate, the general ignorance, illiteracy and coolie poverty of the people, the callousness to social ills induced by the long exploitation of a downtrodden negro population, the ignorance, selfishness and cowardice of "the better elements," the corruptness and flaccid pomposity of past politics, the dry-rot control of decadent plantation barons, and the devious and brutal tactics by which powerful outside corporations have polluted politics.

Long, a human dynamo, if nothing else, put pep into easygoing Louisiana politics. Behind all his moves was, first of all, his own rampaging, driving personality, the rough-roaring, unique back-country man and soap-tosser salesman—"Stick your foot in the crack and talk 'em down and make 'em like it." With his agile brain, his demon-like energy, his limitless personal ambition, his ruthlessness, his power of revivalism, his flare for drama, he was, declares Will Irwin, "the strangest . . . most unpatterned figure . . . since the Civil War." Huey's initial asset then was his energy and capacity. First of all, then, he established *a personal dictatorship.*

364

Aside from that it was a queer mixture of Fascism, bunk and old-fashioned bossism, Tammany style, plus real political wisdom—dictatorship no less real for being hybrid. All political control is hybrid.

Above all else he was a past master in building up a traditional American political machine—but more complete, more all-powerful than any such machine anywhere. His first asset for creating such a machine, also the characteristic which made him a successful leader, was his power to incite allegiance and bind men to him with links of steel, by illusion, fear, self-interest or greed. This was coupled with—despite his physical timidity—unlimited audacity—a kingly demagogue he was, without a crown, except in the cartoons. He accepted, demanded, imposed loyalty, personal loyalty. This was not the loyalty of the artist to beauty, the philosopher to truth, the writer to a creative concept, not loyalty to a cause, but to a person—*gang loyalty* in other words. Gangsters and politicians, in such things, have exactly the same code. Loyalty to the person must transcend any and all loyalty to principle.

Huey rewarded the faithful lavishly. He depended upon no abstract principle of loyalty; he made it pay big dividends.

He punished the unfaithful viciously, without pity. It is said he kept "a son-of-a-bitch book."

This dual generosity and relentlessness is the basic tactic of all dictators: not the best man for the best job, but the most powerful friend for the best job. It is the motto of Paolo Sarpi, which Porfirio Díaz of Mexico took for his own: *"Bread or the Club*—this should be the rule—for the greatest act of justice which the Prince should perform is to sustain himself." This is Caesarism, as Napoleon I defined it—the ambition of one against the ambitions of all—a death struggle against ideas, against parties, opposition, crime, disorder; its weapons are military and bureaucratic force, intrigue, betrayal, opportunism, terror, murder, favoritism, kindness, reward. Means signify nothing; the essential aim is to conserve and increase power at all costs; on the one hand, dictatorial measures directed against and for the masses; on the other, against powerful contestants, finally against obstreperous local "princes" (viz., Walmsley in New Orleans, Thomas in Shreveport, Sanders, Sullivan, Parker, etc.). The process is first to govern with the widest group possible, then to govern with the narrowest clique possible.

Those men whom Huey could not bind to him by such tactics, he bound to him by *a program,* a pseudo-radical program which appealed to many who did not come under the direct sway of his personality. Even sincere radicals swung into his camp, believing his tactic offered a practical way to socialism, which, as we have seen, is tommyrot. It would be folly to deny that Huey had a majority following in Louisiana. If the old crowd hated him, the masses had not yet begun to sniff at the saddle. They adored him. Far better than any of his competitors, he expressed the desire of the poor folk of the South for a better life. He made them feel as though they themselves were spitting in the face of the rich and powerful. He was called by such extravagant phrases as "the Moses of today, destined and inspired by God to lead his people out of the bondage placed upon them by the Pharaohs of today." That the people of Louisiana are economically worse off, despite some worthy reforms, than when he came into power, is plain as a lighthouse on a clear night. But if there are fewer chickens in every garage, Huey more vividly and perhaps more correctly than any prominent man in public life in America diagnosed the evil of our present-day society, and diagnosis is the first claim on the faith of the patient—though the doctor may know not how to cure.

John T. Flynn, the economist, has rightly described the period in which we live as "the era of promisers," and as Oliver Carlson ably puts it:

"The man who can promise most gets the mass support needed. If he can make those promises, and at the same time let the bankers, industrialists, speculators and plantation barons know that they have nothing to fear from him, then his road to power is comparatively sure and easy. Such has been the case with Huey P. Long."

But this appeal to mass following, like everything else, good or ill, was, first of all, handmaiden to the promotion of this personal political machine.

Lastly Huey had the cleverness to break through traditional political groupings and shake them all down for his own benefit. To quote Carlson again:

"Most of the gangs who stole votes and funds from the people of Louisiana have been part and parcel of the Long machine at some period during the past fifteen years. They have shouted for progress and prosperity and reforms in typical Long fashion until Long broke with them."

Unlike other reformers with a set idealistic program, he was willing to, and did, ally himself with any and every political organization of any importance in his state: first with the Independent Regulars, then the New Regulars, then the Maloney Choctaw wing of the Old Regulars, then the Regular Old Regulars. Each in turn he has used to win in a given situation, and when convenient each in turn he dropped with equal facility. Huey would climb into any bed with anybody, but as soon as he got a good leverage on the wall, he gave a jack-knife shove and occupied the whole bed himself. With each desertion he took with him a few key men, politicians, bosses, business men, etc., to form a devoted personal following as a component part of his own personal machine. What is true of political groups was also true of business groups—of bankers, lawyers, public utilities, railroads, etc. In other words clever *coalition and compromise.*

His rise to political importance tactically could be diagramed as a series of violent zigzags becoming less extreme and gradually straightening out to the direct line of personal power. Advance, retreats, side-steps.

Nor was this haphazard. He had the greatest political card index in the country; his machine was organized like a government, a government within a government. The final source of gang-machine politics is *vice;* financial support, vote-getting. Poll-place terrorism is the instrumentality of vice elements. Of the vice elements, Walmsley has said, "Anybody with Huey operates, and everybody who doesn't pay off, doesn't operate." Certainly they operate high and wide in the places

Long controlled. But the Old Ring which put Walmsley into office is scarcely the one to throw stones at Huey.

Connected with all this was Huey's elaborate system of *electoral control,* campaign methods, vote-getting. Before considering this, let us look at his concentration process in government.

The first requisite was *finances,* for himself, his machine and his government.

His personal income cannot be disentangled easily from that of his machine, of which Seymore Weiss is the mysterious Minister of the Exchequer. First came his salary as a senator. With this went numerous prerogatives. Every speech could be written into the Congressional Record, reprinted by the government printing office, the cheapest printing in the world, and sent out under government frank without cost by millions upon millions of copies. Next he collected numerous fees for special legal services to the state government of Louisiana. In his 1927 campaign for governor, Huey denounced past executives for paying out such fat extra fees; when he took charge the state's legal business would have to be done by the attorney-general at no extra cost to the taxpayers. But it is estimated that his fees in the matter of public utility rate adjustments alone in 1935 would have totaled not less than $75,000. Since December last, at least $85,000 was pried out of private companies for such investigation funds.

He frequently represented the state for a fee before the Interstate Commerce Commission and other federal bodies. Several times big appropriations were also made by one of Senator Long's special legislative sessions for an inquiry into the affairs of the city of New Orleans. Senator Long was attorney for the board of inquiry. February 3, 1935, the law firm of Long and Sandoz (Peyton R.), a new combination, was appointed attorneys for the Louisiana Tax Commission. Long was empowered to institute proceedings or effect compromises for the collection of back taxes and to make readjustments with property heretofore incorrectly assessed in return for one-third of all collected. An almost limitless amount could be collected under the contract. The Senator had already demanded $319,338.66 from the Louisiana Central Lumber Company for taxes for the years 1932, 1933 and 1934, and about $400,000 against other concerns throughout the state. He stood to make hundreds of thousands of dollars this year; the estimated gross was at least $215,000, probably $300,000. He justified this: "I admit that I'm the best lawyer in Louisiana, and I don't see why this state should not have a good lawyer. It should also be remembered that my expenses will be terrific. [Not so terrific!] The contract provides that out of my one-third collections I must pay accountants, appraisers, engineers and auditors."

Whether he had any interests in oil, railroads or timber, as some declare (he once did), no one who might know will tell. In addition he received fees from his private law practice, which can easily total over $100,000 a year. I have been told he had a retaining fee as legal advisor to a number of large corporations—most likely a sort of protective insurance. But that he had any appreciable wealth is doubtful. It was all outgo to keep his vast ambitions alive.

His machine collected money from wealthy friends and from state employees. State contractors who build roads, bridges, public buildings, were good campaign contributors. If funds from such sources could not be counted in as his personal income, nevertheless it mostly went to increase his personal power in the state and nationally. With regard to ample state funds, first he increased the war-chest by bond issues totaling over $100,000,000. He got a special federal university loan. He increased taxes.

Second he gained direct control over the expenditure of these enormous sums. The state government had a Department of Accounts, no provision for inspection of its books, to harmonize and keep straight the finances of the various bureaus. Long appointed there one bound to him by long personal association and of undoubted loyalty—Alice Lee Grosjean. As the Legislature passed various tax measures, it handed over the collection of them to this department. Alice at present collects over half the state revenues. In charge of the Highway Commission which was to spend the bulk of the bond issues, he put another intimate of boundless loyalty, O. K. Allen. Last April he set up a tax and bond board with all local finances under its control. Direct local taxation is also controlled through state supervision of assessment rolls. School funds were long ago brought under his control.

In other words every cent of public moneys—local, parish and state—except that going directly to mayors and city councilors for salary, was controlled by intimate agents of Huey P. Long.

Similarly, Huey expanded his Civil Service Commission to pass on all sorts of officials, state and local. He thus struck fear into the hearts of all public employees. Their jobs were bought and preserved only by absolute loyalty to him. Especial coercive use of the board of tax assessments could also strike fear into any who would oppose him. In Louisiana, taxes were a weapon both to reward and punish. Once upon a time a citizen of Louisiana who felt that the state was overtaxing his property had the right to an appeal and a hearing. Long destroyed that right. His Tax Commission had the power to raise, lower, or wipe out an assessment at any time before the tax was paid; and the owner had little recourse.

Furthermore, Huey had the largest *military establishment* of any state in the Union, larger than many a small country's. The National Guard (federally armed), the state militia, the Bureau of Criminal Identification, and the motorcycle highway police, all easy to mobilize, were used frequently during elections and at other times to seize registrar voting lists, to bring indirect pressure on the courts, to oust employees, to raid vice and gambling, to arrest dangerous opponents (the Irby-Terrell "kidnaping," Bourgeois, etc.), to break opposition movements such as the Square Dealers, to destroy local self-government, and above all, for dramatic display.

Another requirement of dictatorship was that he get *complete hold of the Legislature*. His first session in 1928 was a deadlock. The next session brought on impeachment which almost cost his political life. The one after that was deadlocked. But thereafter, having risen triumphant from the shambles of ruin in the senatorial campaign, he had his legislative opponents on the run ever after. Through high-powered electioneering, control of the voting machinery, recall, punishment, lavish patronage, he made it a body so nearly 100 percent Long that the opposition, held in by an iron-clad gag rule, could not even obstruct.

All our states have three branches of government, executive, legislative and judicial; also, in practice, a fourth branch —the administrative and civil service division usually identified with the executive branch, but ordinarily having many checks against immediate executive control, such as civil service, ratification of appointments by the Senate, definite term jobs, etc. Huey, in Louisiana, *completely broke down the divisions between these four branches of government*. All were concentrated in his person. He extended the executive power on every hand. Huey broke down the independence of all state boards and commissions. Where necessary he created entirely new boards. All became merely the rubber stamp of Huey P. Long. He went so far as to provide for direct gubernatorial appointment of the most menial subordinates of those boards. Naturally this control was not changed by the appointment of his home-town friend and partner, O. K. Allen. *Absolute executive control of all boards* was thus an important step in gaining dictatorship.

Huey also expanded the importance and prestige of various *key control bodies*. Thus he greatly augmented the powers of the State Bureau of Criminal Identification, his O.G.P.U., so that it could make arrests anywhere, and ferret out the secrets of his enemies. It also passed on the qualifications of numerous state and local employees such as sheriffs, firemen, policemen, etc.[1]

[1] That body, authorized by anti-Long legislators in 1928, was established in Shreveport, merely as a "fingerprint bureau." In 1932 its headquarters were moved to Baton Rouge. Until 1934, however, it remained a bureau for identification. At the first special session a bill to endow the bureau with "full police powers," including the right to make arrests anywhere in the state and to bear arms, aroused so much protest that for the moment Huey sidetracked it. Everywhere in the state the cry of "cossacks" arose. At the next special session the bill was slipped through. At the following session they were given power over the police, firemen and sheriffs of the entire state. No appointments of such were valid without the approval of the bureau.

More recently, despite the constitution, quite a number of legislators, by one pretext or another, were appointed by the governor.

Naturally, everything he did became "legal." In due time it became also "constitutional."

"They say they don't like my methods," *New York Times* correspondent Raymond F. Daniel quotes him as saying. "Well, I don't like them either. I'll be frank with you. I really don't like to have to do the things the way I do. I'd much rather get up before a legislature and say, 'Now this is a good law; it's for the benefit of the people, and I'd like you to vote for it in the interest of the public welfare.' Only I know that laws ain't made that way. You've got to fight fire with fire."

The judicial system went the same road. Long concentrated on getting judges loyal or obligated to the machine. Others, whom he did not elect, passed under his domination. During 1934 he elected Fournet to the Supreme Court; that body also became his rubber stamp. Whenever it threatened any obstruction, he threatened to increase its personnel or immediately impeach.

A citizen seeking appeal from these dictatorial laws would, since the destruction of the old bar association, have had difficulty in finding a lawyer. The right of any opposition lawyer to practice hung by a thread. Said one attorney: "If a lawyer took a case too obnoxious to Long, he would be walking the street in a week."

If an honest man were "framed" in Louisiana, let us say for stealing chickens, he could have been arrested by a Long-controlled policeman, tried before a Long-controlled judge, and might have found real difficulty securing a competent lawyer to defend him. If the Long machine had wanted to put someone out of circulation "legally" it would have had no trouble. Likewise no suit against the Long outfit would get anywhere. *Absolute control of the judiciary* prevented injuries to Long partisans, coerced enemies, and prevented his laws being declared unconstitutional.

This brings us back to elections. First of all Huey was the greatest campaigner in the history of America. Second, he had *a perfect system of propaganda distribution.* Third, he had unlimited radio publicity by the new station at the university. Fourth, funds could be raised quickly in numerous ways. The state employees were always good for at least $50,000 on short notice.

Formerly in Louisiana, many votes had to be bought. In fact the few dollars received for a vote was all that many citizens ever expected as benefit. Testimony in Judge Borah's court in the Fisher income evasion case showed that members of the Long machine had fake names put on the Highway Commission pay roll and their salaries were used to pay off for campaign purposes.

Witness the April 15 testimony:

"Were you a party to any agreement by which the state highway pay roll was to be used in the political campaign?" was the next question.

"I was," Thompson answered. . . .

"What was the money for?"

"To go around campaigning on the east bank of Jefferson Parish."

"You received the money, but you did not work for the highway department?"

"That's right."

"It was given you as campaign funds?"

Mr. Thompson answered that it was given to him "to go out and get votes."

"Do you realize that you are testifying that you received money illegally obtained from the taxpayers of Louisiana, by forged endorsement?"

But such crude and costly methods were being eliminated. Among other things the poll tax repeal automatically added at least 10,000 voters—the poorest folk, Huey's strongest support—to the ballot-casting population. There were 250,-000 people in Louisiana who couldn't or didn't pay the poll tax. Previously this placed a heavy burden on the Long machine, which had to pay up for any such it wanted to vote.

Louisiana still holds elections, though at times Huey arbitrarily tried to postpone them and they were abolished for

1935 as in any petty Latin American chicken-house country. But henceforth the Long machine was to own all the election machinery. All election commissioners, supervisors, watchers, are appointed by the governor or state boards or parish juries, in turn now made up of executive appointees. All sheriffs are appointed by the state. The local police cannot interfere with a local election. The courts can in no way whatsoever touch or interfere with a registrar of voters or his records.

Thus, however much the federal government might have spent to build up a counter machine and attempt to win elections away from him, Long was preparing for the 1936 general elections so he could not possibly lose. However much money was poured in from Washington to break him, his men would count the votes with no snoopers around; no court action could be successfully brought against the validity of those elections. He had stopped up all possible leaks. One strong man in the opposition, always sure of election, announced he would not run in 1936. "No wise man goes up against a fixed game." Now he may change his mind.

Local self-government was wiped out. Huey gained absolute control. The governor can throw out any mayor and city council in the state. He did so in Alexandria, and that act hung as a heavy sword over all the municipalities in the state. If Huey did not kick out Walmsley and the Old Gang in New Orleans, it was because they were already falling of their own weight. The crash thereof would have added to the Long prestige. Huey was merely picking his teeth till the New Orleans administration cracked up. Now it may not do so.

All local officials were brought under new state civil service or else were in other ways appointed by the state government. All local finances were controlled by him, all school funds and school teacher appointments. Local elected officials could not even appoint their close assistants.

Thus local self-government in Louisiana was made into merely a figurehead luxury with no power. It had become like the dual sort of administration set up in Mexico and Peru where federal officials administer and local officials merely rubber-stamp the wishes of the center.

In Baton Rouge all these measures were accompanied by the establishment of martial law last January and remained in effect while all anti-Long elements were kicked out.

It was irritating to have constant opposition in the very seat of his power. By making a miniature District of Columbia he forever would have ended its power of voting against him.

Through all the ages the safeguard of liberties, of democracy, of honesty, the restraint on centralized authority has been local self-government. However, it is unfair to say that Huey alone destroyed it. Home rule was well shattered before he arrived on the scene. Was there proper self-government in New Orleans? Vice, steamship companies, banana companies, banks, and the Old Ring had run New Orleans as it pleased for thirty years. The Standard Oil ran Baton Rouge. The oil, carbon-black and allied interests ran Shreveport. The sulphur and oil barons ran Lake Charles. The timber wolves ran Bogalusa. The sugar people ran Lafayette. The gamblers and fur kings ran St. Bernard and Jefferson Parishes.

The actions of Huey Long merely announced the deplorable decay of American freedom, the decline of politically conscious manhood, which had already taken place and which bid fair to end all free government in this country. Perhaps the local citizenry had already become too corrupt by the greed of the profit system, petty sharing of the spoils by the "better citizens," ever to take back the reins of self-government in their respective communities. But if they ever desire to do so, they will now have to fight not only the old bosses, but a powerful state machine and restrictive laws. In other words Huey utilized the destruction of local liberties already occurred to build on the ruins of a functioning bureaucratic system of terrible portent for the future.) He showed us what can be done with capable and unscrupulous leadership to the American system. It is a precedent which has been followed in some degree in other states, which has been very much followed nationally, and it is a precedent which, if it spreads, will mean inevitably the development of Fascism and dictatorship in the country at large. The American system—perhaps it was doomed anyway—in Louisiana has been undermined at the very roots. Long merely hauled off the deadwood, and paved over the whole field so not a grass shoot could come up.

We shall consider his control over education subsequently. It is sufficient to say here that he gained control over the appointment and the school budget of every community in the state, that from the very first he began installing his own presidents in all institutions of higher learning, notably the teachers' colleges and the state university. James M. Smith, head of the latter institution, has been one of his most faithful, fawning and useful followers.

Furthermore, since December, 1934, every schoolteacher has had to have her appointment approved by the Civil Service Commission—composed of the governor and other faithful state officials. In the late summer of 1935 the local school boards appointed teachers for the winter session; all who too conspicuously opposed Long passed out into the army of the unemployed. Even the neutrals· had to show enthusiasm. How about private corporations, the government behind government in this country?

Besides his legions of inspectors of one sort and another, Huey in some cases had given to the governor the power at his discretion of *lowering or raising taxes*. The business man who thought of backing an opposition candidate quickly remembered that the assessment on his factory or his building could be doubled in a day. By contract with the State Tax Board Huey gained tax collecting powers and in addition in certain cases could reap personal profit. A big business man knew that when he grew too troublesome, the Legislature could in five days slap a burdensome levy upon him. The state bank examiner was in a position to terrorize any bank and even if everything were open and aboveboard could cause unlimited upset and trouble. Huey used this as one of his weapons to starve out the city of New Orleans from getting funds, to force the banks to take state bonds and other state obligations, and to prevent banks from foreclosing on the obligations of friends.

By these *four coercive whips over business and banking: stern inspection, executive power to raise or lower severance and manufacturing taxes, to raise or lower assessments, and sudden special capital levies,* all business was being brought under subservience to Long. Thus not only did he control the personnel of government, but he could get fired—as was done in the case of Standard Oil—any employee of private business who did not please him. Here again Louisiana had sunk to the lower level of despicable despotism (except for actual torture and murder) of the hated tyranny of Machado in Cuba. The difference is that the mass of Louisianians liked it, while the Cubans, even though Machado was backed by the United States government, had the guts and wisdom to fight and overthrow Machado, and are now fighting to overthrow the inheritor of his system, Batista.

Did Huey interfere with freedom of the press? He threatened to pass a bill putting a tax on the sale of newspapers, and did pass a 2 percent tax on advertising in papers having a circulation of over twenty thousand (New Orleans dailies). It could, of course, be subsequently raised to 10, even 100 percent—not a money-raising project, but one to punish newspaper enemies. The right to tax the press is the right to destroy it, and as such it has not been exercised in Anglo-Saxon countries since the middle of the last century in England.

In Louisiana, persons selling Sender Garlin's Pamphlet (Communist) attacking Long were arrested by state plain-clothesmen and locked up. That they were released almost at once is probably due only to the fact that the police department was not yet then under Long's direct control.

He suppressed an issue of the university student paper and fired the editors. It has been illegal, by martial law order, to criticize the authorities in Baton Rouge. His strong arm men have beaten up reporters and smashed cameramen. He remarked from the public platform that reporters ought to be in the penitentiary. Thus any newspaper man who flattered Long was well on the way toward digging the grave, if not his own, of his fellows. At bottom Huey Long had *a desire to destroy the freedom of the press.*

Long's strongest hold over Louisiana was—*subtle terrorism.* Again and again he dramatically demonstrated his ruthlessness.

Subtle terrorism, patronage, intrigue—there is a Latin flavor to it all, reflex in part of the semi-tropical languor and memories of the Vieux Carré that binds the present inhabitants of King Louis's old colony to their neighbors across the near-by sea. Ships come regularly to New Orleans, not only from Havana, but from Puerto Barrios, Puerto Cortéz, Puerto Limón, Puerto Cabezas and other ports along the Caribbean. And in them often have come political refugees from the banana and coffee countries, to plot the overthrow of the government back home in the security of that seductive and hospitable city. Huey Long may never have eavesdropped at the tables along the Rue Royale, but he nevertheless proved himself an apt pupil, and in some things, a better teacher.

In short, when he attacked the executive centralism of Roosevelt on the national scene, he neglected to state that his own dictatorial powers in Louisiana were greater than those any man has ever exercised in our country, even in war time.

XXXII—KINGFISH KULTUR

BATON ROUGE is in an uproar. Motorcycle cops screech their sirens along the river bluff highway, down the main street, out to the state capitol, out to the Louisiana State University. The Kingfish is coming! The Italian ambassador is coming!

It is the jubilee celebration of the Louisiana State University, the diamond anniversary of the institution.

Huey Long speaks to a Friday luncheon of distinguished guests, politicians, professors, rotarians, writers. The loud-speakers bellow out his words, more sedate than usual, but his turn of phrase is racy. The punch is there.

"I didn't have much to do with the first seventy years of this heah institution, but I've had a lot to do with the last five years, and I'll put my five up against all the other seventy. And jes wait a few more years, and you'll see what I'll do then."

He doesn't waste much time greeting the "Eyetalian" ambassador, but plunges into the question of his own interference with the operation of the university in answer to charges of his destruction of academic liberty.

"Dr. Smith has said I haven't interfered. . . . I am slandered. . . . I wanna assert that as a matter of fact I have interfered. . . .

"Now I wanna give you all this heah advice. I'm the worst politician in the United States. The way I get along with the people of Louisiana is by never denying anything. Of course I interfered with the university."

He tells how he interfered. When professors' salaries all over the country were being cut, he interfered to raise salaries at L.S.U. He interfered to protect the institution against lawsuits. He interfered to increase annual appropriations from

$850,000 to $2,700,000. He soon discovered that it is "impossible to have any institution without a scapegoat," somebody to put "all the tar and dirt on." So he got Dr. James Monroe ("Moron") Smith to be pure, and let himself "get dirtied up." And "I sure got tarred up wide and pretty." Huey threatened that one of these days he "wuz goin' to turn back and stop interfering." He was going to "quit sittin' up with the legislators all night," he was going to "quit huntin' 'em up at two in the mo'nin'." And triumphantly he added, "Jes see all what I've been takin' out of theah hands."

The loud-speaker crackles. "Now you edicated folk think you can get along without politicians. . . . But who's been gittin' money over heah an' spendin' it somewhere else? I'll tell you this about the politician, and they are all pretty bad —if he's a thief, make him steal for the schools, he cain't do much harm then. And I want to tell you, we've just started to upbuild Louisiana edication. Edication comes first in Louisiana. We never economize on schools. We gotta see that a teacher gets as much as a slot-machine man."

And this business of politics. "The schoolteacher otta get into politics. If he's not gettin' into politics he's standin' in his own light and in the light of the people of this heah state. . . . We gotta make edication a business. You can edicate a man for one fifth as much as you can learn him to kill someone."

Following this sadistic rubbing of academic noses in the garbage of politics, the "Eyetalian" ambassador, His Excellency Augusto Rosso, who simulates a happy jerky Fascist youthfulness, speaks extemporaneously in accented but smooth and elegant English to the tables around which are an unusually large number of joyous, glistening-eyed Italians. His words carry a suggestion of pique that Huey has said nothing about him. Fulsomely he praises Dr. Smith and Governor O. K. Allen and *"ridenti"*—"smiling"—Baton Rouge (under martial law), and adds, "In Washington I had heard about Senator Long's interference with the university, and so I have not been so indiscreet as to ask anything about it."

The *New Orleans States* caricatured Huey's speech under

the title, "Beware of Kidnapers." A burly, big-footed, red-nosed man faintly resembling Huey with the famous Maestri stick-pin and labeled "POLITICS" was shown yanking into the air by the collar—books flying off with fluttering leaves—a puny gown and mortar-board figure: "Our schools and colleges."

The whole jubilee celebration was a great political set-up. It marked a high-water mark in what Long considered one of his major achievements—the upbuilding of the State University. It also marked a high-water mark in his ironclad control over education, teachers, professors, students, academic thought, school boards and school finances. It was thus primarily a great political rally looking toward the utilization of the educational system of Louisiana for the control of the state and for the extension of Long propaganda throughout the nation, particularly in intellectual, student, and academic circles, and to help "co-ordinate" the middle class. It also served to pay old political debts and to add credits for the Long machine in many outside influential quarters.

It was all a grand ballyhoo with a fanfare of military parades, hundreds of guests, who traveled, ate, conferred, and speechified at university expense. The city, the capitol, the university grounds, bristled with National Guards, militia highway police, R.O.T.C. platoons of honor, siren motorcycle cops. An ambassador, a university president, and ex-presidents of the Kiwanis, Lions and Rotary Clubs graced the ceremonies. Glenn Frank spoke on academic freedom that wasn't academic freedom. Dr. George S. Counts of Columbia University and of Hearst "red-menace" fame gave a brilliant seasoned address on the school and society, which caused simple villager Governor Allen to nod approvingly in the belief that all Counts said was a confirmation of everything from Share-Our-Wealth to the L.S.U. field house. Underfoot everywhere were poets, writers, bulky Ford Madox Ford, sleek William Allen Tate, un-sleek John Gould Fletcher, the Fugitive Group talking about getting rid of the machine and going back to the good old agrarian traditions of the pre-Confederacy days; journalists, legionnaires, professors, librarians, lawyers, politicians, priests and preachers. The Heidelberg buzzed with them.

Avidly they picked up the pamphlets from the lobby desk, presided over by a pretty coed, regarding academic freedom (a belabored and scarcely convincing argument), and the announcements of the farm-show with its hog-calling contest, cockroach and turtle races, its barn dance with moss-hung rafters and haystacks ("Come in your overalls!"), the Diamond Jubilee Minstrel show and other stunts—"the greatest collection of joy makers this side of Port Allen. . . . Come to the cat-race and get revenge on our professors. . . . Guess how many grains of corn in the cock's crop . . . easy if you know your chickens. . . ."

There was a lengthy farm-show parade with hurriedly improvised floats and more pretty coeds—the hoop-skirted Floradora-hatted coed of last century and the roll-stocking-knee-crossed-cigarette-smoking coed of today, coeds nudely emerging from cotton or sheaves of corn or petals. There was an enormous prize bull and a little runty creature of yesterday before the days of tick-eradication. There were old home looms and new factory looms; there was a rattle-trap cotton gin and a modern cotton gin, a hand saw and a modern sawmill. There were banners about honest toil, righteousness and morals and above all about Huey Long, who back in his 1924 campaign had so bitterly attacked this "Ringling Brothers" institution for which he now claimed all the credit.

2

Nowhere, since my last visit to Italy, have I seen so much military milling around, so many gay uniforms and bands. The "Eyetalian" ambassador, given a doctorate that night, had his heart warmed by so much goose-stepping—in his address he harped on it lengthily in glowing terms. And on the day when the students of nearly every other university in the land (including 600 at the "corporation institution" down in New Orleans, which Huey so hated—Tulane University) were holding peace demonstrations, those at L.S.U.

were out in uniform on parade before the Fascist ambassador, in a city under ironclad martial law.

After the parade and the luncheon Huey descended on the campus store with a mob of students and ransacked it—at his expense—of all its Coca-Colas, candies, chewing gum and cigarettes, and then he took the band to the tailor shops to pick out a new uniform for new and better parades.

Said secret bulletin of a secret "Student Committee," cautious address P. O. Box 465, New Orleans:

"Senator Long paid you a visit, 'distributing good will, promises of football trips, speeches, free cake, candy and soft drinks. And, when it was over, the Senator called for the bill. It was about $100. He paid for it out of his own pocket.'

"Fellow students, are you so credulous as to believe that the tax system, which provides such lucrative revenues for the present political machine of Money Shark Long, is not indirectly coming out of our own pockets as well as the pockets of our fathers, mothers and brothers who must labor and submit to the lowest standard of living in the entire United States despite the fact that the state of Louisiana is one of the richest in raw materials and contains enough mineral wealth to raise the standard of living of each and every citizen, collectively and individually, to the highest per capita level in these United States?"

Some observers saw in the quick-succession visits of German Ambassador Hans Luther and Ambassador Augusto Rosso, an indication of Huey's affinity for Naziism and Fascism, an instinctive desire to pattern his acts and career on those of Mussolini and Hitler, an unconscious (or conscious) consciousness of kind. But the explanation seems farfetched. Huey never hitched his wagon to a Mussolini; he hitched it always to himself, the only star he ever recognized in the firmament. He was ever too astute a politician to wander after alien gods. His political processes were ever more direct.

He had also recently invited the French ambassador, because of the establishment of a maison française on the campus, and because, historically, Louisiana is bound up with France and has many French descendants who are solid voters. Both the French and Italian ambassadors were given degrees, and Ambassador Luther was left out. This tied Huey to the hearts of every man of Italian or French descent—both are numerous in Louisiana. He also intended to establish a Casa Italiana, à la Fascist organization on the Columbia University campus.

And one of Huey's closest lieutenants, "Stick-pin" Robert Maestri, is of Italian origin. The Italians of Louisiana, whatever others may think, constantly compared Huey to Mussolini, and now, more than ever, they adored him. But there are only a few hundred German voters in the state; and though there are only 12,000 Jews, mostly they are wealthy and influential. Many of Long's intimate assistants were Jews who had no love for Hitlerism, for instance Seymore Weiss, colonel of the local Fuehrer's staff; and handler of most of Huey's private and political financial operations, Abe Shushan, etc.

It was rumored that all this fanfare was to give a real backdrop of glory for Huey's receiving of a Doctor of Laws on the basis of his autobiography "Every Man a King." Eight candidates were reported, but only seven received degrees, among them: the Italian and French ambassadors (future political tie-ups), T. H. Harris, State Commissioner of Education (to mollify him for not having been made president of the university and for numerous political services); Leon Weiss, architect of the skyscraper capitol, with its overloading of marble and bronze and its four stone and bronze reliefs of Huey Long (and on which $200,000 in architects' fees have been paid out); Armond Yonge, a professor of radiology, won over from the Tulane University of New Orleans, which Huey hated with all his heart, and several docile professors. The real factor which is said to have deterred Long from accepting a degree after such a stupendous build-up was the published scathing denunciation that day of the convention of Southern student editors in the Roosevelt Hotel, for the suppressing of journalistic freedom among the L.S.U. students, and because of the slight shadows cast by the refusal of Professor Hutchinson of Washington and Jefferson University to come on invitation to the jubilee after publicly denouncing lack of academic liberty at L.S.U.

3

There is no doubt but that Huey did a great deal, along with the harm, for the university, though not all the good he was usually credited with. Much was done before his time. The severance taxes and the mill tax which Huey Long's followers have cited as his achievements for the benefit of the institution were decreed in the 1921 constitution, seven years before Huey became governor. He did, of course, increase them. The impression was also given out that he selected the present university site and erected all its buildings. Actually the plans were made and most of the buildings erected under the administrations of Parker and Fuqua. The university moved from its old pre-Civil War buildings in September, 1925, three years before Huey became governor. Prior to Huey's inauguration as governor there had been erected the Hill Library, the English, chemistry, agriculture, engineering, mechanical, home economics, and veterinary science buildings, the dormitories, Peabody and Cafel Halls, the Dalrample building, the Memorial tower, and the stadium. Huey erected only the girls' dormitory, the music and drama building, the field house and in New Orleans the medical center, the last a truly worthy achievement, but also partly motivated by his hatred for Tulane University. The cost of Huey's erections was disproportionately high to that of the buildings put up by Governor Parker.

Enrollment has increased from 1,600 in 1928 to nearly 5,000, of whom about 4,000 are actually on the present Baton Rouge campus. Huey had arranged to establish a $200,000 industrial plant near the campus to provide worthy employment for poor students and thus raise enrollment to 10,000 and eventually to the largest in the United States, an expansion hardly justified by the economic condition of Louisiana.

This increase in attendance was due neither to the improvement of general economic conditions in Louisiana nor to im-

proved academic rating, though the latter may have contributed, but rather to Huey's political control of the institution
and the giving out of liberal patronage to students. Some three
thousand students have been on the university or state pay
rolls, some with juicy jobs—this alone has been sufficient to
account for the institution's augmented enrollment. In these
hard times L.S.U. has been a good place to attend, especially
if you believed in Huey Long. To give students a chance to
obtain an education is a laudable work, but the price in L.S.U.
has been plenty of hurrah! for Huey P. Long. Various times
he threatened to kick out students wholesale and bring others
in who would toot the Huey horn.

All campus activities were thoroughly controlled through
the fraternities in turn controlled by the secret Theta Nu
Epsilon, the illegal drinking fraternity, the source of Long's
direct control over the students. In the 1934 campus election,
the T.N.E. had two pretty coeds to kiss everyone who would
vote its ticket and advised the students that the only way to
get a campus job was to support its men. All the members of
the students' council have been enthusiastic Long men and
naturally wangled the best jobs. For instance recently a student body vice-president put in a motion that the university
should have a special highway traffic policeman, had it ratified,
approved by the commission, and then himself copped the job.

The head of T.N.E., Joe Cawthorn, who like Huey comes
from the red hills of northern Louisiana, but a more bony,
dry, hard-bitten, unimaginative type, is a henchman, who has
utterly nothing to learn about political manipulation and
camouflage. He accompanied Huey and revivalist Smith on
speaking tours—he took two weeks off from his classes to
assist in the South Carolina drive. Through him many campus
activities were arranged and patronage handled. The plan
pending was to send out to all the universities in the land,
at state or university expense, L.S.U. students who would,
as ardent Long men, with speaking and organizing ability,
found Share-Our-Wealth clubs. Huey was definitely plan-
ning to honeycomb all our universities with a political student machine. At the same time there was founded the *South-*

ern Review as a cultural organ of L.S.U. Few doubted that this was anything else but Huey's ambition to gain mass support in academic circles throughout the land. Also the university put up a powerful radio station—for cultural purposes, of course—which can broadcast to most of the United States. It has been used muchly for propaganda of Louisiana and Huey Long. Huey Long had unlimited access to it (his political opponents none). Many times over it he amused the public with swaggering cocky speeches, bombast and Bible quotations in good cane-brake drawl.

In addition to his student control—and there is no doubt Long was very popular on the campus because of hand-out jobs, promotion of football, free railway tickets to big games and what not—L.S.U. is one of the most ardent R.O.T.C. strongholds in the land. The boys out parading recently for the German, French and Italian ambassador, parade on every other possible occasion: Some Jewish students declined to march for Ambassador Luther and were excused, but immediately after, one of the officers visited the Military Science Class and leaving no doubt as to which of the students he had reference to, intimated that Jews were cowards and pacifists. At the time of the students' nation-wide peace demonstration, the officers gave the L.S.U. students very serious talks against radical foolishness. Well aware of the dangers confronting our noble land, they argued to the boys that the South is the most patriotic portion of the nation, upon which the rest of the country will have to fall back for salvation, once the "red menace in the East" becomes serious.

Some of the more alert students have charged that the R.O.T.C., through a system of demerits, gets rid of any students (such as Arthur Akins Newman) showing signs of independent cerebration. The National Students' League and the League for Industrial Democracy are not allowed on the campus on the grounds that no political organizations are tolerated, in order to preserve "the open mind." But two Democratic Clubs and the more conservative National Student Federation are authorized.

What sort of training did dictator Huey give his students?

First and foremost he went in for all the customary side-show commercialized stunts of university life in vulgar disregard of the deeper significance of education.

Not long ago, following a football match, Huey discovered a unique manner to fill the vacant seat of the senator from Baton Rouge, where he had permitted no elections. He calmly appointed Abe Mickal, the university's star football player, to the post. He ordered Jesse Cutrer, editor of the students' paper, *Reveille,* to call a students' meeting for that purpose. Cutrer not being the student body president, refused. Long snorted. "What relation is he to old Preacher Cutrer?" (his uncle who had opposed Huey in impeachment days).

Huey then had his rough-neck chief of bodyguard, Joe Messina, call and preside over the student meeting. Mickal refused to take the seat, but later in 1935 campus election Abe Mickal was elected president of the student body. The candidates borrowed Long's methods in their fight for votes. Their voices roared loudly across the campus from sound trucks, familiar vehicles of Long expostulation.

Following Huey's strong-arm campus meeting, a student, D. R. Norman, wrote a letter to *Reveille* declaring Huey's action to be a "mockery of free political institutions." Helen Gylkison, Baton Rouge correspondent for the *New Orleans Item,* showed Huey the letter. Huey flew into a rage. "That little ———. I'll fire him and all his family. I'll have a new editor by tomorrow. This is my university. Nobody there is going to criticize Huey Long. . . . I'll fire a thousand of the ——— —— ———. There's ten thousand more waiting to come to L.S.U. Get me Jim Smith."

Smith and E. N. Jackson (business manager) scampered over to the capitol. Men were sent down to the Ortlieb Press where the *Reveille* is published, and 4,000 copies were destroyed.

Huey turned to Helen Gylkison. "I want you to go down and censor the *Reveille*. Smith, you put her on the pay roll."

"O.K. by me," replied Smith.

Miss Gylkison, a handsome woman, with obvious back-stage ambitions, came out dancing. "I'm the censor. I'm the censor." She went down to the *Reveille* office, accompanied by David L. McGuire, former editor of the *Reveille*. There Editors Cutrer and his associates, Cal Abraham and Carl Corbin, refused to let her censor. "You don't know what you're doing when you try to buck Huey Long," she told them.

The editors went to Dean James F. Broussard (a man that day decorated by the French government), who told them "this word 'censorship' grates on my nerves," but advised them that when they got as old as he was they'd find principles didn't amount to much. They called on President Smith, who advised them, "We're now living under a dictatorship and the best thing to do is to submit to those in authority." He also remarked to them he would "dismiss the entire faculty and 4,000 students before he would offend the Louisiana senator."

Helen Gylkison was, until Huey's death, at least, on the university pay roll.

Various students made affidavits to these matters and were fired from the university, among them McGuire, Cutrer and Abraham. Twenty-six students then signed a protest and were suspended.

As most of the students were on the pay roll, particularly the student officers, they were afraid to back up the students in difficulty. A mass meeting was called anyway. It was promptly prohibited by Major Perry Cole, Dean of Men, and the students were dispersed when they arrived.

Student body President Bill Lobdell, who had refused to call any protest meetings and had opposed the students in difficulty in every way (he had a job and was promised another one on the coaching staff the following year) resigned three weeks before his term was up, and came to Cutrer and said his conscience had been hurting him so much he couldn't sleep nights.

On expelling Dave McGuire, Smith characterized him as a "general nuisance" on the campus. Yet he had been editor of the *Reveille* as highest scholar in the school of journalism, he was the university's outstanding military student, and in 1931 had been awarded the president's medal, based on achievement, loyalty, neatness and scholarship, with words of high praise. Cutrer, also fired, was promptly presented a loving cup by the mayor and citizens of his home town, Kentwood, in mass-meeting assembled. It bore the words: "A true American. Well done; you have been faithful." Abraham, ranking Spanish student, by his stand, was cut off from a $1,500 scholarship to study in Spain. Of the twenty-six students suspended, some recanted under duress; others, refusing to apologize, were reinstated anyway. But five of the outstanding students in ethics and principles of journalism refused to go back. All the editors of *Reveille* stood by, except Grace Wilkinson, who had relatives on the state pay roll; she was installed as editor. Saying that two big shots had told her to forget principles and take the job (it carries a good salary), she proceeded to turn out a sublimated bulletin without editorial comment. Her price was ostracism by every intelligent student as a double-crosser, the loss of her Theta Sigma Phi (journalist honor fraternity) pin. But she will easily get a job with Mr. Hearst, if the old boy lives long enough.

After their expulsion the L.S.U. alumni of New Orleans invited them down to speak. Thereupon Dean Broussard, State Alumni Secretary Ray Mobley, and Athletic Director T. P. Heard rushed down to New Orleans and corralled graduate students at Medical Center and other alumni to break up the meeting. The boys were not heard, but a group of alumni raised funds to send them to the University of Missouri where they have all been winning highest honors.

Simultaneously with the jubilee celebration the Southern Student Editors (in convention at the Roosevelt Hotel under the auspices of Tulane University—Grace Wilkinson sent excuses) passed a resolution scathingly denouncing the "subservience of President James M. Smith to Senator Huey P. Long," the "apathy of the L.S.U. student body" and the "indifference of the National Student Federation" while commending the "courage and fearlessness" of Cutrer. In supporting the resolution A. G. Weems, editor of the *Reflector* of Mississippi State College, said that Huey's actions represented "a flagrant example of political control of a university and we, who represent over thirty Southern college publications, should attack and denounce it."

In his autobiography, "Every Man a King," Huey declares that he prevented an improper political appointment to the presidency of L.S.U. and secured a man of high academic standing. Dr. Smith, however, was undoubtedly appointed to do Huey's bidding under very dubious circumstances. "There's not a straight bone in Jim Smith's body," Huey is reported to have said, "but he does what I want him to, so I think he's a good president." Certainly Huey loses few opportunities to insult Dr. Smith in public in the most cynical fashion, and Dr. Smith takes it lying down.

Smith had been dean at a little jerk water college in Louisiana. Soon after he became president of L.S.U., Mrs. Smith developed social ambitions. She persuaded her husband to install a riding academy on the campus. Ten thoroughbred horses were acquired, one of which—"Don"—Mrs. Smith appropriated for her own individual use. The Baton Rouge stores blossomed out with swank riding habits. A riding student was killed and the *Times Picayune* ran a feature story about the academy. At the time, Huey was whacking the brush up state telling the poor share-croppers and bankrupt farmers how he was saving the tax money for them. When he saw the *Times Picayune* piece, he flew into a rage and is said to have wired Smith:

SELL THEM PLUGS

Smith ran around in circles, but he sold them plugs. Thus ended Louisiana's most famous riding academy.

On another occasion when Mrs. Smith was giving a dinner-party with much dog to the social crust of Baton Rouge, Huey burst in with Messina and another bodyguard on his heels and cursed Smith out for wasting the taxpayers' money. While delivering this diatribe he snatched bonbons off the table and crunched them in his mouth. Burly Messina did likewise. The guests soon departed.

On another occasion he barged into a Smith reception with ward-heeler John Brechtel. Putting his arm around him, Huey said: "Gentlemen, I want you to meet John Brechtel, the man who votes for me and supports me and keeps you all in this grandeur."

Once the law fraternity was banqueting at the capitol dining rooms. Dean Flory was speaking. Huey Long burst in with two bodyguards. "What's this going on in my building? Who gave you permission to come in here?"

H. P. Breazeale arose and explained. Huey went off. A law student said loudly on his heels, "Now we know what it is to have the Emperor come in and silence his vassals." The next speaker spoke of famous ghosts that had burst into banquets, and mentioned that of Banquo. "But Banquo's ghost was more silent and more sober."

During the incumbency of the previous President of L.S.U., Atkinson (whom Huey was trying to eliminate along with other professors not his political backers), Long's agent on the campus was the student Kemble K. Kennedy. A scurrilous sheet appeared, called the *Whangdoodle,* which viciously accused various professors of peculation and immoral habits. The president hired a detective, Kennedy was apprehended, and being unable to substantiate his attacks, was sentenced, despite all Huey's efforts, to a year in jail. Huey pardoned him very shortly and ordered President Atkinson to give him his final exams. Atkinson refused. Dean Robert Tullis of the law school refused. Huey had to back down. But presently Huey's machinery became better oiled. President Atkinson was no longer there. Dean Tullis was ousted, later, when scandal broke, was made professor emeritus, and at a June, 1933, board meeting, Kennedy was voted permission to take his exams. But Dean Flory, who succeeded Tullis, likewise refused to sign Kennedy's diploma, and so servile Dr. Smith, the new president, in violation of university regulations, granted him a secret diploma. Many believe that his act was the price of Smith's appointment.

At the time of the *Reveille* incident, Huey, interviewed in Franklinton, denied meddling in university affairs, stating that there had been a student protégé of his in the university, wearing his clothes with his name inside them, and he couldn't even make the university give him a diploma. But at the same time, he said maybe the president was "gonna expel enough students to relieve the overcrowded condition."

In the fall of 1932, Professor Murphy Sylvest of the Department of Government (whose father as a legislator had voted to bring in the articles of Huey's impeachment) was called up by a member of the board of supervisors, and told he was to be dismissed. He wished to fight, but Smith convinced him that this might endanger appropriations for the university, so he resigned.

Dr. John L. Uhler, who wrote the novel "Cane Juice," which reflected on conditions in the sugar industry, was fired by Huey Long at the behest of Catholic priests. After his case was taken up by the American Association of University Professors, he received his year's salary. Later he was reinstated.

Others of the university staff have been appointed because of political pull or because of political trading. Miss Lillian Kelly (mathematics) was imposed by Senator Coleman Lindsey. There was opposition, and her salary had to be paid finally out of the general fund of the university instead of the department. One of the agricultural instructors was imposed by Huey so as to eliminate him as an opposition candidate for some petty office.

At the jubilee celebration the university widely distributed a folder denying charges of political coercion, suppression of academic freedom, or other perversions of customary university ethics. Naturally all the faculty, with the exception of one professor, who had the slender courage of giving a somewhat equivocal reply, denied that there was any abridgment of academic freedom. None dared admit that he had drunk of the hemlock of good jobs and intellectual servitude. It must be admitted, of course, that academic freedom is on the definite decline everywhere in the United States. My own two universities, California and Columbia, have somber records. In this time of social stress, our great institutions of learning, where professors have long been corrupted by fat corporation "investigation" jobs for the Power Trust and other large corporations, who have received large benefactions from wealthy people they do not like to offend, who have made the granting

of honorary degrees a contemptible means of baiting donations from the dumb wealthy, have proven, of all our institutions, perhaps the most cowardly in protecting the American
birthright of freedom of thought and its expression. Why
should ignorant and ambitious politicians place any more value
on academic freedom than the academicians do themselves?
And in Louisiana itself, the record of academic tolerance of
Tulane University has been nearly as dark as that of L.S.U.
Loyola University, of course, instructs in accord with set
Catholic dogma, hence is not a "rational" institution to begin
with.

The difference between the conduct of the students of Louisiana State University and the University of Havana, both
plunged into a dictatorial whirlpool, is striking. In Havana
also Dictator Machado built beautiful new buildings and
stuck up plaques eulogizing himself and his image in bronze
à la Huey, but the students refused to be bought off by jobs
and a few lollipops in the student store; they demanded the
elimination of cheap political appointees from the faculty;
they demanded a curriculum that did not feed the vanity of
the dictator; and they fought for academic freedom, and
when they were humiliated, they fought against the dictatorship. Some of them went to jail, into exile, some were killed—
but they overthrew Machado. In Louisiana, save for the half
a dozen we have mentioned, students merely talk about "the
manhood of the South."

What is the picture of the rest of Louisiana's educational
system, which Huey boasted he had done so much to improve?
His great slogan was that he gave free textbooks to the children of Louisiana. As a matter of fact, New Orleans and most
of the parishes gave free textbooks long before Huey ever
made it a state-wide issue.

The United States Bureau of Education report for 1933
(Huey became governor in 1928) lists Louisiana as compared
to all other states as 44th in general education, 47th in literacy
and 47th in general attendance. Teaching salaries are exceedingly low as compared to most states. In schools for white
students (1931-32) the average salary was $849, for high

school teachers, $1,269. In 1932-33 the average had dropped
to $622 and $977, respectively. By 1933, in negro schools,
it had dropped in one year (that a low) from $288 to $219.
Moreover, as James Rorty has pointed out, unpaid salaries
have mounted up; last year reached a million and a quarter,
double that of the year before. It must also be remembered
that all public employees gave "voluntary" contributions to
the Huey Long campaign war-chest; they were "voluntary"
subscribers and supporters of his paper, *American Progress.*

The Orleans Parish, which was anti-Long and hence not
controlled by him, paid the highest salaries in the state, despite
the Old Ring politics that have reigned there. The salary for
an elementary school is $400 above that of the next highest
parish, and negro high school teachers get $765 above that
of the next highest parish. If the Orleans Parish figures were
deducted from the general average, the salaries paid would
drop to an illusory figure. Teachers' salaries in Louisiana have
been traditionally low, but are disgracefully so since Long
came into power there. In the parishes controlled by him, they
were far lower than in those still independent of his machine.
This school year had declined to only 156 days in white schools
and 100 days in negro schools, and the buildings and equipment are worse than in most Latin American countries.

Huey's political domination over the university, as we have
seen, was duplicated by budget and appointive control in the
elementary and high school set-up. Everything was under his
thumb.

Such is the sad state of education in the great commonwealth of Louisiana, where the Kingfish has so long ruled
supreme. On the inadequate foundation of a backward elementary and high school system politically controlled, he built
up a university of corrupted goose-stepping students and professors. On the basis of an illiterate state, a poverty-stricken
teaching force, a politically vitiated school-system of shameful
meagerness, Huey erected the showy edifice of his great university with an extravagant budget. The millions spent on
L.S.U., much of the money in an improper form, and in a
manner far worse than that for which Long earlier attacked

former Governor Parker, were for the purpose of show, political power, and to provide a basis for a nation-wide conquest of student and professorial support. With this false glitter he was laying plans to seduce higher education everywhere.

Recently he demanded in the United States Senate a billion dollars to send students to universities. It was part of his general program to make a nation-wide bid to college students to buttress up his political power among a group which in a year or so would become voters. The promises he was making to students everywhere—would they have been cast aside as they were in Louisiana, once he gained power? For the university there was primarily a political tool for his greater purposes, not a place for advancing learning or independent thought. L.S.U. was a springboard for bold projects for the glory of Huey P. Long. It was a place of academic whoopla, gaudy parades, and Hitleresque ceremonies, where students and professors did not dare tell you the truth, except in whispers behind closed doors and then piteously beg you not to mention their names. The abiding principle of L.S.U. has been "bigger and better elephants," a bigger subsidized football team, a bigger glee club, a bigger band, the biggest swimming-pool in the world (they forgot the drain when they built it and had to tear it to pieces again); the criterion of the institution was numbers, size and folly. But despite the money it cost, despite its elaborate buildings and its gaudy cloak of grandeur, L.S.U. lacked the spirit of a free institution. So far as real education goes in the Socratic sense, it was an empty shell; a tomb of academic freedom and disinterested scientific education. It was sound and fury signifying first and foremost Kingfish Kultur—Huey P. Long at the heels of motorcycle sirens and surrounded by strong-arm men.

APRIL 27, the Associated Press reported that Huey Long's ally, Joe Fisher, had been sentenced to eighteen months in prison for federal income tax evasion, mostly on money secretly obtained from the Louisiana Highway Commission. On that day Long appeared to attend the annual conference of Milo Reno's Farmers' Holiday Association. He bounced off the train with two bruisers and waded through the little crowd of curious welcoming Iowans.

At the State Fair-Grounds he munched peanuts and sang *Every Man a King* into the microphone, "without anyone throwin' things at me."

Though a Democrat and a Baptist with a family failing to stray over to the Methodists, he found it hard to distinguish between the two major parties—one was skinny from the ankles up, the other from the ears down. He offered his Share-Our-Wealth plan amid much cheering. "If you can't understand this, shut your damned eyes and believe it," he cried and plunged into a lengthy Bible quotation. "Do you believe in the word of God? Put up your hands." Nearly all hands shot up. "Do you believe in the redistribution of wealth?" All hands.

But when the resolution committee of the Holiday Association got down to business little was heard of sharing our wealth. The economic formula, reports Robert Morss Lovett, was production for use rather than profit.

May 2, he was back in Washington thundering over the National Broadcasting Company about Roosevelt's St. Vitus's dance government, and his jaunts on the $5,000,000 *Nourmahal* with Vincent Astor and royalty, while cotton growers were starving. "Hooray for the President's fishing trip. Let's send him off again."

May 13, in the Senate the Farley investigation resolution came up for final decision. With hundreds of spectators clamoring for admission, Huey, in a domineering triumphant mood, tried to swing the members into line.

"Let's see if we're going to whitewash old Jim!" He waved his hand. Brandishing a copy of the P.W.A. reports on the New York investigation, he shouted at Senator Bailey, who was defending Farley, "I don't see how the senator from North Carolina can stand on this floor and say that he's the son of a preacher if he read this report and found nothing in it."

Huey threw new bombshells, affidavits proving that the files of the company involved had been cleared of all documents since the effort to investigate Farley had begun, that with Stewart and Company was kept a contact man, Harry D. Watts, with whom Farley arranged the "manipulating of government business and grants of contracts," and of "insurance premiums." Through him had been arranged the awarding of marble on the federal office building in New York, the giving away of postage stamps to one "Randolph Cook" to get business from the Pennsylvania Railroad. He charged that these stamps had been deposited as security for a loan and that later other stamps were printed "to undo the harm." Farley, it was charged, had grabbed all the papers and correspondence between Ickes, Glavis and Green when they were called for by the committee.

Few more serious charges have ever been made against a high official of the United States. Senators demurred against this "surprise" evidence. In other words, the pilfering of public funds, when and if it occurs, is to be studied only if the evidence is presented when it can't be presented, not on the merits of the case. McKellar, more underhanded, said Huey had only produced a copy of his affidavits, insinuating they were false.

Huey said the originals were in a bank lock-box because his office had been ransacked and the telephone tapped various times since his crusade against Farley had started. He estimated that substitution of marble on the New York job had "swindled" the government out of $383,000. P.W.A. investi-

gator Green's estimate was $410,000. Huey charged that be-
cause of such things the famous architect Cass Gilbert had
died of a broken heart.

McKellar said Long was merely showing "spleen." Long
said McKellar was the sorriest whitewasher he'd ever seen.
Farley was guilty of "swindle, robbery and defalcations."
Waving a fistful of papers, Long jumped up and down the
floor, shouting, "Go ahead and whitewash old Jim. Whatever
you do, you can't make him pure . . . no more than you can
make a rotten egg edible."

Certainly Huey had a prima-facie case. No decent or sane
reply was made. Senator Bailey merely likened Long's out-
bursts "to the barking of a dog," and again tried to push
Farley under the skirts of Roosevelt: Long was merely trying
to "asperse the character . . . and integrity of the President
. . . and destroy the national faith."

And so, May 14, the Senate, by a vote of 62 to 20, rejected Huey's demand for an investigation. Farley was brazenly whitewashed and, as a result, serious implications of guilt
remain. But, as in the case of the attempt to impeach Long,
it was at bottom, merely, dirty politics on both sides. Nobody
concerned was really interested in the welfare of the republic.

Shortly it was simultaneously reported that Long's income
tax record would be investigated again and that Roosevelt
would replace Farley with Frank C. Walker as Postmaster
General, but, of course, not because of any criticism leveled
against him.

2

Huey went back to Louisiana, where he was received by a
big demonstration, principally of war veterans, and hurried
to Baton Rouge to argue the rate-reduction matter. Then back
to Washington.

The N.R.A., already dying, had crashed to ruin with the
Supreme Court decision. It was proposed now to create a
skeletonized body to carry it on to the grave. A rider by Senator Gore worried the administration. It provided for Senate
approval of all government officials and employees with con-

trol over recess appointments, receiving $4,000 or more annually. A blow to the Roosevelt-Farley patronage game. It was unexpectedly passed.

Finally, on reconsideration, it was smashed down and the N.R.A. bill put across, but only after one of the most remarkable one-man filibusters in the history of the republic—by Huey Long, of course.

He began at 12:30 P.M. and talked to 5 A.M. He laughed a good deal when the first-term senators, who forced their elders to hold his feet to the fire without recess, would rise and chant in chorus, "We object. We object."

He told of the concentration of the wealth, of sharing the wealth, of the Farley charges; he quoted poetry and the Bible. As the night wore on he became more and more jocose. He told all his jokes, of his kind-hearted, drink-mixing uncle, of the proper way to fry oysters, how to brew potlikker and make Roquefort cheese salad dressing, some of his information doubtlessly derived from his old Cottolene-selling days.

Someone sent him down a note, reminding him he had not yet mentioned his chief hero in history, Frederick the Great, and how that King had said his generals would take Vienna and his professors at Heidelberg would later justify the violence in law—or was it the professors at L.S.U.? "Whatever became of that sword Frederick presented to Washington?" demanded Huey, munching chocolate and sandwiches which he rolled into tiny pellets so as to continue talking. Now he rolled his eyes to the delight of the gallery and suggested the Senate recess until the whereabouts of the famous weapon could be ascertained.

But the angry Democratic elders, heavy-lidded, more exhausted than Huey, blocked all recess until he dropped or cried quits.

And presently toward dawn, the Kingfish was mumbling instead of speaking and soon afterward his performance was over. Ghastly of countenance, he turned the fight over to blind Senator Schall.

As the clerk read Schall's bitter denunciations of Roosevelt, Huey went out and posed for photographs, but in a few minutes was back, sprawled in a chair, advising Schall how to proceed. The long reading was finally over. The senators hurriedly voted the N.R.A. bill and adjourned at 7:21 A.M.

And so on a day when the Chinese government was defying Japanese occupation, Il Duce tightening the blinkers of censorship on the Italian people, and the health of the King of England was arousing grave concern, Long hit the main headlines of the press. Kirby in the *World-Telegram* cartooned Long in the ropes for a knockout by the Senate. But to people back in the Styx, more than ever he was the brave singlehanded fighter who stood up for their rights to slay the dragons of deceit. Metropolitan East always misjudged the effect of everything Long did on the country at large.

3

Once more in his political career Huey had his clothes stolen while in swimming. Roosevelt unexpectedly came out with a new tax program to radically increase levies in the higher brackets and on inheritances. An attempt was made to make this appear as a sort of Share-Our-Wealth program. Roosevelt said that vast fortunes were contrary to American ideals.

Huey welcomed the President back to the Share-Our-Wealth fold, but feared that his message came at a time to turn the public's mind off the "horrible exposures" made by his former Assistant Secretary of Commerce, implicating a company with which the President's own relatives and his yachting friend Vincent Astor were associated, which had been handed over nearly $2,000,000 government money and given fat ship subsidies.

June 22, Huey published a lengthy open letter to Roosevelt promising support of any sincere Share-Our-Wealth program and in a curious mixture of accusations and praise, asked Roosevelt to define exactly what he wanted, whereupon Huey would back it and it would be enacted before a week had passed. Roosevelt did not reply and proceeded with other measures to try to take the wind out of Huey's sails—projects for youth betterment and education—clever moves all—and yet in them also the faint weary beating of the drums of political demagogy.

For the time being Huey went back to the bayous to round out his absolute power and bring about the final surrender of New Orleans, the badly bullet-ridden last citadel of the opposition.

And so out of the darkness over the airport could be heard the drone of a plane, its green and red lights visible against the dark sky. It circled, dove down the wind in front of the floodlights. With a cordon of guards, Colonel E. P. Roy forced his way to the plane. Two bodyguards came down the gangway. Then emerged Huey. Three bodyguards followed.

Already he was waving both hands; his curly hair ruffled in the breeze. "The Lord and myself sure have been traveling!" he shouted to no one in particular and hurried to his automobile. "Hit 'er up, boy!" he shouted. "I'm used to traveling fast."

At the Roosevelt entrance more guards. He darted through the lobby, up the elevator to his apartment, whipped off his coat, called for secretaries, gave them a list of members of the Legislature: "Get these boys to Baton Rouge tomorrow night at 8 o'clock at the latest. . . . I understand the governor is going to call a special session . . . tomorrow night. . . . Governor Allen wants something like twenty or thirty bills introduced in his Legislature. Wallace and myself will fix 'em up for him; we know what he wants."

After working nearly all night, he was off at dawn for Baton Rouge, his brief case crammed with twenty-six bills that at last were to spell doom to the New Orleans Ring and cement forever and aye his iron-clad dictatorship.

And so in this fashion, Louisiana celebrated Fourth of July, 1935, the one hundred and fifty-ninth year of this country as a free independent republic. The twenty-six bills were approved in forty-five minutes. Despite the shrill protests of a few oppositionists, Huey said with just a note of regret, as the session ended, "It hasn't even given me a light workout.

Things are getting too easy. It must be that my policies are being endorsed by nearly all Louisianians."

He passed a bill making it a criminal offense for anyone to use federal funds for political purposes—"to aid President Roosevelt." But he remarked, "Roosevelt put a half-baked apple in his mouth when he said there'd be no politics in relief. There'd better not be in Louisiana, or we'll fill the jails full of his henchmen." He dashed off a telegram to Roosevelt, at the same time striking a pose for the photographers.

"You know I get mighty lonesome without keeping in touch with Franklin De-la-no Roosevelt. . . . I wonder how this sounds: "Hon. Franklin Delano Roosevelt, White House, Washington, D. C. Your Excellency, greetings. Who tells me I don't know good form? That sounds like hot stuff to me. . . ." He and his cronies laughed uproariously. The telegram said that Louisiana was anxious to help keep politics out of the administration of federal funds, hence the law. "I'm a friend of his. I'm going to be whether he wants me to be or not."

Roosevelt did not answer and indicated Huey's wire would be quietly buried. Presently Huey was saying, after vetoing a pension bill, that Roosevelt's pension scheme was a joke; it would give old folk only $3.60 a year or less than one cent. Roosevelt was just a "liar and a faker." "I'm as big as President Roosevelt. Why, he's copying my Share-the-Wealth speeches now that I was writing when I was fourteen years old. So he's just now getting as smart as I was when I was in knee-breeches."

And now off for the clean-up of that "highbinder bunch" in New Orleans. He jammed through the capitol restaurant, shaking hands right and left, shouting signals to his cronies. "You know that the L.S.U. football team otta watch me. I know how to follow interference."

He slapped a burly bodyguard on the back.

XXXIV—DEATH IN THE CAPITOL

AT 9:20 P.M. Sunday night, September 8, Huey P. Long failed to follow interference.

Stepping from the House Chamber into the corridor of the capitol, after pushing toward completion a number of special session acts further to consolidate his almost ironclad power, he was suddenly confronted by Dr. Carl A. Weiss, a thirty-year-old eye, throat and nose specialist, who pressed a gun into the Senator's side and fired a bullet that tore its way through his intestines.

Before he could fire a second shot, Weiss's arm was deflected. Murphy Roden, one of Huey's bodyguards, grappled with the assailant, trying to wrench his gun away. Unsuccessful, he stepped back and quickly fired several shots at him. The other guards and the highway police promptly riddled Weiss with bullets. The coroner's inquest showed thirty bullet holes in front, twenty-nine in the back, and two through the head.

As Long had stepped out into the corridor with his guards and Supreme Court Justice Fournet, he had called to his aides: "Everybody be here in the morning." A few seconds later he had been shot.

He staggered down the basement steps and was rushed to the hospital. "I wonder why he shot me," said Long.

For thirty-one hours, with the aid of an operation performed by Dr. Vidrine of the Charity Hospital and five blood transfusions, he fought for life, and finally died at 4:06 A.M. Tuesday, September 10.

Following the special session in July, Huey had gone to New Orleans to bring about the final political capitulation of that city. He succeeded in prying loose the whole Old Ring machinery from Mayor Walmsley, leaving him at last in a completely isolated position.

From there he rushed to Washington, where August 9, he told of a murder plot concocted in a political caucus of his enemies—it was listened to derisively—and indulged in a five-and-a-half-hour filibuster up until the time set for closing the session of the Senate, in a vain effort to force consideration of the cotton and wheat bills. He was much criticized for having talked to death the deficiency bill necessary for instituting part of the social security program; but he probably gained more than he lost because of his support to the demands of Southern and Middle-Western farmers.

The federal fight against him was intensified. More federal patronage and money was dished out to his worst enemies in Louisiana. A new Congressional investigation was being pushed. The income tax evasion trials of leading henchmen were soon to continue.

He hurried back to Louisiana to pass more punitive legislation to offset federal patronage and to prepare the scene for the 1936 elections. It was in this special session that he was pushing through a law intended to gerrymander Judge B. H. Pavy, father-in-law of young Dr. Weiss, out of his political job.

Whether this, or deeper motives, were involved in the shooting may never be cleared up. Huey's private secretary, Earl Christenberry, tears in his eyes, promptly charged that the murder of Huey had been decided by lot. "They drew straws and Weiss lost," he declared. Long's Senate declarations that he had an exact record of the political meeting in the De Soto Hotel in New Orleans at which he claimed plans were laid to kill him, at once took on new significance. Long had charged that among those attending was the Baton Rouge district attorney, John Fred Odom. Local Long adherents stated that the Senator had also mentioned Weiss's name.

District Attorney Odom, upon whom fell the duty of investigating the deaths of Long and Weiss, boldly admitted being present at the De Soto meeting, which he declared was also attended by four of Louisiana's congressmen. He did not recall whether Weiss was present or not. He said that as usual violent expressions against Long were voiced, but that these were far from constituting a murder plot and that they had no literal significance. In the hearings over the killing of Weiss, in which Odom showed far more interest than in investigating Long's demise, Reverend Smith, head of the Share-Our-Wealth movement, after being sworn in to testify, branded Odom as "one of the co-plotters of this assassination," and walked out, refusing to be cross-examined by such a person. Odom, white of lips, denounced his statement as a "willful, vicious, deliberate lie."

Smith called upon Congress to institute a proper official investigation of the facts behind the slaying of Huey, which he declared, when revealed, would shake the nation. The night of September 11, Smith went on the air in an impassioned address in which he said that Long's enemies had imported a cash fund of $25,000 into Louisiana "two days before our leader was murdered," and he assailed the "lily-white Congressmen of Louisiana"—presumably referring to those opposed to Huey Long—implying they were present at the De Soto Hotel meeting when "the plot to kill Senator Long was concocted." He repeated these conspiracy charges a few days later in New Orleans. James O'Conner, Sr., an assistant of the state attorney general, declared he had received an affidavit concerning the alleged plot. Earl Long publicly voiced his firm belief in the existence of such a murder conspiracy. Dr. George S. Long, dentist of Tulsa, Oklahoma, declared at a meeting of three thousand Share-Our-Wealthers in De Queen, Arkansas, that Long's followers had voice-recording machine records which revealed that Weiss had drawn "the short straw."

Weiss was buried before Long died. His funeral was attended by, among others, a goodly number of Huey's most bitter political enemies: members of the Square Deal Association, R. L. Tullis, former law school dean of L.S.U., ousted by Long, ex-Governor John M. Parker, Representative J. Y. Sanders, Jr., whom Bozeman testified in the 1929 impeachment activities Long had wished him to kill and on whom

Long last January attempted to fix responsibility for an attempted plot to murder him at that time, Fred Parker, employed by Sanders in Washington, now a federal F.E.R.A. employee, who was also named in January by Long, and later in the Senate, as one of the men who assertedly plotted to kill him.

2

September 11 and 12, the body of Long lay in state in its bronze casket in the capitol he built. 80,000 persons passed by his bier and thousands were turned away. He was dressed in evening clothes, a garb he had boasted he had not worn since becoming governor in 1928.

September 12, at 4:26 P.M., he was laid to rest in a grave in the sunken garden at the foot of the esplanade before the same building in the midst of 100,000 mourners, black and white. The roofs of buildings a quarter of a mile around were crowded; negroes perched all over the live oak trees among the Spanish moss.

The coffin was carried out of the huge bronze entrance doors and down the forty-eight steps, each named for one of the states of the Union, and was accompanied by his family and intimate followers, the members of his bodyguard, who had failed, senators and legislators, all led by Dr. Smith, to the music of a distant dirge, transcribed from Huey Long's own song: *Every Man a King.*

Over his body, before the earth closed it in, Reverend Smith delivered the funeral sermon. "The lives of great men do not end with the grave. . . . This place . . . marks only the burial ground of his body. His spirit shall never rest as long as hungry bodies cry for food, as long as lean human frames stand naked, as long as homeless wretches haunt this land of plenty. . . .

"He fell in the line of duty. . . . The ideals which he planted in our hearts have created a gnawing hunger for a new order. . . ."

He recited the achievements and meaning of Long's life. "The blood which dropped upon this soil shall seal our hearts.

Take up the torch, complete the task, subdue selfish ambition, sacrifice for the sake of victory."

And he closed with Huey Long's favorite poem by Henley:

> "Out of the night that covers me,
>   Black as the Pit from pole to pole,
> I thank whatever gods may be
>   For my unconquerable soul. . . .
> I am the master of my fate:
> I am the captain of my soul."

And thus ended, so far as Huey Long personally was concerned, the Great Crusade.

3

It is too soon to appraise him with proper justice. Nor is it easy to provide a glib summary. For, though his motives may not have been more complex than those of other men, at least all the acts of his life were heightened to an intensity that bears the hallmark of genius. He was a man of Gargantuan energy, overgreedy for experience, action, power. His towering ambition strained against all bonds. He was impatient of anything that hampered his will; he overrode all opposition by almost whatever means came into his hand. A self-appointed humanitarian, he was kind and tolerant to no one who stood in the slightest in his way. He was never too scrupulous about means. Was he scrupulous about ends? His death has, in part, locked the key upon the answer to that question.

But this explains much of his previous personal advancement in Louisiana, where he hitched the crassest machine politics and manipulations to the most idealistic utterances. Certainly, whatever his expressed ideals, in the field of practical politics, every move was made, not primarily toward the advancement of those ideals, but toward the expansion of his personal power.

His announcement, published posthumously by Hearst, of "My First Days in the White House," was a canny attempt to build up a united political front against the Roosevelt régime, without regard for any of the principles Long espoused. Not a man in his proposed cabinet, except possibly Borah, would have had the slightest sympathy for his Share-Our-Wealth program; the government he proposed to establish would have been as ridiculous as a cross between a zebra and a hippopotamus, although Hoover, with doctrines of commercial imperialism, seated at the same table with Franklin D. Roosevelt, big-navy man, is not nearly so incongruous as appears at first glance.

But Huey proposed, so far as personnel went, not a New Deal, but a strange hybrid Old Deal, an administration without ideological unity or purpose. Obviously it was merely a bid for the sympathies and support of the widest and most irreconcilable groups in the country. What is this but the old canny tactics of the Machiavellian dictator, who first seeks power by the widest possible coalition, an absurdity ever doomed, and doubly doomed in times of crisis, in order later to have an excuse to govern with the narrowest possible cliques. Not even the first step toward Sharing-Our-Wealth, were such a thing desirable, could be made with such a set-up.

But few men in history have overcome so many obstacles so rapidly or risen so swiftly to a position of power and importance. The qualities which led to this were his boundless energy, his understanding of human nature and of the common man, his curious coupling of fixed principles with the widest latitude of compromise, opportunism and adaptability, a dazzling and devastating power to attack, boldness and audacity, a thoroughgoing appreciation of dramatics and the ability to act, rapid shifting in tactics, a facile and ready tongue, a prodigious memory, the ability to make strong friends and destroy strong enemies, readiness to let bygones be bygones in return for servility or support, a lightning-quick facility for grasping the implications of any and all situations, a willingness to be ruthless when necessary, a quizzical and irrepressible sense of humor.

Base as have been some of his acts, many have been the instances when he has refrained from using base methods, even when they would have been, at least momentarily, more effective. Though he resorted to typical corrupt machine political methods, though his deeds have rarely corresponded to his creed, though he never carried out any of his major principles in Louisiana, where he had absolute power, nevertheless, unlike most of his vacillating and temporizing political contemporaries, he never swerved verbally for opportunistic reasons from the doctrines he had enunciated since his early youth.

He has been perhaps called a demagogue too freely, or at least without proper examination of the word. Is the man who has the power to rouse the multitude necessarily a demagogue? Is one who promises what he cannot fulfill more of a demagogue than the one who deceives the public without such promises? Certainly no President in the history of the republic has so departed from his original campaign promises as has President Roosevelt. Is there any worse demagogue in America than Herbert Hoover with his inane platitudes about liberty, his colossal ignorance of economics, when he as much as anyone contributed to the destruction of economic liberty for millions of Americans? Is not a demagogue a thousand times more desirable in public life than a gross machine politician like Mr. Farley?

Above all else, whatever his sins, whatever his ultimate purposes, whatever his lack of sincerity, Huey Long has been more courageously frank and outspoken about all public problems than any other man in the ranks of the two major parties. Compared to Hugh Johnson he was a marvel of intelligence and ability. Whatever the folly of his proposals, he will stand as a remarkable social and political critic of the evils and misfortunes of our day. In most of his attacks on national public figures, he was living in a glass house; but if nothing else he has quickened and educated the American electorate. The masses, apparently, can only learn through cumulative disillusionment. What remarkable things Huey Long might have taught them in that line!

He has been freely called a Fascist, a Mussolini. That he was a potential Fascist few can deny. That he brought a species of Fascism, though without many of the worst excesses of that system, to Louisiana, is patent to the man who runs.

But such easy-made clichés and epithets largely serve to blur the issue and the meaning of his rise to power. He was basically a product of Louisiana, of the South and of the Middle West, and he must be defined in American terms before his resemblances and differences to European political practices have any significance. That his success nationally would have precipitated a premature and possibly unnecessary revolution is more than possible. It is, after all is said, perhaps more fortunate for America that Huey Long's crusade goes marching on to be tested on its true merits rather than in the stress of emotionalism of people blinded by passion and hero worship, that it marches on as a crusade rather than that Huey Long himself marches on.

He left as his heritage a political machine as crass as that of Boss Tweed or Pendergast, with all the appurtenances of dictatorship to sustain it, and he left a cause represented by the idealistic Share-Our-Wealth movement with millions of members.

Will his machine survive?

Will his crusade go marching on?

Will his followers be able to maintain their power and to reconcile the essential contradiction involved?

4

Hardly had Huey Long breathed his last than his followers were snarling over the bones of his power, and the opposition was massing to recoup the positions which for eight years they have been steadily losing.

Long had wrought the state into an instrument of absolute power over the lives and property of the people of Louisiana. But he had left that power, except in so far as his successor might be influenced by others, to Oscar K. Allen, a dutiful yes-man, in bad health, of weak will, of mediocre intelligence, without the power to impose respect or obedience upon Long's own cohorts. But whoever can really seize power in Louisiana, and the tale will begin to be told in January, will have ready made for him a mechanism of absolute control, for good or evil, unparalleled in any state in the Union, and unparalleled in Louisiana since Warmoth's days; though bad management, of course, can promptly wreck the most perfected system of absolutism.

The opposition. The opposition in Louisiana has never had any program which would attract the support of anyone with anything over a fourteen-year-old child's I.Q. Its one ambition has been to maintain the old plantation-corporation status quo which had already made the state the most backward entity in the Union, and even far more than the Long cohorts, to grab the spoils. Under the blows of Long, it had disintegrated into factions. It is today not a cohesive group, and it is without talented leadership; its most able speakers are utterly corrupt, without a program, filled purely with petty and selfish ambitions.

The Old New Orleans Ring: the members had largely been browbeaten into the Long camp the month previous to his assassination. They will probably be the first to split off into open opposition.

The Walmsley faction of the Old Ring.

The J. Y. Sanders, Jr., upstate faction of the Old Ring. Sanders is at present Congressman and has been a consistent enemy of Huey Long, as was his father, the former governor, before him. A typical Louisiana politician and corporation lawyer.

The John P. Sullivan New Regulars, into which group the federal government has been pumping so much patronage and so much of the sacred relief and public works money. A man with powerful political connections, but the associations of this group with race-track, gambling and vice activities have led to its complete discrediting.

The Square Dealers, charged by Long with having been fomented by the Standard Oil. Among its members are many Standard Oil employees, disgruntled political outs, and petty agents of men opposed to Long who did not dare play politics in the open. A Ku Klux Klan, night-riding type of organization, with vague tenets of democracy. Into it the federal government had also pumped considerable patronage and money.

The Women's Committee. The nice people. Composed principally of the wives and daughters of political outs and of corporation and plantation heads opposed to Long. Vague tenets of democracy.

The Long Machine.

A. The business-politician group of Seymore Weiss, manager of the Roosevelt Hotel, treasurer of the machine, colonel on Huey Long's staff, member of various boards; Abe Shushan, head of the Levee Board, wealthy businessman and state contractor; Jules Fisher, cannery king and fur magnate, Robert Maestri, millionaire realtor, head of the Conservation Commission, etc., etc.

B. The country politician group: Oscar K. Allen; Charles A. Noe, independent oil man, with strong following in northern Louisiana; Allen J. Ellender, Speaker of the House, with strong political following in southwest Louisiana; young Wade O. Martin of the Public Service Commission, Judge Fournet, etc.

C. The Share-Our-Wealth group, led by Gerald K. Smith. Naturally the various groups partly overlapped.

But if the Long organization had any moral significance and vitality, it was in connection with its Share-Our-Wealth movement, what may be described in vague terms as the group seeking economic justice. The business political group had no interest in this program and was with Long because it paid dividends; naturally it would today make its alliance with any old-line political element which showed any promise of victory stronger than that of the bona fide Long elements.

Apparent at once was the possible alliance of the country politician group with the Share-Our-Wealth forces; and September 19, less than ten days after the Fuehrer's death, Gerald K. Smith, who heretofore has not been so directly active in the inner workings of Louisiana machine politics, muscled in and helped pull off a sudden coup d'état, before a customary caucus could be called. Noe was named candidate for governor and Martin, candidate for the Senate. Seymore Weiss and the business-politician group in general were placed in the position of accepting this independent Putsch or splitting the machine and allying themselves with the previous opposition. In any event they were jockeyed out of leadership of the Long organization. A new compromise eliminated Noe, whereupon others in the machine, including Fournet and Allen, accepted the determination of the Smith-Martin combination, and clambered on the bandwagon.

If the business-political wing of the machine does not follow suit, while they may alienate strong blocs of votes (for instance Maestri has big control in the southeastern parishes), otherwise they are a handicap for carrying on, especially as the successors to Long will have to make a new fervent appeal to the people for support, if they are not routed by old-line coalitions in the January elections, all the discredited outs supported so strongly by Roosevelt, Farley, Hopkins and Ickes. Curiously enough, though, the business-politician wing of the Long group previously received the hardest blows from the federal politicians: most of them are indicted for income-tax evasion. Even so, now Farley doubtless would far rather forge a new alliance with them than with the other Long faction, for thus a new coalition could be formed of the old-style sort in Louisiana which would possibly put the skids under the politician Share-Our-Wealth line-up, for the latter inevitably must remain to a certain extent hostile to the Roosevelt administration.

Thus the new direction of the Long propaganda and machine becomes evident. Thus will the Great Crusade go marching on. With Smith at Martin's elbow in Washington, the franking privileges, in the past worth half a million dollars a year to the movement, will continue to be used to build up the Share-Our-Wealth clans.

But no longer will it be a direct menace to the re-election of Roosevelt. For a time it will be without much direct political expression. Whether it will even continue to expand without Long's vibrant personality is doubtful. Whether eventually the personality of Smith can take his place remains to be seen. Ultimately, if it lives, it will probably be either reconciled to the Democratic Party or will form part of a third party movement.

THE END